Private Security in America

An Introduction

Clifford E. Simonsen

Prentice Hall
Upper Saddle River, NJ 07458

Library of Congress Cataloging-in-Publication Data

Simonsen, Clifford E.
    Private security in America : an introduction / Clifford E.
   Simonsen.
       p.   cm.
   Includes bibliographical references (p.   ) and index.
   ISBN 0-02-410534-1
   1. Private security services--United States. 2. Police, Private-
-United States. I. Title.
  HV8291.U6S55 1998
  363.28'9--dc21

98-52785
CIP

Editorial/Production Supervision,
   Interior Design, and Electronic Paging: *Naomi Sysak*
Acquisitions Editor: *Neil Marquardt*
Cover Designer: *Miguel Ortiz*
Manufacturing Buyer: *Ed O'Dougherty*
Managing Editor: *Mary Carnis*
Marketing Manager: *Frank Mortimer, Jr.*
Director of Production: *Bruce Johnson*

©1998 by Prentice-Hall, Inc.
Simon & Schuster/A Viacom Company
Upper Saddle River, New Jersey 07458

Printed in the United States of America

10 9 8 7 6 5 4 3 2 1

ISBN 0-02-410534-1

Prentice-Hall International (UK) Limited, *London*
Prentice-Hall of Australia Pty. Limited, *Sydney*
Prentice-Hall Canada Inc., *Toronto*
Prentice-Hall Hispanoamericana, S.A., *Mexico*
Prentice-Hall of India Private Limited, *New Delhi*
Prentice-Hall of Japan, Inc., *Tokyo*
Simon & Schuster Asia Pte. Ltd., *Singapore*
Editora Prentice-Hall do Brasil, Ltda., *Rio de Janeiro*

This book is dedicated to all those people, including my father, who worked as "guards" for low pay and little recognition and built the foundation of a giant industry today.

Contents

Chapter 3
The Scope, Organization, and Growth of the Private Security
Industry: 1970–1990   51

Chapter 4
The Dimensions of Security and Loss Prevention: Who Does What
to Whom?   77

Chapter 7
The Organizational Role for Security: A Search for Identity and Respect   179

Chapter 8
Risk Analysis: The Heart and Soul of Security and Loss Prevention   200

Chapter 9
Litigation: The Biggest Threat to Corporate Assets   222

Chapter 10
Physical Security and Access Control: The Wonders of Technology   243

Chapter 14
The Twenty-First Century: Where Next? 343

Glossary 363

Security Resources 391

Subject Index 415

Author index 428

Foreword

When one decides to write an introductory text about an industry as complex and rapidly changing as private security, it becomes a daunting task. The concept of "security" includes a wide range of activities. The most difficult task is to make it short enough to be comprehensible to students, but long enough to satisfy colleagues and professionals that it covers at least some of the depth of this fascinating field. It is like trying to paint a moving bus, with the technologies changing faster than the words rolled off my keyboard. This text, with an intentionally broad scope, examines where security came from, where it is today, and where it seems to be going as we enter the new millennium, as well as some of the issues that need attention to get there. The reader soon appreciates that there is no easy answer to the question, "What is security?" It will be apparent, in the course of reading this text, that private security programs are often a poorly articulated group of independent operations, often with conflicting goals. However, all of them attempt to provide security for the persons, places, and things that are serviced, produced, imported, shipped, stored, sold, and displayed at their place of business. This knowledge will stimulate students to seek out appropriate opportunities, related activities, and solutions for teamwork among those in the private and public sector .

We have attempted to provide an overview for many of the sectors and operations that compose private security. Some subjects we will explore in greater depth than others, in an attempt to cut redundancy and cover as many differences and similarities as possible. The text is presented with the firm belief that this learning experience should be enjoyable as well as educational. For the instructor, the text is presented to make the teaching and learning experience as effective and interesting as possible. This is done to cover the essentials of the subject with an optimal array of pedagogical tools.

Security is a basic need for humans, a rung on the ladder of Maslow's hierarchy of needs. Only now is it budding into a discipline. Just entering the stature of an academic discipline, the available material that presents scientific theory, literature, and research is not extensive in the field of security. (Not too long ago, law enforcement was in the same stage of development as an academic discipline.) The materials available for developing an introductory text have come from a large band of security-oriented magazines and journals, along with a few textbooks dealing with specific operational areas of interest. Much of the information and data come from where the rubber meets the road; that's where the action is in security. Other useful input has come from the vendors and manufacturers of the space-age technology that drives development of operational security at the end of the 1990s. I continue to challenge my colleagues in academia and in security management to conduct the basic research, collect the data, and develop the theories that will transform security into a true discipline.

The Tradition Continues

The methodology for textbook development used by this author on several other successful texts is also the foundation for this one. It will build on the comments of instructors and students to provide a text that works well for both. Features of this text include:

1. An engaging writing style, resulting in a book that is highly readable and effective as a teaching and learning tool

2. A balanced treatment of practical examples, technology, history, and available documents and academic research

3. An eye-pleasing design for easy reading, with features such as clearly understandable tables, figures, graphs, photographs, illustrations, and other supplemental materials to augment textual materials

4. A systems approach to exploring the varied elements of private and public security and safety as a potentially integrated and interrelated series of subsystems

5. An unbiased presentation of a wide range of topics that makes for a text suitable for a wide range of instructors and students with many points of view

6. In-chapter and end-of-chapter materials that augment the textual materials with examples of events, persons, stories, words to remember, and suggestions for further reading

7. An Instructor's Manual that features test banks and other aids for busy instructors, many of whom are adjuncts who work in public safety and private security in a full-time capacity

Organization of the Text

This text has been divided into 14 chapters that build from a historical presentation to predictions for the twenty-first century for the security field. Quoted and extracted materials have been carefully selected for their content and applicability to the subject matter being covered. They should be considered as important as the other textual materials for presentation and study. The extracted materials come from the best available sources in the field, so we have chosen to present them in their original form, not paraphrase them and thereby possibly lessen their impact.

CHAPTER ONE   SECURITY: A CONCEPT IN SEARCH OF A DEFINITION AND DIRECTION

The student examines the development of the rule of law, law enforcement, a system of punishments, and the parallel development of private security and public law enforcement.

CHAPTER TWO   THE MISSION FOR PRIVATE SECURITY: "MAKE MY DAY!" OR "HAVE A NICE DAY"?

This chapter looks at the development of security into a profession, ethics in security, and the growth of security standards and training.

CHAPTER THREE   THE SCOPE, ORGANIZATION, AND GROWTH OF THE PRIVATE SECURITY INDUSTRY: 1970–1990

The development of the two *Hallcrest* reports, crime trends in private security and public safety, and reviews of previous studies give the students an understanding of the vitality and growth of private security in the 1990s.

CHAPTER FOUR   THE DIMENSIONS OF SECURITY AND LOSS PREVENTION: WHO DOES WHAT TO WHOM?

The student is presented an examination of the evolving roles of public police, the citizen, and private security in a nation awash with violent criminal behavior and a shrinking law enforcement sector.

CHAPTER FIVE   THE WIDE RANGE OF SPECIALIZED SECURITY FIELDS AND CAREER OPPORTUNITIES

This chapter looks in depth at a representative, but not exhaustive, range of three specialized fields in security. Aviation and airports security, banking and financial services security, and healthcare security are covered in detail; then several other areas are discussed in a briefer format. They are presented with the intention of providing the student with a range of potential career fields.

CHAPTER SIX   AN EXAMINATION OF GENERALIZED SECURITY TASKS

This chapter follows the last with the presentation of a number of general security tasks and how they affect all kinds of operational environments. Such subjects as crisis management, transportation security, and computer security are discussed in depth, showing how they are incorporated into a total security program in any corporation or institution.

CHAPTER SEVEN   THE ORGANIZATIONAL ROLE FOR SECURITY: A SEARCH FOR IDENTITY AND RESPECT

The role of the security manager and placement of the security operation in the overall organization is covered, with discussions about how this can be changed and some theoretical approaches to security management.

CHAPTER EIGHT   RISK ANALYSIS: THE HEART AND SOUL OF SECURITY AND LOSS PREVENTION

The importance of risk assessment as a foundation for viable and cost-effective security operations is presented, along with the processes and tools needed to conduct them.

CHAPTER NINE   LITIGATION: THE BIGGEST THREAT TO CORPORATE ASSETS

This chapter addresses the tremendous impact that the growth of litigation in security operations has on the companies served by security programs. Case studies and case results show the importance of methods and procedures to prevent litigation before it hits the bottom line of the corporation or institution.

CHAPTER TEN   PHYSICAL SECURITY AND ACCESS CONTROL: THE WONDERS OF TECHNOLOGY

The student examines the marriage of planning, training, and deploying security personnel with the rapidly developing technologies to provide security in depth.

CHAPTER ELEVEN   CRIME PREVENTION: A MAJOR ELEMENT OF SECURITY AND LOSS PREVENTION—ROLES AND PRACTICES

Crime prevention has always been a major part of the security function. This chapter shows the development of crime prevention as a serious part of law enforcement and how private security is becoming a partner in achieving this mission.

CHAPTER TWELVE   SECURITY PRODUCTS, CONSULTANTS, AND VENDORS: THE TECHNOLOGICAL AND SERVICES SECTOR OF PRIVATE SECURITY

The security system's dependence on a symbiotic relationship with the developers and providers of technology, the fastest growing sector of security, is discussed and described. The human element of the person–machine interface is seen as a driving force for better training and use of technology.

CHAPTER THIRTEEN   SECURITY AND LOSS PREVENTION BY ENVIRONMENTAL DESIGN AND SYSTEMS INTEGRATION

This chapter attempts to pull it all together in a discussion of how all the elements of good security planning and operations can be considered in the design phase of any project.

CHAPTER FOURTEEN   THE TWENTY-FIRST CENTURY: WHERE NEXT?

This chapter is a look ahead to the twenty-first century and how the fusion of private security, law enforcement, and technological wonders yet to come can be molded into a partnership that provides security and safety to all citizens.

Acknowledgments

How does one begin to acknowledge all the persons whose love, support, encouragement, and assistance allowed me to develop, refine, and produce a book that has evolved from over thirty-five years in security? To try to acknowledge them individually would take too many pages and I would surely miss some. Any thanks must begin, however, with my wife and best friend of forty-five years whose support has been invaluable. Next, thanks to my close personal friends and colleagues, professionals, and practitioners in security and criminal justice. To all of you, I extend deepest appreciation and gratitude for encouraging me, and helping in the creation of a text that I hope will break the mold for security books.

I would, however, like to mention a few special persons who helped me turn prose, ideas, and concepts for a book about security into a textbook that will reach the instructors and students. First, Prentice Hall's Criminal Justice Editor, Neil Marquardt, gets kudos for leading me through this first edition of a new kind of security text with minimal problems, and a lot of positive support. Neil fought for my ideas and concepts, rather than choosing to stay with the status quo. Mary Carnis, Managing Editor, was always a calm and professional center in the midst of what often became a frantic effort to stay on schedule. Exceptional support and great patience came from Naomi Sysak, my Production Editor, who got me through the resurrection of a book that had languished, and together we made it happen. Her expertise and good humor helped to get it over some serious obstacles. Naomi's layout work and interior design were especially appreciated...we didn't fight over too many of them. Miguel Ortiz , Cover Designer, helped me to understand the importance of visual effect for the great cover of this book. Robert Fiske, our copy editor, gets an extra special "thank you." He used his "magic pencil" assiduously and helped turn the words of this author into a book that reads like the work of a "pro." Frank Mortimer, Jr., Marketing Manager, is busy getting the word out to the sales staff, and will be a great factor in making this text successful in a very competitive field. Judy Casillo, the supplement editor, helped us get the right new tools included with this edition to make it fresh and interesting for the student. Ed O'Dougherty, manufacturing buyer, made sure that everything was in place in the frantic period of final production.

We also must offer special thanks to colleagues, publishers, and manufacturers who gave willingly of their materials, photos, articles, and support to provide the latest information and concepts for this text. Norman Bates, Richard P. Grassie, CPP, Joseph A. Barry, CPP, Lars R. Suneborne, Norman M. Spain, James Kohl, CPP, Mark

Golsby, William C. Cunningham, John J. Strauchs, and Clifford W. Van Meter, and my close friend Rick Nelson, CPP all made generous contributions to this effort. I owe a great debt to the generous use of materials from *Security* magazine, which added a lot of zip to the Security Briefs. Manufacturers of security equipment, too many to thank by name, generously gave photos and descriptions of their latest products and services. Without the help of all of these people and organizations, this book would have been dull and lifeless...and outdated before it was printed. Thank you all!

1

Security

A CONCEPT IN SEARCH OF A DEFINITION AND DIRECTION

> *In examining the origins and development of security, it is both obvious and instructive to observe that security holds a mirror up, not to nature, but to society and its institutions.*
>
> Gion Green

Overview

Security is hardly a new idea. Since the beginning of society, security of some kind has been necessary to protect mankind against threats from nature, creatures, and mostly, of course, humans themselves. Security has caused mankind to seek out a wide variety of psychological, physical, moral, and religious solutions to their fears (real and imagined). These solutions have ranged from comforting stories around the communal fire to nuclear bombs and the threat of total annihilation of life on earth. This text will acquaint the student with the development of societies, the methods for protecting the members of these societies, and the growth of private security, a major player in the entire military–police–private security triad of protection and response to threats. The first chapter gives a brief historical overview of behavior, societies, and the reasons for the development of private security.

Behavior as a Continuum and the Development of Laws

We are about to embark upon a journey into the world of private security. We will first explore the historical context and specific roles society has developed for the provision of security and loss prevention as a factor in the control of criminal and antisocial acts. But before we do, it is useful to look at **social control** from a behavioral viewpoint. Prior to the establishment of social groups—groups in which people gathered for companionship, reproduction, group hunting, and crop growing—we humans probably just wandered around the countryside like all the other animals. Meeting the needs of the reproductive drive and resolving hunger fully occupied our distant ancestors' days and nights. However, with the development of the concept of **territoriality** and **personal property**, along with group social relationships, humans began to worry about the protection of their persons, their places, and their things. From this simple concept has evolved a vast system of controls and processes that define who gets what, and for security measures that have resulted in sometimes frustrating attempts to control the behavior of those who would transgress in these areas of group and individual concern.

Behavior in social groups, whether they are primitive tribes or complex modern nation-states, can be regarded as points on a simple continuum, as shown in Figure 1–1.

In all societies, certain acts or groups of acts have been universally forbidden, discouraged, or **proscribed**. Such acts include murder, rape, kidnapping, and treason (or some form of rebellion against the group's safety and authority). By contrast, most societies have encouraged, sponsored, or **prescribed** other behaviors such as having children, marrying, hunting, growing food, and other actions that benefit the common social welfare.

Behavior that is situated toward the center of the continuum is usually controlled by a set of simple social rules called **folkways**. These rules are enforced by means of mild disapproval (such as the raising of an eyebrow, staring, or a look of shock) or by mild encouragement (such as no reaction, applause, or a smile).

Behaviors that move a bit farther out toward either end of the continuum shown in Figure 1–1 serve to either (1) threaten the group's safety or social order on one end of the scale or (2) contribute to the group's improved existence on the other end.

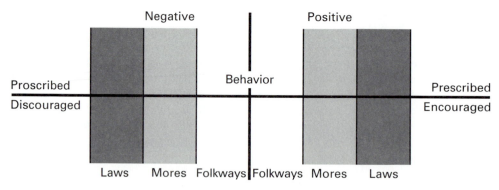

FIGURE 1-1   *The Continuum of Behavior*

These are generally controlled by a stronger set of rules called **mores**. In early human history, mores were enforced by means of strong social disapproval (verbal abuse, beatings, temporary ostracism, banishment, or even death) or strong encouragement (dowries, secure social or financial status, or fertility rites). Many of these informal controls still protect certain mores today.

But as societies became more complex, they were required to devise more structured sanctions in order to prevent violation of the mores (*morals*) that were most essential to the group's survival. These sanctions have generally developed into codified forms of written rules, or **laws**, which formalize and describe certain boundaries of behavior and outline specific punishments for their violation. The reward for obeying laws is simply the ability to continue as a respected and productive member of a social group. Simple definitions of these social controls are as follows:

- *Folkways:* Traditional social customs, including ways of thinking, feeling, or acting common to a social group of people
- *Mores:* Binding moral attitudes, habits, customs, and manners of a particular group of people
- *Laws:* Rules of conduct formally recognized as binding, defined and enforced by a controlling authority

Private security often falls into the range of behaviors that are not a violation of laws, but a violation of the policies, procedures, and practices (*mores*) of a social group or an organization. Often the violation of codified *law* requires that a private security person call a public safety officer to effect an arrest. Some jurisdictions allow limited police powers to security officers and they then work on the continuum that covers both mores and certain specified types of laws. All are related to the ways that social groups or organizations choose to respond to transgressions.

RETALIATION

The earliest remedy for wrongs done to one's person or property was simply to retaliate as an *individual* against the wrongdoer. In primitive societies, personal retaliation was accepted and even encouraged by members of the tribal group. This ancient concept of personal justice or revenge could hardly be considered "law." Yet it has influenced the development of most laws and legal systems, especially English common law, from which most of our American criminal and civil law has been derived.

The practice of personal retaliation was later augmented by the **blood feud**, in which the victim's whole family or tribe took revenge on the offender's family or tribe. Because this form of retaliation could easily escalate and result in an endless *vendetta* between the injured factions, some method of control had to be devised to make blood feuds less costly and damaging.

The practice of retaliation usually begins to develop into a system of criminal law when it becomes customary for the victim of the wrongdoing to accept *money* or *property* in place of blood vengeance. This custom, when established, is usually dictated by tribal tradition and the relative social status and power of the injured party and the wrongdoer.

Custom has always exerted great force among primitive societies. The acceptance of vengeance in the form of a payment (such as cattle, food, or personal services) was usually not compulsory, and victims were still free to take whatever vengeance they wished. Legal historians Albert Kocourek and John Wigmore described this pressure to retaliate:

> It must not be forgotten that the right of personal revenge was also in many cases a duty. A man was bound by all the force of religion to avenge the death of his kinsman. This duty was by universal practice imposed upon the nearest male relative—the avenger of blood, as he is called in the Scripture accounts.[1]

The need to find better ways to deal with retaliation developed into the custom of atonement for wrongs by payment to appease the victim's family or tribe. This custom became known as *lex salica*[2] (or *wergeld*,[3] in Europe). It is still in effect in many Middle Eastern and Far Eastern countries, with the amount of payment based on the injured person's rank and position. Friedensgeld was the practice of paying restitution to the crown, in addition to individuals, for crimes. It later replaced payment to individuals and became the system of fines paid to the state. With fines, the victim disappeared from the criminal justice system, becoming the ignored component of the crime.

FINES AND PUNISHMENTS

How did these simple, voluntary programs become part of an official system of fines and punishments? As tribal leaders, elders, and (later) kings and emperors came into power,[4] they began to exert their acquired authority on the negotiations. Wrongdoers could choose to stay away from the proceedings; this was their right. But if they refused to abide by the decided-upon and imposed sanctions, they were declared to be outside the law of the tribe (nation, family), literally an *outlaw*. There is little doubt that outlawry, or exile, was the first punishment imposed by society,[5] and it heralded the beginning of criminal law as we now know it.

Criminal law, even primitive criminal law, requires an element of *public action* against the wrongdoer—as in a pronouncement of outlawry. Before this element of public action, the backgrounds of criminal law and sanctions seem to have been parallel in most legal systems. The subsequent creation of legal codes and sanctions for different crimes either stressed or refined the vengeance factor, according to the particular society's group values and willingness to enforce the decisions.

BABYLONIAN AND SUMERIAN CODES

Even primitive ethics demanded that a society express its vengeance within a system of regulations and rules. Moses was advised to follow the "eye for eye, and tooth for tooth" doctrine stated in Exodus 21:24, but this concept **(lex talionis)** is far older than the Bible; it appears in the Sumerian codes and in the code of King Hammurabi of Babylon,[6] compiled over five hundred years before the Book of the Covenant.

As early societies developed more refined language and writing skills, they began to make permanent records of the laws of their leaders, elders, and kingdoms. The Hammurabic Code is viewed by most historians as the first comprehensive attempt at codifying social interaction. The Sumerian codes[7] preceded it by about a century, and the principle of *lex talionis* was evident in both. The punishments under these codes were harsh and based on vengeance (or *talion*), in many cases inflicted by the injured party. In the Babylonian code, more than two dozen offenses called for the penalty of death. Both codes also prescribed mutilation, whipping, or forced labor as punishments for numerous crimes. It was felt that the severity of the punishment would act as a general deterrence to violation of the codes. Then, as now, that seldom worked except on the specific individual.

The kinds of punishments applied to slaves and bond servants have been cited by many scholars[8] as the origin of the punishments that in later law applied to all offenders. As historian Gustav Radbruch stated:

> Applied earlier almost exclusively to slaves, [the mutilating penalties] became used more and more on freemen during the Carolinian period (A.D. 640–1012) and specially for offenses which betokened a base and servile mentality. Up to the end of the Carolinian era, punishments "to hide and hair" were overwhelmingly reserved for slaves. Even death penalties occurred as slave punishments and account for the growing popularity of such penalties in Carolinian times. The aggravated death penalties, combining corporal and capital punishments, have their roots in the penal law governing slaves.[9]

The early punishments were considered synonymous with slavery; those punished were often required to even have their heads shaved, indicating the "mark of the slave."[10] In Roman days, the extensive use of penal servitude was spurred by the need for workers to perform hard labor in the great public works demanded by the emperors. The sentence to penal servitude was reserved for the lower classes and usually meant life in chains, working in the mines, rowing in galleys of ships, or building the massive public works planned by the empire. These were generally a sentence of slow death by hard labor. These sentences carried with them the complete loss of citizenship and liberty and were classed, along with exile and death, as capital punishment. Penal servitude became known as **civil death**, which meant that the offender's property was confiscated in the name of the state and that his wife was declared a widow, eligible to remarry. To society, the offender was, in effect, "dead."

CRIME AND SIN

Punishment of the individual in the name of the state also included the concept of superstitious revenge. Here crime was entangled with sin, and punishment in the form of *wergeld* (payment to the victim) or *friedensgeld*[11] (payment to the state) was not sufficient. If society believed the crime might have offended a divinity, the accused had to undergo a long period of progressively harsher punishment in order to appease the gods. Over time, the boundaries between church law and state law became progressively more blurred, and the concept of personal responsibility for one's act was combined with the need to "get right with God."[12] Early codes were designed to make the offender's punishment acceptable to both society and God.

ROMAN AND GREEK CODES

In the sixth century A.D., Emperor Justinian of Rome caused a vast code of laws to be written, one of the most ambitious early efforts to match a desirable amount of punishment to all possible crimes. Roman art of the period depicts a female goddess holding up the "scales of justice" (from Justinian). This metaphor tried to show that codes could be devised that allowed the punishment to perfectly balance the crime, without the need for human deliberation. Justinian's effort, as might be expected, bogged down in the morass of administrative details that were required to enforce it.[13] The Code of Justinian did not survive the fall of the Roman Empire, but it left the foundation upon which most of the Western world's legal codes were finally built.

In Greece, the harsh Code of Draco[14] provided the same penalties for both citizens and slaves, incorporating many of the concepts used in primitive societies (for example, vengeance, outlawry, and blood feuds). To this day, the term *draconian* is understood to mean harsh and cruel administration of punishment. The Greeks were the first society to allow any citizen (not just the victim) to initiate a complaint and prosecution of an offender in the name of the injured party, clearly illustrating that during that period the public interest and protection of the social order were becoming more important than individual injury and individual vengeance.

THE MIDDLE AGES

The Middle Ages were a period of general disorder and chaos. Vast changes in the social structure and the growing influence of the church on everyday life resulted in a divided system of justice. Reformation was viewed as a process of religious, not secular, redemption. As in early civilizations, the sinner had to pay two debts, one to society and another to God. The **ordeal** was the church's substitute for a trial, until the practice was abolished in 1215. In trials by ordeal, guilt or innocence was determined by subjecting the accused to dangerous or painful tests in the belief that the innocent would emerge unscathed, whereas the guilty would suffer agonies and die. The brutality of most trials by ordeal ensured a very high percentage of "convictions," in other words, the suspect died.

The church expanded the concept of crime to include some new areas, still reflected in modern codes. During the Middle Ages, many sexual activities were seen as especially sinful. Sex offenses usually involved either public or "unnatural" acts, and they provoked horrible punishments, as did heresy and witchcraft. The church justified cruel reprisals as a means of saving the unfortunate sinner from the devil. The zealous movement to stamp out heresy brought on the **Inquisition**[15] and its use of the most vicious tortures imaginable to gain "confessions" and "repentance" from alleged heretics. Thousands of persons died at the hands of the inquisitioners. Spain and Holland, where these methods were the most extensively used, were especially devastated. Punishment was not viewed as an end in itself, but as the offender's only hope of pacifying a wrathful God.

The main contribution of the medieval church is the concept of **free will**. This idea assumes that individuals choose to take their actions, good or bad, and thus can be held fully responsible for them. The religious doctrines of eternal punishment,

The Inquisition had many ways to get the "truth."

Courtesy of Culver Pictures, Inc.

atonement, and spiritual conversion rest on the assumption that individuals who commit sins could have acted differently if they had chosen to do so.

The early codes and their administration were usually based on the belief that punishment was necessary to avenge the victim. In early small tribal groups and less complex societies, direct compensation to the victim was used in place of revenge to prevent disintegration of the social structure through extended blood feuds. When those groups began to concentrate their power in a king or similar leader, the concept of crime as an offense against the victim gave way to the idea that crime—however lowly the victim—was an offense against the *state*. In the process, *wergeld* was replaced by *friedensgeld*, and the administration of punishment became the responsibility of the king. Concentrating that power also led to a tendency to ignore victims and their losses, while concentrating on the crime and the criminal.

PUNISHMENT

The most common forms of state punishment over the centuries have been death, torture, mutilation, branding, public humiliation, fines, forfeits of property, banishment, transportation, and imprisonment.[16] These acts, and numerous variations on them, have always symbolized retribution for crimes.

The death penalty (killing the offender) was the most universal form of punishment used among early societies. There was very little knowledge of behavior modification and other modern techniques to control violent persons, and often the feared offenders were condemned to death by hanging, crucifixion, stoning, burning at the stake, drowning, and any other cruel and unusual method the human mind could conceive. As technology advanced, methods for killing offenders became more sophisticated. In the belief that punishment (especially death) would act as a deterrent to others, societies carried out executions and other lesser punishments in public.

Torture, mutilation, and branding are found in the general category of **corporal punishment** (any physical pain inflicted short of death). Many tortures were used to extract a "confession" from the accused, often resulting in the death penalty for an innocent person. Mutilation was often done in an attempt to match the crime with an "appropriate" punishment. (A liar's tongue was ripped out, a rapist's genitals were removed, a thief's hands were cut off, and so on.) Branding was still practiced as late as the nineteenth century in many countries, including the United States. Corporal punishment was believed to act as a deterrent to other potential offenders.

The public humiliation of offenders was a popular practice in early America, utilizing such devices as the stocks, the pillory, ducking stools, lynching, and branding. The most significant aspect of those punishments was their *public* nature. Offenders were placed in the stocks (sitting down, hands and feet fastened into a locked frame) or in the pillory (standing, with head and hands fastened into a locked frame) and were flogged, spat upon, heaped with garbage, and reviled by all who passed by.

The ducking stool and the brank were used as common public punishments for gossips. The ducking stool was a chair or platform placed at the end of a long lever, allowing the operator on the bank of a stream to repeatedly dunk the victim. The brank was a birdcagelike instrument placed over the offender's head, containing a plate of iron with sharp spikes in it that extended into the subject's mouth. Any movement of the mouth or tongue would result in painful injury.

Flogging (or whipping) has been a common punishment in almost all Western civilizations. The method was used particularly to preserve discipline in domestic, military, and academic settings. It was usually administered by a short lash at the end of a solid handle about three feet long or by a whip made of nine knotted lines or cords fastened to a handle (the famed "cat-o'-nine-tails"), sometimes with sharp spikes worked into the knots. Flogging was a popular method of inducing confessions at heresy trials since few victims could stand up long under the tongue of the lash.

DETERRENCE

As noted, the extensive use of capital and corporal punishment during the Middle Ages reflected, in part, a belief that public punishment would deter potential wrongdoers—a belief that the passing years have refuted: "It is plain that, however futile it may be, social revenge is the only honest, straightforward, and logical justification for punishing criminals. The claim for deterrence is belied by both history and logic."[17] No matter how society tried to "beat the devil" out of offenders, in most cases the only criminal deterred was the one tortured to death.

Early Use of the Pillory

Courtesy Federal Bureau of Prisons.

EMERGENCE OF SECULAR LAW

The problem of drawing up a set of laws that applied to the actions of men and women in earthly communities was compounded by Christian philosophers, who insisted that law was made in heaven. In the fourth century A.D., St. Augustine recognized the need for justice, but only as decreed by God. The issue was somewhat clarified by Thomas Aquinas in the thirteenth century, when he distinguished among three laws:

1. Eternal law, or **lex externa**
2. Natural law, or **lex naturalis**
3. Human law, or **lex humana**[18]

All were intended for the support of the common good. The last, *lex humana*, was considered valid only if it did not conflict with the other two.

As time passed and the secular leaders (kings and other monarchs) became more powerful, these rulers wanted to detach themselves from the divine legal order and its restrictions on their personal power. In the early fourteenth century, many scholars advocated the independence of the monarchy from the Pope. Dante, the Italian poet and philosopher, proposed the establishment of a world state, completely under the rule of secular power.

England's lord chancellor, Sir Thomas More, opposed the forces advocating the unification of church and state and died on the executioner's block as a result. He refused to bend ecclesiastical law to suit the marital whims of his king, the fickle Henry VIII. Sir Thomas More was out of line with his day in another sense as well: As an advocate of the seemingly radical theory that punishment could not prevent crime, he was one of the first to see that **prevention** might require a close look at the conditions that gave rise to crime. In the sixteenth century, unfortunately, this line of thought was too far ahead of its time. But Sir Thomas More's ideas persisted and eventually contributed much to the foundation of modern theories in criminology and crime prevention that are the basic principles of modern security and loss prevention.

The idea of punishment to repay society and expiate one's transgressions against God explains in part why most punishments were cruel and barbarous. Presumably, the hardships of physical torture, social degradation, exile, or financial loss (the four fundamental types of punishment[19]) would be rewarded by eternal joy in heaven. Ironically, those punishments did little to halt the spread of crime: "Even in the era when extremely severe punishment was imposed for crimes of minor importance, no evidence can be found to support the view that punitive measures materially curtailed the volume of crime."[20]

As has been shown, the state and the church always seemed to devise punishments for perceived wrongs in early societies. The agents of these sanctions, those designated to observe, detect, and respond to violations of codes, formed the basis for security systems throughout history, both public and private.

A Brief History of Private Security

As we noted in the previous section, the primary role of securing persons, places, and things fell to the individual for many centuries. With the development of more formalized tribes and the concept of leadership power, it became necessary for the king or other type of authority to find ways to protect his tribe—but to also protect his power. This was often accomplished by severe and gruesome punishments. A benevolent dictatorship is considered by many political scientists the finest form of government. But as has happened throughout history, dictatorships seldom remain benevolent for long. Despots of every stripe have always taken from the people with the excuse that they are *protecting* them. Protecting the tribe from outside enemies usually required some kind of a security force. In the early stages of social development, these forces were usually drawn from members of the tribe. As the leaders developed wealth from plunder and taxes, however, they needed to find ways to protect themselves from any would-be successors. This resulted in the leaders needing to spend some of their treasure by hiring retainers, knights, bodyguards, or some other type of personal private security.

These paid members of the king's personal security staff developed into standing armies. But personal armies are usually loyal to the one who pays them rather than the society they allegedly are serving. These mercenary forces nevertheless had legitimate reasons for their existence as well. They protected the populace from roving bands of bandits and outlaws in the Middle Ages, receiving funds from tithing for their services.

ANGLO-SAXON PRACTICES

The concept of **tithing** was organized in detail by the Anglo-Saxons and placed into practice around A.D. 400. This was a system in which the subjects of the king were organized in a specific fashion. Ten families or households were called *tithings*. Ten *tithings* were called a *hundred*. Each of the tithing groups of ten families had a **tithing-man** who represented that specific *tithing* to the *reeve*, a person appointed by the king. The *reeve* was supposed to represent the many *tithings* and to develop ways to maintain order and help collect taxes for the king. Several *hundreds* were organized into a *shire*, and several *shires* formed an *earldom*. The **shire-reeve** was the leader, major tax collector, and law enforcement officer of the king for that shire. (The modern term *sheriff* derived from this position and is still considered the highest elected office in the majority of U.S. counties.)

Under the Anglo-Saxon tithing system, every citizen was expected to be involved with law enforcement and group security, and had to respond to any "hue and cry" that was made by their tithing-man. The hue and cry required every able-bodied person to join in the pursuit and capture of lawbreakers, resulting in the origin of what we now call a **citizen's arrest**.

THE NORMAN PERIOD

William, the Duke of Normandy, defeated the Anglo-Saxons in 1066 at the battle of Hastings and became the King of England. He placed the country under martial law and divided it into military districts headed by a *tenant-in-chief* who was responsible to the king for the similar duties that were formerly handled by the *shire-reeve*. The king set up a traveling court that went throughout the country and heard complaints to the crown. These became the forerunners for our present-day circuit courts. The position of *constable* was established, with one constable assigned to every hundred to help the reeve collect taxes. In A.D. 1116, serious crimes were separated from less serious crimes, and they were designated *felonies* and *misdemeanors*, respectively. The last great contributions of the Normans was the reestablishment of *frankpledge* and the initiation of a *grand jury*. These processes finally did away with the trial by ordeal and trial by combat, and were the forerunners of our present judicial system.

THE MAGNA CARTA

Despite the efforts to block it by the despotic ruler King John, the most significant document in regard to modern jurisprudence was put into effect in 1215. The **Magna Carta** (Great Charter) made the *king* subject to law of the land for the first time. Prior to this event, the king was considered to be responsible only to God, which was the origin of the term **sovereign immunity**. This document also separated *national* from *local* government, established the concept of *due process* for individual rights, and proclaimed liberty for all citizens. Most of the concepts of law and justice in the United States were derived in some form from this great document.

Sheriff of Nottingham

Source: Corbis-Bettmann.

Following the establishment of the Magna Carta, the next four hundred years saw massive social change and chaos in England, as well as the rest of Europe. To provide local security, the system of the **watch and ward** was established, following passage of the Statute of Westminster in 1285. This statute required that every area of England establish a security force for patrolling against bandits and outlaws. The members of the watch were unpaid, and every able-bodied male was required to take his turn at patrolling. As Europe began to be industrialized and cities sprang up, the problems of urban crime and antisocial behavior intensified. The only way that merchants and shippers could protect their goods and cargoes was to hire their own security forces. It was not until 1737, however, that King George II began to pay watchmen with moneys derived from taxes. All paid watchmen prior to that time were paid only by individuals or corporations.

THE ADVENT OF PUBLIC POLICE

In 1748, the first true police force was established in London by Henry Fielding, the chief magistrate of Bow Street, a notorious section of crime and law breaking in London. Fielding established a foot patrol in the urban streets, a mounted patrol for protection of the highways, and the "Bow Street Runners," which was a group of investigators. Although his efforts did help to some degree for Bow Street, his plan did not expand to other areas of London, and the concept of paid police (constables) quietly died.

It was not until Robert Peel was appointed as England's home secretary in 1822 that police reform began to move ahead dramatically. He was not immediately successful and had to overcome strong opposition. The English government had always tried to reduce crime by simply increasing the severity of punishments meted out by the crown. More than two hundred offenses were punishable by death at the time Peel took office.

From 1822 to 1828, fewer than seventeen different parliamentary committees had studied the need for change in policies concerning law enforcement in England. In 1829, following the latest report, Parliament finally passed the Metropolitan Police Act. This act preserved the common-law status of justices and constables. It also provided for the appointment of two police commissioners charged with the authority to organize a new united police force in the Home Office. This became a duty of the home secretary, who, in turn, was directly accountable to Parliament.

This new police force concept went into effect on September 29, 1829. It numbered one hundred men who were clad in distinctive uniforms designed by Peel himself. The uniform consisted of a civilian-type coat, top hat, and black belt. Their only badge of authority was a set of brass buttons that bore the inscription "police." (These brass buttons are believed to be the origin of the term **coppers** or *cops* for police.) This new force initiated a long tradition of carrying out their duties *unarmed*, only broken when the terrorism era of the Irish Republic Army (IRA) began in the latter half of the twentieth century.

Peel promulgated a number of principles of police reform, two of which are worth mentioning:

- No quality is more indispensable to a policeman than a perfect command of temper; a quiet, determined manner has more effect than violent action.
- Good appearance commands respect.[21]

Nevertheless, the populace harbored a good deal of resentment toward the police. A popular ballad of the 1830s lamented:

Oh Mr. Peel what have you done with your police act so grand, sir? 'Twill be the cause I have no doubt of filling Van Damein's Land, sir.[22]

A bobby checks his watch as he guards the main entrance to the Lancaster House in London.

Source: Photo courtesy of Reuters/Corbis-Bettmann.

Peel's new officers were originally referred to derisively as "Bobbies," a play on Peel's first name, Robert. They were also called "Peelers" by those who viewed the police organization as yet another potential source of political patronage. But Peel was determined to create a professional police force that would win the confidence and support of the public. One of the ways he sought to accomplish this objective was to maintain the highest standards for selection and membership of his police force. Some indication of how stringent his standards were is conveyed by an outstanding fact: During the first three years of its operations alone, there were large numbers of dismissals and forced resignations from Peel's new force. Within a few short years, however, Peel's unarmed constables had achieved a reputation for courage, composure, and fair play, which transformed the name *Bobbies* into a term of respect and affection, rather than derision, among Londoners and the world.

THE COLONIAL AND AMERICAN EXPERIENCE

The English experience in both law enforcement and private security is reflected in the colonial experience through the concept of mutual protection, using the town constable and sheriff in the same roles as the parent country. The watch and ward, drawing their watchmen from the community, remained the primary sources of security in the colonies and the fledgling United States until the establishment of full-time police forces in the mid-1800s. The watch and ward system in the new land generally was implemented from dark to dawn.

Many different security issues were faced by the pioneers of the early settlements in the colonies. Threats from drunks, thieves, highwaymen, and robbers were faced along with Indian attacks, wild animals, and escaped slaves. Because the job was long and thankless, it became the general custom for those citizens in the colonies who had work, trades, or independent funds to pay others to pull their shift as a watchman.

Following the model of England's Sir Robert Peel, the first public police force was established in New York City in 1844. Other cities soon followed suit, and police forces were established in Chicago, San Francisco, Boston, Dallas, Los Angeles, and Philadelphia by 1856. The early history of police forces in the United States was not always a model of good training and high ethics. Many were involved in scandals that revealed corruption and inefficiency at all levels. When the Civil Service Act was passed in 1883, some semblance of professionalism and capability began to emerge in the departments springing up across the young nation.

PRIVATE SECURITY AND PARALLEL DEVELOPMENT

Although the emergence of police agencies at every level of government provided some relief to the growing security problems of the brash new United States, the role of the private citizen and private security in the protection of persons, property, and things also continued to grow. The new departments could scarcely grow or develop fast enough to meet the demands for protection by the citizenry of the fastest growing country in the world. Rapid industrialization turned many of the cities of America into cauldrons of crime and corruption. Factories that made the burgeoning economy grow also caused thousands to leave the farm and relocate to the urban areas, often living in squalor and growing slums.

In 1849, the cry of *"There's gold in them thar hills!"* in California opened up the Wild West and created even more problems for the new police agencies. Even the outposts of the territorial army could not control the gun-packing rabble that searched for wealth and a new life on the frontiers of the West. Many villages and towns had to resort to hiring a "gunslinger" to protect their people. Some of those hired were difficult to distinguish from the outlaws they were supposed to fight. Many towns grew so fast that they resorted to vigilantism in an attempt to maintain some order and safety. In the mid-1800s, the components of the private security industry as we know them today began to find their beginnings. The Civil War era only spurred even greater growth of these private security services.

Allen Pinkerton is generally recognized as the "father" of the private security industry in the United States. He formed Chicago's first private detective agency in 1850, and in 1855 he formed the North West Police Agency. This agency provided security for the rapidly growing railroad industry. In 1857, Pinkerton formed the Pinkerton Protection Patrol, providing watchman (guard) services for a variety of industrial clients. Pinkerton, the only vendor to provide interstate security services for more than fifty years, was even called upon by the government to provide intelligence gathering and VIP security for the military during the Civil War. Pinkerton remains

Wells Fargo Shotgun Messengers in Reno, Nevada.

Source: Photo from History Department, Wells Fargo Bank.

one of the largest security guard companies in the world and has been joined by Burns International and Wackenhut as giants in the security guard industry.

Other security pioneers of the 1850s, in the area of providing armed guards for protection of cargo and delivery firms, were Washington Perry Brinks (Brink's Armored Car Service), along with Henry Wells and William G. Fargo (Wells Fargo). These firms became famous throughout the West and in most urban areas, rising to become the world's largest armored car service.

Edwin Holmes started the first central alarm service in 1858, which he called the American Division Telegraph, known today as ADT. His lead caused alarm service companies to be started by thousands of service providers across the nation and gave birth to a whole new industry and technological field. During this dynamic period of growth in the United States, the three parts of the security triangle, the military–police–private security sectors, were trying their best to keep up with the challenge of crime in a society that was a true melting pot.

SECURITY AND LAW ENFORCEMENT IN THE EARLY 1900s

The twentieth century saw a growing need for security services on a number of fronts. Labor disturbances and union rallies in the new factory cities were controlled by private security agencies hired by management to keep order and protect lives and property, often with vigorous use of muscle. The period before and during World War I saw even greater expansion of security for protection of factories, and for help to the government in controlling espionage by politically active national groups. Private security activity dropped off considerably after World War I and reached a low during the Great Depression of the 1930s. At a time when millions of people were out of work, security seemed to be something easy to do without. One bright spot was the formation of the Burglary Protection Council in 1921 to provide standards, specifications, testing, and certification of alarm systems and devices.

The advent of World War II, which sparked the United States to conduct the greatest industrial mobilization in the history of the world, pumped new life into the private security industry as well. The wartime government required all contractors to provide stringent security measures for defense plants to protect them from sabotage and espionage. More than 200,000 plant watchmen were screened by the FBI and awarded the status of auxiliary military police for this crucial mission. These private security guards were trained by local law enforcement, raising awareness of the need for and value of plant security to new levels. The emphasis on plant security continued after the war and expanded from defense plants to all the other segments of the huge new industrial machine that rebuilt the world's economy in the aftermath of that conflagration. The cold war with the Soviet Union and the Peoples Republic of China continued to provide a growing demand for highly trained security forces at

Henry Wells (1805–1878), co-founder of American Express Company (1850), Wells, Fargo & Co. (1852), and Wells College for women in Aurora, New York (1868).

William G. Fargo (1818–1881), co-founder of American Express Company and Wells, Fargo & Co., mayor of Buffalo, New York, and namesake of Fargo, North Dakota.

Source: Photo from History Department, Wells Fargo Bank.

defense industry sites that manufactured trillions of dollars worth of weapons in the following fifty years.

Security in the Last Half of the Twentieth Century

In the second half of the twentieth century, the role of security as an essential element of industrial operations became clear. From the 200,000 security guards in World War II, the industry has grown at a massive rate to more than 1.5 million workers in 1990, with estimates of 1.9 million by the year 2000.[23] The technological advances in electronic and other sophisticated aids to security have provided methods for protecting persons, places, and things that were unimaginable just a generation ago. Today's security professional is no longer the stereotypical "guard" of old, but a highly trained and motivated part of the industrial, retail, medical, government, and services network. Developments from castle keeps to simple alarm systems to computerized access controls required the marriage of people and technology and spurred the growth of the security industry.

PUBLIC AND PRIVATE ROLES FOR SECURITY

As we have shown, security has always been provided in some form or another for our social structures, from early tribal groups to modern nation-states. The first structured providers of security for persons, places, and things were the military organizations. These were first used as all-purpose protectors and controllers, guarding against threats from outside the group and providing control inside. Public safety organizations (police and fire) developed along a parallel track with private security, sometimes at odds with and sometimes in a synergistic fashion to one another. Today, we see these roles and their development as three separate but interrelated and overlapping functions in our society. The three areas of security operations are the military, public safety, and private security. Each has a separate role, but all intersect and overlap at different times and places, sharing some of the same missions and same "clients" at different times. Only a representative sample of these key overlaps is shown in Figure 1–2.

These systems vary in their missions, sources of power and authority, and financing. The military is primarily for the defense of the nation-state against enemies from the outside, deriving authority from the Constitution, and financed by tax monies at the federal level. Public safety has the mission to protect citizens from crimes, disasters, and internal threats to law and order. Most public safety agencies (except federal) derive their authority from state, county, or local legislation, and are funded by local taxes. Private security has many missions, including protection of persons, places, and things; loss prevention; private investigations; and those services not able to be provided by the public sector. Private security gets its authority from the limited powers of a private citizen, but also from local statutes and corporate policies and procedures. Generally funded by private industry, private security is also funded by federal and local tax moneys when hired for contract security services.

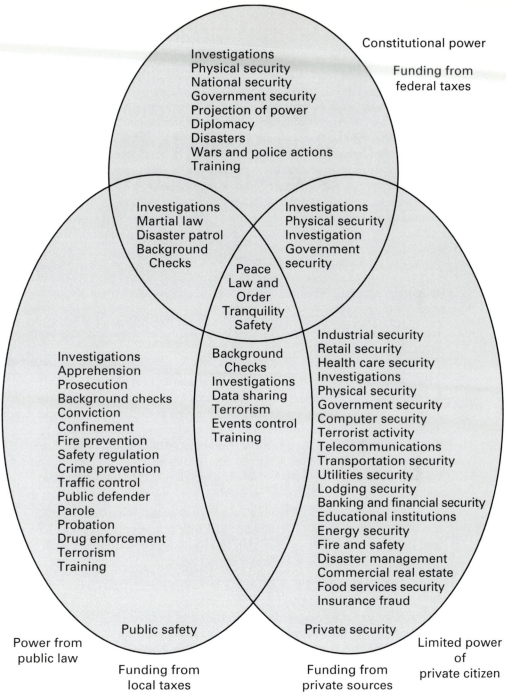

Constitutional power

Funding from
federal taxes

Investigations
Physical security
National security
Government security
Projection of power
Diplomacy
Disasters
Wars and police actions
Training

Investigations
Martial law
Disaster patrol
Background
Checks

Investigations
Physical security
Investigation
Government
security

Peace
Law and
Order
Tranquility
Safety

Investigations
Apprehension
Prosecution
Background checks
Conviction
Confinement
Fire prevention
Safety regulation
Crime prevention
Traffic control
Public defender
Parole
Probation
Drug enforcement
Terrorism
Training

Background
Checks
Investigations
Data sharing
Terrorism
Events control
Training

Industrial security
Retail security
Health care security
Investigations
Physical security
Government security
Computer security
Terrorist activity
Telecommunications
Transportation security
Utilities security
Lodging security
Banking and financial security
Educational institutions
Energy security
Fire and safety
Disaster management
Commercial real estate
Food services security
Insurance fraud

Public safety

Private security

Power from
public law

Funding from
local taxes

Funding from
private sources

Limited power
of
private citizen

FIGURE 1–2 *The Role of Synergism in Providing Crime Prevention and Crime Reduction*

Threats from Strangers: Random, Frightening

The threat of violence from friends and co-workers may not alarm managers and employees as much as the threat of volence from strangers, even though people are more likely to be harmed by someone they know or work with.

Protecting employees from violence perpetuated by strangers seems, in many ways, to be an impossible task. The reality is that it is impossible to protect anyone 100 percent of the time, writes Mark Maggio of the Federal Judiciary Center, Washington, D.C., in an article on workplace violence in Federal Probation Magazine.

The employer and its security department should approach the problem of random violence by strangers on employees with the goal of minimizing the threat rather than alleviating the threat. *The goal should be to reduce the threat as much as possible by taking some measures designed to protect employees and at the same time discourage attackers.*

Among key questions:

- Where is the organization vulnerable to an outside threat? When assessing the organization's vulnerabilities includes human as well as structural assessments.

    The human assessment requires examining several areas. First, determine who, among employees, has training in first aid and CPR. If no one does, offer training. If someone does have the training make that fact known to the other employees. Next, assess the office arrangement. *Have employees placed their desks in such a way as to block an escape route should one be needed? Is there free and clear access to all emergency exits?* Do employees have immediate access to emergency numbers on their desks (security, police, fire, emergency medical services)? Do employees keep on their desks items that could be used as weapons against them?

- Have employees received training on a variety of safety-related topics?

    If the answer is "yes," remember that followup training is critical if employees are to maintain their skill level and establish a level of confidence that will serve them well in a crisis.

- What type of relationship, if any, have you established with your local public safety agencies?

- Are you prepared to deal with the aftermath of a crisis?

    Despite your best efforts, crises can and do occur. Without a process to deal with the aftermath, a crisis of significant proportion can permanently damage your organization and your employees.

Source: O'Toole-Zalud Report. "Threats from Strangers: Random, Frightening." Security (Cahners Publishing Company. Newton, MA, 1997) Vol. 34, No. 3, p. 118.

Since private security has become such a critical part of the protection and enforcement team, far outnumbering its public sector counterpart, it is important to look at the criminal justice system in the United States and where it fits.

Turmoil, crisis, chaos—these are a few of the *milder* terms used to characterize the criminal justice system in the United States today. Terms like these are used by persons who are disposed toward a *sympathetic* view of the system, including many who work within the system itself; *critics* of the system use much harsher expressions. Until recently, it was somewhat of a standing joke among criminal justice specialists to refer to a "criminal injustice nonsystem." Newspapers and television documentaries have introduced the public to some of the more ugly and unpleasant aspects of criminal justice "American-style," and such characterizations are no longer a private matter to be kept within the system. As seen in the Rodney King beatings in Los Angeles, on one end of the spectrum, and syndicated shows showing heroic deeds, today's amateur videocamera user can capture events that are capable of glorifying or vilifying players or agencies in the criminal justice system.

Is there any justification for applying terms such as crisis and chaos to the criminal justice system? The system obviously is at least partially successful, otherwise the structure of our society would have already collapsed. Nevertheless, there is ample cause for concern expressed by private citizens and professionals in the field that the system is becoming increasingly prone to failure. The alarming rise in the incidence of serious crime is only one indicator, but it is the one that has the greatest impact on the public view of the criminal justice system.

CRIMINAL JUSTICE SYSTEMS 1 AND 2

The popular myth is that criminal justice in America is a monolithic, consistent structure that comprises synchronized agencies responding to crime in an interdependent and interrelated manner. This model is, unfortunately, just that—a model—with little relationship to fact. The American criminal justice system is not a single system but rather many separate systems and subsystems of institutions and procedures. Throughout all the thousands of towns, cities, counties, and states in the United States—even throughout the federal government—there are differing types of criminal justice "systems." While they may appear similar in that they all apprehend, prosecute, convict, and confine lawbreakers, no two systems are exactly alike, and few are linked in any comprehensive manner.

There are actually two criminal justice systems in the United States. The first one is highly visible and subject to great controversy. The second is invisible and outside the police, court, and corrections agencies. System 1 comprises the police and sheriffs' departments, judges, prosecutors and their staffs, defense offices, jails and prisons, and probation and parole agencies.

System 2 comprises the many public and private agencies that are outside the police, courts, and corrections, and that are—or should be—involved in the reduction and prevention of crime. This latter mission is the primary goal of the agencies of System 1. Examples of System 2 include legislators who create laws to prevent crime and punish criminals; teachers, ministers, and others who establish the moral fiber of the community; and private security agencies and individuals that fill in the large gaps that are left by the limited capabilities of public criminal justice agencies in the face of a seemingly unlimited growth in crime.

The conflicts, jealousies, and lack of cooperation and coordination between System 1 and System 2 further exacerbate the problems and keep all sectors from reaching optimal effectiveness in the prevention and reduction of crime. In recent years, however, there seems to be a movement toward more cooperation, coordination, and information sharing by participants in both systems. Organizations like the International Association of Chiefs of Police (IACP) and the American Society for Industrial Security (ASIS) now actively pursue cooperative efforts to meet the common goals of crime prevention and reduction. Many of these efforts are now being seen in the broad popularity of "community policing" and "value-oriented policing" programs that embrace the concept of active "partnerships," which involve all sectors of a community to fight crime.

Private Security: A Concept in Search of a Definition

Private security has had a difficult time in overcoming the "guard" label, the one that evokes the image of an elderly, retired person with a pot belly, a timeclock key, and a big gun. As the student will learn in the rest of this text, security today is a sophisticated and complex industry that defies a simple definition. A common definition for the term *private security* is "individual and organizational measures and efforts (as distinguished from public law enforcement agency efforts) that provide protection for persons and property. It also describes business enterprises that provide services and products to achieve this protection."[24]

In today's environment, however, there is much more than that in most security operations. Further, the latest trends have been to find terms that describe specific and general operations in security activities. Some of the latest terms are **loss prevention, assets protection, security services**, and many others that are used for the more esoteric areas of security operation such as *access control, environmental design*, and *biometrics monitoring*. Two excellent definitions that are applicable to most operations are provided by Purpura:

> *Security* is [narrowly] defined as traditional methods (guards, fences, alarms) used to increase the likelihood of a crime-controlled, tranquil, and noninterrupted environment for and individual or organization in pursuit of objectives.
>
> *Loss Prevention* is [broadly] defined as any method (e.g., guards, safety, auditing, insurance) used by an individual or organization to increase the likelihood of preventing and controlling loss (e.g., people, money, productivity, materials) resulting from a host of adverse occurrences (e.g., crime, fire, accident, error, poor supervision or management, bad investment). This broad definition provides a foundation for the loss prevention practitioner whose innovations are limited only by his/her imagination.[25]

Other specific definitions for the many subcategories of security and loss prevention will be examined and discussed in operational terms throughout the text. The student will soon realize that the efforts of "security" are major factors for helping their colleagues in the System 1 agencies to prevent and reduce crime.

Summary

In this chapter, we have seen the principle of punishment for undesirable behavior pass from an individual's response to a wrong, to a blood feud that involved the family, to an abstract action taken by some bureaucracy in the name of the state. We have seen how the development of social groups and societies has required some means to provide control over behavior that is too far out on the proscribed end of the continuum of behavior. Early attempts at codification of behavior resulted in bureaucratic nightmares to administer. The means for enforcement of societal rules and laws have rested in the individual, the social group, the leadership of emerging nation-states, the military, public police agencies, and attempts at private security.

Security has always been provided in some form for our social structures, from early tribal groups to modern nation-states. Although public safety organizations (police and fire) developed along a parallel track with private security, they were often at odds with one another. Only in more recent times have they begun to try to work together in a synergistic fashion. The three areas of security provision are seen as the military, public safety, and private security, each with a separate but overlapping role. Private security has become such a critical part of the protection and enforcement team that it now far outnumbers its public sector counterpart.

The popular myth is that criminal justice in America is a monolithic, consistent structure that comprises totally synchronized agencies responding to crime in an interdependent and interrelated manner. In fact, the criminal justice system is not a single system but rather many separate systems and subsystems of institutions and procedures that are often poorly articulated and seldom meaningfully interrelated. Criminal justice System 2 comprises the many public and private agencies outside the police that are involved in the reduction and prevention of crime, such as legislators that create laws to prevent crime and punish criminals; teachers, ministers, and others who establish the moral fiber of the community; and private security agencies and individuals who fill in the large gaps left by the limited capabilities of public criminal justice agencies in the face of a seemingly unlimited growth in crime.

Security today is a sophisticated and complex industry that defies a simple definition. Several common definitions for the term *private security* were offered in this chapter, and the student will see a great expansion of this definition in latter parts of the text. The efforts of "security" are major factors for helping the public sector agencies in the criminal justice System 1 prevent and reduce crime. To paraphrase the writer and street philosopher Studs Terkel, "A society that does not know its past cannot understand its present, nor shape its future." In this case, the future seems bright for the private security discipline, if those who control its destiny can learn from the successes and failures in the past.

REVIEW QUESTIONS

1. Describe the continuum of behavior and how it affected the development of laws.
2. Why did the role of police develop from former community service by citizens for security needs?
3. Where was the first true police department formed and by whom was it formed?
4. What caused private security to emerge from the Civil War as a new entity?
5. Explain the development and roles of criminal justice System 1 and System 2.

TERMS TO REMEMBER

social control	*free will*	*shire-reeve*
territoriality	*proscribed*	*citizen's arrest*
personal property	*prescribed*	*Magna Carta*
folkways	*corporal punishment*	*sovereign immunity*
mores	*security services*	*watch and ward*
laws	*lex externa*	*coppers*
blood feud	*lex naturalis*	*loss prevention*
lex talionis	*lex humana*	*assets protection*
civil death	*prevention*	*security services*
ordeal	*tithing*	
Inquisition	*tithing-man*	

ENDNOTES

1. Albert Kocourek and John Wigmore, *Evolution of Law, Vol. II: Punitive and Ancient Legal Institutions* (Boston: Little, Brown, 1915), p. 124.
2. *Lex salica* was the fine paid for homicide, and it varied according to the rank, sex, and age of the murdered person. In general, *lex salica* refers to a payment for death or injury.
3. *Wergeld*, which means "man-money," originally referred to the death of an individual and the individual's supposed value to his or her family. It later referred to personal injury as well.
4. Ronald Akers, "Toward a Comparative Definition of Criminal Law," *Journal of Criminal Law, Criminology and Police Science* (1965): 301–306.
5. Kocourek and Wigmore, *Evolution of Law, Vol. II*, p. 126.
6. The Code of Hammurabi is estimated to have been written about 1750 B.C.
7. The Sumerian codes were those of Kings Lipit-Ishtar and Eshnunna and are estimated to date from about 1860 B.C.
8. Thorsten Sellin, "A Look at Prison History," *Federal Probation* (September 1967): 18.
9. Gustav Radbruch, *Elegantiae Juris Criminalis*, 2d ed. (Basel, Switzerland: Verlag für Recht und Gesellschaft A.G., 1950), p. 5.
10. Slaves were also marked by branding on the forehead or by metal collars that could not easily be removed.

11. *Friedensgeld* was the practice of paying restitution to the crown, in addition to individuals, for crimes. It later replaced payment to individuals and became the system of fines paid to the state. With fines, the victim disappeared from the criminal justice system, becoming the ignored component of the crime.

12. This religious requirement brought the two issues of sin and crime into the same arena and broadened the scope of the church courts. The offender was obligated to make retribution to both God and the state.

13. Emperor Justinian I A.D. 483–565 was a great preserver of Roman law who collected all imperial statutes, issued a digest of all writings of Roman jurists, and wrote a revised code and a textbook for students. His *Corpus Juris Civilis* became the foundation of law in most of continental Europe.

14. Draco, ruler of Greece in 621 B.C., drew up a very harsh and cruel code that used corporal punishment so extensively that it was said to be written not in ink but in blood.

15. The Inquisition was a tribunal established by the Catholic church in the Middle Ages with very wide powers for the suppression of heresy. The tribunal searched out heretics and other offenders rather than waiting for charges to be brought forward (somewhat in the manner of former Senator Joseph McCarthy, who rooted out "Communists" in the early 1950s). Emperor Frederick II made the Inquisition a formal institution in 1224, and it came to an end in 1834.

16. Walter C. Reckless, *The Crime Problem*, 4th ed. (New York: Appleton-Century-Crofts, 1969), p. 497.

17. Harry Elmer Barnes and Negley K. Teeters, *New Horizons in Criminology*, 3d ed. (Englewood Cliffs, N.J.: Prentice-Hall, 1959), p. 286. For a more recent update on deterrence, see Steven Klepper and Daniel Nagin, "The Deterrent Effect of Perceived Certainty and Severity of Punishment Revisited," *Criminology* 36 (1989): 721–746.

18. Stephen Schafer, *Theories in Criminology* (New York: Random House, 1969), p. 25.

19. Edwin H. Sutherland, *Criminology* (Philadelphia: Lippincott, 1924), p. 317.

20. Reckless, *The Crime Problem*, p. 504. There is no evidence that increased use of incarceration will lead to lower levels of crime. See David Biles, "Crime and the Use of Prisons," *Federal Probation* (June 1979): 39–43.

21. H. Vetter and C. Simonsen. *Criminal Justice in America: The System, the Process, the People* (Philadelphia: W.B. Saunders, 1976), p. 89.

22. W. H. Hewett. *British Police Administration* (Springfield, Illinois: Charles C. Thomas, 1965), p. 64.

23. William C. Cunningham, John J. Strauchs, and Clifford Van Meter. *Private Security Trends 1970 to 2000: The Hallcrest Report II* (Boston: Butterworth Heinemann, 1990), p. 229.

24. National Advisory Committee on Criminal Justice Standards and Goals, *Private Security: Report of the Task Force on Private Security* (U.S. Government Printing Office, Washington, D.C., 1976), p. 3.

25. Philip P. Purpura. *Security & Loss Prevention* (Boston: Butterworth-Heinemann, 1984), p. 30.

2

The Mission for Private Security

"MAKE MY DAY!" OR "HAVE A NICE DAY"?

The opinions of respected individuals and groups within the security community indicate the time is right for interested parties to initiate a push toward codifying the discipline. The acceptance of security management as a concept rather than a function will be an indisputable signal to the field of management: security is ready for appropriate academic attention and professional management recognition.

— C. H. Davidson

Overview

Clearly, society was slow to develop protection for its groups and individuals. Law enforcement has been rapidly accepted because of clear and defined laws, rules, and procedures to detect and apprehend anyone who violates those laws. The force and power of the state were a foundation stone for law enforcement and provided prestige, often beyond the reality, to police agencies and their officers. Law enforcement became a regular academic discipline in the 1930s, and the Law Enforcement Assistance Administration (**LEAA**), following the President's Commission on Criminal Justice Standards and Goals in the 1960s, even provided a program to finance advanced education for police. This program, the Law Enforcement Education Program (LEEP), provided an opportunity for thousands of those in pubic safety to acquire bachelors', masters', and even Ph.D degrees though federal financing.

This certainly gave a boost to that part of professionalism in the law enforcement field. Private security took longer to move in that direction, and this chapter discusses the reasons for that, as well as the missions for both law enforcement and private security.

Private Security: A Profession or Just a Job?

Private security has sometimes been defined as a "function in search of a discipline." We have seen that the history of private security has been one of feast and famine, rising and falling with the economic seas. Perhaps another definition might be "a discipline looking for professional standing." Too often the businessperson looks at security operations as a luxury, one that can be afforded in good times, but the first to be cut during economic downturns. Part of this fault lies with the security professionals who fail to clearly demonstrate the *value* of security and loss prevention throughout the year, often discussing the *cost* of these vital services only at budget time. A relevant discussion of the problems involved with defining security management as a profession is presented by C. H. Davidson:

> Security management has developed to the point where it deserves recognition as a free-standing management science. To that end, it clearly needs specialized professional training and universal recognition as an academic discipline. A review of current literature substantiates this point. To date, academics in general have placed security management under the rubric of criminal justice curricula. The complex issue of privatization may ultimately focus attention on the increasingly distinct differences between security management as a private sector organizational specialty and criminal justice as a field limited to public administration. If security management deserves the mantle of an academic discipline [profession], recognizable market trends in the credentials expected of entry and mid-level security professionals should lend credence to this contention. The opinions of respected individuals and groups within the security community indicate the time is right for interested parties to initiate a push toward codifying the discipline. The acceptance of security management as a concept rather than a function will be an indisputable signal to the field of management: security is ready for appropriate academic attention and professional management recognition.[1]

The generally accepted test of a **profession** comprises five specific guidelines:

1. Specific standards and a code of ethics and conduct that governs the actions of the members of that profession.

2. A body of knowledge, professional journals, and a historical perspective that acts as a guide for new members of the profession.

3. A recognized association that provides a forum for the continuing discussion and development of the profession.

4. A certification program that ensures that the members of the profession are competent to practice in the field.

5. An educational discipline that prepares students in the specific functions and philosophies of that profession.

This may seem to be quite a menu for private security, but much progress has already been made on all these points in the past couple of decades. Criscouli attests to this fact in a thoughtful essay:

Security can be considered a profession because it requires advanced training of a mental rather than manual nature. This claim is not made to suggest that all security practitioners demonstrate full professional competence; no profession could seriously make that claim. Rather, it is made to point out a fact many people seem unaware of—that security is not merely a matter of intuition or common sense; it involves a complex body of knowledge, analytical abilities, and the know-how to prescribe suitable security measures for individual circumstances as well as the effective use of an array of other managerial skills.[2]

In this chapter, we examine some of the important issues faced by security managers and practitioners in the movement toward professional status and recognition in a world that often takes a viewpoint of security and loss prevention that is far from reality. Let us examine these five guidelines for a profession.

1. *Specific standards and a code of ethics and conduct that governs the actions of the members of that profession.* The security field has a plethora of organizations that profess to represent one or several segments of the industry. That seems to be one of the major problems in describing the security "profession" as a unitary entity. It is actually more like a swarm of bees, an entity comprising many different individual organizations. If one examines the standing committees of the **American Society for Industrial Security** (ASIS), it reveals the vast diversity found in that one association:

> Academic Programs in Colleges and Universities
> Banking and Financial Services
> Commercial Real Estate
> Computer Security
> Crime/Loss Prevention
> Disaster Management
> Educational Institutions
> Energy
> Fire Prevention and Safety
> Food Services
> Government Security
> Health Care Services
> Insurance Fraud
> Investigations
> Law Enforcement Liaison Council
> Lodging
> Museum, Library and Archives
> Physical Security
> Privacy and Personnel Information Management

Private Security Services Council

Retail Services

Safeguarding Proprietary Information

Security Architecture and Engineering

Substance Abuse

Telecommunications

Terrorist Activities

Transportation

Utilities

White-Collar Crime

This patchwork would hardly seem to have specific standards of conduct, if only because the individual committee's missions are so diverse. But in defense of ASIS, it does best approach the model of the American Medical Association or the American Bar Association in trying to make the sum greater than the whole. Surely doctors and lawyers of every type are considered professionals. Therefore, it seems possible that the individual groups of security activity are moving toward the adoption of standards to meet this first point.

2. *A body of knowledge, professional journals, and a historical perspective that acts as a guide for new members of the profession.* The body of knowledge in security has grown rapidly in the past decade. Until recently, most of the books and treatises on this broad discipline were simply modified versions borrowed from law enforcement and criminal justice. This has changed, and now there is a continuing demand by publishers and academic institutions for texts that are "security pure" and juried journals that will publish intellectual research and writings about all aspects of security. Many texts have developed historical perspectives on security as a potential profession, and the small, but growing, cadre of scholars with an eye on security are building a strong database of knowledge. In the United States, the two editions of the *Hallcrest Report* have shown a new crop of security leaders just how the field has developed and where it is going.

   The growth of quality magazines and journals in the security field has produced a veritable library of reference and guidance materials ranging from extremely technical (*Security, Access Control*), to legal (*Security Management Bulletin, The Lipmann Report, Security Law Newsletter, Canadian Security*), to general security and management (*Security Management Today, Security Management, INTERSEC*), to academic (*International Journal of Risk, Security and Crime Prevention, Security Journal, Journal of Healthcare Protection Management*).

3. *A recognized association that provides a forum for the continuing discussion and development of the profession.* We have seen the ASIS become a leader in the field of security associations. This does not mean that many other fine security organizations have not been working diligently to provide leadership in their nations, or specific fields of security activity. Although the American Society for Industrial Security has done a great job in pulling many of them together, not all have responded.

The Canadian Society for Industrial Security and a similar association in New Zealand are two national types of associations, and they do a fine job. The International Association of Hospital Security Supervisors and the Association of Certified Fraud Examiners are two that deal with specific tasks in security. All these organizations provide forums for discussion and seem to meet the qualifications for this definition.

4. *A certification program that ensures that the members of the profession are competent to practice in the field.* Most of the associations mentioned, and many others, have some kind of certification program. The **Certified Protection Professional** (CPP) designation is perhaps best known and is open for examination to anyone in the security profession who meets the Professional Certification Board's criteria. The **Certified Hospital Protection Administrator** (CHPA) designation is awarded only to those who are security administrators in the hospital field. The Canadian Society for Industrial Security also has a professional accreditation program for its members that is rigorous and extensive. Many other organizations have also developed professional certifications for their associations and specific fields of security, such as the **Certified Fraud Investigator** (CFI) designation.

5. *An educational discipline that prepares students in the specific functions and philosophies of that profession.* It is in this last category that perhaps the most development still needs to be made. Even though numerous two-year certificate programs or associate degrees are offered at community colleges and other educational institutions, the movement toward a clearly defined security administration undergraduate degree and graduate degree has been slow and limited. Part of this appears to have been because of the limited cost benefit for the effort. Security wages, especially at the line level, have been slow to catch up with the public safety agencies. Only in the past couple of decades have management and technical skills become demanding enough to cause salaries for security administrators to rise at a rate to impress or attract college-educated applicants. Despite the belief of many that little is needed to be a security person, this is no longer so. The past vision of the aging **rent-a-cop** has long given way to the need for technically capable and well-trained security officers. They need to be experts in management, risk analysis, and in the installation and use of high-tech gadgets for security and loss prevention. Former police officers and military personnel now find themselves in a *proactive* rather than a *reactive* environment, one that requires managerial and technical skills unthought of just a few years ago.

All this is happening in a climate of downsizing of security operators in the corporate world, while the threat of violence in the workplace seems to be increasing every day. This means the security professional can no longer survive as someone with a high school diploma and twenty years in law enforcement or the military. The security professional of the twenty-first century will need to be a keen thinker with the management and technical skills relative to his or her position in the hierarchy of the security organization. These kinds of skills must be garnered not just from training classes but also from solid educational programs that address the business skills required to survive in today's corporate environment. Doing *more with less* means that those who compose the "less" be better educated, trained, and prepared to work *smarter*, not harder.

It seems that the professionalization of security is not quite a *fait accompli*, but it now has all the pieces in place. The threats from criminals, terrorists, and perpetrators of fraud to assets around the world demand that the industry provide security professionals the tools and knowledge to use them to meet these threats. To be regarded as professionals, security personnel must expunge the image of the rent-a-cop and replace it with levels of skill backed by experience, education, ethics, and technical abilities. Only when security managers and staff are able to back the claim of professionalism with the test of these five guidelines will they get the respect and clout they need to do their jobs most efficiently.

Ethics and the Security Profession

The student should recognize that the vast majority of persons in any organization are ethical and moral, with security professionals even more so on the average. However, lest we forget that some do choose to set a different value on ethical behavior, we must accept the value and need for ethics in security work. Although not the sole representative of the private security profession, the American Society for Industrial Security is the largest and acts as the major force for all segments of security and loss prevention as all work toward its recognition as a true profession. In the area of ethics, ASIS has published the code of ethics, shown as Figure 2–1. We learned in Chapter 1 that what is considered right or wrong can be placed on a behavior scale from prescribed to proscribed. The balance point of the behavioral continuum is not constant, however, and changes **over time**, at **different times**, and in **different societies**.

CHANGES IN BEHAVIORAL DEFINITIONS

Changes can be observed *over time* in the folkways, mores, and laws in regard to what is considered to be pornographic material. Not long ago, the material now found on sale at almost every bookstall would have gotten the publisher burned at the stake, or at least driven out of town. As attitudes toward the viewing of the human body gradually changed, these new attitudes were reflected in what appeared in print, plays, movies, and dress.

In regard to reaction to behaviors at *different times*, one need look no further than the Eighteenth Amendment to the U.S. Constitution, commonly referred to as the Volstead Act (or the Prohibition Act) which, in 1919, prohibited the sale of alcohol under punishment of law. Prior to 1919, alcohol was perfectly legal to sell and consume in the United States. From that date on, until repeal of Prohibition in 1933, the sale of alcohol was illegal but *consumption* was legal and therefore created a flourishing crime industry supplying "bootleg" alcoholic beverages to those who did not agree with the law.

In the first example, the folkways and mores of the society changed over time, and its members came to agree that the previously strict pornography laws were unnecessary and needed to be relaxed. In the example of legal prohibition of the sale of alcoholic beverages, a minority of private interest groups were able to get the Eighteenth Amendment passed. But since the law was not in sync with the folkways

FIGURE 2–1 *ASIS Code of Ethics*

Preamble

I. A member shall perform professional duties in accordance with the law and the highest moral principles.

Ethical Considerations

1. A member shall abide by the law of the land in which the services are rendered and perform all duties in an honorable manner.
2. A member shall not knowingly become associated in responsibility for work with colleagues who do not conform to the law and these ethical standards.
3. A member shall be just and respect the rights of others in performing professional responsibilities.

II. A member shall observe the precepts of truthfulness, honesty, and integrity.

Ethical Considerations

1. A member shall disclose all relevant information to those having a right to know.
2. A right to know is a legally enforceable claim or demand by a person for disclosure of information by a member. Such a right does not depend upon prior knowledge by the person of the existence of the information to be disclosed.
3. A member shall not knowingly release misleading information nor encourage or otherwise participate in the release of such information.

III. A member shall be faithful and diligent in discharging professional responsibilities.

Ethical Considerations

1. A member is faithful when fair and steadfast in adherence to promises and commitments.
2. A member is diligent when employing best efforts in an assignment.
3. A member shall not act in matters involving conflicts of interest without appropriate disclosure and approval.
4. A member shall represent services or products fairly and truthfully.

IV. A member shall be competent in discharging professional responsibilities.

Ethical Considerations

1. A member is competent who possesses and applies the skills and knowledge required for the task.
2. A member shall not accept a task beyond the member's competence nor shall competence be claimed when not possessed.

V. A member shall safeguard confidential information and exercise due care to prevent its improper disclosure.

Ethical Considerations

1. Confidential information is nonpublic information the disclosure of which is restricted.
2. Due care requires that the professional must not knowingly reveal confidential information or use a confidence to the disadvantage of the principal or to the disadvantage of the member or a third person unless the principal consents after full disclosure of all the facts. This confidentiality continues after the business relationship between the member and his principal has terminated.
3. A member who receives information and has not agreed to be bound by confidentiality is not bound from disclosing it. A member is not bound by confidential disclosures made of acts or omissions which constitute a violation of the law.
4. Confidential disclosures made by a principal to a member are not recognized by law as privileged in a legal proceeding. The member may be required to testify in a legal proceeding as to information received in confidence from his principal over the objection of his principal's counsel.
5. A member shall not disclose confidential information for personal gain without appropriate authorizations.

VI. A member shall not maliciously injure the professional reputation or practice of colleagues, clients, or employers.

Ethical Considerations

1. A member shall not comment falsely and with malice concerning a colleague's competence, performance, or professional capabilities.
2. A member who knows, or has reasonable grounds to believe, that another member has failed to conform to the Society's Code of Ethics shall present such information to the Ethical Standards Committee in accordance with Article XIV of the ASIS Bylaws.

Source: Courtesy of American Society for Industrial Security (International).

and mores of the society, it was generally ignored. As a result, most of the people continued to get their alcohol from illegal sources until the laws were finally repealed.

CULTURAL DIFFERENCES IN DEFINITIONS

Different societies (sometimes even subcultures within societies) move the centerpoint on the behavioral continuum based on their perceived needs. For example, the birth–death ratio in the United States is almost even with or below the maintenance of a zero growth population. The growth of industrialization, incredible increases in the productivity and replacement of manual labor with machinery in factories and farms, and social welfare programs that secured old age made it unnecessary to have large families to provide a workforce and old-age security for family heads. As a result, family planning was encouraged and family size shrank. However, in many third-world nations where high infant mortality, lack of social welfare, and no security in old-age security exist, large families seem to continue as the primary means of supplying a large unskilled workforce and security in old age for the senior members of their social groupings.

RIGHT OR WRONG?

So what is the appropriate definition of "right" and "wrong"? Why is it "right" to take pencils and paper from the office for your children to use in school, but "wrong" to use that same company's vehicles and fuel for your personal use as a self-awarded "perk"? The private security practitioner is constantly faced, as are other professionals, with the conflict between **organizational ethics** and standards and **professional ethics** and standards. Although many say you must follow the organizational "golden rule" (whoever has the gold makes the rules), this simplistic statement falls into the trap of **situational ethics** and hardly denotes a sense of ethical professionalism. The private security professional is often encouraged by less ethical colleagues in the organization to "go along to get along." This usually means making a compromise of personal and professional standards in situations that are clearly unethical, even illegal.

We all are subjected to a constant barrage of sordid investigative journalism about unethical behavior by our congressional representatives, televangelists, police, bankers, doctors, teachers, businesspersons, financial advisors, union leaders, and even presidential candidates. It is therefore not surprising that security professionals must strive to be extra vigilant about their own ethics. It is always easy to say "everyone is doing it" and look the other way, or even join in. As professionals charged with the protection of life, property, and possessions, we must constantly consider the rightness and wrongness of what we observe and do. As noted by Foster:

> As a security professional I have grown increasingly concerned about something we seem to have lost sight of in America. It has been the mortar between the bricks of our national character and our industrial strength, and it is represented by one small word, a word that encompasses the best qualities we have always expected of ourselves, our peers, and our leaders—*ethics*. That word lives among a select group of

Security managers must handle many tasks at the same time.

Source: C. Simonsen. Courtesy of Northwest Protective Services, Inc.

small, powerful words like *duty*, *honor*, and *country*, words that carry meanings far beyond their humble dictionary definition....ethics are the binding threads that are interwoven through every fold in the fabric of human endeavor, providing strength and trust. Ethics are inseparably linked to the laws of our land, to statutory requirements, and to social acceptability. Behavior that is unethical is often also illegal.[3]

The late 1990s is a time in history when ethics are often scoffed at, bypassed, or ignored. Security professionals have an additional obligation to maintain basic ideas of ethical standards for themselves and their employees at a very high level; security professionals who think otherwise perhaps should consider another line of work. It is critical that the security professional act as a positive example and advisor to organizational leaders and members, however difficult it may become.

A CODE OF ETHICS

Analysis of the code of ethics supplied by ASIS, as shown in Figure 2–1, is a useful exercise. Although only one of many excellent codes, it highlights the need to inform your corporate administration that failure to follow ethical practices in security can often cost the company more in the long run in litigation awards than it would save in shortcuts to profit. A recent analysis of this code of ethics states:

At times you may disagree with corporate administration when the incident merits such action. Protecting a human life is required of everyone. Only recently have heads of corporations been found guilty in court for business decisions. If you make decisions inside the business and corporate setting [or abet them] that can cause death or harm to someone, then you are guilty too.

The bottom line is this: If your professional code of ethics conflicts with company policy and management's behavioral standards, you may have to stop being a part of the management team and uphold your professional ethics. You must observe special standards of conduct and manifest good faith in professional relationships with all individuals you encounter while working.

…Whether you work in an industrial, retail, military, or security education setting, you will be expected to make ethical decisions that may conflict with administration or corporate policy. Making them won't be easy, but it is the only way to live up to—and with—your professional ethics.[4]

In later chapters, we will examine the financial cost to industry from unethical behavior by employees. In the government, this cost is passed on to the taxpayer; in business, to the consumer. Those who report such unethical or illegal behavior are called **whistle-blowers**, a perhaps inauspicious name that tends to make those who report such behavior seem like "tattle-tales." Unfortunately, this makes the outcome of much whistle-blowing, both in the government and in the corporate world, often harder on the informant than it is on the violators. Corporate and governmental tolerance of such behavior and protection of the violators make one think before taking action that may be seen as counterproductive to the company's bottom line. However, although the security professional may understandably feel that whistle-blowing can be a situation that is not career enhancing, always remember that the security person *is the one with the whistle*.

STANDARDS: A CURSE OR BLESSING?

Almost three decades ago, the federal government issued *Private Security: Report of the Task Force on Private Security* as one volume in the huge examination of criminal justice standards and goals. The issuance of this massive report, truly a "how-to" document in most sectors of the so-called criminal justice system, was also hailed as a great breakthrough for private security. Then it was, like so many "blue ribbon" reports, filed and forgotten, and too often unread. A number of goals for private security were proposed and seventy-six standards presented for activities from selection of personnel to sanctions and criminal punishments. The depth of this classic report is amazing, and it should be on the bookshelf of any serious student of private security. However, as with many blue ribbon reports, it raises more questions than it answers. Response to the standards proposed by the commission report has been less than thunderous, but for practical reasons. Standards in private security must be considered in the context of a profit-oriented industry that has to answer to some kind of a bottom line and is often looking for those services from the lowest bidder.

Implementation of the goals and standards in the *Report of the Task Force on Private Security* fell into the morass of city, county, or state legislation and has had limited success, still dependent upon economic trends. Unfortunately, as in the implementation of similar recommendations in other sectors of the criminal justice system, the major influence on change has been litigation resulting in court-ordered change. Much of this litigation has used the establishment of standards and goals that are probably impossible to reach, and were not provided with adequate resources to implement, as justification for massive court judgments. (This will be discussed in some detail in a Chapter 9). This type of "commission-speak" report is a standard method for politicians to implement in order to highlight a problem, study it, make a report on the problem, and then let the industry or agency involved twist in the wind as it tries to implement cost-effective solutions. As noted by Bureau of Business Practices:

> …as we know, standards, training and economics are all tied together. As security head, you have to make sure that your top management understands the functions of private security officers and the training necessitated by those functions. Items that are among them include deterring crime, maintaining order, preserving safety, and in some business interacting with and assisting visitors to the facility. Then there are special functions that vary with the work setting. The amount and type of training needed by a security officer will depend on whether the officer guards a warehouse or office building after dark, drives an armored car, or works in an amusement park, museum, or busy shopping center. The person perfect for one assignment could be very wrong for another.[5]

TRAINING

The standards for one specific type of security position may be quite different from others. *Training*, therefore, seems to be the first area of standards creating problems that can result in mistakes and litigation. The *Report of the Task Force on Private Security* recommended thirty-two to forty hours of training for *armed* security guards, but left whole areas of security with little or no standards for training. The state of Washington passed legislation in 1992 that requires eight hours of training for licensed security officers. And it took twenty-six years of effort by security professionals for even this minimum standard to be passed. A sample of the list of standards for training, as described in the *Report of the Task Force on Private Security*, shows the amount of work required to meet "minimums":

> 2.3 Private security employers should develop job descriptions for each private security position.

> 2.4 Private security employers should ensure that training programs are designed, presented, and evaluated in relation to the job functions to be performed.

> 2.7 Private security employers should ensure that private security personnel are given ongoing training by using roll call training, training bulletins, and other training media.

2.8 Private security employers should provide effective job-related training for supervisory and managerial employees. Appropriate prior training, education, or professional certification should be accepted to meet this requirement.

2.9   A state government regulatory agency should have the authority and responsibility to accredit training schools, approve training curriculums, and certify instructors for the private security industry.

2.10 Appropriate State boards and agencies should coordinate efforts to provide training opportunities for private security personnel and persons interested in preparing for security employment, through utilization of physical and personnel resources of area vocational schools and colleges and universities.[6]

A more recent commentary is to be found in *The Hallcrest Report II* of 1990, regarding the explosion of litigation in the security industry for **inadequate security**. A logical definition of inadequate security is difficult without any clear standards for what is "adequate." *The Hallcrest Report II* concludes:

> Perhaps during the 1990s, as a secondary outcome of litigation, we will see evaluative research into the crime prevention research into the crime prevention effectiveness of security guards, alarms, locks, cameras, lighting, and employee training…. the litigation explosion may also be the catalyst for long overdue *security standards* and/or codes which should help reduce the claims of inadequate security and ultimately may improve security services and products [emphasis added].[7]

STANDARDS LEGISLATION

On June 11, 1991, U.S. Senator Al Gore introduced Senate Bill 1258 to require the administrator of general services to issue regulations to establish standards for the hiring of federal security officers, to establish a grant program to assist states in establishing standards for the hiring of security officers by public and private employers, to require a study and report by the administrator of the general services administration, and for other purposes.[8]

Earlier, on April 11, 1991, the Washington State Legislature passed House Bill 1180 and Senate Bill 5125 to regulate procedures for licensing of private security guards and private detectives within Washington State. The purpose of these efforts at legislation was to describe the requirements of these governmental rules for the federal, state, county, and city levels as they affect or may affect the private and proprietary security industry in general, and the local municipality level in particular. The central question is, "Do these laws serve the public good?"

Attempting to answer this question requires comparing the various proposed or enacted laws across the nation. Because these laws cover a broad spectrum of licensing requirements, we will examine the training standards to be implemented as a point of focus. Let's first look at the federal act. U.S. Senate and House of Representative staffers, in researching the issue of security officer employment standards, found that:

1. More than 1,100,000 security personnel in the United States protect the citizens and property of the Nation.

2. For many entities, private security officers from private security companies are rapidly replacing public sector law enforcement officers.

3. Such private security officers provide protection, on a proprietary or contract basis, to such diverse operations as banks, hospitals, chemical companies, airlines, and nuclear installations; and protect individuals, tangible and intangible property and proprietary information.

4. The trend in this Nation towards privatization in such security services has accelerated rapidly as the per capita number of public sector law enforcement officers has decreased.

5. The trend towards such privatization is to be applauded, as such privatization frees up public sector law enforcement officers to combat serious and violent crimes.

6. Such trend creates concomitant increase in the need for highly qualified professional private security officers.

7. Possible applicants for such private security officer positions should be screened as thoroughly as possible.

8. Industry standards in the private security industry are essential for the selection, training, and supervision of qualified security personnel.

9. If such standards are not developed, there will be an excessive burden on public sector law enforcement officers.

10. There is a need to balance the rights of an applicant for a security officer position and the need of the private security industry to ensure highly qualified professional service.[9]

Screening requirements would require applicants for security officer positions to undergo a check of references from former employers, a physical fitness test, a proof of U.S. citizenship or intent to achieve this status, a credit check, a psychological test, and a criminal background check.

A basic training provision would require officers to be trained and tested (and be given adequate refresher training on an ongoing basis) in subjects including fire protection and prevention, first aid, legal information relevant to providing security services, investigation and detention procedures, building safety, methods of handling crisis situations, methods of crowd control, the use of equipment needed in providing security services, and technical writing of reports. The proposed federal law clearly defines that "Nothing [in this bill]... shall preclude any State from adopting more stringent rules than those required... [by this bill]."

An ambitious research project was launched in 1988 by William Hamill to detail the laws and statutes that affect private investigators and security guard agencies in the United States. First published in 1989 and revised in December 1991, Hamill's herculean effort provides an excellent single source for statistics in this area. His report, nearly 900 pages long, will not be detailed here. However, to provide a sense of regional laws, we will examine data from four Pacific Northwest states (Alaska, Idaho,

Oregon, and Washington; see Table 2–1) and five states with major metropolitan population centers (California, Florida, Illinois, New York, and Texas; see Table 2–2).

WASHINGTON STATE'S LEGISLATION

It is useful here to track some of the problems encountered by trying to establish mandated standards. Washington State is a good example. In 1986, a meeting of security industry officials was convened for the purpose of drafting language to establish a statewide law to regulate the private security industry in the state of Washington. Within the industry, there had long been concern that no consistent standards or licensing existed. Several meetings over many months failed to yield a successful sponsor at the legislative level. In the fall of 1990, the Washington State Security Council and the Pacific Northwest Association of Investigators, two groups that represented the major suppliers of private security services in Washington, engaged the services of a professional lobbyist to move efforts for legislation forward. The Department of Licensing suggested dividing the proposed legislation into a bill to regulate private security guards and a separate bill to regulate private detectives. Representatives of the state patrol, police chiefs, sheriffs, Criminal Justice Training Commission, the House

Table 2–1	
COMPARATIVE SECURITY LICENSING REQUIREMENTS OF FOUR PACIFIC NORTHWEST STATES	
Alaska	(Hamill, 1991: 9–12) No state license. No distinction between private investigators and other members of the public.
Idaho	(Hamill, 1991: 285–287) No state license. Some Idaho counties and cities do have licensing requirements. Follow county laws pertaining to public carrying of firearms.
Oregon	(Hamill, 1991: 671–676) No state license. Licensing left to county and city discretion. Follow laws pertaining to public carrying of firearms.
Washington	Data for Washington taken from new laws (18.170RCW and 18.165RCW, effective December 1991).
	State licensing required. Includes fingerprinting and no disqualifying convictions. Counties and cities may impose business taxes and limited regulations. Minimum four (4) hours preassignment training and testing. Additional weapons permit training and range qualification for armed guards. Unarmed guard minimum age eighteen (18). Armed guard minimum age twenty-one (21). Director, Department of Licensing, shall consult with the private security industry and law enforcement before adopting or amending preassignment or continuing education requirements. Law does not apply to law enforcement or proprietary security.

COMPARATIVE SECURITY LICENSING REQUIREMENTS OF MAJOR METROPOLITAN POPULATION STATES

California (Hamill, 1991: 105–140)	State licensing required. Includes fingerprinting and no disqualifying convictions. Counties and cities may impose business taxes and limited regulations. Two (2) hour class and test in Powers of Arrest required. May require written/oral preassignment test for guards using any of the following: baton, tear gas, dogs, or other specialized equipment. Minimum fourteen (14) hours of classroom/range qualifying for armed guards. Governor appoints nine-member Advisory Board on Private Security Services for four year terms. Two members are licensed private patrol operators, two members are licensed alarm company operators, and five members from the public. Only one public member may have active connection with law enforcement. No public member may have active private security connections. Members review and recommend to Chief, Bureau of Collection and Investigative Services. Disciplinary review board is appointed by Advisory Board. Law does not apply to law enforcement or proprietary security.
Florida (Hamill, 1991: 163–182)	State licensing required. Includes fingerprinting, and no disqualifying convictions. Counties and cities may impose business taxes only. State is phasing in additional training requirements. Sixteen (16) hours of classroom training as of October 1991. Four (4) hours is added every two years until October 2003, when forty (40) hours of classroom training becomes minimum requirement, or until amended. Weapons permit requires twenty-four (24) hours training—only eight (8) hours may be range hours. Effective October 1992, four hours are added and four hours every two years until forty-eight hours minimum is reached in 1998. Four (4) hours of annual firearms refresher training is also required. Department of State appoints an eleven-member Private Security Advisory Council for four-year terms. One member shall be a law enforcement officer having statewide jurisdiction, or representing a statewide law enforcement association, one member shall be an owner or an operator of a business which regularly contracts for security from a licensee, other members shall represent the state geographically, and two members shall be from the security profession (one from an agency with 20 or fewer employees), two members shall be from the private investigative profession (one from an agency with five or less investigators), one member shall be from the repossession profession; the remaining four members may come from any of the professions regulated by the law. The Director, Division on Licensing, or designee, shall serve as a nonvoting Secretary. Members review and recommend only, to the Department of State. Law does not apply to law enforcement. However, proprietary officers must be licensed. They do not have to have the 14–40 hours of training noted above, except, if they are armed they must complete the same weapons training *and* the minimum officer training.

TABLE 2–2 (CONT'D)

Illinois (Hamill, 1991: 238–284)	State licensing required. Counties and cities expressly prohibited from regulating. Includes fingerprinting and no disqualifying convictions. Twenty (20) hours of classroom instruction during first ninety days' employment required. Additional forty (40) hours of classroom and range qualifying for armed positions required. Director, Department of Professional Regulation appoints a nine-member Board for four-year terms. Three members shall be licensed security alarm contractors, one shall be a public member with no active affiliation with the security industry. The Board reviews and recommends only. Law does not apply to law enforcement or proprietary security.
New York (Hamill, 1991: 551–558)	State licensing limited to agency. Guards/officers must submit fingerprints and have no disqualifying convictions. No training requirements. Weapons permits regulated by counties and cities. Law does not apply to law enforcement or proprietary security.
Texas (Hamill, 1991: 769–829)	State licensing required. Counties and cities expressly prohibited from regulating. Thirty (30) hours of combined classroom and range qualification is required. All security officers must be commissioned security officers. If position requires a weapon, additional physical and mental tests may be required. The Governor appoints a Texas Board of Private Investigators and Private Security Services of ten (10) members. (Sunset law expires September 1999 unless reinstated.) Membership includes an *ex officio* Director. The director is a paid state employee, having no financial or direct active interest in any agency covered by the law. Other members are Director, Texas Department of Public Safety or designee serving *ex officio*; the Attorney General or designee serving *ex officio*; three public members; two private investigator or security services contractors; one member who is an owner or operator of a guard company; one member who is a security industry expert. All appointments must have Senate consultation and approval. The Board administers the program. The law does not apply to law enforcement or proprietary security.

and Senate (especially respective law and justice committees) were all consulted, and changes were adapted to attempt to meet all concerns.[10]

On April 11, 1991, the Washington House Bill ESHB 1180 passed the House 94–1. The Senate Bill SB 5125 passed the Senate days later. The governor signed into law two codes: *The Law Relating to Private Security Guard 18.170RCW* and *The Law Relating to Private Detective 18.165RCW*. Regulations affecting the owners of private security industry companies took effect January 1, 1992. Regulations affecting the individual private security guard or detective took effect June 1, 1992. The president of the Washington State Security Council stated on April 24, 1991, "The formula for our success has been simply persistence combined with a network of informed communication."[11]

Prior to enactment of the new legislation, more than three hundred companies were paying local authority business operator fees within the state. An unknown number were operating in areas where business licenses were not required. In an effort to help these and other companies meet the training standard requirements, a task force was established, with representatives of the Washington Law Enforcement Executive Forum (WLEEF) and the Washington State Security Council (WSSC). Their purpose was to further redefine the training requirements and to develop a credible list of speakers for a proposed four-hour training video that would fulfill minimum training requirements of the laws. According to the president of the Washington State Security Council:

> This is an exciting project, as it is the first instance in the United States where public law enforcement and private security professionals have formally shared expertise and resources with the intent of improving the quality of guard training and bridging the gap between the two usually exclusive services.[12]

With the passage of the new bills, previous county ordinances regulating the security industry were repealed. In King County, for instance, fees had ranged from $200 to $500 for an agency and $15 to $25 for an individual. No previous training standards were required. The county required demonstrated firearm proficiency if the security position required a handgun. Testing was administered at the King County Firing Range by the Sheriff's Office.

Previous city ordinances regulating the security industry were also repealed. Fees had ranged from $200 to $500 for an agency and $15 to $25 for an individual. No previous training standards were required. In Seattle, for example, the city complied with King County requirements for firearm proficiency if the security officer position required a handgun. Testing was administered by the county.

Security managers, especially those in the proprietary sector, where little regulation exists, are faced with the unknown. Since they may be subject to litigation at any time and have no direct standard or law they must comply with, they must remain aware of court decisions and trends. Keeping up with such issues requires attendance at professional seminars, active participation in industry professional societies or associations, and reviewing and maintaining written and video material.

A central theme of all such conferences, seminars, lectures, and the literature remains clear: The proprietary security service that develops a proactive posture in training its personnel and the people they serve will be far ahead of any potential harm from a lawsuit. And a proprietary security service that accomplishes this important attribute will have adequately and faithfully provided security protection to its employer.

Several international, national, state, and local organizations are reacting to this theme of providing professional standards.

The American Society for Industrial Security (ASIS):   Founded in 1955, ASIS is the world's largest organization of security professionals, with more than 25,000 members. ASIS is dedicated to the protection of people, property, and assets of a wide array of private and public organizations. ASIS publishes three periodicals: *Security Journal, Security Management,* and *Security Dynamics.* Each of these publications provides insightful security articles written by well-known and highly competent professionals. ASIS conducts a series of professional education seminars, such as Asset Protection I, II, III and Executive Update courses. Attendance at these courses can lead to successful completion of the rigorous Certified Protection Professional (CPP) examination and designation, clearly the most sought-after professional designation in the security industry today. As mentioned earlier in this chapter, because the membership of ASIS crosses many disciplines, it has established specialized councils and committees to ensure that members are kept abreast of many fields and points of view.

International Foundation for Protection Officers (IFPO):   This international foundation, based in Canada, was formed in 1988 to address the direct needs of security officers and first-line supervisors. These groups were seen as underrepresented in the various industry professional management associations and societies. IFPO provides two certification programs available by home study and centralized testing. The Certified Protection Officer (CPO) program consists of a series of lessons ranging from the history of security to investigative technique, report writing, legal issues, and physical fitness. Any officer or first-line supervisor who completes two 250-question examinations successfully is awarded the CPO distinction, an attractive shoulder patch and pin, and a certificate. But most important, the department he or she works for will have a better qualified officer.

Private security patrols can often prevent crime by alert action.

Source: C. Simonsen, Courtesy of Northwest Protective Services, Inc.

The second program offered by IFPO is a Security Supervisor course geared specifically toward the first-line supervisor or highly motivated and promotable officer. Rather than focus on as many direct security topics, the course's intent is to develop competent managers.

International Association for Healthcare Security and Safety (IAHSS):
Founded in 1968, the IAHSS membership includes about 1500 professional security directors, managers, and supervisors in the healthcare industry. IAHSS has taken a leadership role in two principal areas: standards and training. These are worth some examination.

IAHSS STANDARDS

I. A security program shall be developed that is consistent with the environment within which the facility is located. Consideration should be given but not limited to moral and legal responsibilities, vehicular and pedestrian traffic, neighborhood crime rate, frequency of police patrol and response capability and finally, the perception of the security requirements of patients, employees, visitors and vendors.

II. Each health care institution, regardless of size, should have a person at an administrative level responsible for the security function. It is preferred that the Director/Manager be a full time position. However minimally, the percentage of time devoted should be consistent with the security requirements of Standard I.

III. Readily identifiable Hospital Identification Badges will be issued to all hospital employees and medical staff. Badges should contain a photograph, job title, department and employee identification number. Wearing of the identification badge must be required whenever employee is on hospital property.

IV. A standardized key/locking program must be developed that is consistently utilized throughout the facility. The key system should be designed to provide optimum retrieval and tracking of issued keys. It should be designed to provide for anticipated facility expansion and be upgraded/evaluated every 5 years.

V. A security operations plan will be maintained by all hospitals of 50 licensed beds or more. This plan will be maintained by the administrative officer responsible for organizing security and contain a written statement pertaining to scope, responsibilities, activities, and functions of the security protection effort. It will also contain a written directive from the chief operating officer or chief executive officer designating the specific administrative officers responsible for security.

VI. All hospitals employing either full-time or part-time security officers will maintain a record of training activities which will have taken place under the direction and control of the hospital. This record will contain, as a minimum, the date of training, subject matter of the training, length of time individual spent in training and the instructor's name and affiliation. This individual training record shall be maintained as long as the security officer is employed and for five years following termination of the security officer. The security officer will be furnished a copy of his training record upon termination.

Standards I, II, III and IV adopted November 1985. Standards V and VI adopted June 1986. All Standards were adopted by the consensus of the membership.[13]

These standards were provided to the Joint Commission on Accreditation of Healthcare Organizations (JCAHO), which is the central inspection authority for healthcare licensing to meet governmental standards to receive grants (Medicare reimbursement).

IAHSS TRAINING

To meet professional training needs, IAHSS publishes the *Journal of Healthcare Protection Management* and a newsletter. Seminars and an annual meeting are held throughout the world. IAHSS has produced three training certifications:

> **Basic Security Officer Training Standard:** This forty (40) hour self-study and centralized monitored program provides historical perspective, legal issues, report writing, and many other topics. It is considered the minimum level required for all officer personnel.

> **Supervisory Development Standard:** This twenty (20) hour self-study and centralized training program provides necessary skill training designed for first-line supervisors, aspiring supervisors, and as a base of knowledge for any officer.

> **Certified Healthcare Protection Administrator (CHPA):** Although no central training program leads to the CHPA, it remains the most sought after professional designation in healthcare security. A full-day test must be passed. Since inception in 1986, fewer than one hundred CHPAs have been awarded.

Many more professional security associations and publications exist than have been highlighted here. Many of them are listed in Appendix A.

Summary

The political and fiscal restraints public servants face in achieving their individual or agency goals have become increasingly difficult to deal with. Our nation's national and local political campaigns send a clear message that citizens are unhappy about how they are lead and in how their tax dollars are spent. State and local governments are experiencing cutbacks in federal grant monies, which forces them to fund more and more public services independent of outside aid. Shifting responsibility for managing many service functions to the private sector is seen by some as a method of solving part of the political and fiscal problems faced by state and local governments.

Security is caught up in the impact of the trend toward private funding of public services, popularly referred to as **privatization**. If a city can no longer allocate sufficient police staffing or patrol activity in and around the area of a private facility, the burden for protection service shifts. The private security in and around the area must manage to protect patients, visitors, and staff over large areas encompassing many blocks—which is often public or privately held property not at all affiliated with the private security agency's mission or client. But since clients have satellite buildings and parking areas near the main focus of their business, they cannot ignore the risks inherent in persons and property in proximity to or on these facilities.

We can no longer rely on the public police to provide total protection for persons, property, and things. Police agencies are hard pressed to meet demands for very serious crime and must carefully prioritize their efforts and resources. Businesses often must take action on their own. Does this serve the public good? Are they aware of the new risks? What else can we do about it? These are just a few of the questions needing answers. Although we may not be able to answer the questions precisely, this chapter has shed some light on the magnitude of the issues. And we have opened the topic for further investigation and research into the public and private missions.

The responsibility for the public's safety depends, in increasing magnitude, on private security. *The Hallcrest Report II* indicates that private security companies employ 1.5 million people, compared to 600,000 people who work in public law enforcement.[14] Proprietary security personnel, those hired directly by and for a person or company, provide additional nonpublic law enforcement. The exact number of proprietary personnel has never been calculated. This is primarily because these security forces are seldom required to be licensed.

For example, five major medical centers in Seattle, Washington, employ collectively more than one hundred proprietary security personnel to protect citizens using their facilities, as well as passing through their areas in the First Hill and Capitol Hill neighborhoods. These staffing patterns are not recorded in any statistical database because such proprietary departments are not required to be licensed in Washington State.

The resistance to standards for security often comes from the very industry that is in need of security. Because the cost of security personnel, services, and equipment is often viewed as a total drain on the bottom line, operational managers try to keep this cost to a minimum. The *recovery* factors of security are easy to document, but the *deterrence* aspect of security takes creative analysis and presentation to management in order to justify the costs of services. Standards that raise this cost are too often looked upon as negative because it is so difficult to document something that *didn't* happen because of the type, amount, and *standard* of security services. This is especially evident when you compare the two major ways that security is provided: **proprietary** and **contract**.

The hiring of security personnel on a contract basis goes back deep into the history of security, from knights in armor to the watch and ward. Contract security lost some of its appeal in the era following World War II, and many businesses chose to create their own (proprietary) security programs. Contract guards and proprietary security personnel make up almost 75 percent of the employment in the security field. Technology in the proprietary security areas has helped cut into the costly personnel portion of this sector. The *Hallcrest Report II* predicts the portion of personnel in the proprietary sector of security will drop from 25 percent of total security employment in the 1980s to less than 20 percent by the end of the 1990s. Contract security is expected to remain fairly constant or show some modest growth.[15] The fastest growing sectors will be those involved with the technology of the security industry. As more sophisticated devices are developed to supplement or supplant more and more personnel assets—assets that become increasingly expensive each year—the shift will be toward more technically qualified personnel. This shift has been seen in the other sectors of employment as well, and can be expected to continue into the twenty-first century.

Contract security seems to be the interim option for the corporate security manager. Contract services are based on a strict contractual fees-for-services basis that generally results in a smaller hourly cost than for proprietary personnel. This is generally because the hourly rate offered by contract guard services is usually less than that for corporate employees. The benefit packages for the contract personnel are provided by the contractor and are usually less than they would be for a full-time corporate employee. In addition, it is much easier for contract services to be expanded or cut, as the situation requires. A corporate employee is much more of a long-term commitment by the company and results in costly severance pay, vacation and sick leave reimbursement, and other continuing benefits when they must be terminated. The contract guard company, on the other hand, can simply move the contract employee to another work site at no cost to the former contracting corporation. This has become the most desirable feature of the contracted service agency. Yet another feature of contract security services is that the contract agency is often able to provide technical equipment on a short-term basis and save that cost to their clients. Patrol services may be contracted at a number of client sites, even sites that involve **shared services** with other clients that help provide a way to distribute cost among several clients.

Some states have indicated that they believe the licensing of security services is necessary for the public good. Florida, which has the most restrictive laws—and includes proprietary security as well as private security licensure—indicates this factor directly in their law:

Florida, 493.6103 Authority to make rules.
The department shall adopt rules necessary to administer this chapter. However, no rule shall be adopted that unreasonably restricts competition for the availability of services requiring licensure pursuant to this chapter or that unnecessarily increases the cost of services without corresponding or equivalent public benefit.[16]

Illinois states even clearer their position on public good:

Illinois (2653) Legislative intent Section 3.
The intent of the General Assembly in enacting this statute is to regulate persons or businesses licensed under this Act for the protection of the public. These practices are declared to be practices affecting the public health, safety, and welfare and subject to State regulation. This Act shall be construed to best carry out these purposes.[17]

Washington State also has referenced the public aspect of their new law in that the Director, under RCW 18.170.180, has authority to adopt standards of professional conduct and practice. Under RCW 18.170.25, the Director may issue cease and desist orders to any business not operating in the public interest; and under RCW 18.170.170, grounds for disciplinary action, including suspension or revocation of license, can be made if there is a failure to adequately supervise employees to the extent that the public health or safety is at risk.

The trend, and properly so, of states is to define security as a public good regardless of the provider. The public expectation when seeing an officer with a uniform, badge, and other equipment is that they will be protected. It makes little difference, nor should it, whether or not the officer is a public, private, or proprietary provider of security protection. This being the case, it naturally follows that the person should be well trained and monitored by some authority. Standards and licensing would help accomplish this task. Responsible security professionals in all facets of the criminal justice field will be best served if they educate themselves to the complexities involving regulations, standards, and training. Only by making an honest effort in this regard will the public good truly be served.

A few specific recommendations are suggested:

- Federal and state authorities should cooperate more fully in developing an integrated regulatory approach that includes private and proprietary input.
- Federal and state authorities should cooperate more fully in developing a common minimum training standard with input from the private and proprietary sectors.
- A federal-level Private/Proprietary Security Services Advisory Board should be appointed (the Florida, Illinois, and Texas models are referenced) to coordinate the efforts of developing regulations, standards, and training.
- Professional security societies and associations should lobby federal, state, and local authorities, as well as the public, to accomplish these tasks.

Efforts across the nation have been underway to provide statutory standards for security operations and security products. Although these efforts may seem less than optimal compared to the hours of training and restrictions applied to hiring in the public law enforcement sector, they have grown rapidly in the 1980s because of litigation that has shown the weaknesses in so many programs. The days of "mom and pop" security agencies, where a person was given a uniform and keys and put on post, are clearly numbered. These are being replaced by agencies that must follow rules for licensing, training, insurance, bonding, and performance standards that will, over time, create a more professional security industry. This professionalism will eventually extend from the security manager (or security contract firm management) to the entry-level security officer. As noted by Dalton:

The United States has woefully lagged. It's both ironic and sad that we are the front runner in the development of equipment and hardware standards, yet we commonly turn over operations to people who can barely read or write.

The need for a national standard actually transcends the contract industry. Businesses and organizations employing their own forces would do well to consider adopting one as well. Generally, it is believed that a company's own staff subscribes to a higher standard since security personnel are recruited in accordance with a firm's hiring criteria. For many this may be true; however, such standardization is largely confined to hiring alone.[18]

Only when strong standards of professional security services are accepted and implemented, and when these standards lead to training and academic programs for security personnel, will we be able to call security a profession. Then it will no longer be just a "job" but a desirable and satisfying career pattern for well-educated and professional leadership.

REVIEW QUESTIONS

1. What impact did the Law Enforcement Assistance Administration have on the police?
2. What is the current status of private security as a profession?
3. Explain how laws and behaviors can change over time.
4. What are the differences between organizational ethics and professional ethics?
5. What are the major factors in choosing proprietary security or contract guard services?

TERMS TO REMEMBER

LEAA

profession

American Society for Industrial Security

Certified Protection Professional

Certified Hospital Protection Administrator

Certified Fraud Investigator

rent-a-cop

over time

different times

different societies

organizational ethics

professional ethics

situational ethics

whistle-blowers

inadequate security

privatization

proprietary

contract

shared services

ENDNOTES

1. C. H. Davidson, "Toward a New Discipline of Security Management: The Need for Security to Stand Alone as a Management Science," *Security Management* (Stoneham, Mass.: Butterworth), Vol. 1, No.1, pp. 3–13).
2. E. J. Criscouli, Jr., "The Time Has Come to Acknowledge Security as a Profession," *Annals* (AAPSS, 1988), pp. 498–499).

3. Al Foster, "What Ever Happened to Right and Wrong," *Security Management* (ASIS, Arlington, Va.), Vol. 33, No. 11, November 1989, p. 152).

4. Delores Cassidy-Ervin, "Ethically Speaking…" *Security Management* (ASIS, Arlington, Va.), Vol. 33, No. 2, February 1989, p. 100.

5. Bureau of Business Practices N.F.I., "Security Management, Protecting Property, People and Assets" (Waterford, Conn.), October 1988, p. 8.

6. National Advisory Committee on Criminal Justice Standards and Goals, *Private Security: Report of the Task Force on Private Security* (Washington, D.C.: U.S. Government Printing Office, 1976), pp. 89–120).

7. William C. Cunningham, John J. Strauchs, and Clifford W. Van Meter, *Private Security Trends 1970 to 2000: The Hallcrest Report II* (Boston: Butterworth-Heinemann, 1990), p. 38.

8. *Security Officer Employment Standards Act of 1991: S.1258*, pp. 1–14.

9. Ibid., p. 15.

10. Paul J. Dockendorff, "Two New Bills May Change State Licensing Requirements," *Around the Sound* (May 1991), pp. 1, 6.

11. Jeff Kirby, "Passage of ESHB1180 & Senate Bill 5125," *Around the Sound* (May 1991), p. 7.

12. William Cottringer, "Training File," *Around the Sound* (April 1992), p. 14.

13. International Association for Healthcare Security and Safety, *1991 Directory*, pp. 1–107.

14. William C. Cunningham, John J. Strauchs, and Clifford W. Van Meter, *Private Security Trends 1970 to 2000: The Hallcrest Report II* (Boston: Butterworth-Heinemann, 1990), p. 229.

15. Ibid., p. 38.

16. William Hamill, *National Laws and Statutes for Private Investigators & Security Guard Agencies* (Edmond, Okla.: Oklahoma Investigators, 1991), pp. 163.

17. Ibid., p. 238.

18. Dennis Dalton, "Professional Consultants Challenge Industry with Proposed, Workable Officer Standard," *Security* (March, 1991), p. 21.

3

The Scope, Organization, and Growth of the Private Security Industry: 1970–1990

No police force can ever be large enough, no court system can provide adequate justice, no correctional scheme can afford the necessary services to cope with a society in which citizens do not respect or obey the laws.

—Arthur J. Bilek

Overview

In 1976, the chairman of the massive *Report of the Task Force on Private Security* was probably unaware of the impact the citizens' lack of respect for the laws of the nation would eventually have on private security. The lack of data on just how many persons are involved in private security, what it costs, and how it is being accomplished make it difficult at best to determine where and when growth rates in the private security industry take place. In 1985 and 1990, however, two truly comprehensive examinations of the field, funded by the **National Institute of Justice** (NIJ), yielded a glimpse of a dynamic industry and some amazing data. This chapter will examine those landmark studies and give the student a solid basis for looking at the scope of this gigantic industry.

Hallcrest I and Hallcrest II

In the early 1980s, the National Institute of Justice tasked Hallcrest Systems, Inc. to conduct one of the first truly in-depth studies of the private security industry in the United States. The task was threefold:

1. Gather information on the general character of the private security industry in the United States, updating previous work completed on the subject

2. Describe the contribution private security makes to the overall problem of crime control and order maintenance and identify opportunities for improvement

3. Describe the working relationships between private security and public law enforcement agencies and develop recommendations for improving these operating relationships[1]

The final report, generally referred to as **The Hallcrest Report**, was published in 1985 and caused an immediate stir in law enforcement and the private security industry. Five years later, in 1990, a second version of the *Hallcrest Report* (referred to as **Hallcrest II**) was released and has shown even more dramatic statistics that describe a security industry that is rapidly growing and changing as it looks ahead to the twenty-first century.

As we have seen in previous chapters, the almost exponential growth of private security from the 1960s to the mid 1990s resulted from a number of causes, not the least of which was a continuous growth of crime in America. This created staggering costs in dollars and personnel for defending against it. As shown in Table 3–1, however, statistics based on victimization studies have shown a decline in rates since 1993...a break in a long trend of continual increases. Victimization studies tend to show a broader view of crime than police statistics, since they reflect the huge amount of crime never reported to the police. Table 3–1 gives a detailed breakout of these crimes by year since 1992 and the encouraging trends over that time. It may be too early to make a statement that law-abiding behavior is on the rise, but at least victimization was down in 1995. In this same general time frame, the expenditures for private security grew from around $19.2 billion to more than an estimated $51.6 billion.[2] Few industries can boast of that kind of fiscal growth. *The Hallcrest Report II* estimates that figure will grow to more than $103 billion by the year 2000.[3] In terms of employment, though, only 500,000 persons were employed by security in 1980. *Hallcrest II* estimates the number will increase to 1.8 million by the year 2000.[4] These figures seem turgid compared to the growth in security equipment sales revenues involving new services and technology. Estimated at $4.5 billion in 1980, *Hallcrest II* puts that figure at almost 500 percent higher or $23.7 billion by the year 2000.[5] This latter figure largely reflects the high cost of technology in the securing of persons, property, and places.

One of the most difficult aspects of trying to understand the true picture of economic crime in America is that the statistics are inadequate for any serious analysis. As noted in *Hallcrest II*, this issue needs to be addressed before we can have the same type of reliable statistical data as can be found in, for instance, the FBI's Uniform Crime Reports, or the National Crime Statistics of the Bureau of Justice Statistics:

Government must focus its attention and initiatives on filling the data and information gaps.... Any proposal for improving data suffers from the necessity to impose reporting requirements on the private sector...most importantly, the private sector must develop comprehensive crime loss measurement.[6]

CRIMINAL VICTIMIZATIONS AND VICTIMIZATION RATES, 1992–95

Type of crime	Number of victimizations (1,000's)				Victimization rates (per 1,000 persons age 12 or older or per 1,000 households)				Percent change	
	1992	1993	1994	1995	1992	1993	1994	1995	1993–95	1994–95
All crimes	42,834	43,547	42,362	38,446	...	...	...	...		
Personal crimes*	10,618	11,365	11,350	9,966	50.7	53.7	53.1	46.2	-14.0%*	-13.0%*
Crimes of violence	10,249	10,848	10,861	9,601	49.0	51.3	50.8	44.5	-13.3*	-12.4*
Completed violence	3,290	3,213	3,205	2,779	15.7	15.2	15.0	12.9	-15.1*	-14.0
Attempted/ threatened violence	6,958	7,635	7,655	6,822	33.2	36.1	35.8	31.6	-12.5*	-11.7
Rape/sexual asssault	607	485	433	340	2.9	2.3	2.0	1.6	-30.4*	-20.0‡
Rape/attempted rape	374	313	316	234	1.8	1.5	1.5	1.1	-26.7*	-26.7*
Rape	175	160	168	141	.8	.8	.8	.7	-12.5	-12.5
Attempted rape	200	152	149	93	1.0	.7	.7	.4	-42.9*	-42.9*
Sexual assault	233	173	117	106	1.1	.8	.5	.5	-37.5*	0
Robbery	1,272	1,291	1,299	1,142	6.1	6.1	6.1	5.3	-13.1‡	-13.1‡
Completed/property taken	844	815	795	745	4.0	3.9	3.7	3.5	-10.3	-5.4
With injury	307	274	288	218	1.5	1.3	1.3	1.0	-23.1	-23.1‡
Without injury	538	541	507	527	2.6	2.6	2.4	2.4	-7.7	0
Attempted to take property	428	476	504	397	2.0	2.3	2.4	1.8	-21.7‡	-25.0*
With injury	81	96	122	95	.4	.5	.6	.4	-20.0	-33.3‡
Without injury	346	381	382	302	1.7	1.8	1.8	1.4	-22.2‡	-22.2‡
Assault	8,370	9,072	9,129	8,119	40.0	42.9	42.7	37.6	-12.4*	-11.9*
Aggravated	2,317	2,563	2,478	1,892	11.1	12.1	11.6	8.8	-27.3*	-24.1*
With injury	671	713	679	509	3.2	3.4	3.2	2.4	-29.4*	-25.0*
Threatened with weapon	1,646	1,850	1,800	1,382	7.9	8.7	8.4	6.4	-26.4*	-23.8*
Simple	6,053	6,509	6,651	6,227	28.9	30.8	31.1	28.9	-6.2	-7.1*
With minor injury	1,142	1,356	1,466	1,291	6.9	6.4	6.9	6.0	-6.3	-13.0*
Without injury	4,611	5,153	5,185	4,936	22.0	24.4	24.3	22.9	-6.1	-5.8
Personal theft[b]	369	517	489	365	1.8	2.4	2.3	1.7	-29.2*	-26.1*
Property crimes	32,217	32,182	31,012	28,480	325.3	322.1	307.6	279.5	-13.2%*	-9.1%*
Household burglary	5,803	5,984	5,483	4,825	58.6	59.9	54.4	47.4	-20.9*	-12.9*
Completed	4,744	4,824	4,573	4,072	47.9	48.3	45.4	40.0	-17.2*	-11.9*
Forcible entry	1,841	1,856	1,725	1,507	18.6	18.6	17.1	14.8	-20.4*	-13.5*
Unlawful entry without force	2,903	2,968	2,847	2,566	29.3	29.7	28.2	25.2	-15.2*	-10.6*
Attempted forcible entry	1,059	1,160	910	752	10.7	11.6	9.0	7.4	-36.2*	-17.8*

Type of crime	Number of victimizations (1,000's)				Victimization rates (per 1,000 persons age 12 or older or per 1,000 households)				Percent change	
	1992	1993	1994	1995	1992	1993	1994	1995	1993–95	1994–95
Motor vehicle theft	1,835	1,961	1,764	1,654	18.5	19.6	17.5	16.2	-17.3*	-7.4
Completed	1,200	1,291	1,172	1,098	12.1	12.9	11.6	10.8	-16.38	-6.9
Attempted	635	670	591	556	6.4	6.7	5.9	5.5	-17.9*	-6.8
Theft	24,579	24,238	23,766	22,002	248.2	242.6	2335.7	215.9	-11.0*	-8.4*
Completed[c]	23,488	23,020	22,744	21,149	237.1	230.4	225.6	207.6	-9.9*	-8.0*
Less than $50	10,318	9,653	9,377	8,238	104.2	96.6	93.0	80.9	16.2*	-13.0*
$50–$249	7,992	7,682	7,874	7,589	80.7	76.9	78.1	74.5	-3.1	-4.6[‡]
$250 or more	4,145	4,253	4,251	4,163	41.8	42.6	42.2	40.9	-4.0	-3.1
Attempted	1,091	1,218	1.022	852	11.0	14.3	10.1	8.4	-41.3*	-16.8*

Note: Completed violent crimes include rape, sexual assault, robbery with or without injury, aggravated assault with injury, and simple assault with minor injury. In 1993 the total population age 12 or older was 211,524,770; in 1994, 213,747,400; and in 1995, 215,709, 450. The total number of households in 1993 was 99,926,400; in 1994, 100,808, 030; and in 1995, 101,888,380.

...Not applicable.

*The difference is significant at the 95% confidence level.

‡The difference is significant at the 90% confidence level.

ªThe victimization survey cannot measure murder because of the inability to question the victim.

ᵇIncludes pocket picking, purse snatching, and attempted purse snatching.

ᶜIncludes thefts with unknown losses. In 1993 this category accounted for 1,433,000 victimizations; in 1994, 1,241,000; and in 1995, 1,159,100.

Source: Bruce M. Taylor, *Changes in Criminal Victimization, 1994–1995* (U.S. Department of Justice, Washington, D.C., April 1997), p. 2.

With information sources and data collection scattered and fragmented, major obstacles stand in the way of a crime reporting system that would truly define economic and business crime in America:

1. The lack of mutually accepted definitions for business crimes.

2. Lack of a comprehensive data base upon which to build or to measure trends.

3. The difficulty to get businesses to develop and implement methods of data collection and reporting of losses.

4. Businesses are too often reluctant to release financial loss data that might reflect negatively on them.[7]

These obstacles explain why it is difficult to make accurate assessments about loss data provided from these kinds of sources, sources on which a researcher must depend in order to assess the price tag for economic crime.

THE PRICE TAG FOR CRIME IN AMERICA

The primary task of private security is to deal with **economic crime**, crime that tends to disrupt the normal commercial and industrial activities that contribute to the overall economy of the nation. *Hallcrest II* offers two excellent definitions of economic crime:

> Economic crime is illicit behavior having as its object the unjust enrichment of the perpetrator at the expense of the economic system as a whole and its individual

components. The consequences of economic crime are increased costs that are passed on to consumers and taxpayers and that place a financial burden upon business, the government, and, ultimately, the public. This working definition of economic crime is intended to encompass the terms of white-collar crime, crimes against business, management fraud, ordinary workplace crimes, and fraud against the government, business, and consumers.

Economic crime is financially motivated crime that has a direct impact on the economy. Such crime destroys public and private assets or diverts them from legitimate channels, thereby imposing higher costs on all consumer goods and services. It especially affects private business and government contracting programs.[8]

Economic crime is measured in two basic categories: **white-collar crime** and **ordinary crime**. White-collar crime is crime that violates a private or public trust, usually in the course of one's occupation, and results in the theft of information, property, or money by stealth and secrecy. Examples of white-collar crime include fraud, embezzlement, trading insider information, computer crime, tax evasion, bribery, and corruption. Ordinary crime that has an economic impact is usually committed by persons who are not in positions of special trust, nor does it involve the stealth found in white-collar crime. Examples of ordinary crime include arson, burglary, shoplifting, employee theft, and vandalism. It is very difficult to come to any specific estimate of the cost of economic crime because of the inadequate loss data statistics for both white-collar and ordinary crime. Many of these crimes are settled by insurance claims, negotiated plea bargaining, administratively, or in some way that is not well documented.

Hallcrest II examined a potpourri of data from a wide variety of sources and came up with an estimate of the cost of economic crime that projects a loss of $200 billion in the year 2000, as shown in Figure 3–1.

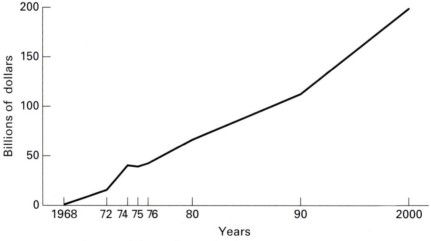

FIGURE 3–1   *Estimated Costs of Economic Crimes*

In fact, as shown in another estimate from *Hallcrest II*, this figure may be only the tip of the iceberg. As shown in Figure 3–2, costs to business and the public that are estimated from a wide range of sources could total as much as $1.737 trillion. The weakness of these data is clear: There is often overlapping and duplicated reporting of the same losses; nonetheless, the derived figures are astounding. The cost to businesses for failures due to economic crime and the cost for bonding and insurance are not even calculated into these incredible losses. Since such losses are often made up by increased cost to consumers, these estimates, as inaccurate as they maybe, could be costing every man, woman, and child in the United States a **hidden business tax** of $7000 a year. Little wonder that the security industry has grown to the levels that it has, and will continue to grow.

Crime/loss	Amount (annually)
Employee theft, "time theft," and drug abuse on the job	$320 billion
White-collar crime	$ Hundreds of billions
Computer crime	$200 billion
Time theft	$170 billion
Bogus sick days, late arrivals, early departures, excessive socializing on the job, etc.	
Lost worker productivity due to drug use	$130 billion
Business property theft	$100 billion
Savings and loan (S&L) fraud	$100 billion
Worldwide product counterfeiting	$100 billion
U.S. product counterfeiting	$8–$20 billion
Federal income tax evasion	$81.5 billion
Workplace drug abuse	$60–$100 billion
Income of organized crime	$46.6 billion
Theft of intellectual property	$40 billion
Retail theft	$30 billion
Retail shrinkage	$16–$24 billion
Employee theft	$15–$25 billion
Bank crime	$17–21 billion
Check fraud	$7–$10 billion
Loan fraud	$6–$7 billion
Embezzlement	$2.1 billion
Credit card fraud	$1.2 billion
ATM fraud	$70–$100 million
Bank robbery	$60–$70 million
Commercial bribery (kickbacks)	$3.5–$10 billion
Telephone fraud	$500 million
Business failures due to economic crime	20%–30%

Source: William C. Cunningham, John J. Strauch, and Clifford W. Van Meter. *The Hallcrest Report II: Private Security Trends 1990–2000* (Butterworth-Heinemann, Hallcrest Systems Inc., 1990), p. 29.

FIGURE 3–2   *Estimates of Losses from Various Categories of Economic Crime*

CRIME TRENDS IN PRIVATE SECURITY

Behavioral trends of crime in America today seem to result in more and more violence and attacks on property as a response to perceived repression, or simply lack of control by citizens. The riots following the decision in the Rodney King beating trial in Los Angeles resulted in massive destruction of property, looting, and more than fifty deaths. The security and safety of south central Los Angeles was clearly sacrificed to the seemingly mindless and wanton destruction that descended on that community.

This kind of mindless destruction was seen again, not two weeks later, in the "celebration" following the Chicago Bulls victory in the championship game of the National Basketball Association. In what should have been a joyous occasion, the crowd became a violent and mindless mob that destroyed cars, set fires, injured people, and looted businesses in the name of a "victory celebration." These two events were separated by thousands of miles and two entirely different motivations, but both seem to demonstrate the violence that lingers just below the surface of our society. What can private security do in this environment of fear, violence, and hate? To examine this challenge, we must consider the threats to persons, places, and things.

EXTERNAL THREATS

The general public perceives the major crime problems in America exist only as they are shown on television or written about in the newspapers and tabloids. If one were to categorize the *economic* impact of crime, however, the **headline crimes** would fall far down the list. **External threats** are those that originate outside the facility or operation that is being secured (or not secured). External threats include such crimes as:

- Homicide by an ex-employee
- Assault on employees near the facility
- Robbery in parking areas or on grounds
- Rape in parking areas or on grounds
- Burglary from offices or storage areas
- Car theft in parking areas
- Hijacking of goods or supplies enroute
- Bomb threats that disrupt operations
- Hostage taking or kidnapping of executives
- Riots and disturbances
- Vandalism to vehicles, plant, or grounds
- Computer crime by "hackers" into company system
- Industrial espionage by electronic means or stealth
- Shoplifting from retail establishments
- Drug trafficking in the area around the facility

SECURITY BYTE 3 – 2

Crime Fear Still Keeps Shoppers Home

Fear of crime still's dampening the number of shoppers at night all across America; and one in five Americans now say they carry a security device when they do go out after dark.

America's Research Group, which primarily conducts shopping and retail studies, discovered crime's negative influence on shopping last year, in a joint project with a security industry trade group.

The firm's most recent study, released in May, still shows shoppers staying home at night, shopping closer to home and cutting down the hours they shop—all because, in part, of a fear of street and violent crime. *But there's also a decline, for the first time, in impact of the "crime fear factor."*

Most American shoppers polled still don't believe crime's really going down. About 71% reported "nothing's" made them feel safer than they did a year ago.

In the retail business, perception's the thing.

A typical mall, according to some security experts, now spends about $400,000 a year on security, double 1991.

RETAIL SUFFERS FROM CRIME FEAR

Changed way shop due to crime?
Yes
22%

Changes are:
Don't Shop After Dark
49%

Eat Out Less Often
9%

Carry Security Device
6%

Source: America's Research Group

Fear's still negatively affecting public use of stores and restaurants.

Source: O'Toole-Zalud Report. "Crime Fear Still Keeps Shoppers Home." *Security* (Cahners Publishing Company. Newton, MA, 1996), Vol. 33, No. 7, p. 94.

To develop countermeasures against outside threats, the security manager must look at elements of risk analysis that identify the item to be secured, the probability of the threat taking place, and the damage that would result if it were to occur. All this is generally covered by the term **foreseeability**. To determine foreseeability as a factor in liability suits, courts try to decide if there has been a similar case that a responsible security director should have either known about or done something about. Courts review the following to determine foreseeability:

- Prior crimes
- Local crime statistics
- Industry crime statistics

- Company crime statistics
- Type of neighborhood
- Proximity of major roads
- Employee complaints
- Use of security officers
- Employee crime awareness programs

Courts also try to determine how aware the security service was of the particular crime environment and what actions were or were not taken. They will then look for specific local and national industry standards to determine how other security operations or professionals may have reacted.

INTERNAL THREATS

The threat from outside the organization is fairly well known, and generally accepted as the source of most economic crime activity. Actually, the greater threat is not from external sources, but from **internal threats**, those within the organization itself. Internal threats include such crimes as:

- Theft of time by employees through false records
- Theft of time by employees malingering or loafing
- Theft of time by poorly managed or false overtime
- Theft of supplies and equipment
- Misuse of supplies and equipment
- Use of supplies and equipment for personal business
- Misuse and sale of proprietary information
- Theft of money or products by employees
- Skimming money in a retail business by clerks
- Use and abuse of drugs or alcohol in the workplace

It is always prudent to look first to the possibility of an internal source for economic crime when it is not immediately obvious that the threat was from an outside source.

Hallcrest II, as Reviewed by ASIS

As the leading professional journal in the security and loss prevention management field, *Security Management* magazine, a publication of the American Society for Industrial Security (ASIS), was quick to take a hard look at *The Hallcrest Report II*. The material in this section is drawn from a special report on *Hallcrest II* that was published in the December 1990 issue of the magazine.[9]

Workplace Violence: A Growing Exaggeration?

There's discord over workplace violence.

In the face of bloody headlines and the exploding business in violence prevention, some experts in demographics, human resources (HR) and statistics now suggest the problem's mis-focused, if not exaggerated.

"Behind closed doors, when HR executives speak frankly with one another, workplace violence is rarely a pressing topic," says Gene Remoff, a nationally-recognized HR practitioner.

Yet in the media and at conferences, it's red hot. "There's no lack of lawyers and consultants on the topic," adds Remoff.

At a recent midwestern security seminar, for instance, one speaker started her speech, "Is Your Company Turning Into a Battleground," by explaining away the

WORKPLACE VIOLENCE COMPARING THREATS	
In Perspective:	
Event	Rate Per 1,000 Adults Per Year
• Accident	220
• Personal theft	61
• Assault	31
• Death—all causes	11
• Robbery	6
• Death from cancer	3
• Homicide	0.1

Source: Bureau of Justice Statistics
Analysis by The Zalud Report

Workplace violence must be measured against all threats.

incendiary title. "I just wanted your attention!"

No doubt: workplace violence grabs attention.

"Epidemic," says the Centers for Disease Control. "The number one killer of women at work," says the National Institute for Occupational Safety and Health. "Fear and Violence in the Workplace" is the label of an often-quoted study. Author turned consultant Joe Kinney parlayed several hot buttons in his book: "Breaking Point: The Workplace Violence Epidemic and What To Do About It."

Questioning the Scenario

Only recently have some questioned the facts, figures and consultant opinions.

WORKPLACE VIOLENCE THE "UNREAL" SPIN
Put Homicides Into Perspective:
→ 120.8 million U.S. workers
→ 1,063 workers "murdered"
→ 33% of 1,063 murdered workers were self-employed
→ Only 59 of 1,063 workers killed by co-workers, former co-workers
→ Vast majority: males killed in robberies

Source: Bureau of Justice Statistics

The reality of workplace homicide: very few killings; mostly robberies of males.

Workplace Violence: A Growing Exaggeration?

The Wall Street Journal, for instance, just reported how fuzzy the numbers have become.

Take the 1,063 U.S. workers "murdered on job" in 1993.

And then take another, closer look: at least one-third were self-employed; the vast majority were males killed in robberies. When such subtractions are made, there were only 59 workers killed by co-workers or former co-workers.

Too much focus on homicides, says Dr. Dennis Johnson, whose firm, Behavior Analysts & Consultants, Stuart, Fla., has covered the issue for more than a decade. He co-wrote and promoted the Kinney book but now warns against "inexperienced consultants" flooding the field.

Threats and Harassment

Johnson wants attention to shift to nonfatal physical and psychological incidents: "the stalkings, the sexual harassment, the threats that affect morale and cost firms money," he contends.

The "Fear and Violence" Northwestern National Life Insurance study, forever quoted, deduced that 2.2 million workers had been "physically attacked" on the job in the 12 months ended July 1993 and that a remarkable, some now say unbelievable, one in four workers had some type of violent incident at work.

Source: Editor, "Workplace Violence: A Growing Exaggeration?" *Security* (Cahners Publishing Company, Newton, MA, 1995), Vol. 32, No. 1, p. 9.

Among the report's major findings:

- The increasing growth of private security and the limited growth of private law enforcement are due to three main factors: increasing workplace crime, decreasing rate of government spending for public protection, and increasing awareness and use of private security products and services as cost-effective protective measures.

- The cost of economic crime in 1990 is estimated at $114 billion. At "2 percent or more of the gross national product, economic crime is out of control and on the rise," the report states.

- Drug abuse is a major cause of economic crime in the workplace, yet drug prevention and treatment programs are rare in the small companies for which most employees work.

- The use of locks, security lighting, burglar alarms, citizen patrols, and other measures suggests the public's fear of crime is increasing even while the rate of most property crimes is stable or declining.

- The computer security equipment market was $224 million in 1990, and the figure is growing at an annual rate of 17 percent.

Security measures displace some terrorist incidents but have little effect on reducing their number. Although the threat from internal and external terrorism is real and has been severely tested since 1990, government and business have seldom addressed these problems dispassionately. The vast sums being spent on counter-terrorism programs, though important, seem out of proportion to the benefits gained.

Although private security personnel are younger and better educated than they used to be, the field's low wages continue to draw minimally qualified workers and keep turnover high. For proprietary and contract unarmed security officers, the average wage is $7.70 per hour. Equally distressing, the typical officer receives only four to six hours of preassignment training.

The number of academic security programs has grown significantly. In the mid-1970s, only 33 certificate and degree programs were offered in the United States. In late 1990s, 164 such programs are available.

To expand on just how big private security is, the report estimates that the average annual rate of revenue growth for the private security industry will be 8 percent to the year 2000. In that year, private security expenditures will reach $104 billion. Expenditures for public law enforcement, by contrast, will grow at an annual rate of 4 percent during the same period, reaching $44 billion by the end of the century.

Employment in private security is forecast to grow at 2.3 percent annually to the year 2000, whereas law enforcement employment is expected to grow at an annual rate of only 1 percent. The U.S. Department of Labor predicts the national workforce will grow by 1.2 percent over the same period. In the year 2000, the total employment in protective services (private security plus law enforcement) will be 2.5 million people.

One of the major sections of *The Hallcrest Report II* focuses on the relationship between private security and the police. Four topics it explores in that relationship are privatization, false alarms, police moonlighting, and private justice.

PRIVATIZATION

The report notes that law enforcement administrators have shown much interest in transferring certain responsibilities to the private sector, such as responding to burglar alarms and completing incident reports when the victim declines prosecution or files for insurance purposes only.

In a survey by the report's authors, private security executives reported they are already performing a number of such tasks, including parking enforcement, special events security, funeral escorts, and court security. The report notes that "crime-related law enforcement services are rooted in constitutional responsibilities and may be one of the truly mandated functions that should not or cannot be contracted away. More likely…is a return of non-crime and nonemergency services to the private sector, thus removing extraneous activities from the work load of police agencies."

FALSE ALARMS

The report notes that the percentage of residences with alarm systems might double to 20 percent before the year 2000. That increase raises this question: Could the police, the alarm industry, and the public tolerate double the current number of false and nuisance alarms?

The burden that excessive false alarms creates for the police is a major problem in developing good working relationships between law enforcement and private security, the report notes. Some law enforcement officials view alarm response, especially residential, not as police business but as a special consideration for the few citizens who can afford alarm systems or as a free service for alarm companies.

More than 2000 communities have alarm ordinances. Typically, these allow three to five false alarms per system per year, a graduated scale of fines, and untimely nonresponse to problem locations. *The Hallcrest Report II* suggests that such ordinances are most successful when they foster communication among the user, the alarm company, and the police, rather than levy harsh penalties against the user and the alarm company.

POLICE MOONLIGHTING

Many businesses hire off-duty police officers for guard, patrol, traffic direction, crowd control, and other security functions. However, the report notes, such **moonlighting** evokes negative feelings among most contract security company owners, who see it as unfair competition.

At least 80 percent of U.S. police departments allow moonlighting, the report found. In fact, in some areas of the country, more than 50 percent of police officers moonlight.

Interestingly, some police officers earn more from moonlighting than they do from their regular jobs. Annual police income from moonlighting in security is estimated at $1.8 billion, equal to the combined 1988 revenues of the nation's four largest security officer companies.

PRIVATE JUSTICE

Much economic crime is resolved privately, not through the public criminal justice system, the report notes. Yet little is known about the fairness, structure, or dynamics of private justice systems, in different types of businesses and institutions.

One important reason that police play little role in solving such crimes as fraud, employee theft, and computer crime is their workload of street crime and other calls for service. Moreover, police often lack the training and resources required for investigating business crimes.[10]

The National Institute of Justice Looks at Private Security

In August 1991, the National Institute of Justice (NIJ) published an excellent synopsis of *The Hallcrest Report II* in their *Research in Brief* series. The director of the NIJ made a strong comment on this monumental report:

Public safety demands that the police concentrate on crime prevention and criminal apprehension. While priorities compel state and local agencies to focus on enforcing the law, they must also provide other public services that do not necessarily warrant the attention of sworn law enforcement personnel.

Because of this gap in public services delivery, private security forces have evolved to the point that they now routinely perform some of the tasks traditionally performed by law enforcement, such as guard, patrol, and investigative services. Indeed, the private security industry has grown to where it now dwarfs public law enforcement: it employs 2 1/2 times the personnel of public agencies and outspends them by 73 percent.

But where is the line to be drawn between the responsibilities of law enforcement and the opportunities for private security agencies? Will private security and public law enforcement work together effectively for the public good?

Private security agencies now investigate crimes against business as a matter of course. These crimes include computer offenses, copyright and trademark infringement, industrial espionage, and even fraud and embezzlement.

Serious and violent crimes, on the other hand, are undeniably within the purview of the public sector. Rape, murder, and drug trafficking must be dealt with by

Off-duty policemen often provide higher levels of security in parking garages.

Source: C. Simonsen. Courtesy of Seattle Police Department.

public law enforcement agencies. Consequently, NIJ's research is intended to explore areas in which private security can assume some of the burden now borne by overworked public law enforcement agencies, thereby freeing them to concentrate their efforts in areas where their involvement is essential.[11]

The synopsis of the larger and more complete *Hallcrest II* document was prepared by the original authors under an NIJ grant and is included in large part here as it was presented in the August 1991 *Research in Brief*.

Private security is now clearly the nation's primary protective resource, outspending public law enforcement by 73 percent and employing two and a half times the workforce, according to a new NIJ study of the private security industry. Currently, annual spending for private security is $52 billion, and private security agencies employ 1.5 million people. Public law enforcement spends $30 billion a year and has a workforce of approximately 600,000.

In 1980, NIJ research revealed that the private security industry had annual expenditures 57 percent larger than public law enforcement.[12] In 1990, a new NIJ-sponsored descriptive study of the years 1970 through 2000 confirmed the trends noted earlier and forecast that they would continue at least another decade.[13]

Private security executives perceive their industry's role as a supplementary one, protecting property and assets in ways that exceed the resources of public law enforcement. Crimes against business that are commonly investigated by private security personnel, but seldom by law enforcement, include many computer crimes, fraud, and industrial espionage.

According to one definition, private security includes "those individuals, organizations, and services other than public law enforcement and regulatory agencies, that are engaged in the prevention and investigation of crime, loss, or harm to specific individuals, organizations, or facilities."[14] That definition, however, excludes the fastest-growing segment of private security—the manufacture, distribution, and installation of security equipment and technology.

For the purpose of the 1990 study, researchers identified nine categories as part of the security industry:

- Proprietary (in-house) security
- Guard and patrol services
- Alarm services
- Private investigations
- Armored car services
- Manufacturers of security equipment
- Locksmiths
- Security consultants and engineers
- "Other," which includes categories such as guard dogs, drug testing, forensic analysis, and honesty testing

The *Sourcebook of Criminal Justice Statistics 1988*[15] estimated the cost of police protection—federal, state, and local—at $13.8 billion for 1979. The Key Market Coverage, 1981, for *Security World* magazine, listed private protection costs for 1980 at $21.7 billion.

Conservative methods of extrapolation from the current (1990) figures yield the growth pattern shown in Figure 3–3.

Even though public expenditures for law enforcement will reach $44 billion by the year 2000, they will be dwarfed by private security expenditures, which will reach $104 billion. The average annual rate of growth in private security will be 8 percent, or double that of public law enforcement.

SECURITY–POLICE COOPERATION

NIJ-sponsored research in the early 1980s revealed few collaborative efforts between police and private security groups, with the exception of crime prevention programs. Public law enforcement officials described their relationship with private security managers as fair to good at best. Few police chiefs and sheriffs even had lists of the names of security managers at area companies or contract security firms. Security personnel, on the other hand, said they had excellent working relations with police.

In the 1980s, however, the International Association of Chiefs of Police, the National Sheriffs Association, and the American Society for Industrial Security began joint meetings to foster better cooperation between the public and private sectors. In

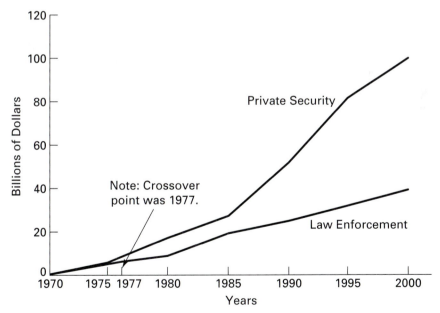

Source: NIJ, Research in Brief, *Private Security: Patterns and Trends*, August 1991, p. 3.

FIGURE 3–3   *Private Security and Law Enforcement Spending*

1986, with funding from the National Institute of Justice, these organizations set up the Joint Council of Law Enforcement and Private Security Associations. A number of local and regional groups also set up cooperative programs involving the police and private security.

POLICE–PRIVATE SECURITY ISSUES

Many in both law enforcement and private security consider privatization, false alarms, police moonlighting, and private justice to be the key issues that must be addressed in building improved relationships between the two sectors. These issues, though briefly introduced earlier, need to be addressed in the context of the study itself.

PRIVATIZATION

As an indication of the growing interdependence of the public and private sectors, state and local government spending for a wide variety of private sector services has increased dramatically over the past fifteen years, from $27 billion in 1975 to $81 billion in 1982 and an estimated $100 billion by 1988. Federal expenditures for all types of private sector services totaled $197 billion in 1987.[16]

Crime-related services provided by public law enforcement are rooted in constitutional responsibilities and perhaps should never be contracted away. Law enforcement officials, however, might welcome a fuller partnership with private security if contracting out some support services would free up their officers for basic crime fighting.

Services frequently identified as candidates for privatization are public building security, parking enforcement, patrolling of public parks, animal control, special events security, funeral escorts, court security, prisoner transport, and public housing development patrol. Private security executives report they already perform a number of these police support services. And though such privatization is occurring slowly, the study found that at least eighteen states perform some form of it.

FALSE ALARMS

The smaller the law enforcement department, the greater its interest in transferring authority to private security for all tasks except responding to burglar alarms. Large police departments, nearly 70 percent of them, were most interested in transferring responsibility for responding to burglar alarms to private security.

Residential use of burglar alarms, already found at most businesses, is on the rise. False alarms from security systems are a common police complaint. Police studies consistently show that 95 to 99 percent of alarm calls are false, and that alarm responses account for 10 to 30 percent of all calls for police services.

In the early 1980s, only 2 to 5 percent of residences had alarm systems. By the end of the decade, this figure was up to 10 percent. As alarm systems become less expensive, the installation of residential alarm systems could double by the year 2000. Can the police, the alarm industry, and the public tolerate twice the number of false and nuisance alarms?

Interviews reveal that some law enforcement officials view alarm response, especially at residential sites, as a special consideration for a few citizens who can afford

Information Services Link Private, Public

On-line information services are among ways private security and public law enforcement share and work together.

Sharing Critical Information

Always a strategy of savvy security directors, it's taken on increased urgency with threats ranging from sophisticated frauds and terrorism to corporate espionage and product counterfeiting. Security's not only sharing more information among themselves but also finding more and better ways to cozy up to their law enforcement and public safety colleagues.

Information Convergence

At its core, what's happening is the converging of two trends: the growing use of on-line information services and the growing closeness of private and public security.

Spurred by information technology advances, security professionals, sometimes sharing the same neighborhood, type of business or threat, are linking together. These emerging security information services go beyond mutual asociations, a data base of former employees accessed by retail security screeners, or computer-accessible consumer credit-reporting data bases.

One example, and a most ambitious one, is The Security Network, or SeNet, of Schaumburg, Ill., which links together private security and public law enforcment in a real-time information exchange network, what founder Tom Hines, CPP, calls "the equivalent of a private APB system." A unique, and necessary, SeNet twist: it's a secured network, what Hines labels a "private, closed-circuit computer-based information service."

Sensitive information shared among security and law enforcement is kept confidential.

Government Advances

For law enforcement, specialized information-sharing among federal, state and local public safety officials also's on the rise. Two examples: evolutionary Automated Fingerprint Identification Systems, ignited by advances in fingerprint imaging, and on-line data base experiments in several border states to determine more quickly and accurately the 'alien' status of suspects or potential employees.

Computer-based information-sharing complements, and in some respects drives, the growing closeness of private security and public law enforcement agencies. One recent milestone: one of the nation's most recognized police officers, William J. Bratton, former New York City and Boston Police Commissioner, has brought his computer and community policing outlook to First Security Services of Boston.

Association Synergy

The Security Industry Association, a manufacturers' trade group, and the American Society for Industrial Security, composed of security professionals as well as product and service vendors, have "front-burner" private-public projects.

It's with SeNet, however, where the concept of a connected security-police community is most intriguging and stands in contrast to the still-forming services available on the unsecured Internet World Wide Web.

SeNet's concept is simple enough: create an information network so that security executives and law enforcement can work together to stop fraud, theft, vandalism and other loss threats.

Information Services Link Private, Public

Filling a Need

Started about four years ago by SeNet President and Chief Executive Officer Thomas N. Hines, CPP, The Security Network provides subscribers instantaneous reporting of crime incidents through its high-technology broadcast network created to bring real-time security information to private security and public law enforcement.

The service, delivered over landlines, wireless and satellite communications, is in essence the equivalent of a private "All Points Bulletin."

"I started the service because as a 20-year veteran of security and law enforcement, I found that these entities were missing the information they needed. We take a proactive approach," he says. Designed for a variety of clientele, including banks, retailers, medical facilities, college campuses, hotels, office buildings and others, the service allows subscribers to receive "Flash Bulletins" of incidents that might range from counterfeiting, bad check writing and credit card fraud to smash and grab, bomb threats and abductions.

For example, a retailer who has just had a customer try to cash or use a bad check can send an immediate bulletin to others on the network, warning subscribers of this individual, and even providing information and graphics to help identify the person.

Going Real-time

Hines says that private security has been communicating incidents for years, but via telephone, fax and informal networking. "With the assistance of The Security Network, the communication can be more helpful and timely because data is transmitted simultaneously and instantaneously, with other search and reporting functions enhancing the system."

Flash Bulletins can be custom tailored to the subscriber's specifications. A Flash Bulletin may include the subscriber number and area, the alleged incident, incident status, details on the suspect such as whether armed or unarmed, as well as a detailed description. When a crime occurs, the affected subscriber issues the bulletin regarding the crime. That's transmitted to all other subscribers in the area requesting information on that type of activity. The bulletin, including graphics, can be sent in approximately 60 to 90 seconds, so other subscribers have immediate information on the incident and are forewarned so that they can take a proactive approach.

The Security Network is generally sold in clusters or blocks throughout various geographic areas. Subscribers can receive bulletins through a computer, called DataLink; by telephone, called TeleLink; or by pager, called PageLink. A fourth, wireless service called PortaLink is scheduled for roll-out in November. It will use emerging personal computer service (PCS) devices.

Source: Bill Zalud. "Information Services Link Private, Public." *Security* (Cahners Publishing Company. Newton, MA, 1996), Vol. 33, No. 9, pp. 25–26.

alarm systems rather than as a communitywide police function. Others see alarm response as a free service for the alarm companies, who profit at police expense. Meanwhile, eight of ten local managers of guard and patrol services reported they would be willing to take over alarm response on a contract basis.

The National Burglar and Fire Alarm Association estimates that more than 2000 communities have alarm ordinances. These typically involve alarm system permits, allow three to five false alarms per system per year, and levy fines for excessive false alarms. Under some ordinances, police can refuse to respond to alarms at problem locations. Some manufacturers and vendors have taken significant steps to reduce the number of false alarms through improved design and user training for customers.

POLICE MOONLIGHTING

Businesses frequently hire off-duty law enforcement officers for guard and patrol duties, traffic direction, crowd control, and other security functions. For more than fifteen years, contract security company owners have objected to this as unfair competition.[17] Although 15 to 20 percent of U.S. police departments prohibit or severely restrict such activity,[18] law enforcement administrators estimate that about 20 percent of their personnel supplement their police salaries with regular outside security employment. This means that some 150,000 local police officers perform regular off-duty private security work (roughly 10 percent of the total private security employees in the United States).

Three-quarters of the police departments that permit the practice allow officers to wear their uniforms while employed outside. Many also permit off-duty use of other department equipment, including radios and vehicles.

Opponents of police moonlighting say that despite putting more police on the street at no public cost, such private financial arrangements with employees of public agencies raise questions of liability and conflict of interest. And they maintain, in the long run, the practice undermines the notion of equal protection for all. However, proponents of the practice argue that police officers are better trained than private security personnel and possess greater inherent authority.

PRIVATE JUSTICE

Interviews in both 1980 and 1990 confirmed that much economic crime is disposed of privately instead of through the public criminal justice system. As the Task Force on Private Security observed in 1976:

> It would appear that a large percentage of criminal violators known to private security personnel are not referred to the criminal justice system. A logical conclusion would be that there is a "private" criminal justice system where employer reprimands, restrictions, suspensions, demotions, job transfers, or employment termination take the place of censure by the public system.[19]

Both the 1980 and the 1990 NIJ studies indicated that the workplace crimes most frequently reported to law enforcement are Uniform Crime Report "index crimes" such as arson, burglary, and robbery.

Employee crimes such as fraud, employee theft, and computer crime typically are resolved internally by firing the employee, obtaining restitution, or absorbing the loss. Businesses may report employee crime directly to the prosecutor, not to the police first. Both security executives and business officials may be unwilling to report employee crimes out of concern for the negative publicity that such events might generate.

Of course, little is known about the fairness, structure, or dynamics of these practices. But when the offenders are not publicly identified or prosecuted, there may be no record of their criminal activity to which others should be alerted.

STANDARDS AND TRAINING

The five-volume 1971 Rand Corporation study of the security industry described "the typical private guard" in terms recalling the negative stereotype of the night watchman that still exists among some segments of the law enforcement community and the public:

> ...an aging white male who is poorly educated and poorly paid...between 40 [and] 55; he has little education beyond the ninth grade; he has had a few years' experience in private security; he earns a marginal wage...some have retired from a low level civil service or military career....

By 1989, however, the first issue of *Security Journal* reported the education and experience characteristics of one proprietary security organization approached those of the public police. The private security organization also employed more female officers, and the staff had a greater diversity of ethnic backgrounds than found in local police departments.[20]

The 1990 NIJ study found the turnover rate for contract guards ranged from 100 to 300 percent. (Proprietary guard turnover is lower, although no figures are available.) This means that the entire force is replaced one to three times a year. However, it is believed that until significant advances are made in training, salary, promotional opportunities, and personnel supervision, this high attrition rate will continue, undermining efforts to upgrade private security.

FIREARMS AND TRAINING

A study conducted twenty years ago[21] found that 50 percent of both contract and proprietary guards carried firearms at least a quarter of the time. The 1980 NIJ study found that only 10 percent of the guards were armed, and the rise in insurance premiums and liability litigation suggests that by the year 2000 perhaps only 5 percent will be armed.

In 1976, the Task Force on Private Security recommended that private security personnel receive twenty-four hours of firearms training, including three hours of instruction on legal and policy restraints, before assignment. Fewer than ten states have such stringent requirements. However, twenty-three states mandate some firearms training for armed guards; only fourteen require unarmed training for guards. Surveys and interviews indicate that the typical uniformed guard receives an estimated four to six hours of training before assignment.

In 1976, the task force found that five colleges offered a bachelor's degree; no masters' programs were available. By 1990, according to the *Journal of Security Administration*, forty-six institutions offered bachelor's degrees in private security, and fourteen offered a master's.

RECOMMENDATIONS

The 1990 NIJ study recommended that all security employers have access to criminal history records to screen applicants for guard jobs. The study also recommended more effective licensing through state, not local, regulations and licensing reciprocity between states.

As a step toward upgrading security training and advancement opportunity, the 1990 report recommended that the private security industry consider setting its own national standards similar to those adopted by the British Security Industry Association. The report also suggested that the industry promote professional accreditation, as does the Commission on Accreditation for Law Enforcement Agencies.

FORECASTS

The NIJ report forecasted that more sophisticated and technical white-collar crimes will emerge in the 1990s, with higher dollar losses than before. Computer crimes, the report stated, will rise, but by the mid-1990s, most networks and systems should be protected, making computer threats a diminishing concern by the year 2000.

The rapid growth of closed-circuit television, sophisticated alarm systems, access control, and other technology will not necessarily mean a reduction in the number of security personnel, but may change the functions they perform. By the year 2000, there will be an estimated 750,000 contract guards and 410,000 proprietary security personnel, of which 280,000 will be guards.[22]

Summary

Hallcrest I and *II* make it abundantly clear that the private security sector will far outstrip its public police counterpart in both its funding and the raw numbers of persons employed. More recent history has shown that these projections may be too conservative. As can be seen in Figure 3–4, the number of persons employed in the field of private security will approach two million by the start of the next century. On the other hand, there will be only slight growth, which does not even match the growth in population, in the public police sector. This can mean only that efforts to meet the growing threat of crime must be met with even greater efforts at cooperation between the major sectors that provide public safety and security in the United States.

When one examines the average annual rates of growth for the private security industry, as shown in Table 3–2, it is even clearer that contract guard services are leading

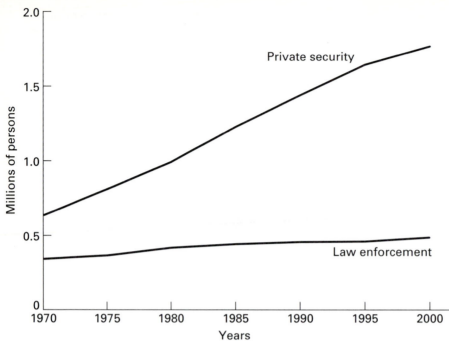

Source: NIJ, Research in Brief, *Private Security: Patterns and Trends*, August 1991, p. 3.

FIGURE 3–4   *Private Security and Law Enforcement Employment*

the way with a rate of 4 to 6 percent a year. This is more significant to public police agencies when you consider that 68 percent of those employed in private security are security officers or guards. This annual growth is even more amazing when contrasted

TABLE 3 – 2

NUMBER OF EMPLOYEES IN PRIVATE SECURITY INDUSTRY, 1980–2000

Year	Contract Service and Manufacturing Employees	Average Annual Rate of Growth	Proprietary Security Organization Employees	Average Annual Rate of Growth	Total Private Security Employment	Total Average Annual Rate of Growth
1980	556,000	NA	420,000	NA	976,000	NA
1990	965,000	6%	528,000	2%	1,493,000	4%
2000	1,473,000	4%	410,000	–2%	1,883,000	2%

Source: The Hallcrest Report II, p. 176.

to the flat rate of growth, even negative rates in some major urban areas, for public police agencies.

Some glimmering of hope for public police funding and growth hinges upon the growing debate over equal protection opportunities for all citizens. This may force already strapped governmental bodies to provide more funding for public safety. Efforts by the Clinton administration to provide funds for putting 100,000 new police officers on the street show great promise. The Federal bureaucracy has moved slowly to provide them. The notion that protection is available for only the few who can afford it stirs up the issue of how far can private security go in helping with the public safety issue.

The push across the nation for tighter regulation of the private security industry, with standards for operations and training, is on. Although there are fears that this might drive up the cost of private security, there is still a public demand for more regulation. Many states are upgrading their standards for licensing guard service companies, guards themselves, private investigation agencies, and all other aspects of private security. This may draw the requirements for police and private security closer to each other and foster greater mutual respect.

A clear message rings out from all this. The message is that the private and public security sectors need each other as never before. They must open up lines of communication and cooperation. The challenge for these next few years is to search for and find ways to meld these resources into a coherent and cooperative venture that provides greater safety and security for all citizens. What kinds of joint activities and ventures can be developed and applied? How can we break down the stereotypes that have plagued the drawing together of the public and private sectors? These will be the tasks of the student of security and criminal justice for the twenty-first century.

REVIEW QUESTIONS

1. What are the major benefits derived from the *Hallcrest* reports?
2. Describe the societal differences between economic crimes.
3. Why do white-collar criminals not lose their self-respect when caught?
4. What is meant by the term *foreseeability*?
5. What are the differences between internal threats and external threats?

TERMS TO REMEMBER

National Institute of Justice
The Hallcrest Report
Hallcrest II
economic crime

white-collar crime
ordinary crime
hidden business tax
headline crimes
foreseeability

external threats
internal threats
moonlighting

E N D N O T E S

1. William C. Cunningham and Todd H. Taylor, *Private Security and Police in America: The Hallcrest Report I* (Boston: Butterworth-Heinemann, 1985), pp. 4–5.

2. William C. Cunningham, John J. Strauchs, and Clifford W. Van Meter, *Private Security Trends 1970 to 2000: The Hallcrest Report II* (Boston: Butterworth-Heinemann, 1990), p. 175.

3. Ibid., p. 175.

4. Ibid., p. 237.

5. Ibid., p. 205.

6. Ibid., p. 20.

7. Ibid., p. 26.

8. Ibid., p. 26.

9. The author is grateful for being allowed to use these materials that describe the future for security, as it is presented by the Hallcrest team and analyzed by the professional leaders at ASIS. Some editorial additions are used to maintain the flow for this text.

10. Staff writers, "Hallcrest II: The State of Security." *Security Management* (Arlington, Va.: December 1990), Vol. 34, No. 12, pp. 68–70.

11. Charles B. DeWitt, "Private Security: Patterns and Trends." *Research in Brief* (Washington, D.C.: U.S. Department of Justice, August 1991), p. 1.

12. William C. Cunningham and Todd H. Taylor, "The Growing Role of Private Security." *Research in Brief* (Washington, D.C.: NIJ, 1984).

13. Gion Green, *Introduction to Security*, 3rd ed. (Boston: Butterworth-Heinemann, 1981).

14. Bureau of Justice Statistics, *Soucebook of Criminal Justice Statistics* (Washington, D.C.: BJS, 1981).

15. Bureau of Justice Statistics, *Report to the Nation on Crime and Justice*, 2nd ed., (Washington, D.C.: BJS, 1988), p. 118.

16. Albert J. Reiss, *Private Employment of Public Police*. In this document, the practice is generally favored (Washington, D.C.: NIJ, 1988).

17. Ibid. Reiss also notes that New York City, with the largest police department, permits no uniformed outside employment.

18. National Advisory Commission on Criminal Justice Standards and Goals, *Report of the Task Force on Private Security* (Washington, D.C.: U.S. Government Printing Office, 1976).

19. James Kakalik and Sorrell Wildhorn, *Private Police in the United States: Five Volumes* (Washington, D.C.: NIJ, 1971).

20. William Walsh, "Private/Public Police Stereotypes: A Different Perspective." *Security Journal* (Boston: Butterworth, 1989), Vol. 1, No. 1, pp. 22–27.

21. Kakalik and Wildhorn, supra. (Specifically in *Volume 2, The Private Police Industry: Its Nature and Extent*, pp. 133, 135, 137.)

22. Kakalik and Wildhorn, supra.

4

The Dimensions of Security and Loss Prevention

WHO DOES WHAT TO WHOM?

Crime related services provided by public law enforcement are rooted in constitutional responsibilities and perhaps should never be contracted away. Law enforcement officials, however, might welcome a fuller partnership with private security if contracting out some support services would free up their officers for basic crimefighting.

—Hallcrest II

Overview

Crime in America, as seen in the previous chapter, is no longer the exclusive venue of public law enforcement. Although the constitutional roles of law enforcement have been defined to protect the citizen, the growth of violent crime and the subsequent drain on finite resources in the public sector have required a rethinking of the roles of various sectors in the protection against, investigation of, and apprehension of perpetrators of a broad spectrum of activity we classify as "crime." Recall from Chapter 1 that crime is a *legal* definition of behavior, depending upon where that behavior falls along the behavioral continuum.

This leaves a wide range of choices to the government. The behavior could be redefined as noncriminal and therefore no longer a governmental problem. Unfortunately, this choice does not remove the behavior, nor does it protect the potential victims of such crimes. In such a situation, the citizens may be tempted to use vigilantism to gain revenge or retribution. Another choice is to redefine the severity of the crime, reducing the behavior from a felony to a misdemeanor, or from a misdemeanor to an administrative ticket. Again, the citizen may become dissatisfied and feel that the selected approach is nonresponsive, and may also resort to personal vengeance or vigilantism.

Jails and prisons are now so full that only the most violent offenders will be kept incarcerated for any length of time. This problem has been exacerbated by **get tough** and **three strikes and you're out** sentencing attitudes and practices that have emerged from public frustration about crime rates. Recent crime statistics have, however, shown a slight decline. But it is far too soon to attempt to relate these factors as cause and effect. The concerned citizen often sees a "revolving door" of justice, with the victim of crime often spending more time in the station house than the offender. Investigative resources are allocated to the most serious crimes, and the millions of offenses against the average citizen (simple burglary, theft, minor assault, and so on), those that are considered unlikely to be solved, are often put on "hold" from sheer volume. Because of this situation, understaffed and outgunned police departments must often resort to looking for new ways to do old things. This issue was noted as a serious problem in the *Report of the Task Force on Private Security*:

> A grave dilemma is arising across the Nation. In the face of ever-rising crime rates, communities are finding that the limits of their fiscal resources have been reached. Additionally, it is now apparent that police alone cannot control crime. As aptly pointed out by Louis Radelet, Michigan State University professor of criminal justice, in the December 8, *1975*, issue of *Crime Control Digest*, "The police alone are futile in the prevention of crime....They need to work in partnership endeavors with community forces." One such force possessing the potential to significantly contribute to the reduction of national crime is the private security industry.
>
> Considering the mutual interests and common linkages between the public law enforcement and private security sectors, a close working relationship could enhance the efficiency and effectiveness of both forces, adding impetus to the efforts to curb crime in our society.[1]

Rigid role models for deciding just who does, should, or can provide protection, investigation, and incarceration services to the citizens are being reexamined. To see where public and private protection services have been, and where they are now, we will take a look at the traditional roles of each sector and put them in context with movements for change (see Figure 4–1). In this chapter, we first examine the police role.

The Police Role

Police work is a phrase that conjures up a mental image of dramatic confrontation between a police officer and a lawbreaker, with victory going to the party with the stronger arm, faster gun, or craftier wit. Although, especially in large urban areas, there are plenty of heroic moments in police work—more than one hundred police officers a year are killed in the line of duty—the majority of situations to which a police officer responds are not *criminal* (that is, those that call for arrest and the

Security	Law Enforcement
Prevention	Apprehension
General services	Prosecution
Proactive	Reactive
Organization defined	Statute defined
Protect an organization	Protect a society
Private funding	Tax supported

FIGURE 4–1 *Security and Law Enforcement Tasks*

possibility of prosecution, trial, and punishment). Rather, many of these situations involve public nuisances that the community wants stopped: the blaring stereo, radio, or television in the middle of the night, the barking dog, the revelers filled with party (and other) spirits. As long ago as 1967, it was noted:

> Many situations involve people who need help whether they want it or not: Helpless drunks [and homeless] out in freezing weather, runaway boys [and girls] who refuse to go home, tourists in search of exciting night life in a dangerous neighborhood. Many of them involve conduct that, while unlawful, cannot be prevented or deterred to any great degree by means now at the disposal of the criminal justice system: Using narcotics, prostitution, gambling, alcoholism. Many situations, whether or not they involve lawful conduct, may be threatening: A sidewalk orator exercising the right of free speech in the midst of a hostile crowd, a midnight street corner gathering of youths whose intentions are questionable, an offering by a belligerent drunk to lick any man in the house.
>
> All of these situations could invoke the violation of some ordinance or statute. All of them could lead to serious breach of public order, or for that matter to a serious crime. Much of police work is seeing that they do not lead to this extreme. This means becoming involved in the most intimate, personal way with the lives and problems of citizens of all kinds.[2]

The intimate personal involvement is the inevitable consequence of "calling the cops"—an idiom that refers to one of the methods employed by citizens to cope with a large variety of problems. "What are police officers supposed to do?" cannot be distinguished meaningfully from "What kinds of situations require remedies that are nonnegotiably coercible?" This means simply that when the law enforcement officer determines that force is necessary, he or she is not accountable to anyone or required to listen to arguments against that option. This may not always be a legal rule, but it is a practical application of what police often have to do. So far as this view is widely held by police officers, two unfortunate consequences can occur:

1. All sorts of problems, if they involve culpable offenses, can always appropriately be handled by quasi-legal methods.

2. Crime control is the only serious, important, and necessary role of police work, and it deleteriously affects the morale of police officers.

Police have traditionally based their operational policies on the goals of (1) eliminating or substantially reducing crime, and (2) apprehending all perpetrators of crimes. We question whether crime prevention is a realistic objective for the police, particularly in view of the limitations of the police to act against the causes of crime. What is true today was just as true when noted in the *Task Force Report* in 1967:

> The police did not create and cannot resolve the social conditions that stimulate crime. They did not start and cannot stop the convulsive social changes that are taking place in America. They do not enact the laws that they are required to enforce, nor do they dispose of the criminals they arrest. The police are only one part of the criminal justice system; the criminal justice system is only one part of government; and the government is only one part of society. Insofar as a crime is a social phenomenon, crime prevention is the responsibility of every part of society.[3]

Even in theory, deterrence of crime is a responsibility that the police share with the entire criminal justice system—even the entire society. The police are specifically responsible for only the initial stage of the process: the arrest of the perpetrator of the crime. The police have no control over the subsequent actions of the prosecutors, the courts, or the correctional system.

A LOOK AT POLICE PRODUCTIVITY: A THREE-STAGE SYSTEMS MODEL

If police effectiveness is to be defined operationally in terms of the objective of arresting all perpetrators of crime, the measurement becomes fairly straightforward. In this model of police effectiveness, one employs a **three-stage systems model** and a simple formula that makes **productivity** the result of *output* divided by *input*, as shown in Figure 4–2.

As can be seen in Security Byte 4-1, the relationship between **efficiency** (*inputs*) and **effectiveness** (*outputs*) can be a quantitative measure of productivity. This model is often applied to law enforcement in an attempt to objectively measure police activity. The most common measurement is *clearance by arrest of crimes known to the police*. A kind of productivity measure is derived by dividing the crimes (*inputs*) by the arrests (*outputs*), then dividing the total cost of police services by that number. This gives a rough estimate of the cost per arrest. This method works fine for manufacturing widgets, but it is a shaky measure for justifying police budgets. If the effectiveness or productivity of police is determined in terms of arresting all perpetrators of crime, then as this measurement figure approaches zero, police productivity approaches the ideal.

Unfortunately, for a long time now, the *Uniform Crime Reports* of the FBI have indicated that only about 25 percent of all offenses known to the police are cleared by arrest. This dismal record of arrest might be attributed to the defensive strategy of police activity that guides most conventional police forces. The principal tactic for a defensive operation is *investigation*, which assumes certain things about relationships in the crime and that the perpetrator has made some fatal error. Commitment to a

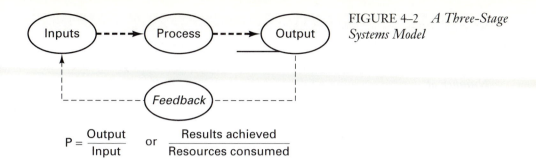

FIGURE 4–2 *A Three-Stage Systems Model*

$$P = \frac{\text{Output}}{\text{Input}} \quad \text{or} \quad \frac{\text{Results achieved}}{\text{Resources consumed}}$$

defensive (*reactive*) strategy in periods of increasing crime is a vicious circle in which a greater proportion of available personnel is diverted from crime prevention to crime investigation as more crimes occur, thus leading to even more crime. Tables 4-1 and 4-2 indicate the numbers of local police on guard against crime in America, and the massive number of persons served by a diminishing number of agencies and officers.

With the advent of the importation, sale, and use of drugs on an unprecedented scale, especially since the arrival of crack cocaine in the mid-1980s, the system of reactive law enforcement has overwhelmed the major cities and urban centers of America. The **war on drugs** has been difficult to pursue because the enemy is difficult to identify. If we return to the question, "What do police do?" it will be seen that police work is inherently committed to a tremendously variegated range of activities and tasks by the unique nature of the responsibilities assigned to the police as *the* mechanism in our society for the "distribution of a situationally justifiable force."[4]

One of the seven basic objectives identified by the *Task Force Report* of 1967 was to immediately develop and apply all available police agency, community; and other criminal justice resources to apprehend criminal offenders.[5] Despite the priority of that goal a quarter of a century ago, it remains obvious that most police agencies continue to be called upon to respond to and carry out a number of tasks that fall outside the range of either crime prevention or apprehension of criminals. If police are to

S E C U R I T Y   B Y T E   4 – 1

Productivity as Related to Efficiency and Effectiveness

- Efficiency is getting the most tasks completed with the least expenditure of resources and time.
- Effectiveness is getting the tasks completed with the least number of failures closest to the goals established.
- Productivity is the measure of the relationship of how efficiently and effectively resources are used in the production of goods or services as related to goals.

TABLE 4-1

LOCAL POLICE DEPARTMENTS, BY NUMBER OF SWORN PERSONNEL, 1993

Number of sworn personnel*	Agencies		Full-time sworn personnel	
	Number	Percent	Number	Percent
Total	12,361	100%	373,554	100%
1,000 or more	38	0.3%	118,460	31.7%
500–999	38	0.3	27,351	7.3
250–499	86	0.7	29,344	7.9
100–249	326	2.6	46,983	12.6
50–99	692	5.6	45,779	12.3
25–49	1,443	11.7	45,160	12.1
10–24	3,361	27.2	40,913	11.0
5–9	2,940	23.8	13,906	3.7
2–4	2,587	20.9	5,085	1.4
1	851	6.9	594	0.2

Note: Detail may not add to total because of rounding.
*Includes both full-time and part-time employees.

Source: BJS. Sourcebook of Criminal Justice Statistics—1994 (U.S. Government Printing Office, Washington, DC, 1995), p. 38.

evolve into professional specialists in crime fighting, as some authorities agree they should, we are left with the question of who shall assume the responsibility for discharging the duties currently demanded of them. In the meanwhile, the police officer is given a great deal of **discretionary power** in the performance of police work.

Discretion is essential to the continued operation of a criminal justice system that is overwhelmed by crime at every other point in the process. Every offense that comes to the attention of the police does not result in an arrest; every arrest does not result in a prosecution; every prosecution does not result in a conviction; and every conviction does not result in incarceration. Judge Charles Brettel addressed this situation:

> If every policeman, every prosecutor, every court, and every post-sentence agency performed his or its responsibility in strict accordance with the rules of law, precisely and narrowly laid down, the criminal law would be ordered but intolerable.[6]

It is also clear that such application of the law would swamp a system already bursting at the seams. Public fears of the actual exercise of arbitrary power in conventional

TABLE 4-2

LOCAL POLICE DEPARTMENTS AND FULL-TIME SWORN PERSONNEL, BY SIZE OF POPULATION SERVED, 1993

Population served	Agencies		Full-time sworn personnel	
	Number	Percent	Number	Percent
All size	12,381	100%	373,554	100%
1,000,000 or more	12	0.1%	75,496	20.2%
500,000–999,999	27	0.2	37,856	10.1
250,000–499,999	45	0.4	33,261	8.9
100,000–249,999	147	1.2	39,057	10.5
50,000–99,999	340	2.7	40,493	10.8
25,000–49,999	703	5.7	42,864	11.5
10,000–24,999	1,662	13.4	47,405	12.7
2,500–9,999	4,099	33.2	42,879	11.5
Under 2,500	5,327	43.1	14,243	3.8

Note: Detail may not add to total because of rounding.

Source: *BJS, Sourcebook of Criminal Justice Statistics—1994 (U.S. Government Printing Office, Washington, DC, 1995), p. 38.*

police practice are forestalled by the low visibility of police activity. The camcorder seems to have thrown further light on this less savory aspect of police discretion that contributes to such events as the Rodney King beating and riots. The insular character of police activity sometimes shields their practices from the general populace and even from the prosecution and courts, which enjoy a greater latitude in the exercise of discretionary judgment as a matter of course. A small percentage of police can be expected to rationalize the use of **back-alley justice** when they see the system not keeping the criminal elements with which they deal off the streets.

Law enforcement officers struggle to meet their missions with limited budgets, reduced personnel, little administrative support, and no real consensus on just what the citizen wants them to do. Law enforcement has a code of ethics developed by the International Association of Chiefs of Police, given in Figure 4-3. It is time for a re-examination and *implementation* of some of the prophetic ideas suggested in a number of studies on the police–community role, some now collecting dust for over twenty-five years.

THE CITIZEN'S ROLE

As we noted in Chapter 1, the problems of crime and criminal behavior were handled for centuries by individuals or by tribal groupings in the name of the individual. As

FIGURE 4–3   *Law Enforcement Code of Ethics*

various kinds of law developed, along with the development of agencies with the power and mission of providing law and *order*, however, the citizen's role seemed to recede to that of victim and perpetrator. The police were charged with preventing and investigating crime, the prosecutors and courts with conviction and judgment, and the penal system with punishment. This seemed to work fairly well for a long time, before crime exploded and overwhelmed every segment of the justice system. More and more police, more and more laws and judges, even more and more jails and prisons failed to stem the tide. In the mid-1990s, one of thirty-eight adults and one of twenty-eight adults in the United States are either incarcerated or under the supervision of probation or parole. Figure 4–4 shows how the system has worked to remove the vast majority from punishment in correctional institutions in 1994. Even with this "funnel" effect, the United States still incarcerates more citizens per 100,000 than any developed country in the world.

The public began to explore cooperative activity with some segments of the criminal justice system. Community crime prevention—a concept encouraged, initiated, and fine-tuned by the efforts of the National Advisory Commission on Criminal Justice Standards and Goals—is a movement that has had fits and starts for a couple of

The Evolution of the Law Enforcement Code of Ethics

The establishment of a code of ethics to govern the conduct of its members is essential in a professional association. In recognition of this, the membership of the IACP first considered the language of such a code more than 30 years ago. During the 64th Annual IACP Conference in Honolulu, Hawaii, September 29–October 3, 1957, the association passed the following resolution:

Whereas, A constitutional object of the International Association of Chiefs of Police is to encourage adherence of all police officers to high professional standards of conduct; and

Whereas, A Law Enforcement Code of Ethics has been developed jointly and adopted by the Peace Officers Association of California and the Peace Officers Research Association of California; and

Whereas, The Law Enforcement Code of Ethics has since been adopted by the National Conference of Police Associations; and

Whereas, The Board of Officers of the IACP at Chicago in June 1957 did endorse the Law Enforcement Code of Ethics and recommend its adoption at the 64th Annual Conference at Honolulu, Hawaii; now, therefore, be it

Resolved, That the IACP, at its 64th Annual Conference, does hereby adopt the Law Enforcement Code of Ethics, a copy of which is appended to this Resolution; and be it

Further Resolved, That the Association does express its appreciation to those who phrased the Code in its final form, all of whom were active members of this Assocation; and be it

Further Resolved, That the Code of Ethics be implemented by the Canon of Ethics as authored by the IACP.

In 1989, in an attempt to increase the code's relevance to modern policing, the Executive Committee of the IACP adopted a new Law Enforcement Code of Ethics during its October 17 meeting at the 96th Annual IACP Conference in Louisville, Kentucky. Drafted by an ad hoc committee, the new code drew much of its language from the Royal Ulster Constabulary's "Professional Policing Ethics," with the permission and assistance of Sir John C. Hermon, former chief constable.

While the new code made revisions sought by many, it also raised some concerns. The new code's length was one concern—it was considered to be too long for use as an oath of office during graduation ceremonies at police academies. Additionally, there was the fact that not all of the values and statements contained in the new document were reflected in the 1957 code. Some association members were also concerned that the membership had not voted on the revision of the code of ethics.

The solution was to edit the 1957 code, making only those changes necessary for consistency with the new version, and retitle the 1989 Law Enforcement Code of Ethics the "Police Code of Conduct." These changes were presented to the membership in the form of a resolution at the 98th Annual IACP Conference in Minneapolis, Minnesota, October 5–10, 1991, where it received unanimous approval.

Source: IACP, Public Relations, Alexandria, VA, 1997.

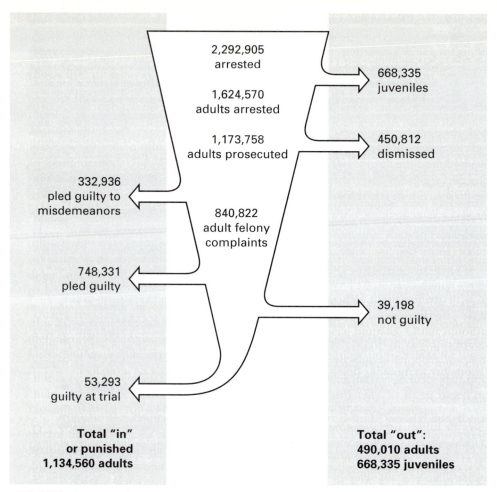

2,292,905
arrested

1,624,570
adults arrested

668,335
juveniles

1,173,758
adults prosecuted

450,812
dismissed

332,936
pled guilty to
misdemeanors

840,822
adult felony
complaints

748,331
pled guilty

39,198
not guilty

53,293
guilty at trial

**Total "in"
or punished
1,134,560 adults**

**Total "out":
490,010 adults
668,335 juveniles**

Source: FBI. UCR: *Crime in the United States: 1995* (Washington, D.C.: U.S. Department of Justice, 1995).

FIGURE 4–4   *Outcomes for Arrest: Felony Crimes, 1994.*

decades. Some programs have been relatively successful, however, and are being re-examined in the 1990s as a way to take back neighborhoods from the criminal elements.

The concept of "community policing" has grown from the storefront police station to a partnership with the total community environment in some cities. Research is now being conducted to determine the most effective protocols and procedures to harness the energy of the community to fight crime. Community crime prevention can range from neighborhood watch programs, to community patrols by volunteers, to campaigns to improve street lighting and clean up parks. It can involve joint efforts to renovate slums, volunteers in schools, jobs for the unemployed, or counseling for disturbed and troubled youth. Any public or private activity outside the conventional criminal justice system that is directed toward reducing crime is, in fact, community crime prevention.[7]

Crime prevention has long been a less than desirable position for conventional police officers. For this reason, and others that involve budgets and perceptions of how police agencies should spend them, crime prevention has not been given the attention it deserves by police agencies. As violent crimes have increased and numbers of police personnel have decreased, smart police administrators are looking for better ways to use limited sworn police officer resources for response to the most serious crimes, and alternatives for the rest. This may also involve a new way to measure crime in terms of community *values*. The current movement, though slow in building, is toward value-oriented policing, with support from the community in which those values are represented.

ANOTHER LOOK AT POLICE PRODUCTIVITY: A FOUR-STAGE SYSTEMS MODEL

As shown in Figure 4–5, the way to look at productivity in terms of values is to develop a **four-stage systems model**. The three-stage model we examined earlier is okay for determining quantitative measures of police activity. Since most measures in this model are derived from the estimated 20 percent of crimes that become **known to the police**, and from the less than 25 percent of those that are **cleared by arrest**, the figures do not well reflect what is occurring in the communities. People who live in those communities are not affected by numbers alone, but by their personal perceptions of criminal activity, personal safety, and protection provided by the police. These are reflected in their *values* in regard to crime and its impact on their community. Values are not *quantitative*, they are *qualitative*.

In examining this four-stage model, we find it works more effectively in measuring a public service (police) as related to an expected *outcome* or *value* as predetermined by the community in which the service is provided. In a sense, this model goes beyond the concept of answering just the question "What happened?" (in *quantitative* terms). The fourth stage addresses the more important question of "So what?" (in *qualitative* terms). This establishes the relation to the implicit and explicit values that were determined before the effort was taken. Outcome is not a "destination" but a "direction" toward which any set or subset of actions should move to be considered *productive*. For example, if the traffic division has shown their quantitative productivity by greatly increasing the number of tickets per officer, but the public is very unhappy

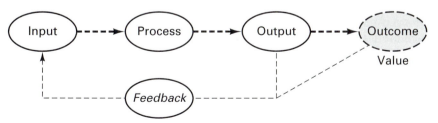

FIGURE 4–5   *A Value-Oriented Four-Stage Systems Model*

because the department is not moving toward the value "reduce street crime," then **value productivity goals** have not been met.

Because too many police officials ignore this concept of citizen values, citizens often take an adversarial role to police. The values of one community in a city may be quite different from those of a community several blocks away. When citizens are ignored, they either take the law into their own hands or simply try to stay neutral and survive in crime-ravaged areas. A number of positive alternatives have come about across the nation in the past several years since the studies on community crime prevention have been written. Some of the major recommendations of a study were the following:

- Citizen volunteers in criminal justice
- Expanded public employment programs in areas of high unemployment
- Career education in elementary and secondary schools
- Individualized community drug abuse treatment services
- Physical design of buildings, parks, and thoroughfares to reduce criminal opportunities
- Ethical codes of conduct for governmental officials[8]

To think that citizens do not care about their community and will not work with the police to solve problems is incorrect. Many cities, however, do not know how to gain access to the private or public services and assistance that can be used to help. The mere presence of police in the community does not make it community policing. One example of how community policing, based on values, can be effective is found in Honolulu, Hawaii.

ANOTHER EXAMPLE OF EFFECTIVE COMMUNITY POLICING

The Kalihi Police District in Honolulu developed a pilot program for community policing in the Kuhio Park Terrace, a low-income housing development that had been a police "hot spot" since its opening days in the early 1960s. It was the first and only low-to-no income high-rise building on Oahu, with all the chronic crime problems associated with such housing. Public alcohol abuse, drugs, fighting, and a youth gang culture infested the neighborhood. Five months after the Hawaiian model of community policing was installed, it made dramatic strides at Kuhio Park: Children were in their apartments by 10:00 P.M., there were no "beer runs" (snatch-and-run thefts from a local 7-11 store), and police were rarely called. The residents started night security patrols to reduce noise and public drinking, drug dealing, and defacing of the property. A beautification project, coordinated by the community police team, arranged for a graffiti paint-out by gang members, brush-and-trash clearing through the correctional authorities, and a general cleanup by the residents. How did they accomplish all this in what was considered a "throw-away "neighborhood?

The strength of the Honolulu Police Department community policing program can best be described by *involvement*. They have recognized that traditional methods of police work do not seem to affect crime rates. Thefts, burglaries, assaults, disorderly complaints, and so on still occur in some locations. Citizen involvement seems to be an answer for dealing more effectively with crime. The key in Kalihi was found in four critical elements: community involvement, problem-solving orientation, community-based deployment strategies, and increased police accountability.

COMMUNITY INVOLVEMENT

There is a growing realization that the police cannot work in isolation from the community they are supposedly serving. That is, they cannot simply come through a neighborhood to handle an incident and leave directly after. Neighborhood crime problems are, in fact, community problems. Many more issues other than enforcement affect crime, such as education, economics, family life, neighborhood organization and dynamics, and cultural values.

Community policing should inculcate the idea that the police *alone* do not stand as the last line of defense against crime. What is needed is *real* community involvement in the fight against crime, not just speeches, brochures, and pretty pictures. This concept does not mean that the police want citizens to take unnecessary risks or to do the police officer's job. The police remain as the primary anticrime agent, but with a lot of citizen backup. Neighborhood associations, business groups, churches, civic organizations, and public and private agencies have a shared partnership in establishing priorities for anticrime efforts involving the police and other agencies.

The concept of **partnership with people** means that citizen-based anticrime efforts such as Neighborhood Watch, task forces, and community-based alternative programs (basketball leagues, family counseling, tutoring, and so on) will receive recognition and support by the police. Neither the police nor citizens can do the job alone, but together they can make a big difference.

PROBLEM-SOLVING ORIENTATION

Responding to emergency calls for service remains a priority for the police. Police are organized in a reactive mode, responding to as many calls for service as possible. They are problem solvers by nature and training and should continue to be. The task is to enlarge the problem-solving abilities of patrol officers, supervisors, commanders, and even detectives so that they have more success with chronic crime problems in areas like Kalihi by techniques that go beyond the easy answers such as more police patrols, more arrests, and searching for the underlying reasons for the crime problem.

By using these techniques, the crime rates will decline, calls for police service will decline (freeing them to respond to major crimes), and the reactive workload of the police officers will decrease so that they can use the time for problem solving and crime prevention in concert with citizens and groups in the community.

COMMUNITY-BASED DEPLOYMENT STRATEGIES

Police placed in the community must be trained to realize that they are there to work with their partnership members, not to be a conscience or to push their weight around. Cities have used police officers in many ways to meet the goals of community policing, including projects such as miniprecincts, permanent beat officers, bicycle patrols, and horse and foot patrols. Only a few cities have implemented the concept of community partnership that makes Hawaii's plan unique. In Kalihi, they have frequent meetings, attended by every possible faction in the community, during which they develop plans that best fit the problems of that community. The police partners do not have to live in the community (though that would be ideal), but they must be committed to working with the community to solve the crime problem.

INCREASED POLICE ACCOUNTABILITY

True community policing requires the increased involvement of the community in deciding the police role and what values should drive that role. The public must be part of the decision making when developing priorities, in determining how police resources will be used, in selecting strategies, and in developing and executing programs designed to restore neighborhoods as strong components of a safe neighborhood. Since the whole point of community policing is that it is designed around neighborhood problems, police officers, their supervisors, and their command will be responsible for working with citizens to resolve problems.

Police and community members must also work together to identify crime and noncrime problems and draft accountable plans to solve them. Supervisors in the police hierarchy will review these partnership plans to determine that resources from the police budget are identified in the plans to make them happen. Support units such as narcotics and vice officers and juvenile officers will also be made available as appropriate.

Actions other than a community policing program that can involve concerned citizens in helping to solve the problems of crime are many and varied. The local community is being redefined throughout America, but concerned citizens remain one of the nation's most underdeveloped and underutilized crime fighting resources. This resource must be considered by public and private protection agencies and used by everyone concerned about the growing cancer of crime in the community.

A community may translate its concern about crime into action through the individual and group efforts of its citizens; through the local industries, businesses, and institutions such as schools, youth service bureaus, and religious organizations; and through the responsible and responsive efforts of its governing bodies.

These options in no way exhaust the possible approaches that a community may take to reduce and prevent crime. Indeed, there are as many viable approaches to community crime prevention as there are citizens who deplore the conditions that have been shown to cause crime. What is needed is a commitment to involvement in solving the problems rather than continuing to be a part of them. One sector that is part of the formula for solutions, and a part of the communities in which they serve, is the private security industry—the subject of the next section.

The Role of Private Security

It is a popular myth that public police do, or can, police any and all areas of a community that they wish. Public law enforcement, unless asked to enter or unless in "hot

Easy-Wash Windows, Walls Defeat Graffiti Artists

How do you stop a graffiti artist from displaying his "talents" on your walls or windows? Unfortunately, you probably can't. Not permanently.

But by taking the fun out of it, you might succeed in "encouraging" him to go elsewhere.

Coatings such as Durapoxy from Garon Products, Wall, N.J., make cleanup easy, wiping off with a special Durapoxy cleaner. The coating can be used on new concrete as well as on painted surfaces that have been properly prepared. By erasing the graffiti soon after it is done, the artist is denied the satisfaction of having his work "displayed."

Window Treatment

An increasingly prolific area for graffiti artists is windows. Spray Paint, crayons, soap and sharp objects are common "tools" of the window artist.

A special kind of window film can sharply reduce the cost of replacing a defaced or scratched window, says Bill Bigelow, product manager of Metalized Products, St. Petersburg, Fla.

Part of the ArmorCoat line of films, Graffiti-Gard, unlike safety and security film, goes on the outside of the window. The 7 mil film is toughened with a weatherable coat to increase resistance to the elements.

Depending on the type of graffiti, the film works in different ways. If it is a wax-based instrument, the marking can just be wiped off. Paint or scratches, and the film can be easily removed and replaced. "When the vandal tries to use a sharp object, the film grabs the object and he is not able to maneuver it," Bigelow says.

New Developments

On the horizon is a product that will make graffiti almost self-cleaning. The non-stick coating was developed by Dow Chemical, and has been licensed to two companies for manufacture and release.

One company, Michigan Molecular Institute (MMI), Midland, Mich., plans to sublicense the technology to customers interested in developing applications. One such application, says Conrad Balazs, project manager for new ventures, will likely be anti-graffiti. "Typically, graffiti material will not stick to a building coated with this material," he says.

The other company, 3M, St. Paul, Minn., purchased the license in 1993. Development on a final product is still in the "embryonic stage," according to the company, and it is expected to be at least a year before commercial products become available.

While none of these products may stop the artist from performing his craft, they will have an effect on where he does it, Bigelow says. "People who are out there doing graffiti are going to find ways to try to get around different safeguards. They have no respect for other people's property. Thus, they are not hindered by a whole lot.

"But what a lot of these products do is to make your property less desirable for the graffiti artist. They are encouraged to move on to another target."

Source: Karyn Hodgson. "Easy-Wash Windows, Walls Defeat Graffiti Artists," *Security* (Cahners Publishing Company. Newton, MA, 1995), Vol. 32, No. 8, p. 69.

pursuit" of a fleeing felon, need a warrant or subpoena to enter private property on police business. This is usually a satisfactory arrangement for urban police since they are busy with the full plate of crimes they already have. As mentioned earlier, the conditions for crime and criminal behavior in the cities of America have become a critical mass over the past couple of decades. The same problems of crime, drugs, and violence have also faced the private business sector, prompting the growth of private security to a level that far exceeds that of public police, both in numbers and budget.

So what is private security's role in the overall mission of crime prevention and control in America? And where does it fit into the emerging new concepts of community policing? Two decades ago, a *U.S. News and World Report* stated, "…the number one need is to overcome the public's misconception that they can leave crime fighting entirely to the police."[9] Since those words were written, the battle against crime has been lost many times, but the war goes on. Only recently, however, is there a growing awareness in the trenches that readily available reinforcements for police are everywhere. This awareness and new respect has encouraged public–private cooperation in crime prevention to become a viable concept in the twenty-first century.

In fact, many, if not most, of the security managers for America's corporations and institutions have come from the ranks of the federal (both civilian and military), state, and local law enforcement agencies. These leaders are well aware of the problems facing the policing of America and are reaching out to cooperate with their beleaguered comrades.

Police have traditionally been slow to ask for help or to relinquish their "turf" to nonsworn personnel. Their concept of private security has been less than favorably viewed, generally referring to them as rent-a-cops. The trend toward civilianization of all but the most essential sworn positions in law enforcement (a budgetary necessity), however, has caused some serious rethinking by progressive law enforcement leaders. The tidal wave of drugs and drug-related crime that has washed over the country has increased the need for cooperation and the redistribution of at least some public police responsibilities.

POLICING: PUBLIC OR PRIVATE?

To decide whether policing ought to be public or private takes asking some serious questions:

- Where does the policing occur—in public, private, or mixed space?
- Whose interest is served by the policing—the general public, a private interest, or both?
- What is the function of the policing?
- Who pays for, or sponsors, the policing—public or private interests, or both?
- Who carries it out—regular sworn agents of the state with full police powers, special-purpose deputies with more limited powers, or citizens with no official powers?
- Who controls and directs the policing?

- Where the policing involves data collection and investigations, who has access to the results?
- What popular and self-definitions characterize those doing the policing?
- What organizational form does the policing take?
- To what extent are social control agents linked in informal networks that transcend their nominal definition as public or private?[10]

Although it may sound easy to have the private–public sector working together in harmony, one has to realize that there are basic differences between public and private orientations in financial objectives, populations served, specific missions and functions, funding sources, and sources of police powers. We compared some of these factors in Chapter 1, to include the military, but Figure 4–6 shows this relationship with the other elements added.

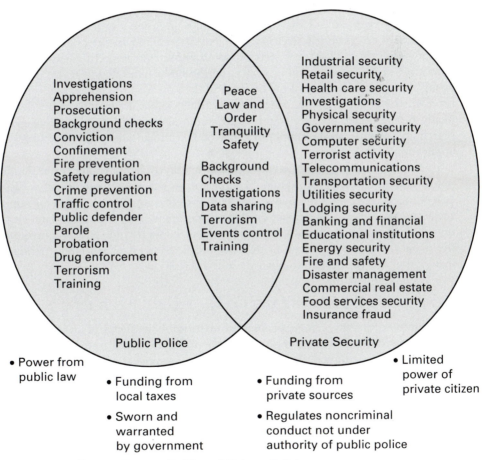

FIGURE 4–6   *Differences Between Public and Private Policing*

In the cases of financial orientation and missions, the private security organization has a profit-oriented motivation in two ways: (1) if a proprietary security force, it helps with preventing crimes, protecting assets, and providing loss prevention to enhance the profitability of the corporation or institution served in a cost-effective manner, and (2) if a contract guard service, it helps with meeting these same goals for their client while making a profit for the security service. In this situation, the security provider and the client must decide whether their relationship is profitable for both and worth pursuing. On the other hand, government is a nonprofit entity and, in many cases, has no choice but to expend vast resources to conduct massive investigations, so as to enforce the law. The principle is that the law must be upheld, perpetrators must be caught, and justice must be served regardless of cost.

The private security provider is expected to serve specific, contracted clients in the private sector (although many do provide contracted security services for various levels of government on a contract basis as well). In this role, the security officer, with some limited exceptions, has only the arrest power of an ordinary citizen. In regard to the client served, however, the power of investigation and access to information may approach or even exceed that of public police in some cases. Generally speaking, unless a serious crime has occurred that requires calling in the police, most private security results in administrative actions (for example, restriction from entry, restitution, demotion, or firing). The public police, on the other hand, being sworn government agents, have the full power of public law and the power of the government in order to serve all the general public. Since their actions can result in loss of freedom, even death, public police are also highly restricted and limited by the rules of evidence, search and seizure, and a myriad of other constitutional and public law issues in the application of this power.

In one area, the private security officer has a power not usually exercised by the public police. Generally speaking, the police must act upon some directive of law to enforce their powers on the public. In the case of private security, behavior not under the authority of police to enforce (such as corporate mores) can be regulated as determined by corporate policy and procedure. This would include access controls within the property of the corporation or institution, dress codes, assigned parking, and many other behaviors that do not violate laws.

POSSIBLE CONFUSION FOR PUBLIC?

These differences often create problems for the public in terms of understanding how far private security officers can go to help them. Public and private officers both wear uniforms and badges, and carry security gear and even weapons, making it sometimes difficult to tell one from the other. The public often assumes that private security officers have more legal authority than a private citizen. This *appearance* of a higher level of authority can be frustrating to the citizen who wants police-type action to be taken. As a general rule, private security officers have much less training than their public police counterparts and must be limited in what they can do by state law in regard to security licensing and by the rules of their corporate or contract executives.

Potent Training Professionalizes Security Staff

You want to train your security force, but don't know where to begin.

You recognize the need to professionalize subordinates. What you cannot come to grips with is how to implement a training program.

And therein lies the problem.

Over the years I've developed a set of "Standard Training Recommendations" that security and facility managers in virtually any type of business can use in some manner to make training happen.

Offer Training Beforehand

Point One—Provide a new officer as much instruction as possible beforehand. Doing so accomplishes several things:

- It prepares the officer for the job and reduces the number of unfamiliar and uncomforable situations to which he/she may be exposed.
- It strengthens the socialization process so that the new employee is "brought into the fold" in a more efficient manner.
- It speaks volumes about management's commitment to the new officer.

Use CPO Program

Point Two—Use the Certified Protection Officer (CPO) program developed by the International Foundation for Protection Officers. This process reaps several rewards. It:

- Eliminates scheduling/overtime hassles, as studying is done on the employee's own time. Provide some form of a reward from the organization.
- Eliminates course development costs. Generally speaking, courses often don't ever get developed due to budget and operational constraints.

Point Three—Tap into inhouse resources as much as possible.

Most organizations provide employees some type of customer service, memo writing, computer, interviewing or safety training. All of these areas are relevant to the security function. Having security personnel, proprietary or contract, sit in on this training has several advantages:

- Enhancement of the security department image within the parent organization as security is seen engaging in professional development activities.
- Improved training of officers as the previous training is both reiterated and expanded.

Source: Chris Hertog. "Potent Training Professionalizes Security Staff," *Security* (Cahners Publishing Company. Newton, MA, 1996), Vol. 33, No. 3, p. 85.

It seems to be time to try to determine whether or not public police and private security can work in a complementary role. In an era of shrinking budgets at the federal, state, and local levels of government, it is finally time for a partnership to take place in the public–private security sectors that provide many of the same services. The following are some of the several duties of both professions:

> Personal safety: The private sector has a responsibility to ensure the safety of its employees, its clients, and anyone else with whom it comes into contact. That responsibility rests largely on the shoulders of employers, not local police.
>
> Crime prevention activities: Both professions have an obligation to develop crime prevention initiatives. More and more police departments have acknowledged that it is better to prevent crime than to combat it after the fact. That philosophy is a founding principle of the security profession.
>
> Order maintenance: The police are responsible for maintaining public order. In areas maintained by private industry, the job of order maintenance falls to private security.[11]

In these times of limited resources, public police must deal with crimes that most affect the public's concept of safety and security. This creates an inability to deal with what is referred to as minor crime. This, in turn, creates an additional burden on the private security sector since these minor crimes do not just go away, and a more assertive attitude by private security officers is often required to try to better *prevent* such crimes. Privatization of more of the traditional police services (discussed later in this chapter) is but one answer. Another method being used more and more is contracting with public agencies for performance of some of the following activities:

- Public building security
- Parking enforcement
- Parking lot patrol
- School crossing protection
- Public park control
- Non-injury accident investigations
- Animal control
- Traffic control
- Special event security
- Funeral escorts
- Executive protection
- Housing project patrols[12]

If this seems to echo the recommendations from the *Report of the Task Force on Private Security*, it does. It is always amazing how long the recommendations of such "blue ribbon panels" take to be responded to. As noted by the chairman of the American Society for Industrial Security's Law Enforcement Council in 1991:

> Particularly in urban and suburban areas, traditional police responsibilities are increasingly a shared activity. Many police administrators look favorably on such an exchange, which permits the police to focus on more serious crime concerns.
>
> Police are not the only ones who must adapt. Businesspeople must recognize that traditional police protection may not be available. Executives must adjust to the notion that, despite the taxes paid, the demand for protection will be met primarily outside the public arena. Private security activities will need to be expanded to fill the vacuum created by police responses elsewhere. Compromise, negotiation, and partnership will be the key activities in future public/private enforcement roles.
>
> Where should we be, and how can we get there? The need for security simply can't be satisfied by the traditional systems of public and private protection. It's time for both protection professions to explore their opportunities—at the local, state, and federal levels—for cooperative options of mutual benefit. It's time for police and security administrators to develop broad cooperative strategies.[13]

Clearly, it is the right time to implement the partnerships with people kind of community policing developed by the program in Kalihi, Hawaii, drawing on *all* the public and private resources available to make our cities and neighborhoods free from fear of crime, clean, and safe. Private security is an often forgotten element in that concept, but one that could be of great help in the goals of the community. Not only in the big cities could the help from private security be useful, however. With 80 percent of the nation's police agencies employing 10 or fewer sworn officers, help from any source might be considered useful. Small towns near big factories may find that the security department there has more sophisticated equipment and well-trained officers than the police. These efforts may be strengthened by awarding limited police powers to the private security officers.

SPECIAL POLICE POWERS: PROS AND CONS

Thousands of security officers across the country exercise full police powers granted to them by a state agency or local community. A security officer who has been licensed as a **special police officer** can, in most locations, exercise authority equivalent to that of a regular police officer in the same jurisdiction. However, the security officer's authority is limited to the geographical boundaries of his or her location, whereas public police officers are able to assert their authority throughout the jurisdictional boundaries. Since the licensed security officer and the public police officer possess similar authority, both the private company and the municipality gain. However, a number of potential problems may be created when private citizens act like police officers.

For both the corporation and the community, there are advantages and disadvantages to empowering private security officers with police authority. Each entity should carefully weigh both sides of the issues before the authority, its inherent responsibilities, and the associated risks are assumed.

The private company gains several potential advantages when its security force has full police authority. The decision to license a private staff will depend on the company's business, location, amount of crime experienced, corporate philosophy, and other factors.

SOME ADVANTAGES TO ENHANCED POWERS

The arguments in favor of police powers include the following:

INCREASED AUTHORITY

With full police powers, the security staff becomes more than a guard force. Specially licensed security officers may make arrests that ordinary citizens are generally not allowed to make. The difference between the inherent authority of a private citizen's arrest and that of a licensed officer usually depends on whether the offense was a felony or a misdemeanor.

In many states, citizens may arrest someone whom they have witnessed committing a felony. In some areas, this authority includes arrests based on probable cause if in fact the felony was committed.

Generally, a private citizen may not arrest someone who has committed a misdemeanor except where local legislatures have passed special provisions allowing such arrests. The most common example of this law is found in the merchants statutes, which state that retail merchants or their employees may arrest for shoplifting, a misdemeanor.

With full police powers, security officers may arrest for felonies committed in their presence, felonies based on probable cause, and certain misdemeanors as provided by statute. In brief, their authority is enhanced considerably to encompass a wide range of criminal activity.

REDUCED RISK OF LIABILITY

Tort liability caused by arrests that are later ruled illegal because the officer did not possess the requisite authority can be reduced or eliminated. A misdemeanor arrest that was accomplished consistent with the officer's special powers would be valid. The same arrest made by an unlicensed private security officer would be invalid and hence illegal.

SECURITY EMPLOYEE MORALE

Security personnel who are entrusted with police powers may perceive themselves as being more professional. Although this factor is subjective, security officers who have positive attitudes about their work and employers are more likely to perform better and stay longer with a company. In an industry noted for high employee turnover, any corporate action that reduces turnover and improves performance should be considered.

QUALITY OF STAFF

When a prospective applicant is investigating employment opportunities as a security officer within a private company—whether contract or proprietary—he or she might favor a position that offers a greater level of authority. Further, since increased authority should be synonymous with greater responsibility, the position may pay more. It may also help retain personnel who would otherwise want to move on to public law enforcement positions.

RELATIONSHIP WITH LAW ENFORCEMENT

If the local police do not have to make arrests, conduct investigations, and testify in court for the private company, a better relationship may be created between the two. Police officials complain that their limited resources are burdened by having to handle the crime-related problems of private businesses, which the companies could deal with themselves through enhanced powers.

Relations can be further strained when a company decides not to prosecute and instead pursues its own system of corporate justice. Arrests made by police officers that result in dismissals because the company no longer wants to prosecute cause unnecessary friction and are likely to result in reduced cooperation. Businesses may be able to operate without police support much of the time, but they will be unlikely to survive a major crime wave, labor dispute, or terrorist attack without police help.

DETERRENCE TO CRIME

The reputation of a security department, inside or outside an organization, will affect the level of crime it experiences. If shoplifters know they will be prosecuted to the limits of the law, or dishonest employees know they may be arrested in front of their peers, they may be less inclined to commit the act. If a private company has the reputation of arresting and prosecuting offenders, potential offenders will probably be deterred.

SOME DISADVANTAGES FROM ENHANCED POWERS

On the other hand, a private company can face a number of potential disadvantages by having a security staff with full police authority. Some of the arguments against private citizens having police powers include the following.

NEGATIVE IMAGE

Security officers may become too policelike if they have full arrest authority. In most businesses, the role of private security is primarily loss prevention and investigations. Many security professionals take pride in the fact that they are able to control losses within their companies without having to resort to arrest and prosecution.

Furthermore, many businesses would prefer to project a positive public relations image with their customers, guests, employees, and the community. A high frequency of arrests may not be the best means of accomplishing that.

UNDESIRABLE CANDIDATES

The private security industry often attracts people who would prefer to work in public law enforcement because of the appeal of having arrest authority and a police officer's powers. But because of a lack of opportunity or inadequate personal qualifications, some of these individuals have found it easier to gain employment in the private sector.

One concern voiced by many security professionals is that if their officers are given arrest powers, they may be prone to abuse their authority. Aside from the legal implications of such abuse, the wrong type of candidate may be attracted to this kind of authority.

It would not be unusual, for example, for a newly empowered security officer to be eager to make his or her first arrest. Although this attitude may disappear after the first or second experience with the criminal justice system, some individuals are strongly attracted to having authority over others.

UNNECESSARY ARRESTS

When the security staff is licensed with police authority, the company may see an increase in the number of unnecessary arrests. Although retail businesses may choose to measure performance by the number of arrests made, in most businesses, a less dramatic and public way of handling problems is preferred. The more arrests made, the greater the risk of civil liability for false arrest and other torts. Further, overtime hours may be needed when the arresting officer has to appear in court.

CONSTITUTIONAL RESTRAINTS AND CIVIL RIGHTS LIABILITY

Generally, the provisions and restrictions imposed by the U.S. Constitution and its amendments apply to the actions of law enforcement officers—not to the activities of private security employees. For example, if an unlicensed security officer conducted a search and seizure that was later ruled illegal under the Fourth Amendment, the evidence seized would not be subject to exclusion as it would be if conducted by a public law enforcement officer. The evidence would still be admissible and carry its full weight in the criminal proceedings.

Across the country, however, some courts are ruling that if the private security officer is operating pursuant to special police powers, the search may be subjected to a stricter constitutional review. Such a review would require the court to apply the more stringent rules of due process and probable cause, resulting in excluded evidence and lost cases.

Having private individuals empowered with police authority increases the risk of application of the federal law prohibiting civil rights violations. *Federal law 42 US Code section 1983* provides monetary damages to anyone whose civil rights have been violated by a person acting **under color of law**. Although section 1983 liability should not be imposed unless the color of law requirement is met, some courts have been willing, to a limited extent, to impose this sanction.

Color of law requires the plaintiff to establish that the defendant officer was acting pursuant to authority conferred by law. In the South Carolina decision *Thompson* v.

FIGURE 4–7 *Police Code of Conduct*

All law enforcement officers must be fully aware of the ethical responsibilities of their position and must strive constantly to live up to the highest possible standards of professional policing. The International Association of Chiefs of Police believes it important that police officers have clear advice and counsel available to assist them in performing their duties consistent with these standards, and has adopted the following ethical mandates as guidelines to meet these standards.

Primary Responsibilities of a Police Officer

A police officer acts as an official representative of government who is required and trusted to work within the law. The officer's powers and duties are conferred by statute. The fundamental duties of a police officer include serving the community, safeguarding lives and property, protecting the innocent, keeping the peace and ensuring the rights of all to liberty, equality and justice.

Performance of the Duties of a Police Officer

A police officer shall perform all duties impartially, without favor or affection or ill will and without regard to sex, race, religion, political belief or aspiration. All citizens will be treated equally with courtesy, consideration and dignity.

Officers will never allow personal feelings, animosities or friendships to influence official conduct. Laws will be enforced appropriately and courteously and, in carrying out their responsibilities, officers will strive to obtain maximum cooperation from the public. They will conduct themselves in appearance and deportment in such a manner as to inspire confidence and respect for the position of public trust they hold.

Discretion

A police officer will use responsibly the discretion vested in his position and exercise it within the law. The principle of reasonableness will guide the officer's determinations, and the officer will consider all surrounding circumstances in determining whether any legal action shall be taken

Consistent and wise use of discretion, based on professional policing competence, will do much to preserve good relationships and retain the confidence of the public. There can be difficulty in choosing between conflicting courses of action. It is important to remember that a timely word of advice rather than arrest—which may be correct in appropriate circumstances—can be a more effective means of achieving a desired end.

Use of Force

A police officer will never employ unnecessary force or violence and will use only such force in the discharge of duty as is reasonable in all circumstances.

The use of force should be used only with the greatest restraint and only after discussion, negotiation and persuasion have been found to be inappropriate or ineffective. While the use of force is occasionally unavoidable, every police officer will refrain from unnecessary infliction of pain or suffering and will never engage in cruel, degrading or inhuman treatment of any person.

Confidentiality

Whatever a police officer sees, hears or learns of that is of a confidential nature will be kept secret unless the performance of duty or legal provision requires otherwise. Members of the public have a right to security and privacy, and information obtained about them must not be improperly divulged.

FIGURE 4–7 (cont'd)

Integrity

A police officer will not engage in acts of corruption or bribery, nor will an officer condone such acts by other police officers.

The public demands that the integrity of police officers be above reproach. Police officers must, therefore, avoid any conduct that might compromise integrity and thus undercut the public confidence in a law enforcement agency. Officers will refuse to accept any gifts, presents, subscriptions, favors, gratuities or promises that could be interpreted as seeking to cause the officer to refrain from performing official responsibilities honestly and within the law. Police officers must not receive private or special advantage from their official status. Respect from the public cannot be bought; it can only be earned and cultivated.

Cooperation with Other Police Officers and Agencies

Police officers will cooperate with all legally authorized agencies and their representatives in the pursuit of justice.

An officer or agency may be one among many organizations that may provide law enforcement services to a jurisdiction. It is imperative that a police officer assist colleagues fully and completely with respect and consideration at all times.

Personal-Professional Capabilities

Police officers will be responsible for their own standard of professional performance and will take every reasonable opportunity to enhance and improve their level of knowledge and competence.

Through study and experience, a police officer can acquire the high level of knowledge and competence that is essential for the efficient and effective performance of duty. The acquisition of knowledge is a never-ending process of personal and professional development that should be pursued constantly.

Private Life

Police officers will behave in a manner that does not bring discredit to their agencies or themselves.

A police officer's character and conduct while off duty must always be exemplary, thus maintaining a position of respect in the community in which he or she lives and serves. The officer's personal behavior must be beyond reproach.

Source: IACP, Public Information, Arlington, VA, 1997.

McCoy, 425 F. Supp. 407 (1976), the federal court was willing to apply section 1983 liability since the offending officer was licensed with police powers under South Carolina statute and acted pursuant to that authority.

In contrast, the Massachusetts Supreme Judicial Court ruled in *Commonwealth* v. *Leone* 386 Mass. 329 (1982) that color of law is not established on the basis of special police status alone but on whether the private security officer was fulfilling a public function, one usually performed by police officers for the public good. If the officer's actions were simply intended to further the interests of the private employer, color of law would not be present, and constitutional restraints and penalties would not apply. Clearly, these suggest that a security manager should check carefully before deciding to obtain police authority.

ISSUES THAT FAVOR PUBLIC OFFICIALS

The existence of specially empowered officers may assist a municipality and its law enforcement efforts in a variety of ways. Some of the arguments in favor of a system of licensing private citizens with these powers include the following.

SUPPLEMENTAL PERSONNEL

With licensed officers in the private sector, local police personnel are not as likely to be involved in private business matters and can concentrate their limited resources on public law enforcement issues. Additionally, in an emergency the municipality may be able to enlist the aid of private citizens to assist the regular police.

REDUCED OVERTIME

In municipalities where local security departments are able to make their own arrests, the police department may only have to transport the arrested person. Otherwise, if a security officer has detained someone suspected of committing a crime, the local police must transport the subject, effect the arrest, and appear in court to testify. The court time involved in such circumstances is often at overtime rates and is paid for by the municipality.

REVENUE SOURCE

Most licensing procedures have associated fees that are paid for by the applicant. In communities that issue large numbers of special police licenses, a significant amount of revenue can be produced. These licenses are often renewable annually, so a municipality can look forward to these revenues as a regular source of income.

CONTROL MECHANISM

Although roughly two or three times as many people are employed in private security-related functions as are employed in public policing, little or no control over the former group's activities exist. If the municipality issues special police powers, however, it can set requirements and standards for licensee qualification and training.

For example, cities may limit the type of weapon carried, specify the color of uniforms worn, require written examinations, conduct background checks, and even request a short training course be completed. Such requirements may not provide for maximum control, but if a licensee violates department rules, penalties can be levied against the officer and his or her employer.

REDUCED CRIME

Special police powers may help a security department control and eventually reduce crime within its organization or institution. Although many offenses committed within the confines of a private property may not affect the citizens of a particular community, the statistics for such crime should be included in reported crime rates for the entire municipality. If the private security departments of businesses located in that municipality are more effective in reducing crimes, the reduction will be favorable for the community overall.

ISSUES THAT CONCERN PUBLIC OFFICIALS

Any community that allows its private citizens to hold police powers without controlling them can anticipate a variety of problems. Some of the issues that public officials have expressed concern with or already encountered include the following.

GREATER LIABILITY

Both attorneys and municipal leaders have argued that granting special police powers to individuals in the private sector increases the likelihood of suits against the community for negligence and civil rights violations. The legal theory behind this argument is that though municipalities are granting these powers and receiving revenues, they are not regulating those who exercise them. Whether a civil suit would be successful based on this theory is not now known, but the potential has been real enough to inspire some cities to consider elimination of licensing programs.

At issue is the fact that these people are not trained or supervised to the extent needed to reduce the likelihood of an illegal arrest, search, or excessive use of force. Although some government units have established minimum training standards for these officers, all too often the newly licensed officer is turned loose on an unsuspecting community.

ADMINISTRATIVE RESPONSIBILITY

Some municipal administrators have expressed concern about the responsibilities involved with licensing, which may include checking applicants' criminal records, maintaining records, assigning staff to manage details, and so forth. They often see this task as another burden on the community's limited resources.

INEQUITABLE PERFORMANCE

Unsupervised and poorly trained special officers may enforce the law in a discriminatory and uneven manner. Inequitable enforcement of laws may result in unfair treatment of individuals, which in turn reflects poorly on the community. Poor treatment can increase citizen complaints against the police department.[14]

Each security manager must determine the applicability of each of these arguments and issues on his or her organization before deciding to use special police powers for security officers. If the *Hallcrest II* predictions about the size of the police and private security by the year 2000 are correct, however, a mutually acceptable resolution of these issues would likely have to be found, since crime has shown only small decreases in recent years.

Privatization: The Wave of the Twenty-First Century?

The costs of many services previously handled by government personnel have been reexamined in light of the costs for supplying these services in a period of shrinking budgets at all levels. It is not too difficult to find examples of privatization of services in many parts of the criminal justice system. Many of these are seen in the corrections system, but the advantages and disadvantages can be interpolated into law enforcement for serious examination.

Prison crowding, lawsuits over conditions and practices, high staff turnover rates, increased rates of incarceration of offenders, explosive budgetary growth, and perceived lack of innovation in institutionalized corrections have provided an environment in which a new correctional approach has arisen: a movement toward **privatization**. Privatization is the delivery of correctional services to governmental agencies by for-profit or nonprofit entities. This innovation can take four forms: operation of prison industries by private enterprise, private-sector financing of correctional construction, contract services (such as health care or food services), and the total management and operation of correctional institutions by private enterprise. Of the four, the most controversial is the total management and operation of prisons and jails.

The private sector is believed to be more cost effective by providing equal services at lower cost than states and counties. Such service providers can cut through the bureaucratic "red tape" more easily than the public sector might be able to do. They are seen as better able than public agencies to hire the most competent people, provide training, and fire personnel who cannot perform to standards. Private-sector providers, such as the Corrections Corporation of America and Wackenhut, Inc. (which also provide security services), argue that they can furnish improved services, greater access to special services, more responsive personnel, and flexible programming, and at a lower cost than that offered by the public sector.

Whether those claims will be validated over time and across the many different types of clientele that corrections must serve remains to be seen. This innovative approach has been most actively applied to juvenile corrections and by the halfway house movement in the United States. But only a handful of correctional institutions have been completely managed by private correctional service agencies over many years. This is an area of criminal justice that students and practitioners should observe carefully for future developments in the twenty-first century.

A report by the National Institute of Justice points out five circumstances under which careful experimentation with private sector facilities may work out:

1. Rapid mobilization. Given the widely acknowledged ability of the private sector to move more rapidly to bring additional facilities and man-power on-line, combined with the uncertainty that surrounds future population trends, contracting may be useful at the State level to avoid permanent facility expansion but still accommodate near-term population shifts.

2. Experimentation. An agency can test new models of institutional corrections practice without making a permanent commitment or laboring under the constraints to innovation typically present in traditional corrections bureaucracies.

3. Decentralization. Greater geographic and programmatic diversity may be possible by calling on local contractors rather than trying to provide the same community-oriented services under the direct control of a centralized agency.

4. Specialization. The flexibility of private contractors to satisfy unique demands suggests that contracting for the confinement of offenders with special needs may offer significant relief to general-purpose institutions as well as more opportunities for the successful treatment of the "special management" inmate.

5. Regionalization. Finally, the private sector is not typically bound by the jurisdictional politics that might otherwise impede efforts to develop shared facilities among States or counties within a State.[15]

As governments continue to search for innovative ways to serve their constituencies, without burdening them with excessive taxes and adding more public employees, they are turning increasingly to private companies. The experiences with corrections, and the growing interest in community policing, seem to be heading in the same direction. They are seeking to do business with private firms that offer high levels of expertise, adequate financial resources, and a quality service for a reasonable return on their investment.

Summary

In an era of shrinking public resources, productivity has been a difficult cross to bear by public safety agencies whose mission includes the *prevention* of criminal behavior. How do you measure productivity by something that *didn't happen*? This quandary also bedevils the efforts of security and loss prevention practitioners, especially at budget time and when they have to justify staff or equipment. This is sometimes referred to as the fireman syndrome, in which the local government observes that there have been no fires for a long time, so they reduce the fire department to zero. But when fires begin to occur, the firemen are soon brought back. This problem is one of trying to measure such services in *quantitative* terms alone. The trend today should be toward meeting the "values" of the community (or commercial organization in the private case) and trying to determine how close the course is to the desired *direction*. When you use such *qualitative* measurement to determine the productivity of a police or security organization, it becomes clearer what impact enforcement and preventive measures are having.

Community involvement is generally referred to as community policing and has been found to be efficient and effective when used with involvement of all elements of the community served. The same techniques (covered again in Chapter 7) are effective in describing what the private security agency does in its role of *preventing corporate losses* through security and loss prevention strategies and tactics. This is especially critical when the security department is tagged as having no "profit center" and contribution to the bottom line. These efforts are also better articulated by using a value-oriented measure and then seeing how close the aim is on that value.

The age-old issue of who does what, to whom, and with what powers creates some real barriers to effective integration of public and private protection issues in the twenty-first century. As some states try to give more and more policelike powers to security agencies, the problems and liabilities for such a strategy mount. Privatization seems to be "pushing the envelope" when it is considered for full police powers to private security services in the community. Not until the next century will many of these issues be resolved. In the remaining chapters, we shall return to this theme of integration and cooperation as we try to find the best way to provide public safety and security in the United States.

REVIEW QUESTIONS

1. Describe the differences between efficiency and effectiveness.
2. Explain the elements of a three-stage systems model.
3. What is the ratio of crimes known to police and crimes cleared by arrest?
4. Discuss the partnership with people program in Hawaii.
5. What is meant by "three strikes and you're out"?

TERMS TO REMEMBER

get tough	*war on drugs*	*value productivity*
three strikes and you're out	*discretionary power*	*partnership with people*
police work	*back-alley justice*	*special police officer*
three-stage systems model	*four-stage systems model*	*under color of law*
efficiency	*known to the police*	*privatization*
effectiveness	*cleared by arrest*	

ENDNOTES

1. National Advisory Commission on Criminal Justice Standards and Goals, *Report of the Task Force on Private Security* (Washington, D.C.: U.S. Govt. Printing Office, 1976), p. 205.
2. President's Commission on Law Enforcement and the Administration of Justice, *Task Force Report: The Police* (Washington, D.C.: U.S. Govt. Printing Office, 1967), p. 91.
3. Ibid., p. 1.
4. E. Bittner, *The Function of the Police in a Modern Society* (Chevy Chase, Md.: NIMH, 1970), p. 42.
5. President's Commission on Law Enforcement, p. 91.
6. President's Commission on Law Enforcement, p. 130.

7. National Advisory Commission on Criminal Justice Standards and Goals, *A National Strategy to Reduce Crime* (Washington, D.C.: U.S. Govt. Printing Office, Washington, DC, 1973). Much of the material in this section is drawn from this report, edited and updated to meet the needs of this text.

8. Ibid., p. 45.

9. "The Losing Battle Against Crime in America," *U.S. News and World Report*, Vol. LXXCII, No. 25 (Dec. 16, 1974), p. 43.

10. Gary T. Marx. "The Interweaving of Public and Private Police in Undercover Work." *Private Policing* (Los Angeles: Sage, 1987), p. 187.

11. Charles P. Connolly. "Working Together," *Security Management*, ASIS, Vol. 35, No. 1 (January 1991), p. 50.

12. Ibid., p. 52.

13. Ibid., p. 52.

14. Norman D. Bates. "Special Police Powers: Pros and Cons," *Security Management*, Vol. 33, No. 8 (August 1989), pp. 54–58. This article has been used in its entirety, thanks to the kindness of my friend Norm Bates. The author is especially grateful for the use of this material, upon which there could be no improvement.

15. J. K. Stewart, *Corrections and the Private Sector* (Washington, D.C.: NIJ, Washington, DC: 1984), p. 1.

5

The Wide Range of Specialized Security Fields and Career Opportunities

Indeed, the private security industry has grown to where it now dwarfs public law enforcement; it employs 2 1/2 times the personnel of public agencies and outspends them by 73 percent.

—Charles B. DeWitt

Overview

With this statement, the former director of the National Institute of Justice summarized the growth of the private security industry over the past two decades. The image of a uniformed security guard as the only manifestation of "security" has long been replaced by trained, experienced, and professional security practitioners in a broad range of industries and many narrow specialties within those industries. The present-day security expert is more likely to be carrying a laptop computer than an old rusty pistol.

This chapter examines a few representative areas within the general security task that have been identified as developing into specialty areas, most of which have been officially recognized by the American Society for Industrial Security by the establishing of permanent standing committees tasked to describe and prescribe the missions and standards for each identified category. Many of the basic concepts of private security clearly overlap these less than discrete divisions, but we shall examine a few of the more interesting differences that separate these functions and missions in security.

Since all students of public safety and security wonder what they might do when they graduate, they need to examine what fields seem right for them. This chapter will cover a few areas in quite some detail, some in less, and some only in passing mention. Our main interest is in describing some of the career opportunities for each category. Trying to describe any part of this dynamic industry, however, is sometimes like trying to paint a moving bus. Rapid development of new technology and the attendant security issues that develop from each of them make the field of security an exciting and growing opportunity for career innovation. Though the selection of topics for in-depth analyses is arbitrary, we try to cover those that seem to offer the most striking differences.

Airports and Aviation Security

Beginning with the first commercial airliner skyjacking in the 1960s, to the bombing of Pan American flight 103 over Lockerbee, Scotland, in 1989, to the still unresolved crash of **TWA 800** in 1995, the former *laissez-faire* attitude toward security in the aviation industry has done a sharp about-face. The security for airliners and airports has grown from the placing of air marshals on the planes themselves to a complete system of security for airports, parking, transports, baggage, passengers, and the aircraft themselves. Whole new technologies have been developed to deter, detect, and divert potential threats to the air traveler.

Since 1987, the Federal Aviation Administration (FAA) has been tasked to develop standards for security for the aviation industry and standard airport security programs. In late 1988, Congress passed **FAR 107.14**, a rule that requires all U.S. airports to raise the level of security and access to airports. FAR 107.14 states that they should "control by computer the access to aeronautical operational areas." These aeronautical operational areas (AOAs) are generally seen as those places where there is access to the aircraft. Since thousands of employees and vendors must access the AOAs, with hundreds of points of ingress and egress, this has stimulated a lot of activity among security professionals to find ways to accomplish the mandates of the FAA rules.

The problems with jurisdiction, ownership, and operations at U.S. airports further complicates the process of providing proper security. As noted by Stump:

> Ownership and operation of U.S. airports vary considerably. Airports can be either public or privately owned. When public, they are usually operated by a city, county, state, or airport authority. The Port Authority of New York and New Jersey, for example, operates LaGuardia, Kennedy, and Newark airports.
>
> Ownership also determines an airport's law enforcement structure. State and local police forces or special airport authority forces are used primarily. The FAA also requires airports to meet criteria to ensure a consistent level of service. Most airports employ forces responsible for physical security, and private contractors often provide security forces.
>
> Security is further subdivided between an airport operator and air carriers by exclusive area agreements. Carriers are responsible for physical security in areas they lease from the airport, including air operations areas, cargo buildings, and

airline spaces within the terminal. As many as 25 organizations may share security responsibility at a single airport, according to the President's Commission on Aviation Security and Terrorism.[1]

Figure 5–1 displays the problems with explosives aboard aircraft from 1977 to 1995. As can be seen, the wide fluctuations tend to make the task of the aviation security manager a real high-wire act in providing consistent security. During times of few problems, the cry is to reduce costs (especially in the turbulent times when U.S. airlines find themselves fighting for market share of the passenger business); then, invariably, an incident causes another flurry of activity to increase security.

Although the threat of skyjacking or airborne terrorism seizes most of the headlines, the security task at airports and in the air includes many other serious and not-so-serious threats and problems. Airports and aircraft are subject to all the crimes that affect any large community, from murder to purse-snatching. In addition to the "normal" crimes found in cities and towns (and an airport has every aspect of

FIGURE 5–1   *Baggage Universe*

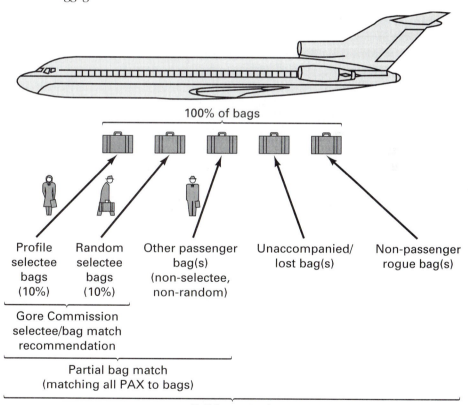

Source: Billie Vincent, *Access Control* (Intertec Publishing, Pittsfield, MA, 1988), p. 33.

a fairly large city), there are crimes such as cargo theft, ticket fraud, drug smuggling, stowaways, luggage theft and pilfering, sabotage, escaped criminals, and many other specialized types of crimes. This, combined with fragmented responsibilities, makes it difficult for the multijurisdictional components of security to work together in a common effort.

PROFILING

A recent trend in airport screening is the development of **profiling** passengers, which is aimed at spotting probable terrorists and smugglers. The concept of profiling has received a lot of publicity through the FBI's behavioral program in its efforts to profile serial killers and rapists. Similar concepts can be applied to profiling smugglers at customs points and used by specially trained security personnel. These security officers are trained to resolve suspicious signs so as to reduce the number of people who are searched and catch the approximately four of four hundred passengers who may be up to something. The vice president of aviation security for the firm of International Consults on Targeted Security (ICTS) describes the system:

> One of the basic rules we set for the system is to have as few people as possible selected for a search, so we can have all our resources and efforts devoted to a small number of passengers who really present a high risk. When you enter a country, customs officials may search your bags as if you have diamonds or gold or drugs in them. After three or four minutes, if they don't find anything, they will treat you as if everything is okay and let you enter the country.[2]

Figure 5–2 clearly shows that the terrorist threat from the 1 billion airline passengers a year is less than .0000001 percent, but the results can be disastrous when a terrorist event occurs. This figure also shows that probably more than half the threatening passengers are **unaware passengers**, ranging from naive passengers to framed terrorists. Knowing this allows trained profilers to question unaware passengers without creating friction or distress.

DETECTION OF EXPLOSIVES

In addition to proper use of profiling, the task of detecting explosives is attacked from a number of fronts beyond visual inspection and use of dogs. As a matter of fact, public law 101-604 required that the FAA undertake an extensive review of threats to civil aviation and have new equipment and procedures to meet the technological challenges presented by terrorism in place at all major airports by November 1993. Such devices are at the leading edge of technology and include:

- *X-ray absorption:* This method involves measuring the density and shape of various kinds of explosives and comparing the result with computerized data. Several such devices have been used on an experimental basis.

FIGURE 5–2 *Passenger Typologies*

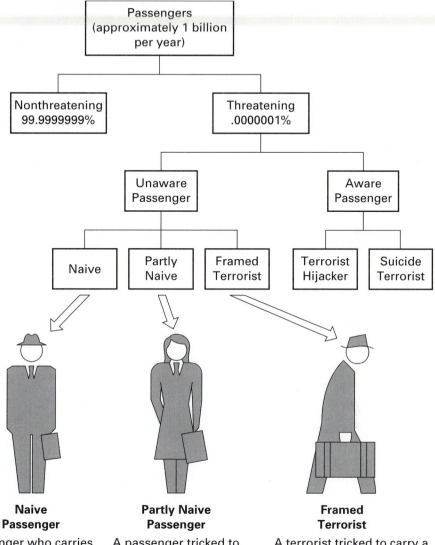

Naive Passenger

A passenger who carries a bomb in his or her baggage without being aware of it.

Example: A passenger transfers a bag or a gift for a friend.

Partly Naive Passenger

A passenger tricked to believe that his or her baggage contains contraband but in reality is carrying a bomb.

Example: A passenger who transfers a load of contraband, such as diamonds, cash, or drugs.

Framed Terrorist

A terrorist tricked to carry a bomb on board an aircraft without being aware of it.

Example: The terrorist believes he or she is transferring explosives only on a flight but in fact is carrying a complete working bomb, set to go off in midair.

Source: ICTS, Cleveland, Ohio.

- *Nuclear magnetic resonance:* This method combines both an electromagnetic field and a superimposed radio frequency field that interact with the hydrogen atoms in explosives. The system is designed to detect the byproduct of the interaction.

- *Thermal neutron activation:* In this system, the low-energy, thermalized neutrons produced by a radioactive source interact with the nitrogen contained in explosives. The byproduct of the interaction is then detected.

- *Fast neutron analysis:* This is more costly than the thermal neutron analysis and is based on a different source for detecting explosives.

- *Pulsed fast neutron analysis:* This method is similar to the fast neutron analysis, except a pulsed beam of neutrons is used to detect the explosive material.

- *Vapor detection systems:* This is a system based on gas chromatography, which samples molecules from air samples obtained from baggage. A collector, about the size of a mailbox, sucks in an air sample from baggage. The collector is then inserted into a 4-foot-high console that mixes the sample with ozone in the chamber. A weak light is produced if explosive is present. The analysis of the sample takes only a few seconds.

- *Enhanced x-ray detection:* The current x-ray scanners have been used for many years to detect weapons and less sophisticated explosive systems. More advanced systems are already in use or under development. These include dual- or multienergy scanners, backscatter x-rays, and computerized tomography systems.

AIRPORT PERSONNEL AND SECURITY

In the end, however, the real key to security in airports and on airliners is wrapped in two key elements: (1) informed management and (2) dedicated, motivated, security-aware, and *trained* personnel at all levels of the organization. As an example, United Airlines, the largest U.S. carrier, feels that the security mission is not limited to just security officers, but includes staff such as their skycaps and ticket agents:

> They [skycaps] are the first people, generally speaking, to meet the passenger. They meet and greet people all day long, and they are certainly well qualified to look at people who will be flying with us. There are a number of things we can have skycaps do for us in security and still not be members of the security department.

> They [ticket agents] also meet people all day and are very good at maintaining order. They are probably the primary group, along with flight attendants, to deal with irate passengers, people who are intoxicated or under the influence of narcotics, and those that have a penchant to cause us a problem.[3]

United Airlines has initiated extensive training for its personnel, including many hours of training on security-related subjects. For example, skycaps receive six hours of ticket recognition alone.

While you can apply profiles to inanimate objects such as cargo, baggage, etc., you ultimately have to tie the profile to an organization, and finally, to an individual or group.

BAGGAGE/PASSENGER MATCHING

There are many reasons for a bag becoming separated from its owner's flight. Most of these are legitimate and the unaccompanied bag presents no threat to the safety of flight.

In rare instances, however, the separation is deliberate and the unaccompanied bag may present a dire threat to the safety of flight. In still others a bag may be surreptitiously inserted into an airline's baggage system for criminal purposes such as movement of drugs or sabotage.

There are basically two types of security processes focusing on bags and passengers matching passengers to bags and matching bags to passengers.

ORIGINATING PASSENGER/BAG MATCH

In this process all passengers are matched with their checked bags. An originating passenger checks in with an airline at an airport, uses a ticket to get a boarding pass, checks one or more bags and proceeds to the departure gate. The airline then ensures that the passenger boards the flight; if he does not, his bags are located and removed from the flight. This process is generally known as the originating passenger/baggage match and does not consider any bag that may already be in the belly of the aircraft. An originating passenger/baggage match is a partial bag match process if it does not reconcile the baggage and passengers already on board the aircraft at each stop.

PROFILE SELECTEE OR RANDOM PASSENGER/BAGGAGE MATCH

The Gore Commission recommended this process as an interim measure until it could be determined through research that a full passenger/baggage match was operationally feasible in the U.S. domestic aviation System. This process tracks only those passengers that have been singled out for added scrutiny through a profile process or a random selection. If the passenger meets the U.S. profile, or is selected on a random basis, that passenger's bags may receive security screening using an x-ray, Explosives Detection System (EDS), or a physical search, after which the passenger proceeds to the departure gate.

In the case of a "profile selectee" or a "random selectee," the airline must ensure that the passenger actually boards the aircraft or have the passenger's bags removed from the flight.

Not addressed by the Gore Commission was whether "profile selectees" or a "random selectees" would be matched to their bags on multi-segmented flight stopovers. In any event, this process is a partial passenger/baggage match as it ignores the majority of passengers.[4]

Clearly, there are many opportunities in the field of airport and aviation security for the student of security management. These careers range from security director of the airport complex, to security director for each airline, to contract security management at the airport sites. There are also great career opportunities in training and technology to meet the threats that loom large for a world that has become not only easier to travel, but also more dangerous.

Banking and Financial Services Security

The banking industry has grown from the corner bank to huge financial conglomerates, with downsizing and takeovers occurring almost monthly. The industry has been forced, by sheer volume, to make giant steps in using technology for handling the massive financial transactions necessary to keep an industrialized society moving ahead. The use of **electronic fund transfers**, **automatic teller machines** (ATM), and the whole host of advantages that come with modern computer technology have created new security specialization in banks. We will discuss the relationship between computer crime and banking security in later parts of this chapter, but the ability to move billions of dollars across the airwaves, with attendant risks, makes the problems of armed bank robbers pale by comparison.

Indeed, the armed bank robber is still a problem, and the number of actual bank robberies continues to grow. There were 9000 bank robberies in 1994.[5] Actually, however, when looked at from the perspective of all financial crime, robbery is small potatoes. Estimated losses from major loss categories in the banking industry find four of the top five are crimes of fraud:

- Robbery: $60 million to $70 million
- Credit card fraud: $1.2 billion
- Inside abuse (defalcation): $2.1 billion
- Loan fraud: $6 billion to $7 billion
- Check fraud: $7 billion to $10 billion[6]

The **Bank Protection Act of 1968** (revised in 1992) requires all banks to have a security officer. This responsibility is somewhat mixed up in most banks, however.

In many cases, physical security responsibilities are distinct from fraud loss prevention and investigation. Also, internal defalcations are often the responsibility of the internal audit section, and commercial loan fraud is the concern of the commercial loan department. Despite these initiatives, fraud losses have skyrocketed over the past decade.[7]

FRAUD IN THE FINANCIAL INDUSTRY

Since fraud is the big loser for banks and financial institutions, it is important to look at some of the various types of fraud. Check fraud is one of the oldest kinds. This category includes theft of checks, counterfeiting of checks, and kiting checks against a quick deposit. Computers have made these kinds of fraud not only more profitable, but also harder to detect.

AUTOMATIC TELLER MACHINE (ATM) FRAUD

Automatic teller machines (ATMs), which dispense funds at booths outside banks, in airports, in your local grocery chain, and anywhere money is needed quickly, is a real convenience to the bank customer. But in major urban areas, they have become a nightmare. As fast as schemes for protection of ATMs and their customers are devised, criminals come up with new ways to defeat them. ATM robbery and killings caused New York City to pass some of the toughest legislation in the country in regard to ATMs (Int. No. 787-A) calling for:

- No new outdoor ATM locations in New York City
- Adequate lighting around existing ATMs, their parking lots, and the interior portions of buildings where ATMs are accessible after hours
- A surveillance camera and recorder at every New York City ATM
- Card access entry doors to outdoor ATMs for after-hours use
- At least one glass exterior wall at all ATM enclosures
- Reflective mirrors mounted above ATMs to allow the customer a rear view of the surrounding area
- A sign stating the ATM is monitored for security, customers must close the entry door completely before using the machine, customers must pocket their cash securely before leaving the ATM, and where complaints about ATM safety should be directed
- Each ATM cardholder be given a written copy of basic ATM safety information
- Penalties of up to $500 for a first violation of rules, up to $1000 for a second violation, and a minimum of $2000 for a third and subsequent violations (banks would be given three days to correct a violation) [8]

Similar legislation has been adopted in California and Nevada, and the trend seems to be strong for such legislation to spread. ATM crime has become so prevalent that some police jurisdictions have begun listing it as a separate category, broken down by ATM type. An examination of ATM robbery has shown the following characteristics:

- Ninety-six percent of the crimes involve a single ATM customer.
- About fifty percent of the crimes occur between 7:00 P.M. and 12:00 A.M.
- Most of the crimes began as the customer was using the ATM (54 percent) or leaving the ATM (33 percent).
- Customers refused or resisted the perpetrator in 13 percent of the incidents.
- Customers were injured in about 14 percent of the crimes.[9]

It is clear that, with hundreds of thousands of ATMs in service in the United States, and more than 500 million cards that can be used at ATMs, there will be a continuing need to find ways to better protect those who use them. Not just bank customers are targets of ATM crime, however. Those who service the machines and collect or load money are also prime targets. Three caveats should be written into every bank's policies and procedures and carefully drilled into all employee's minds:

1. Never attempt to transport currency for ATMs without an escort. Transporting should be done with at least two people, one to carry the currency cassette and one to look out
2. Never transport currency through areas that are open to the public
3. Never transport cash containers openly to an ATM site away from the bank. Instead, keep the currency cassette covered in a way that does not reveal its contents (robbers know what cassettes look like). Vary the way that you conceal it.

ATM crime is also subject to the same kinds of fraud as any other cash-handling system.

CREDIT CARD FRAUD

At a rate of $1.2 billion a year, credit card fraud is another major problem in which crime follows opportunity. Credit cards are also ATM cards in most cases, so these two types of fraud seem to work together to further hurt the financial institutions.

INSIDE ABUSE (DEFALCATION)

Inside abuse, also called **defalcation**, which accounts for annual losses of some $2 billion, is a problem that is usually kept low profile in the industry. Investigations and whistle-blowers bring these huge losses to light, but seldom are the guilty employees. Instead, the institution chooses to dismiss the employee and lower the level of publicity and bad image created by prosecution.

LOAN FRAUD

Loan fraud, already at a $6 billion to $7 billion annual rate, was rocked by the savings and loan scandals that showed just how greedy some managers had gotten, and how loose the controls were on such loans. Fraudulent loans in the savings and loan industry have resulted in a massive bailout by the taxpayers in the neighborhood of $500 billion, which threatened the stability of all other types of financial institutions. That money, which was attracted to savings and loan coffers by inflated interest rates and put aside for homes and retirement, wasn't taken at the point of a gun, but by telex, wire, and bank transfers. A scandal of this size rocks the financial industry, but the fraud goes on at a cost of billions more.

CHECK FRAUD

The many types of **check fraud**, estimated at a staggering $7 billion to $10 billion annually, have a major impact on American business. The cost of bad checks to business sales is growing at a rate approaching 25 percent a year and accounts for as much as 1 percent of sales. Some suggestions for cutting bad check losses are offered by Hale:

- Verify all checks electronically before accepting or guaranteeing them if verification can be cost justified.
- Don't drive away good customers with policies, actions, and attitudes that are intended for bad check writers.
- Formalize and enforce check and ID acceptance policies at all locations.
- Provide prompt feedback to individual cashiers on uncollectible checks they accepted.
- Follow up with managers who approved checks that should not have been accepted.
- File all uncollected checks for criminal prosecution.
- Don't automatically redeposit returned checks without testing to determine how many checks clear on redeposit.
- Assign responsibility to one person at each store for ensuring that administrative functions for bad checks are performed by those responsible.
- Adopt the procedural safeguards necessary to prevent employee theft of customer payments for bad checks.
- Electronically verify merchandise returned for cash refund.
- Compare in-house costs for verifying and collecting checks with the cost of using a reputable outside service.
- Use customer data compiled from check verification for a positive database and for merchandising purposes as well.[10]

Check fraud spreads to more than just the issues described here. Stolen checks, counterfeit checks, and even use of checks by financial industry employees make the totals mount up.

SECURITY'S PLACEMENT IN A BANKING INSTITUTION

banking industry is dynamic, but volatile. Hale suggests some of the ways that security can help banking get through future crises and attacks from within and without through the twenty-first century. Forces such as the evolution of banking, technological advances in banking and security, crime trends in society against banks, legislation and regulations relevant to the industry, how security defines its role, and how bank management defines the role of security are crucial.[11] These forces will determine the directions taken by security to help stop the hemorrhaging of funds from our most trusted financial institutions. The role of security in this evolution can be of great help, but only if properly positioned in the organization. As noted by Hale:

> Security is suffering from an identity crisis. When security directors get together it is not uncommon to find that none share the same reporting structure within a bank and no two have the same responsibilities. Security can, and does, report

Americans: Crime Over Privacy; More Security, More Police

More than 9 of 10 Americans feel safer when monitored by video cameras while shopping, according to a national survey of consumers released exclusively at the just-completed International Security Conference (ISC) in New York.

Safety More Critical

The study also shows that 86.6 percent of American workers prefer safety over privacy in the workplace.

The survey was conducted by America's Research Group, the leading consumer survey research firm in retailing. The ISC press conference was called by the Washington, D.C.-based Security Industry Association. SECURITY Magazine and its editor, Bill Zalud, have played a significant role in an effort to reposition opposition to the proposed federal privacy for Consumers and Workers Act.

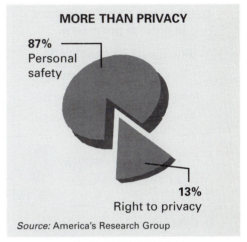

MORE THAN PRIVACY

87%
Personal safety

13%
Right to privacy

Source: America's Research Group

Vast majority of people rank their security over more intangible privacy concerns.

At the ISC press briefing, Zalud called the proposed privacy bill "pro-crime legislation that simply provides a blueprint for criminals."

Shoppers in the survey were asked which was most important in a retail store, personal safety or the right to privacy. Of those interviewed, 90.7 percent answered safety, while only 9.3 percent said privacy.

Britt Beemer, founder and chairman of America's Research Group, a Charleston, South Carolina-based consumer survey research firm, said, "A 91 percent response is rare in research, and politicians in Washington would be wise to pay attention to the mood of consumers on this issue."

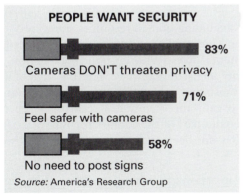

PEOPLE WANT SECURITY

83%
Cameras DON'T threaten privacy

71%
Feel safer with cameras

58%
No need to post signs

Source: America's Research Group

People are more concerned with their security in stores and in the workplace.

Americans: Crime Over Privacy; More Security, More Police

DEMANDING MORE SECURITY
In order of preference:

Bright parking to lighting

Three strikes you're out

More police walking streets

More police in patrol cars

More CCTV

More police visibility

CCTV in parking lots

Curfews for young

More security patrols

More death penalty

Source: America's Research Group

People want more visible signs of police and security.

John Galante, executive director of SIA, noted the research confirms that the Association's position "sides with a majority of Americans in opposing government interference in securing where people work and shop."

Other Survey Data

- 71.3 percent of shoppers say they feel safer in stores using security cameras.

- 82.7 percent don't feel security cameras threaten their privacy.

- Almost half the respondents (47.3 percent) said they most definitely would like to see more security personnel patrolling parking lots at stores and malls.

Source: Editors. "Americans: Crime Over Privacy; More Security, More Police," *Security*. (Cahners Publishing Company. Newton, MA, 1994), Vol. 31, No. 10, p. 7.

through a variety of organizations—including human resources, audit, property management, and operations. Some security organizations are limited to physical security, guard management, investigations, fraud prevention, or information security. Other security departments have nothing to do with alarms and surveillance cameras because they are considered a property administration function. In many large organizations, physical security is separate from investigations, which then becomes part of the audit department. Security rarely performs any function that has not been and is not performed by some other department.

Security's placement within an organization's reporting structure often determines what security will be able to achieve. If security is placed too far below senior management, selling any proposal will be an uphill battle. Placing security within the context of building management limits the ability of security to deal with fraud and embezzlement.[12]

The career field for the student is wide open in the banking industry. The impact of the savings and loan scandals, along with the confusing and shaky status of the banking industry in the late 1990s, demands well-educated and well-trained security managers and officers in our financial institutions. It is essential for those calling themselves professional in the security industry to acquire an in-depth knowledge of computers and computer security principles. It is even more critical in the era of electronic transfer of funds, ATMs, and direct transfer of funds as more and more transactions overwhelm the systems. As we shall see in Chapter 7, this applies to placement of security in almost any kind of company or agency.

Security in Healthcare

As this is being written, President Clinton is beginning his second term, and politicians from every point on the political compass are arguing about the cost of our healthcare system and its failure to provide quality medical care at a reasonable price to every American. Those who must spend time in a healthcare facility—as a patient, visitor, or employee—also deserve to be safe and secure during their stay. As the prestigious *Lipman Report* reveals, the problems of hospital security in the 1990s are rising with the tide of crime and violence in America:

> The unique characteristics and responsibilities of a hospital environment create multiple and thorny risks, and make security particularly difficult to provide. As a prelude to this report, it is perhaps useful to review some of these difficulties:
>
> - A hospital is never closed. Access to the physical facility and its services must be provided around the clock. Access control is complicated by the availability of multiple points of entry to the premises and by high levels of legitimate vehicle and pedestrian traffic.
> - A hospital is obligated by federal law to provide emergency treatment to virtually every patient, a growing number of whom are (or accompanied by people who are) aggressive, addicted, or deranged.
> - A hospital has multifaceted security needs. A gift shop, a pharmacy with its need to monitor controlled substances, a newborn nursery, and operating room, a medical records library, an emergency room, and a cafeteria each require much different forms of security and protection.
> - A hospital's valuable equipment and powerful drugs are magnetic attractions for misuse and theft.
> - Access by all persons inside a hospital to numerous small and relatively valuable items increases exponentially the difficulty in securing and protecting them.
> - The immobility or helplessness of many of the hospital's constituents makes them more vulnerable to victimization. In the case of Children's Hospital infants and children who are critically or terminally ill are particularly at risk.

Hot and Cold Biometrics Heat Up Again

The hot and cold world of biometrics for security access is hot again.

New and emerging biometric approaches—ranging from finger, hand and eye, to face—were prominent at this year's American Society for Industrial Security (ASIS) conference and business exposition in Las Vegas.

New players included signature, fingerprint and retinal scanning.

Signing In

Signature verification had seemed to disappear for a while as an access tool. But a new offering from Cadix International Inc., Newport Beach, Calif., is about to change that. The ID-007 is an on-line signature verification system that bases access decisions on three different criteria: the actual signature, the pressure of the pen and the speed of the signing.

To accommodate changes in signatures, the enrollment process requires between three and five signatures. In addition, the computer has a "learn mode," enabling it to accept the variations and changes that naturally occur over time, says company president Ben Lee.

"Signing is a very natural way to do things," Lee says. "It has a trust factor in business applications, whereas other types of biometrics, such as fingerprinting, have very different connotations."

Touch of a Finger

The use of fingerprints for access often gets a bad rap, so to speak. The association of fingerprinting with criminal activities can give users the wrong idea.

But there is a real difference between digitized fingerprint files in a law enforcement data base and use of a fingerprint biometric for secure access.

"When we're able to talk to people, they see tht it's not a forensic fingerprint," says David Scott at Indentix Inc., Sunnyvale, Calif. "It's a mathematical characterization of a fingerprint. It can't be used to compare with an FBI database, for example."

TouchLock II from Identix is a new access control product incorporating the fingerprint biometric principle. The employee punches in an ID number to call up their record, then places their finger on the optical window. Authentication occurs within half a second.

Focus on Access

According to Melvin Womack at EyeDentify Inc., Baton Rouge, La., the eye is one of the most stable biometric identifiers. "The eye shares the same stable environment as the brain, and only a small number of diseases or serious physical injuries can alter the pattern."

Both EyeDentify and IriScan, Mt. Laurel, N.J., use the eye as a biometric tool. EyeDentify scans the retina, while IriScan mathematically encodes information contained in the iris.

Another company, Data Link of Herndon, Va., expanded its imaging approach to include biometrics. The company's TrueFace system is based on facial biometric verification.

Source: Karyn Hodgson, "Hot and Cold Biometrics Heat Up Again," *Security* (Cahners Publishing Company, Newton, MA, 1994), Vol. 31, No. 11, p. 17.

- Hospital staff, patients, and visitors are exposed routinely to highly stressful, emotionally charged situations which can easily result in inappropriate or violent behavior. Stress may be exacerbated by anger about the high cost of health care, about a long wait before receiving treatment, about crowded conditions at the facility, about the perception that staff is too hurried or noncaring, by the effects of substance abuse among those who seek care or accompany patients, or by the number of other related or unrelated circumstances.

- The need to be easily accessible to population centers leads to the location of hospitals in transitional areas where crime rates tend to be growing.

- The population's natural tendency to consider a hospital off-limits to unlawful or violent behavior and activity is changing. In 1990, emergency departments in Philadelphia confiscated loaded guns, knives, box cutters, piano wire, brass knuckles, razors, and hand grenades.

- On average, 70 percent of hospital employees are female, more vulnerable to sexual assault and robbery than males in general. It is increasingly difficult to retain female staff in what appears to them to be an unsafe environment.

There are many reasons to act quickly and conscientiously to respond to security problems at hospitals when they are revealed. These range from moral issues, to legal issues, to an effort to maintain a positive image. In recent years, however, the most ominous kind of reason has emerged. Between 1987 and 1989, the number of *security-related lawsuits* grew by 27 percent. At the rate they are now expanding, one-half of all hospitals will have faced one or more **security-related** lawsuit by the end of 1992!

Recent court rulings indicate that, increasingly, hospitals are being found liable for damages when crimes that occur on their premises are judged to result from *inadequate security*. In such cases, a jury may award compensatory damages to the plaintiff to cover medical and related expenses, lost wages, and pain and suffering. But that is seldom the end of the story. Sometimes the jury finds that a hospital's *inadequate security* is the result of gross negligence. In these cases, the jury may grant the plaintiff *punitive* as well as compensatory damages. Punitive awards are particularly significant because they tend to be larger than compensatory awards, because they have no upper cap, *and because they are not insurable*.

Liability is not limited to the institution alone, either. Directors, managers, and even members of hospital boards could be held *personally liable* for crimes that occur on hospital property if such crimes are deemed to have resulted from breach of duty. Of particular interest to hospitals is the fact that workers' compensation laws may not always prevent a suit from being filed or temper an award against an employer. (See: Hudson v. Americus/Sumpter County Hospital Authority as a case in point.)

There are a number of things that can be done in the hospital environment to help improve security and safety for patients, visitors, and staff, many of which are covered in this report, and many have been cited in litigation, such as:

- After hours, limit the number of access points into the hospital and onto the hospital grounds to channel traffic away from isolated areas and into areas that can be controlled and monitored.

- Improve lighting on parking lots and grounds surrounding hospital buildings.

- Arrange for close-in parking for employees who are on call or who work the night shift. (More than 90 percent of those who work in hospitals after normal business hours are female.)

- At all times, limit available points of entry into hospital buildings by channeling routes with signs and use of access control cards. Ensure that all designated entry points are either attended by a receptionist or a security officer, or are controlled by card access and television systems (CCTV).

- Lock storage areas. Lock all areas that are not regularly used for patient care and limit access to them.

- Require staff to wear photo-identification badges at all times.

- Require after-hours visitors to register on entry and obtain identification materials for use while in the hospital.

- Consider installation of "panic buttons" at vulnerable work stations or to be worn on vulnerable persons in isolated or remote areas of the hospital.

These basic and essential security efforts are helpful, but just physical changes are not enough. *Hospital management* must make a deliberate and visible commitment to improve the overall quality of *hospital security. Management* must insist that its security program meet the stringent requirements and achieve the level of training, education, and expertise expected from other healthcare practitioners. Management must recognize security officers not just as "background support personnel" who protect people and assets, but as front-line ambassadors of hospital policy as liaisons to the hospital's public, and who have the highest visibility.[13]

The healthcare industry has become a "target" of the media and worried citizens because of the high cost of medical care and hospitals in general, along with fear and confusion about Medicare and Medicaid. The healthcare industry been doubly burdened by the skyrocketing costs of malpractice insurance and defense attorneys for such litigation. Now, the healthcare industry is being hit with litigation for negligence in many areas other than medical malpractice. For the purposes of this text, we shall consider the problems that affect security in today's hospitals.

Because hospitals are necessarily open facilities, the roles of security personnel and loss prevention specialists are made more difficult. The invitees who are found on the hospital grounds and in the buildings are staff, patients, visitors, vendors, construction crews, and transients. The legalistic model of strict enforcement is difficult for security to employ with this potpourri of persons, especially when most hospital administrators do not want to project a **fortress hospital** image to the public. Usually understaffed and kept in the background, healthcare security must be extremely dedicated to proving their value in protecting the assets of the hospitals and clinics of America.

Hospitals Find New "Tracking" Uses for Delayed Egress

By now, most people are used to seeing delayed egress on back doors and "emergency exits." When someone tries to exit, the door will alarm, and delay opening for several seconds, allowing security personnel time to respond.

This method has proven popular with retail stores and hospitals with Alzheimer's patients. But now, there is a new twist on the delayed egress front. Instea of remaining locked, the doors are open to all but the people who are not allowed to go through them.

RF/Delayed Egress Combo

Security Door Controls, Westlake Village, Calif., and RF Technologies, Brookfield, Wis., have teamed up to produce a unit that ties patients wandering or infant monitoring tags to the electromagnetic locks.

"There are three different types of hospital applications for this system," says Bob Finnie, sales manager for RF Technologies. One is a wandering patient, where they have some form of mental impairment and you want to make sure they don't wander outside the unit.

Another is infant monitoring. The tags will automatically alarm and lock the door if the abductor gets near it with the baby. The tags themselves are also alarmed, automatically locking the doors if they are cut.

Finally, medical staff wearing transmitters for emergencies can activate the doors in certain situations by the press of a button.

Control/Convenience

The addition of delayed egress to patient wandering provides an added level of control for hospital staff, says Glenn Jonas, president of RF Technologies. "Normally, if someone walks up to the door wearing a transmitter, it will alarm. But with the lock, it not only alarms, it will momentarily lock that door so they cannot exit. With the alarm only, by the time a staff member gets there, they could be out the door."

Integration like this is becoming a greater issue, particularly in hospitals where the financial situation is difficult, Finnie adds. "Hospitals may not have the staffing to retrieve a wandering patient. This system helps stop the situation from occurring in the first place."

Other Advantages

According to Bill McGinty, national sales manager for SDC, hospitals aren't the only facilities where this combination is desirable.

"For example, take a Target store that may have tag detectors on merchandise. We can tie that in to start the time delay if the alarm sounds."

Another advantage is flexibility. Because the system can be set up to be either always locked or always open, it can be tailored to the facility's needs, McGinty says. "Security by definition is inconvenient. You are always locking doors, or causing people to move in a certain way.

Hospitals Find New "Tracking" Uses for Delayed Egress

This system provides some convenience, with a relatively high level of control."

On the healthcare front, this is particularly important. "The overall goal is the protection of the patient. The hospital staff and visitors can move freely, but the patients are protected," McGinty says.

Hospitals are also finding more opportunities to integrate access control with other uses, Finnie says. In the future, things like medical equipment, personal computers and other valuable items may be tagged to prevent theft.

"More and more hospitals are going to an open environment," Finnie says. "This is a way of eliminating the complete lockdown situation."

Source: Karyn Hodgson. "Hospitals Find New "Tracking" Uses for Delayed Egress," *Security* (Cahners Publishing Company, Newton, MA, 1996), Vol. 33, No. 2, p. 17.

LITIGATION IN HOSPITAL SECURITY

In recent years, there has been a growing number of negligent security, **negligent training**, and negligent supervision litigation against hospitals. Major security concerns in the healthcare industry are much different from the average manufacturing or retail operation and include protection for narcotics and dangerous drugs, newborn babies, emergency rooms, and parking lots. In addition, special security concerns include medical records, computers and high-tech equipment, materials management, laundry and linen controls, research labs and data, medical waste and hazardous materials, and even guest rooms belonging to the hospital. All this is in addition to the normal duties of access control, parking control, escort and informational duties, physical security, and investigations.

WHY HOSPITAL SECURITY?

Hospitals are often called "houses of mercy." Why should such places need to have a security program? In his landmark text, *Hospital Security*, Russell Colling gives five rationales for hospital security in the last decade of the twentieth century:

> The first of several basic reasons for providing a protection system is moral responsibility. Every organization, especially those serving the public, has an obligation to manage its environment in such a way that it minimizes the possibility of injury or death to all people on the premises. It is also the organization's responsibility to take reasonable steps to preclude the destruction, misuse, or theft of property, so that the physical facility remains intact to carry on business.

A second justification for providing protection services is legal responsibility. The hospital corporation has the duty to exercise care and skill in the day-to-day management of corporate affairs. A specific example of this general obligation is the duty to preserve its property by preventing fire and safety hazards and to protect people from the actions of others.

The hospital's obligation to its patients is contractual in that the hospital assumes certain responsibilities toward them. The duty of protection becomes even greater when patients are unable to take care of themselves, as in the case of the critically ill, the elderly, infants, and children.

The issue of liability in the management of patient care facilities has become more acute in recent years. A hospital may be held liable for the *negligence* of an individual employee under the doctrine of "respondeant superior," or for corporate negligence. In terms of employee negligence, two general factors are requisite for imposing liability on the corporation. An employer-employee relationship must exist, and the employee's act or failure to act must occur within the scope of his or her employment. Corporate negligence occurs when the hospital maintains its buildings and grounds in a negligent fashion, furnishes defective supplies or equipment, hires incompetent employees, or in some other manner fails to meet accepted standards, and such failure results in harm or injury to a person to whom the hospital owes a duty.

One aspect of the legal rationale is of growing concern for hospitals: punitive damages. Jury awards that punish hospitals for not taking appropriate security measures are increasing in frequency and size. An added concern is that in many jurisdictions punitive damages awards will not be covered by insurance and must be paid from the hospital's funds.

A third important reason for maintaining a safe and secure environment is the responsibility of complying with requirements imposed by JCAHO [Joint Commission for Accreditation of Hospital Operations], the Occupational Safety and Health Act, and other federal, state, and local codes.

The fourth rationale for providing a protection system is to maintain a sound economic foundation for the organization. In this regard, healthcare has faced mounting criticism, especially in regard to the rapidly escalating costs of delivering quality medical care. Critics often cite the lack of cost-containment measures, that in part relate to preventing theft and the waste of supplies and equipment. Authorities estimate that between 3 and 20 percent of hospital expenditures could be saved if proper security controls were implemented. Yet, in most cases, the protection budget for healthcare facilities is generally less than 3 percent of the total operating budget.

It would seem that the economic stimulus of increased profits would be especially important to proprietary hospitals. Yet as a group they go no further than other hospitals in providing adequate loss prevention and protection systems.

Last [fifth], a safe and secure environment is required to maintain good public and employee relations. Although this reason does not appear to be as important as the others, it has probably been responsible for providing more funds for the security budget than the other four justifications combined. Hospital administrators who face bad media coverage of a security problem or restless employees threatening to walk out over a security incident somehow find the money to make necessary adjustments in the protection plan. [emphasis added][14]

It is clear that one of the most serious threats to healthcare providers is litigation, and the new hospital security manager needs to be thoroughly informed on how to minimize that threat.

DEVELOPMENT OF HOSPITAL SECURITY

Hospital security has gone through a long developmental period in the twentieth century. In the first half of the century, the role of security was handled by the maintenance staff of the facility as a minor part of their other duties. In some of the larger hospitals, the concept of a fire-watch guard was sometimes used, but the staff was still reporting to maintenance. Later, in the 1950s to the mid-1960s, the emphasis was shifted to law enforcement, using on-duty police in most cases stationed at the hospital or frequently patrolling it. With the shrinking size of law enforcement agencies from the 1960s to the 1980s, the role of security slowly shifted back to the healthcare corporations themselves. From these new beginnings, the present concept of security as a specialized management service has grown into an integral and respected activity in many hospitals. Spurred by litigation and the advent of a more professional structure in healthcare security, *safety* became another important aspect of the healthcare security operation.

The International Association for Healthcare Security and Safety (**IAHSS**) was established in 1968 to provide a professional forum for the healthcare security professional. The IAHSS, which has grown to more than 1500 members, released its code of ethics in 1989 as a model for security and safety managers. Shown in Figure 5–3, this code of ethics guides the growth of professionalism in this important field that now serves about 6500 hospitals, 21,000 nursing homes, and thousands of outpatient clinics and doctors' offices serving the sick in the United States.[15]

Hospitals have always been looked upon as a sort of sanctuary, a place where one could feel safe and secure, and where violence is virtually unknown. Alcohol and drugs, poverty, domestic violence, and a general frustration in society has changed all that. In 1987, a survey was conducted by the IAHSS on the annual frequency of violent incidents, meaning extreme, sudden, unjust, or improper force exerted so as to cause damage, abuse, or injury. Of the hospitals polled, 99 percent reported thefts, 58 percent reported assaults, 52 percent reported bomb threats, 29 percent reported suicides, 12 percent reported armed robberies, 8 percent reported rapes, 7 percent reported arson incidents, and 4 percent reported kidnappings.[16]—hardly the kinds of

FIGURE 5–3 *IAHSS Code of Ethics*

IAHSS Code of Ethics

Preamble

"Recognizing that the overall quality of health care delivery is directly related to the professional service rendered by the hospital security department, the International Association for Healthcare Security & Safety adopts the following Code of Ethics and mandates adherence to its basic tenets as a consideration of membership with this association."

As a health care security professional, I pledge to dedicate myself to providing a safe and secure environment to the people and institution I serve by:

Promoting "total" patient care and awareness within my health care facility;

Recognizing that my principal responsibilities are security service to the hospital patients, visitors, staff and personnel; to protect life and property and reduce crime through the implementation of recognized crime prevention and investigative techniques;

Respecting the moral and constitutional rights of all persons;

Performing my duties in accordance with the highest moral principles, and observing the precepts of truth, accuracy and prudence, without allowing personal feelings, prejudices, animosities or friendships to influence my judgments;

Recognizing and protecting the confidential and privileged information of employers, patients and medical staff of my institution;

Maintaining a professional posture with other security professionals, recognized law enforcement agencies, and other professionals with whom I conduct business;

Striving faithfully to further my education, both academically and technically in order to render optimum security services to my institution;

Encouraging the professional advancement of my personnel by assisting them to acquire appropriate security knowledge, education, and training;

Applying uniform and equitable standards of employment in recruiting and selecting personnel regardless of race, creed, color, sex, or age;

Promoting and exemplifying the highest standards of integrity, honor, justice, morality and loyalty to those whom I serve, dedicating myself in my chosen profession...Health Care Security.

---

activities that one expects to be handled by a maintenance worker or fire-watch guard. Dealing with a disturbed person is much more likely to occur in the climate of the 1990s; security officers need to know how to do that.

VIOLENCE COMES TO HOSPITALS

As violence becomes a more common form of social communication in the United States, we see it creeping into hospitals, where the only violence we expect is in the psychiatric wards. Turner points out this growth and, perhaps, how we got there:

> Violence and aggressive behavior are becoming a primary and, frighteningly, an acceptable form of communication in our society. The public seems to accept this mode of action when other more socially acceptable methods do not seem to be working or are working too slowly. In the larger society, health care is seen as something everyone is entitled to, and the legitimacy of aggressive behavior to gain what you need is growing. A number of factors have led to this acceptance of aggression as a form of communication:
>
> - The violent content of films and television
> - Contradictions in our legal system that appear to link behavior and its consequences only minimally
> - The legitimacy of some forms of aggression (wars of liberation, terrorism, vigilantism)
> - The romantic American myth of the individual against the institution
> - The role of the news media in shaping our attitudes toward what constitutes legitimate and illegitimate violence
>
> In spite of the increasing acceptance of violence, a clear consensus is developing that violence should not be viewed as just a hazard of employment. Legal concerns delineate the need to train staff to manage and defuse aggressive behavior.[17]

Service-Oriented Security

Hospital security and safety requires that the security manager see that a broad range of services is provided. For hospital security to be considered a vital function, it must find more ways to be of service to the organization as a whole, allowing it to meet its mission and improve its image. These services may include maintenance of order at the hospital, preventive patrol, control and reporting of incidents, response to service calls, escort of staff to and from parking areas, injury and accident reports, investigations, security awareness training for all staff, pedestrian and vehicle traffic control, emergency planning and testing, access control and identification badges, internal audits and surveys, liaison with law enforcement and other security agencies, key control, security lighting, and various interdepartmental supportive services.

For the student seeking a career that has a broad base of responsibilities, that offers a challenge of leadership, and that is growing and expanding at a fantastic rate, the healthcare security field has great potential. It is important that the security professional seek support and document services provided to let the largely educated and professional staff know that security services can be a very positive part of the hospital's mission, and can even help with the bottom line. Hospital security needs to be alert to whatever can be done to provide maximum protection and services with minimum interference with the life-saving and care-giving missions for the overall organization.

Retail Security

Perhaps no industry has a higher visibility in the security business than retail operations. The local shopping mall is likely to have a security presence that is uniformed and visible. The term *retail security* does, indeed, cover a very wide spectrum of businesses and business activities at the retail (point-of-sale) level. **Retail security** is not just for the major department store, it is applied to shopping malls, auto part stores, candy counters, drug and sundry stores, food stores and supermarkets, minimarts, discount stores, appliance and furniture stores, clothing stores, and almost every kind of point-of-sale retail outlet that can be imagined. All have the same problem: They are targets for crime, both from without and within.

Aislekeeper by Sensormatic provides an electronic shield

Photo courtesy of Sensormatic.

The costs of these crimes, primarily from shoplifting and employee theft, are staggering. In *Hallcrest II*, it was noted how difficult it is to separate the exact sources of crime data from the large number of varied sources. As they stated, however, "If just a few of these crime cost figures are plausible, then the impact of economic crime is, indeed, profound and represents a cancer in the economy."[18] In the case of retail theft, the estimates are as high as $30 billion a year from both categories. The cost of economic crime, from sources other than crime index data, has been placed at $200–300 billion a year.[19] The total estimated losses to economic crime could have paid off 50 to 75 percent of the nation's deficit, with retail losses accounting for some 10 percent of this. Since the deficit problem was such a major political factor in the 1992 elections, it would seem prudent to bring these losses under control.

Retail crime is so pervasive and costly that it plays a big role in the rise in costs, but these are usually just passed on to the consumer. If this was not done, many retailers would soon be out of business from the losses incurred by shoplifting and employee theft. According to a leading consultant on retail shrinkage, the average theft by shoplifters is two or two and a half times the average sale for the "big three" of retailing: department stores, apparel specialty stores, and drug stores.[20] In the case of employee theft, the average is found to be about two times that of shoplifting, but shoplifting exceeds employee theft by a three-to-one margin.[21] Even though billions of dollars are lost to retailers by shoplifting and employee theft, these crimes are generally considered a security problem and seldom handled by law enforcement. Most experts agree that this is a serious mistake by retailers and that more prosecutions would probably have a greater impact on those who chose "retail theft" (as it is known in some states) as a way to acquire what they want is not small-time theft. Results of a major study on shoplifting disclosed the following profile for the average **shoplifter**:

> The average respondent was an 18-year-old white female, observed by an investigator concealing $86 worth of clothes, taking merchandise from the cash register area past salespeople and point-of-sales terminals.
>
> Each shoplifter was apprehended by a loss prevention investigator…and asked a series of questions relating to the shoplifter, and found that:
>
> - Most thieves stole for themselves because they liked the merchandise and not for economic gain.
> - Many casually tempted thieves can be deterred by security or selling measures. Not all, of course, but about one-half of the thieves indicated that they were influenced by theft prevention strategies and actions.
> - Most shoplifters knew what they were doing was wrong.[22]

It must be noted, however, that not all losses in retail operations come from shoplifters and robbers. A major threat, perhaps the most critical one, comes from within. Employee theft in one single retail area, the supermarket, shows that the average employee admitted to stealing $143 a year from the store. Interestingly, the same people estimated that the coworkers were stealing about $1176 each per year.[23]

Although the actual amount probably falls somewhere between these two figures, the calculations suggest losses for a large chain of stores exceed $2 million a year. For an industry with such a low profit margin, this is a major loss.

The retail industry in America is different from other industries in its approach to security. Not only must they deal with employee theft and competition from those who would steal their ideas for marketing, but they must move thousands of customers through their shops without alienating them or restricting their movements through excessive security measures. The security profession has developed a number of excellent theft prevention tools for the retail manager to use. However, the way these are applied to customers and staff can, for most small retailers, make the difference between staying in business and going bankrupt. The student should see the vast potential for helping retailers walk the fine line between success and failure by finding newer and better ways to prevent losses, both from without and within.

Security for Educational Institutions

Universities and colleges in the United States today, and to a great extent the community colleges and small colleges, resemble large and complex communities within the larger community they serve. The campus is no longer a safe haven but is a problem-laden municipality itself, rife with the same problems that beset any outside community. These "hallowed halls" now are faced with real-world problems—economic problems, problems with political effectiveness, and problems of crime and traffic similar to that of a city.[24] In fact, the problem of escalating crime on college and university campuses has been identified as the unique challenge to campus police departments in the late 1990s. They have had to accept the fact that the basic function of campus police and security officers is dealing with problems related to crime.

There are indications that, as early as fifteen years ago, more than 36,000 violent assaults, 7500 sexual attacks, dozens of homicides, and some 200,000 thefts of such diverse items as money, jewelry, computers, and stereo equipment occurred each year on these campuses.[25] Does this startling volume of crime mean that it is no longer safe to try to get an education on campus in the 1990s? No. But it does mean that institutions, students, and the community should take campus crime very seriously. Although college and university administrators are addressing the problems of campus crime head on, there is much that students, faculty, and support staff can do to ensure that learning takes place in a safe environment.

The history of security on the campuses of America is quite vague prior to the 1950s, but seemed to revolve around the war between students and faculty, often resulting in civil disorder. The main thrust of security was to control the students, and it is not difficult to appreciate why such a harsh disciplinary approach to student control was resented by the students. The primary role of the early security officer on the campus was as a fire-watch guard up to the end of World War II. Following that conflict, more colleges and universities began to establish formal security departments. After the turmoil of the 1960s, culminating in the infamous shooting

Retail Stats Point to Parking Lot, Back Door Security

It's a chilling reminder of what can happen. At a recent conference on retail security, one chain store security director shared a CCTV video with his peers.

The video showed a violent crime in action. One associate was shot and killed in the incident, which occurred when the perpetrators walked in through the back door (which was monitored by a person at a desk) dressed as employees.

In addition to actual crime, the fear of crime by potential customers is another worry to retailers.

According to Loss Prevention Specialists, Winter Park, Fla., who hosted the conference in Orlando, 47 percent of customers fear shopping in the evening. "The fear of crime can be as costly as crime itself," says Read Hayes, a consultant with Loss Prevention Specialists.

More Bad News

Crime incidents and statistics point to a future that will unfortunately not be brighter. "Crime now is probably the lowest it will ever be," Hayes says.

According to Hayes, one reason is the youth factor. The fastest growing violent offenders in the U.S. by age are 14 to 17 year-olds. And, population predictions point to an increase by the year 2010—at least 30,000 more habitual, violent offenders than today.

Other reasons include predictions for increases in urban and metro areas; gangs; racial tensions; quantity of weapons and drugs; and violent terrorist attacks.

Technology Solutions

According to LPS, several existing and upcoming technologies could help retailers both now and in the future.

They include: Access control to parking areas, as well as surveillance and lighting of those areas; and access control and surveillance of back doors and vulnerable inside locations.

Top 10 States with Fastest Growing Crime Rates
1. Forida*
2. Texas
3. Arizona
4. Washington
5. California
b. New Mexico
7. Nevada
8. Georgia
9. Colorado
10. Hawaii
(*Already highest per capita Since 1984)
Source: Loss Preventing Specialists

Growing crime rates combined with other predicted factors, mean that security demands will increase.

Source: Read Hayes, *Security*. (Calines Publishing, Des Plaines, IL, 1995), Vol. 32, No. 12, p. 16.

of students at Kent State, the role of campus security began to resemble that of other security operations that deal with places for people to live. The concept of **in loco parentis,** or the institution serving as a substitute parent, gave way to civil rights and freedom on the campus.

The growth of security staffing in educational institutions has been seen as a function of the kind of crime or violence that occurs.

As noted by the security director of Transylvania University in Lexington, KY:

> Campus security can best be described as a service infrastructure that has evolved in response to a perceived obligation by the administration to provide a safe and secure environment for the campus community.
>
> The service orientation refers to the handling of a variety of situations in which the law may have been violated but the campus security officer chooses to deal with the situation without resorting to the criminal justice system.
>
> For example, an officer may intervene to arbitrate quarrels, pacify the unruly, and aid people in trouble. With a service orientation the officer continuously looks for violations so that he or she can intervene and perhaps avoid the need for an arrest.
>
> In contrast, campus security officers with a law enforcement orientation often approach situations by invoking criminal statutes. Their goal is to make an arrest or report a person's actions so that punishment can be meted out. That orientation is consistent with student control and emphasizes a need to maintain law and order within the campus community.[26]

With the fantastic growth of some of the major universities in the 1970s and 1980s, some security departments became separate police departments inside the larger community and were given full police powers. Most of these agencies follow the law enforcement model, but with the added issues that are unique to a major campus.

The majority of security departments on community college, four-year college, and university campuses are still small, however, and most still use the service-oriented approach. These campus positions offer an opportunity for the student to become involved as an employee while getting his or her education in some sector of law and justice.

Security for Commercial Office Buildings

Most security programs in the early part of the 1900s concentrated on industrial manufacturing, shipping, and storage sites. Over the last couple of decades, the economy has shifted from manufacturing and basic materials to a service type of effort. Commercial office buildings, skyscrapers, and business parks throughout the country now have salespeople, commercial bankers, lawyers, architects, stockbrokers, telemarketers, and a myriad of other office workers. A vast system of supporting services has also had to move into these complexes. All these layers are primary users for some kind of security and loss prevention protection.

College, Country, Biometric IDs Push Imaging Advances

The antagonistic debate in the U.S. over immigration controls and potential use of a national ID card stands in sharp contrast to the quickening movement by countries as varied as Spain and China to create security multi-technology ID cards for their citizens.

The huge IDing projects, no matter how American politics sway in the national ID card wind, will drive much of the security imaging ID developments over the next several years.

One-card with Biometrics

Emerging: one-pass card production on PVC stock, images printed by dye sublimation, magnetic stripe slowly losing out to smart card and inclusion of fingerprint and retinal biometrics.

Earlier this year, Lasertechnics told *Security* Magazine that its Sandia Imaging

Systems unit received an order for 15 high speed multi-station card printers for use by the Ministry of Public Security of Shenzhen in the Province of Canton, China. These cards will carry an encoded mag stripe.

Sandia, just weeks earlier, had received a similar contract from the U.S. Immigration and Naturalization Service for new alien credentials.

About the same time, Unisys Corp., Blue Bell, Pa., said its systems integrator for a national social security identification card project for Spain's Ministry of Labor and Social Security. That project will include fingerprint ID as well as smart cards.

In the U.S., Florida State University is in the midst of an upgrade of its multi-purpose, mag stripe ID cards. Through the university's Card Application Technology Center, one-card systems have been developed to handle security as well as financial transactions, debt purchases, vending and other tasks. This year, the university plans to roll out Smart ID—a new generation smart card. The project includes: Sensormatic Electronics, Deerfield Beach, Fla.; Software House, Waltham, Mass.; and Dallas-based Amtech for parking controls.

Pending immigration control legislation (S. 1394) introduced by Sen. Alan Simpson (R.-Wyo.) has drawn fire. Primarily conservative groups strongly oppose what they see as a federal program leading to a national ID card with a fingerprint or retinal biometric data base.

College ID

Instant photo ID for students	69%
Imaging ID for students	21.5%
Instant ID for staff, faculty	64.1%
Imaging ID for staff, faculty	23.1%

College ID developments include imaging, multi-tasking and some smart cards.

Source: Bill Zalud, "College, Country, Biometric Ids Push Imaging Advances," *Security* (Cahners Publishing Company, Newton, MA, 1996), Vol. 33, No. 3, p. 71.

With such a large variety of tenants, commercial office buildings create a multitude of problems for the owners and operators of these complexes. One business tenant may have a strong need for effective security (for example, a wholesale diamond broker), whereas another may feel there is no need for security and is reluctant to pay for it (for example, a typing service). A further problem is that these two very different tenants may be located across the hall from each other. If allowed to be on their own in the provision of security, there can well be gaping "holes" in any security effort to protect all the tenants, further muddying the difficult problem of *tenant liability* for the building owners and management.

When the entire building is occupied by a single corporate tenant, the level of security can be decided by that entity and a uniform policy applied. Centralized security services, most often provided by security guard companies, make the task of providing protection and loss prevention much easier. Liability to the owner and managers can be somewhat reduced when dealing with a single tenant.

In most cases, however, a **commercial office building** is more likely to have a wide variety of tenants with an equally wide range of security needs. Often, this will also include shops and restaurant facilities open to the public. This requires that the commercial building's owners and managers either create a single security program that meets all tenant needs or allow tenants to deal individually with security needs. The trends in security-related litigation, however, seem to indicate that the landowner–tenant relationship drives commercial office building owners–managers to provide at least minimal access controls, observation capability, and security patrols. They fail to do so at their peril. Urban areas are subject to high rates of crime, violent crime is growing, and commercial office buildings are often situated in the center of such activities.

Since most office buildings are open to the public, they are easy to "case" by criminals who want to exploit any weaknesses. Major targets of criminal behavior in commercial office complexes are:

- Assaults and rapes of tenants
- Robbery of tenants with valuable commodities
- Kidnapping or extortion of executives
- Burglary and theft from offices
- Theft from one tenant by another's employees
- Theft by service, maintenance, and custodial persons
- Theft of opportunity by lack of visitor control
- Bomb threats and arson

The targets of theft are as varied as the types of tenants in a commercial office building. Assets range from typewriters, calculators, and computers to more complex items such as stocks and bonds, check writing equipment, and industrial secrets.

As noted, most security for commercial office buildings is provided by contract guard companies. This does not preclude the use of proprietary guard services in very large complexes, especially if they are part of a series of buildings owned or managed by a single group. The patrol by unarmed security officers and the use of closed circuit television for entrances, elevators, stairwells, and service areas are the most common ways to secure such complexes. The key to success is the involvement of the tenants in the security program and their sharing in the development and implementation of security and loss prevention strategies. As corporate America becomes more of a service and less of a smokestack economy, the need is to provide security for the growing number of multipurpose commercial office complexes in a cost-effective and efficient manner.

Other Specialized Fields

If one tried to describe in detail the many fields of endeavor in which security has specialized methods and means, it would take a book twice the length of this one. There are many other significant areas of interest, however, and we will give some of them passing mention.

One of the most litigious areas of security involves the lodging industry. Hotels, motels, resorts, lodges, apartments, and other types of lodging are beginning to see the value of more professional security services and are responding to the rising tide of negligent security suits that are plaguing the field. As the lodging chains grow, the field is wide open for educated and experienced security professionals to advance.

Some of the more interesting kinds of security positions are to be found in museum, library, and archive security. Fine art, objects from antiquity, and rare books are prime targets of thieves around the world. When a masterwork is stolen, the effort is more likely to be aimed at recovery and not so much on catching the thief. This is a rapidly expanding field that sorely needs security professionals who understand the ways in which these treasures must be preserved and protected.

The use of digital communications, fiber optics, and instant communications worldwide from office, home, car, boat, or walking makes telecommunications security a fascinating and exciting field for security professionals. The transmission of computer data alone creates a whole new set of parameters for security. Fraud in the use of cellular phones is a $350–$500 million a year problem for telecommunications security providers. Wire transfer of funds, classified transmissions, and other issues make this one of the security positions for the twenty-first century and beyond. Those who want to enter this promising field for security managers must know about technology and always be one step ahead of the hackers and technocriminals.

Other fields for the student looking for a career in the security profession are almost without limit. From spacecraft centers to basic utilities and power plants, to off-shore oil rigs and deep sea exploration, to movie and television studios, to garbage and toxic waste disposal, the security profession has a part to play in protecting persons, places, and things in a way that does not disrupt the industry or interfere with the basic purpose of the operation.

Summary

This chapter was designed to whet the student's curiosity about security as a field, but we have only scratched the surface of the possibilities that are available for the security professional in a number of industries and specialties. It should be clear by now that security must be a part of every endeavor. It may not require a security force, but simply an awareness by that industry that security truly is everybody's job, and good security and loss prevention can actually add to the bottom line in terms of how it prevents theft and fraud, and how it recovers losses when they do occur.

The next chapter will show the student how various kinds of security issues "cross over" into almost all kinds of industries. When these two chapters have been studied, the student will see how to correlate these factors and apply them to the industry of his or her choice.

REVIEW QUESTIONS

1. What are the basic elements of a profiling program?
2. What was the result of the Bank Protection Act of 1968?
3. Explain the meaning of the term *defalcation* in the banking industry.
4. What are the major threats to automatic teller machines (ATMs)?
5. What is the meaning of the term *in loco parentis*?

TERMS TO REMEMBER

TWA 800
FAR 107.14
profiling
unaware passengers
electronic fund transfers
automatic teller machines

Bank Protection Act of 1968
defalcation
check fraud
fortress hospital
negligent training

IAHSS
retail security
shoplifter
in loco parentis
commercial office building

ENDNOTES

1. William P. Stump, "Airport Security: The Challenges Ahead," *Security Management*, Vol. 35, No. 7 (July 1991), p. 76.
2. Karen K. Addis, "Profiling for Terrorists," *Security Management*, Vol. 36, No. 5 (May 1992), p. 29.
3. Karen K. Addis, "Security the Friendly Skies," *Security Management*, Vol. 35, No. 7 (July 1991), pp. 28–29.
4. Billie H. Vincent, "About Profiles and Baggage Match," *Access Control* (Intertec/K-3 Publications, Pittsfield, MA, May 1997), pp. 32–33.
5. Department of Commerce, *Statistical Abstract of the United States* (Washington, D.C.: U.S. Government Printing Office, 1996), p. 305.
6. Carl P. Brown, "Crisis of the Vault," *Security Management*, Vol. 34, No. 1 (January 1990), p. 31.
7. Ibid., p. 31.
8. F. Barry Schreiber, "Tough Trends for ATMs," *Security Management*, Vol. 36, No. 4 (April 1992), p. 29.

9. Ibid., p. 29.

10. Ronald K. Hale, "Banking on Security's Future," *Security Management*, Vol. 34, No. 3 (March 1990), p. 48.

11. Ibid., p. 46.

12. Ibid., p. 47.

13. Ira Lipman, *The Lipman Report*, (Memphis: Guardsmark, Inc., May 15, 1992).

14. Russel L. Colling, *Hospital Security*, 3rd ed. (Boston: Butterworth-Heinemann, 1992), pp. 56–57.

15. Ibid. p. 3.

16. Anthony L. Best, "Securing Hospital Halls," *Security Management*, Vol. 34, No. 8 (August 1990), p.41.

17. James T. Turner, "Is Violence Holding Health Care Hostage?" *Security Management*, Vol. 30, No. 30 (March 1986), p. 26.

18. William C. Cunningham, John J. Strauchs, and Clifford W. Van Meter, *Private Security Trends 1970 to 2000: The Hallcrest Report II* (Boston: Butterworth-Heinemann, 1990), p. 29.

19. Ibid., p. 31.

20. Peter Berlin, *Shrinkage Control Seminar* (Jericho, N.Y.: The Peter Berlin Consulting Group, October 15, 1992), p. 19.

21. Ibid., p. 15.

22. P. James Carolin, Jr., "Survey of Shoplifters." Special Supplement, *Security Management* (March 1992), pp.11a–12a.

23. Food Marketing Institute, "Picking Out the Bad Tomatoes," Special Supplement, *Security Management* (March 1992), pp.6a–7a.

24. Diana C. Bordner and David M. Petersen, *Campus Policing the Nature of University Police Work* (CITI, Md.: University Press of America, 1983), p. 181.

25. James W. Fox, "Crime on the Campus," *Journal of College Student Personnel*, Vol. 18 (1977), p. 345.

26. Pam Collins, "Big Plan on Campus," *Security Management*, Vol. 36, No. 3 (March 1992), p. 30.

6

An Examination of Generalized Security Tasks

Unlike other business professions such as purchasing, finance, and personnel recruiting, in which the application of fundamentals is much the same from one organization to another, security differs considerably according to the specifics of the organization where it is applied.

— E.J. Criscuoli, Jr., CPP

Overview

In the previous chapter, we examined, at various depths of inquiry, some of the major fields of security management for specific kinds of industries. In this chapter, we shall examine some of the major tasks within a security operation that span the spectrum of almost all industries and institutions. The security manager must be fully capable of applying the right principles to the same tasks at different locations, departments, and functions of a company. These tasks might be repetitive, and locations might be all in one area. Or the organization might be a multinational giant, with dozens of products and hundreds of dissimilar locations. The student must be aware that security is seldom one dimensional or simplistic, making knowledge about and mastery of a number of tasks and technical skills essential to successfully securing a company's or institution's assets. We will start with the concept of crisis management and how to apply it to the myriad details of the security mission.

Crisis Management

Almost all the activities that involve security and loss prevention are aimed at situations that can or do result in a **crisis**. The newspaper headlines during the time we have spent on this text make the point of how important crisis management can be in a way that the words in a textbook find hard to compete with. The lurid pictures on television of military troops lining the streets in Los Angeles in order to prevent looting during the Rodney King riots, the massive destruction by tornadoes in the Midwest, the devastation from earthquakes approaching the size of the predicted "big one" in Southern California, the crushing destruction from Hurricane Andrew in southern Florida, and the devastation of the bombing of the Federal Building in Oklahoma City have highlighted security planning. The need for better *beforehand* security planning to protect persons

In commercial buildings security officers must have intimate knowledge of "who" and "where."

Source: C. Simonsen. Courtesy of Northwest Protective Services, Inc.

as well as private and public property during man-made and natural disasters has been driven home to the public. Other disasters, such as the chemical release of poison gas in Bophal, India, or the collapse of a hotel balcony in Kansas City, which both resulted in large losses of life, negatively influence the image of their corporate owners. Such matters must be handled very carefully to prevent them from being perceived any worse than they actually are. Other crisis situations may not be as spectacular as these, but they all negatively affect the company's image if not handled properly. These days, crises can range from sexual harassment by executives, to fraud or theft by key employees, and even to improper behavior by security personnel.

As shown in Figure 6–1, a crisis situation builds like a pyramid. This pyramid begins with thinking about what might happen if a crisis situation occurs and developing appropriate plans for dealing with it. We refer to this as the *if…then* model of planning: *If* this happens, *then* we will do this. This kind of linear thinking will ensure that the involved security professional can be brought into the overall response plan and contribute to the return to normalcy. Figure 6–2 shows the logical and sequential

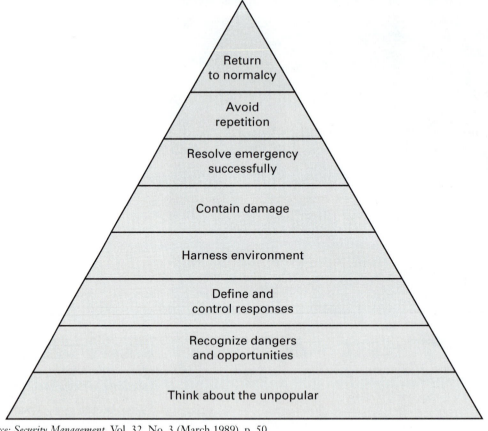

Source: *Security Management*, Vol. 32, No. 3 (March 1989), p. 50.

FIGURE 6–1 *Crisis Management Pyramid*

actions that security personnel must consider in doing disaster planning and reaction. Traditional methods and stages for disaster planning are often just traps for trouble.

Far too many organizations discount the idea that some type of emergency situation will occur. While most government agencies and large corporations may recognize that such situations occur, the press of everyday requirements mitigates the amount of time and thought devoted to such eventualities. In order not to ignore the matter completely, emergency planning may be delegated to middle-level or junior employees. These people are generally overworked, but accept this additional responsibility because:

- they have no other choice,
- they recognize the importance of planning for these contingencies,
- or they realize that, should anything happen during their watch, career advancement will weigh in the balance.

True crisis management is more than reflex and luck. Having a well-considered, well-tested contingency plan is important, but the planning process should occur in conjunction with effective, proactive crisis management to make policy decisions.[1]

CRISES AND CRISIS MANAGEMENT

Disaster or crisis situations fall into three general categories: *accidental*, *natural*, and *manmade*. **Man-made disasters** can also be further broken down to internal (from within the organization), or external (from outside the organization) crises. In

Good planning	**Maintain control**
• Consider all possibilities	• Stay ahead of the flow
• Don't focus only on immediate problems	• Schedule and pace yourself
• Establish contacts now	• Look for the real problems
	• Be creative
Good personnel	• Retain public affairs initiative
• Look for experience and knowledge	• Rely on your people
• Train, test, and evaluate	• Have confidence in the plan
• Use people effectively and humanely	• Keep records
• Organize to mitigate stress	
	Get back to normal
Good shakedowns	• Evaluate and document
• Test plans and people	• Reward
• Evaluate and revise plans	• Analyze implications
• Keep an open mind	

Source: Security Management, Vol. 32, No. 3 (March 1989), p. 51.

FIGURE 6–2   *Crisis Management Highlights*

any case, the ten basic steps for effective crisis management, with some customization to a particular situation, are essentially the same. It is essential that crisis management planning include not only technical solutions to the crisis, but effective ways of maintaining communications with all concerned. Jonathan Bernstein outlines his especially well done ten steps in a clear and understandable manner:

1. *Identify your crisis management team:* A small team of senior executives should be identified as your company's crisis management team. Typically, the team is led by the company CEO, with the firm's top marketing or public relations executive as his/her advisor. Other team members should be the heads of major company divisions, including legal, financial, personnel, and operations departments. The same principle applies in a small firm, but some individuals may wear several hats. If your in-house resources are not sufficient to handle the work, a crisis may generate. You should identify outside consultants such as law firms, accounting firms, or public relations agencies that can supply senior executives for your crisis management on short notice.

2. *Identify spokespersons:* Within each team, individuals should be authorized as the only ones to speak for the company in times of crisis. The CEO should be one spokesperson, but not necessarily the primary one. The fact is that some chief executives are brilliant businesspeople but not very effective in-person communicators. That doesn't matter in written communication and may not matter for some audiences. Often, however, image communicates as strongly or more strongly than facts, as politicians know well. Hence, communications skills are one of the primary criteria in choosing a spokesperson.

3. *Train spokespersons:* Spokesperson training is the Boy Scouts of media interviews. It teaches you to be prepared, to be ready to respond in a way that maximizes the chance of a story being reported the way you want it to be. Expert spokesperson trainers can be found in most major metropolitan areas, working either as independent consultants or in public relations agencies.

4. *Establish communication protocols:* Initial and crisis-related news can be received by anyone in a company . A guard on outpost or someone in personnel may be the first person aware of the problem. Word could come by way of a midnight phone call from an out-of-town salesperson. Who should be notified, and where do you reach them?

    An emergency communication tree should be distributed to all company employees telling them precisely what to do and whom to call in case of a potential or actual crisis. In addition to appropriate supervisors, at least one member of the crisis management team and an alternate member should include their office and home numbers on the emergency contact list.

    Some companies prefer not to use the term *crisis* with non-management personnel, thinking it may cause panic. Frankly, using "potentially embarrassing situations" or similar phrases doesn't fool anyone. If you prepare in advance, your employees will learn that a crisis doesn't necessarily mean bad news but simply something very important to the company requiring quick action.

5. *Identify your audiences:* What are the audiences that matter to your firm? Most firms care about the media, employees, clients, prospects, and vendors. Private investors may be involved. Publicly held companies have to comply with Securities and Exchange Commission public information requirements. You may answer to local, state, or federal regulatory agencies.

   For each audience, you need complete mailing, fax, and phone number lists for rapid communication in time of crisis. Ideally, lists are prepared in advance. You also need to know what type of information each person on the list is looking for and brief personnel on your emergency communication tree appropriately.

6. *Anticipate crises:* Gather your crisis management team for a long brainstorming session or two on all potential crises that can occur in your business. This exercise provides two immediate benefits. First, you may realize that some situations are preventable by simply modifying existing methods of operation. Second, you can begin to think about possible responses and about best case/worse case scenarios— better now than when under the pressure of an actual crisis. As a result of such anticipation, each watch commander can have a list of possible scenarios delineating which can handle themselves and which they must notify a senior company executive about.

In some cases, of course, you know that a crisis will occur because you're planning to create it by laying off employees or making a major acquisition. You can proceed with steps 7 through 10 ahead of time.

7. *Assess the situation:* Reacting without adequate information is classic shoot-first-ask-questions-later behavior. You could be the primary victim. But if you've done all the preceding steps first, assessment is simply ensuring that the crisis management team receives all incoming information and the right type of information is being provided. Then you can proceed to determine your reaction. If you haven't prepared in advance, steps 1 through 6 can be accomplished fairly quickly with the help of professional crisis management counselors.

8. *Identify key messages:* You already know what type of information your audiences are looking for. Now, what do you want them to know about the crisis? Keep it simple. Have no more than three main messages for all audiences and perhaps a few messages targeted for special audiences. In the "guard commits a crime" situation, for example, key messages to communicate may include the following:

   - We are very concerned and are cooperating fully with the authorities.
   - This is an isolated case that in no way reflects our ability to serve our clients fully.
   - We are conducting an immediate internal investigation to find out how this situation occurred and who is responsible for hiring the individual and placing him or her in this situation. (This message would be aimed at private investors.)

9. *Decide on communication methods:* You can use many different ways to communicate during an internal or external crisis. Employees, clients, prospects, and investors can be briefed in person or receive letters, newsletters, or faxed messages. The media can receive press releases and explanatory letters or attend one-on-one briefings and press conferences. Each of the many options available has a different impact. They must be evaluated by a professional who thoroughly understands the pros and cons of the methodologies as applied to your company's needs.

10. *Ride out the storm:* No matter what the names of a crisis, no matter whether it's good news or bad, no matter how carefully you've prepared and responded, some members of your audience are not going to react the way you want them to. This misunderstanding can be immensely frustrating. That is the time to do the following:

   - Take a deep breath.

   - Take an objective look at the reactions in question. Are they your fault or a unique interpretation?

   - Decide if another communication to that audience is likely to change that impression for the better.

   - Decide if another communication to that audience could make that impression worse.

   - Decide if additional communication is worth the effort.

   - While in some situations additional communication is definitely worth the effort, this evaluation process rules out further contact 90 percent of the time.[2]

DISASTERS

The definition of a **disaster** has many variations, but here's one that covers most kinds: (1) an unplanned interruption of service; (2) an extended time that is not covered by normal problem management procedures.[3] Generally speaking, the difference between a crisis and a disaster is that a disaster creates a situation that could be fatal to the company, its employees, or its operations. The movement from a situation to a crisis to a disaster is neither consistent nor restricted to rules that can predict timing or impact. Crisis management can deal with occurrences that may result in problems or embarrassment, but disaster planning and recovery management deal with major natural or man-made events. Security managers in every industry must be able to assist in prevention, in crisis or disaster management, and in recovery activities that are aimed at minimizing impact to the company. Three key elements that must be included in any disaster plan are selection of an alternative site, depth of personnel and their availability following the disaster, and safety of company records and restoration of operations. The "onion model" of crisis management, shown in Figure 6–3, is a simple graphic portrayal of the levels needed.

The kind of response one takes to protect against a particular potential crisis or disaster depends on three factors: (1) the *asset* being protected, (2) the *risk* to the

FIGURE 6-3   *The Onion Model of Crisis Management*

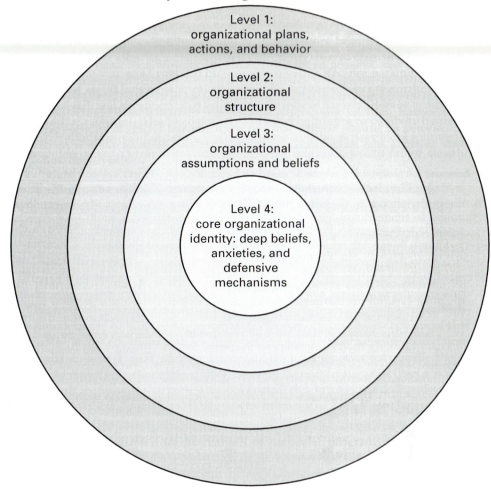

Level 1:
organizational plans,
actions, and behavior

Level 2:
organizational
structure

Level 3:
organizational
assumptions and beliefs

Level 4:
core organizational
identity: deep beliefs,
anxieties, and
defensive
mechanisms

Source: Security Management, Vol. 33, No. 9 (September 1990), p. 76.

company if that asset is destroyed or compromised, and (3) the cost of the *counter-measures* against potential loss. (The concept of risk assessment will be discussed in greater detail in Chapter 7.) This last factor can be considered a method for objectivizing common sense. If an asset costs $10,000, and the risk to the company would be high were it is lost or destroyed, then a countermeasure that costs $50,000 would be a poor use of funds. On the other hand, if an asset costs only $3500 and the risk to the company would be disastrous were it lost or destroyed, then countermeasures that cost much more than the asset would be justified.

All this adds up to the concept of **vulnerability**. If your company is vulnerable to many kinds of crises or disasters, you must do some planning for protection before the crisis or disaster, during the crisis or disaster, and during the recovery phases. In addition to accidents and natural disasters, the more probable kinds of vulnerabilities are shown in Figure 6–4.

The concept of "be prepared," combined with a strong set of policies, procedures, and post orders will ensure that the security department will be ready to make a major contribution to a crisis or disaster. Training for all security staff in the importance of proper communication and information practices to all parties involved with the event will make sure that the company image is preserved and recovery can move ahead without unnecessary problems.

Source: Labor Relations	Malfeasance	Isolated stations
Bargaining	Anticompetitive behavior	Unattended equipment
Strikes	Business recovery insurance	Choke network fraud
Safety	Judge Harold Greene	
Kidnapping		Source: Security
Video display terminals	Source: Regulatory	Vulnerabilities
Office locations	Vulnerabilities	Kidnapping
Asbestos	Pornography	Liaison with local law
Vehicles	Rates	enforcement
Accidents	Organized opposition	Bomb threats
Work environment	Disorganized opposition	Decision to evacuate
Clothing	Lack of preparation	Who decides
Drugs/chemical abuse	Interaction with unregulated	Loss prevention
Undercover drug	entities and their associates	Safety
surveillance	Product liability	Guards (perception of
Age		safety)
Contracting out	Source: Network	Limits of authority
Layoffs	Vulnerabilities	Sabotage
Plant closings	Earthquakes	Terrorism
Privacy	Weather	Strikes/employee actions
Cultural differences	Fire	Liaison with local authorities
	Nuclear plant incidents	Data security (hackers)
	Evacuation	Privacy
Source: Legal Vulnerabilities	Service continuation	
Labor	Chemical spills	Source: Larger Issues
Discrimination	Commercial power failure	Toll interruption
Drug testing	Major event	Office loss (major switching
Personal injury	Plane crash	loss)
Liability	Public event	Problems of worldwide net-
Political	Assassination	working
Ethics	National emergencies	Computerization
Criminal behavior	War	Network diversity
Civil matters	Terrorist activity	Switch diversity
Regulation	Industrial accidents	Superfund Amendments and
Competition (business	No-ring architecture	Reauthorization Act laws
conduct)		

Source: Security Management, Vol. 34, No. 12 (December 1991), p. 65.

FIGURE 6–4   *Vulnerability Catalog*

"No Surprises" Is Best Disaster Plan

It is the nature of many disasters that they strike with little or no warning. Pre-planning can help minimize the impact such crises will have on employees, tenants and business.

Some helpful resources: ITI/Meggitt Controls, Wilmington, Mass., has a Total Recovery Planning System, including Emergency Planning Software; Emergency Film Group, Plymouth, Mass., offers "Industrial Incident Management," a three part video series; and Asset Recovery Technologies (ART), Elk Grove Village, Ill., offers restoration services for computers and other electronic equipment.

In addition, there is a lot companies can do themselves to help avert or better manage disasters when they occur, says Vincent Papi, vice president of sales for Allied Security, Inc., Pittsburgh, Pa. Through primarily a contract officer firm, Allied has frequently helped clients with contingency planning, Papi says. And the firm has had experience with clients facing Hurricane Andrew, the recent California earthquake and the L.A. riots.

Papi recently spoke with SECURITY Magazine about what companies can do to plan for such events.

Q: How do you plan for something that may be a complete surprise?

A: First of all, you must determine where and how you are most at risk. Begin by taking an inventory of your physical location. Carefully consider the physical characteristics of the building, the type of operations performed there, the tenant population, the hours of operation and the public access to the facility. Even more important, evaluate the risk to people.

Q: How do you evaluate these risks?

A: Each risk should be evaluated based on the likelihood of occurrence, the downtime that could result, the impact on people and corporate liability.

When assessing each risk, look at both the near and long term impact. For example, a natural disaster might not simply close a business for several days. The infrastructure could be damaged, requiring weeks or months to repair. The downtime for the business could be the real disaster.

Q: What about contingency plans?

A: "What if..." scenarios should be created for each of the risks identified. For instance, a bank we worked with in Florida knew that one contingency should include hurricanes. We analyzed what could be done to provide security for them in that event, including how to get officers from unaffected areas if the airports were closed, living accommodations once there, etc. When Hurricane Andrew hit, everything went smoothly.

Q: What other considerations are there?

A: The final step in the crisis management process is to devise a system for resuming normal operations. In cases of natural disasters, operations may be disrupted for months. Determine how and where business can resume operation in the event of a total shutdown, as well as how you are going to communicate those changes in operation to employees, customers and vendors.

Source: Editors. "No Surprises Is Best Disaster Plan," *Security* (Cahners Publishing Company, Newton, MA, 1994), Vol. 31, No. 10, p. 27

TRANSPORTATION FACILITIES AND EQUIPMENT

Every company that manufactures, imports, or sells a product must be able to move it from the place of manufacture to the point of sale with some assurance that it will arrive. An important security function deals with the movement and storage of assets. All businesses have to transport their products to market, receive cargo from vendors and suppliers, and maintain docking and storage areas that contain valuable products or supplies. The transportation function has seen such threats as vandalism, hijacking, internal theft, and fraud in transporting goods and products that are manufactured or imported in the United States. It is clear that no single approach to transportation security can deal with every industry. New technologies and new ideas must be used to attack the most vulnerable link in security in almost every environment. In large corporations—those with their own transportation department—this could be an intracompany problem. In most companies, it is staying on top of what the carriers, whether land, sea, or air, are doing to reduce shrinkage as goods move from place to place. Security plays a vital role in loss prevention for shipments in transit, during loading and unloading, and while in storage facilities. Generally speaking, **transportation** can be divided into seven phases:

1. Movement to storage area prior to shipment
2. Movement from storage to docking area
3. Loading onto form of transportation
4. Movement to destination
5. Unloading and storage at destination site
6. Loading onto local transportation for delivery
7. Transport and delivery to ultimate receiver

In each of these phases, another critical element is added, *documentation and an audit trail* for the item(s) being shipped. Although there are obvious weaknesses in every stage of transportation, perhaps the weakest link is this last item.

MOVEMENT TO STORAGE AREA PRIOR TO SHIPMENT

The movement of the item to be transported from where it is manufactured, imported, assembled, or packaged is critical in terms of accurate identification, tagging, documentation, and tracking through or between the corporate facilities to temporary storage. Modern technology, using bar codes and other types of inventory equipment, can reduce the possible losses from shrinkage in these early stages. This is almost always a situation that requires insider assistance, and security can be a big help in assisting in and monitoring this activity for the corporation. Sometimes the only way that this type of shrinkage activity can be detected is by planting covert investigators in the workforce to detect where the losses are occurring.

MOVEMENT FROM STORAGE TO DOCKING AREA

Possibly the most vulnerable point in the transportation process is the movement to a docking or staging area for onward shipping by common carrier, road or rail. It is at this point where both inside and outside threats are found to the assets being transported, often in combination and collusion. And it is usually at this point that documentation is shifted from a corporate function to that of the carrier. Security has to be alert to the **falsification of documents**, the placing of items or packages at remote areas of the loading docks, and the removal of items from the packaging before loading. In this last-named case, it is often the dumpsters or trash receptacles in which these items are hidden after removal from the packaging. This is especially true with small and expensive electronics. Again, this point of transfer may require an undercover investigator in order to discover the method of diversion or outright theft.

LOADING ONTO MODE OF TRANSPORTATION

Whether the mode of transportation is by land (truck or rail), sea, or air, it is essential that careful loading and documentation take place. In today's transportation systems, the use of 20- and 40-foot **intermodal cargo containers** makes intermodal transportation possible with a much higher degree of control and security. These containers can be loaded at the company's facility, and double-checked and secured by locking and sealing them to be shipped as a single unit. This puts more of the burden on the carrier for the entire container in terms of liability and loss while in transit. In other cases, where the company's cargo goods are placed in **break bulk** with other items on the same carrier, the problem with shrinkage is multiplied by every stop that the form of transport makes. Again, the documentation and transfer of responsibility for the cargo is critical and must be carefully checked by security guards before the carrier leaves.

MOVEMENT TO DESTINATION

As we noted, the use of intermodal containers, which revolutionized the shipping industry in the early 1960s, make the movement of goods in transit much easier to secure. On the other hand, it has also made hijacking an entire load of expensive goods easier. All the hijacker needs today is a tractor-truck and the knowledge of what is in a container to make off with the whole shipment. For this reason, it is good security to maintain tight control over exactly what is in a particular container. This requires the use of coded, or encrypted, documentation that lets only the shipper, specific agents of the carrier, and the receiver know *exactly* the nature of high value and vulnerable cargo (see Figure 6–5). This allows the audit of an informational trail that makes pinpointing the losses to specific persons. Mixed cargo, carried with other commodities in the same mode of transportation, is much more difficult to pinpoint, but can also be coded as to the exact contents. In some cases, it is not a good idea to ship all of a highly valuable, critical, or classified commodity in the same vehicular mode or in the same shipment. Security can work with operational staff to advise them in this regard.

FIGURE 6–5   *Crisis Management Checklist*

It is imperative that the following information be obtained and forwarded to the crisis management team in order to reduce and/or eliminate any injuries to employees and law enforcement personnel involved in the incident. It will be the duty of the security duty office to determine:

A. Nature of call: Barricade_____   Hostage_____   Other _____

B. Call initiated by: _____

C. Date: _____   Time: _____

D. Arrival of responding security officer: _____

E. Location of:
    1. Incident
    2. Suspects
    3. Hostage(s)

F. Security/police (name and location within inner perimeter)
    1. _____
    2. _____
    3. _____
    4. _____

G. Description of:
    1. Suspect
        a. _____
        b. _____
        c. _____
    2. Hostages
        a. _____
        b. _____
        c. _____

H. Injuries to:
    1. Police/security
    2. Hostages
    3. Suspects
    4. Other

I. Is evacuation necessary?   Yes _____   No _____
    1. Authorized by: _____
    2. Date: _____   Time: _____

J. Weapon

Command Response

Notification
_____ Security director
_____ Assistant security director
_____ Local law enforcement
_____ Fire department
_____ Any other notification

Source: Security Management, Vol. 33, No. 9 (September 1990), p. 51.

UNLOADING AND STORAGE AT DESTINATION SITE

The same vulnerabilities are present, in reverse order, when being unloaded, inventoried, and stored (temporarily or permanently) at the point of destination. It is very important for the security personnel of the intermodal holding areas to assist at this point when any discrepancies are found. If the shipment is international in nature, it can often be held in these areas for long periods. Coordination between the receiving company security personnel and the port or carrier holding site security is critical when this occurs. Properly coordinated investigation and confirmation of losses will assist in clearly demonstrating that the losses or shrinkage occurred in transit while in control of the common carrier. Such actions will determine where liability rests for the losses and help both the company and the carrier prevent further such losses in the future.

LOADING ONTO LOCAL TRANSPORTATION FOR DELIVERY

Whether it is the company's own transportation or that of a short-haul common carrier, this is another critical period in which the cargo is highly vulnerable. This is true if the cargo is still sealed in an intermodal container or if it is now being broken down into several smaller loads for delivery to diverse, multiple sites. Again, documentation is critical and must be checked and rechecked before being accepted as complete. Many of these large staging areas are under constant pressure to move cargo as quickly as possible and rush the documentation. Security can work with their counterparts at the site and the drivers, both company and common carrier, to be sure that inspection of cargo, verification, and documentation are done in an efficient and thorough manner.

TRANSPORT AND DELIVERY TO ULTIMATE RECEIVER

The final phase of transportation is what gets the cargo to the receiver or user of the product being shipped. After careful documentation and verification all through the shipment, it is not wise to become lax on the process at the point of delivery. Even if it has been shipped only by local carrier for a few miles, there is always the concern that a short stop in that trip could result in shrinkage. The danger at this point is that normally alert and thorough inventory, inspection, and documentation procedures will become less lax and "assumptions" of delivery will blind the receiving personnel. Security staff must coordinate and train staff to appreciate that this final link in the chain of shipment must be as systematic and thorough at this point as at any other.

As can be seen, there are many ways to lose items in the transportation process. The task of finding a viable way to secure parked trucks and service fleets, and prevent millions of dollars from damage and theft at distribution centers for ground transportation remains very important. As noted by Hackler, this often starts at the perimeter and tells how a better mix of personnel and technology can be used:

> No consistent approach has been able to protect distribution centers, transportation and service vehicles, or their contents. Typically, security officers are hired to patrol parking areas or monitor surveillance systems, such as CCTV. For deterrence, empty camera housings are sometimes employed, often in combination with patrols. To complicate the picture, distribution centers are frequently protected separately by interior motion sensors, such as passive infrared, or by door-entry systems.

SECURITY BRIEF 6–2

Smarter Tags, Seals Computerized Advantages

Smarter integrated security systems that tag articles or seal cargo are decreasing losses at businesses as varied as drug stores and truck fleets.

Integrated Security Packaging

Loss prevention technologies now let stores shelve smaller packages of higher priced goods. One example: Pharmacia & Upjohn's shrink-wrapped Rogaine.

The firm recently integrated several security approaches in its shrink-wrap packaging on cartons of Rogaine hair regrowth products. In addition to shrink-wrapping, P&U provides two other anti-theft initiatives.

The first: Electronic Article Surveillance (EAS) tags on Rogaine products during the manufacturing process. Two widely used Systems, Sensormatic and Checkpoint, are offered. P&U has designed a shelf organizer unit that will allow only one carton of Rogaine at a time to be taken from the dispenser.

This display guards against thieves who may attempt to "sweep" the product off the shelf in large quantities.

"The shrink wrap is the final piece in this anti-theft puzzle," says Harold Milliken, vice president of OTC sales for Rogaine in the United States. "Now it will be much more difficult for thieves to lift the bottles from the boxes."

Bringing more expensive items from behind counters to store shelves is highly important in the margin-sensitive retail environment. Market research, for example, shows that more Rogaine is sold when it's in the hair care aisle than when it is behind a service counter.

In the United Kingdom, the advance is smarter electronic seals on trucks.

City Link, one of the UK's leading parcel distribution companies, has equipped its fleet with electronic seals from Encrypta Electronics Ltd. of Newport, Gwent. Over 70 vehicles are now fitted with Crypta III seals replacing the previous system that used plastic disposable seals.

"Plastic seals can be tampered with," says Phil Duckworth at City Link. "We also had the problem of distributing stocks of seals out to each of the depots and ensuring that they were stored securely. Now, once a vehicle is sealed at a depot, the seal number is read by pressing the button on the unit," says Duckworth.

Source: Bill Zalud. "Smarter Tags, Seals Computerized Advantages." *Security* (Cahners Publishing, Newton, MA, 1997) Vol. 34, No. 3, p 65.

Over the years, problems with these approaches have become apparent. For example, security officers have become costly. In addition, the effectiveness of post-mounted systems is limited because vehicles cannot be parked between the posts without breaking the beam and setting off the alarm.

Using two or three types of security systems to cover the distribution center, parked vehicles, and the loading dock results in the proliferation of detection and assessment monitors, the need for security officers or monitoring personnel, and, ultimately, higher costs.

Effectively addressing these problems requires a security system that has a proven high probability-of-detection rate and is cost effective. The technology involved must not interfere with the movement of vehicles, be adaptable to a wide range of site sizes and configurations, and be covert and unobtrusive.[4]

These caveats are clearly good advice to the security planner for the shipment of goods in the United States. One way if not to ensure that cargo has not been tampered with, then to monitor whether it has been, is the use of cargo seals on trailers and containers used in transport (see Figure 6–6). Seals do not protect the loading doors of trailers or containers from being broken into, they simply let you know at each point of inspection if they were. Seals must be carefully inventoried, documented, and issued to trusted personnel for use in sealing or resealing cargo doors at each point in the shipping process. Seals are serially numbered items, and the numbers must be carefully recorded on the shipping documents for them to be effective. This is especially important when trailers have been loaded to make several deliveries along the route. The driver carries enough seals to reseal the cargo areas after each stop.

FIGURE 6–6 *Two Types of Cargo Seals*

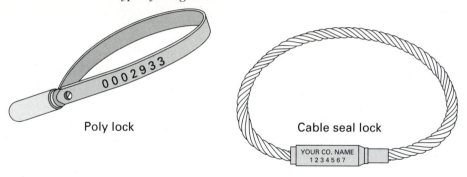

Poly lock

Cable seal lock

The receiving area will verify the seals have not been broken and note the resealing upon completion of delivery. The highest possible security must be afforded for the seals, and security must be involved with their use and control. Serial numbers must be carefully recorded after each breaking and resealing for the system to establish just where any shrinkage occurred.

The estimated losses in the transportation of goods in the United States is $8–$10 billion a year.[5] Often the cost of these losses is simply passed along to the customer and kept quiet to prevent embarrassment to the manufacturer or shippers. The indirect costs that accrue from cargo theft are also staggering, and tied up in insurance investigations, litigation, and claims processing.

Shipping goods and products is an essential element for a strong economy. The **infrastructure** of roads, rail, seaways, and airways moving commodities in America is what makes it so strong. When such an infrastructure breaks down, as seen in the countries of Somalia and Yugoslavia in recent years, chaos can reign. The security and loss prevention student can find plenty of room for growth and development in assisting the economy to move goods safely and with minimum shrinkage—a problem that is part of every security operation in the world.

Computer Security

Computers, or computer microchips, are ubiquitous today and affect our lives in a million ways. Cars have on-board computers to run all the various components: televisions and VCRs are marvels only imagined a few years ago; post offices weigh our Christmas packages, and a built-in computer issues the correct amount of postage on a bar-coded, self-sticking "stamp." The wonders of the computer age make easier and simpler the modern production of goods, transfer of funds, ordering of goods, and transmission of data. But there is a dark side to this silicon miracle—computer crime.

COMPUTER CRIME

Computer crime is any illegal act for which knowledge of computer technology is used to commit the offense. No longer is computer crime confined to the activities of a few hackers in their college dorm rooms or to an occasional bank fraud. In all parts of the country, computers have been tools in crimes of unprecedented economic cost, from electronic funds transfer fraud to inventory loss. A recent study by the accounting firm of Ernst and Whitney estimated that high-tech thieves in the United States steal $3–$5 billion annually. It has also been estimated that the average bank robbery yields about $6600, but the average computer bank fraud yields $600,000. One of the most famous bank robbers of the 1930s, Willie Sutton, was asked when caught why he robbed banks. His calm reply was, "That's where the money is." If Willie Sutton were alive today, he would surely have a computer and a modem.

Computers are not tools just for traditional white-collar crimes. Increasingly, computers are being used in the illegal activities of drug networks. Drug traffickers use them to communicate with each other, to record their transactions, and to transfer and launder money.

Many law enforcement administrators have become concerned about increases in computer-related crime. In the 1986 National Assessment Program survey sponsored by the National Institute of Justice and conducted by the Institute for Law and Justice, 75 percent of the police chiefs and 63 percent of the sheriffs surveyed said computer crime investigations were likely to have a significant impact on their workloads in the future. In jurisdictions having populations of 500,000 or more, the proportion was even higher: 84 percent of police chiefs and 75 percent of sheriffs.[6]

CATEGORIES OF COMPUTER CRIME

As shown in Figure 6–7, the categories of computer crime vary greatly and can be easily related to the security function in almost any commercial endeavor or institution today.

INTERNAL COMPUTER CRIMES

Internal computer crimes are alterations to computer programs that can result in the performance of unauthorized functions. These crimes have acquired names like

FIGURE 6–7   *Categories of Computer Crime*

Internal computer crimes	Support of criminal enterprises
• Trojan horses	• Databases to support drug distributions
• Logic bombs	
• Trap doors	• Databases to keep records of client transactions
• Viruses	
Telecommunication crimes	• Money laundering
• Phone phreaking	
• Hacking	Hardware and software thefts
• Illegal bulletin boards	• Software piracy
• Misuse of telephone systems	• Thefts of computers
Computer manipulation crimes	• Thefts of microprocessor chips
• Embezzlements	• Thefts of trade secrets
• Frauds	

those listed in Figure 6-7 to indicate different programming techniques for carrying out the unauthorized functions.[7]

TELECOMMUNICATIONS CRIMES

Telecommunications crimes involve the illegal access or use of computer systems over telephone lines. A hacking program tries to find valid access codes for a computer system by continually calling the system with randomly generated codes. Use of a hacking program constitutes unauthorized access to a system, and access codes generated by a hacking program are stolen property. Misuse of telephone systems also falls into this category. Phone phreaking is the use of computers or electronic devices to trick the phone into charging long-distance tolls to a legitimate number.[8]

COMPUTER MANIPULATION CRIMES

Computer manipulation crimes involve changing data or creating records in a system for the specific advancement of another crime. Virtually all embezzlement in financial institutions requires the creation of false accounts or modifications of data in existing accounts. The perpetrator need not know computer programming but must have a

---

S E C U R I T Y   B Y T E   6 – 2

Computer Security Spending Grows

Companies of all sizes are equally vulnerable to security breaches, according to a just released 1997 Industry Survey by Deloitte & Touche LLP, and Infosecurity News, which also reports extraordinary growth in computer security budgets.

Companies ranging in size from very large to very small reported a significant percentage of security breaches within the past year. This rise may link to another finding: Computer security budgets jumped 50 percent in 1996, with continued growth anticipated in 1997. That's more than 40 points higher than the budget growth of corporate security departments supporting more traditional asset-protection assignments.

Of all size firms, almost half (49 percent) reported experiencing some sort of information security breach last year. Of those breaches, 40 percent were internal and 27 percent were external. Ironically, a majority (62 percent) cite "budget constraints" as the top obstacle to obtaining adequate levels of security for their organizations, surpassing "lack of end-user awareness" in previous years.

Despite budget concerns, a majority (80 percent) agree that information security has improved over the past two years, and 90 percent believe it will continue to improve over the next two years.

Source: Security (Cahners Publishing, Des Plaines, Il., 1996) Vol. 33, No. 11, p. 93.

good sense of how to operate the system. The embezzlement offense is always the main charge, but charges of computer crime, such as unauthorized access to a computer system, may be added.[9]

SUPPORT OF CRIMINAL ENTERPRISES

Computer systems now play a key role in support of criminal enterprises. Prostitution, drug dealing, stolen cars, and many other criminal enterprises now use computers to make their "work" easier. Hate crime-organizations such as the KKK, Aryan Nations, and Neo-nazis also use computers extensively.

HARDWARE AND SOFTWARE THEFTS

There is a thriving industry involved with stolen or pirated (illegally copied) software, theft of computer hardware and related equipment, and industrial espionage to steal trade secrets in the computer industry and from other industries using computers. It is essential for the security manager to have a firm working knowledge of computers and how they can be compromised. In the twenty-first century it will be a main skill for consideration to higher levels of leadership in security.

COMPUTER CRIME STRATEGIES

The computer crime strategies adopted by police and security agencies depend on their size, budgets, technical abilities, and the wishes of the community served. It will be many years until we have a type of security officer or police officer who will have the specialized technical skills to fight computer criminals. There are strategies, however, that can be adopted to fight computer crime more effectively:

1. Make a top management commitment to respond to computer crime. The highest level officials—[CEOs, security directors], chiefs of police, sheriffs, and district attorneys—must commit to establishing the capability to address this kind of crime.

2. Determine the level of commitment feasible. The investment can range from sharing of resources with other jurisdictions [or departments], through developing expert on-staff investigative skills, to assigning investigators full time to computer cases.

3. Conduct a skills and interest survey and identify at least one investigator and one prosecutor with an interest in computer-related crime.

4. Assure that the individual receives at least basic level training. This will mean participating in the courses available at the federal level, if feasible, and training opportunities available from the state, computer associations, or consultants.

5. Establish clear operating procedures or organizational requirements to ensure all computer crime cases are referred to trained staff.

6. Identify technical support resources. First determine if these resources exist within the agency (not necessarily in investigation and prosecution), and then identify technical experts and investigators in the community and at state and federal levels.

7. Whenever possible coordinate [security], law enforcement, and prosecution efforts.

8. Work closely wherever possible with other [security], law enforcement officers, and prosecution to form a local or state association of computer-related investigators and prosecutors.

9. Don't neglect prevention. Allow time for public speaking engagements with businesses, schools, and agencies to increase potential victims' awareness of the [security] justice system's attention to the issue.[10]

Safeguarding computer systems and the information they gather, process, store, and transmit is a pressing and critical issue facing security managers today. Without secure computer systems and information, the fundamental processes of business and government can no longer function in a modern, technological environment. The business, social, and economic upheaval that can result from the loss

---

SECURITY BRIEF 6–3

Electronic Commerce: New Security, New Threats

About half of all U.S. businesses plan to conduct e-commerce business in 1998. And some feel e-commerce revenue could reach $100 billion by 2001.

But businesses using the Internet for sales and financial transactions may not come close to reaching that figure without a significant customer-perception turnaround, especially for security of personal information and transaction data on the Web. According to IDG research, 65 percent of businesses already using the Web for e-commerce feel that low customer confidence is a primary obstacle to more revenue. And of these Web-savvy firms, 58 percent believe that security concerns also are major impediment.

Businesses not yet on the Web are more wary.

The IDG study found that 82 percent of these respondents view e-commerce security as a major obstacle to future use and growth, while 65 percent see "availability to customers" as another problem that's kept them out of the Internet and Web.

Privacy Concerns

One problem that may not easily go away is the concern the public has over personal privacy issues over the Web.

Released in late March, the eTRUST Internet Privacy Study, conducted by The Boston Group, found that over 70 percent of consumers who responded to the on-line survey are more concerned about privacy on the Internet than they are about the invasion of privacy by telephone or mail. Ironically, a high number of Web users react to this privacy concern by refusing to provide personal information or by giving intentionally incorrect information—practices that add to the perception of mistrust and insecurity that consumers and businesses hold.

Source: Bill Zalud. *Security* (Cahners Publishing, Des Plaines, Il., 1996), Vol. 33, No. 11, p. 93.

of a major information technology system, such as in a large banking institution, is immeasurable. Beyond the loss of a system, the everyday threats to the confidentiality, integrity, and availability of information in today's world can be equally harmful and disruptive.

Security managers need to be acutely aware of the value and sensitivity of information assets under their protection. Many security managers do not fully understand the threats to the information assets of their companies, nor to they understand the countermeasures that can and must be taken to protect these assets. The components of a security program for computers and computer systems must be defined, and procedures must be provided for developing, implementing, and maintaining a security program that (1) complies with the laws, policies, regulations, standards, and guidelines influencing or directing computer security policy, and (2) provides reasonable assurance that assets are protected from potential threats.

COMPUTER SECURITY ENVIRONMENT

The computer security environment, in order to be effectively applied, must be related to the following objectives:

1. *Prevention:* The security procedure/countermeasure is intended to prevent an undesirable event such as an unauthorized access to information technology assets. Use of keys to control physical access, user identifiers and passwords, and encryption are examples of preventive countermeasures.

2. *Detection:* The security procedure/countermeasure is intended to detect the occurrence of an undesirable event such as a fire or unauthorized alteration of data or computer programs. Smoke detectors, record counts, and audits are detective countermeasures.

3. *Protection/correction:* The security procedure/countermeasure is intended to protect and recover information technology from the effects of an undesirable event. Sprinkler systems, equipment covers, and backup files are protective/corrective countermeasures.

4. *Accountability:* The security procedure/countermeasure is intended to assure that the individual taking an action (for example, making a change to a computer program or authorizing a disbursement) can be identified. User identifiers, signature cards, and program change logs are accountability countermeasures.[11]

It is helpful, as shown in Figure 6-8, to visualize the computer security environment not as a single entity, but as three areas: the facility, electronic environment, and procedural environment. Each of these areas can be divided into separate security zones by type and potential threat. Then, as shown in Figure 6-9, each zone can be considered for possible countermeasures.

Computer-related crime is one of the most challenging problems facing U.S. industries today. Although computer crime it is escalating at a dramatic rate, the detection of it is very low. Experts estimate that less than 20 percent of computer crime is detected, and less than 5 percent of that results in the apprehension of the

FIGURE 6–8   *Information Technology Installation Security Areas*

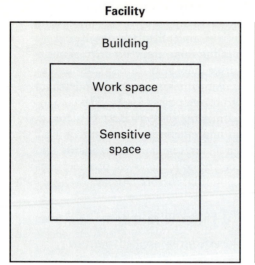

Facility

Building

Work space

Sensitive space

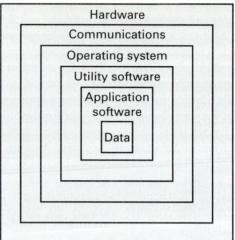

Electronic Environment

Hardware

Communications

Operating system

Utility software

Application software

Data

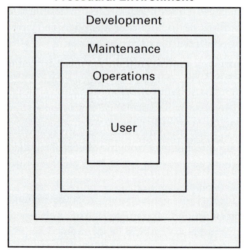

Procedural Environment

Development

Maintenance

Operations

User

person who committed it. Computer criminals seldom leave fingerprints, footprints, or any kind of physical evidence. The daunting task of solving computer crimes should not create despair but opportunity for the wise security manager. You *can* do something. By developing an investigative team, you can reduce the effect that computer-related, white-collar crime has on your company. This team comprises a coordinator, an investigator, an information systems specialist, and an attorney:

Coordinator: Depending on how the company is organized, the director or manager of security should be the team's leader or coordinator. The coordinator's responsibility is to

FIGURE 6–9   *Possible Control Techniques by Security Area*

	Facility	**Electronic Environment**	**Procedural Environment**
Prevention	Keys, cardkeys Guards	Protected memory Encryption Passwords	Separation of duties Training Background checks
Detection	Smoke detectors Moisture detectors	Control totals Exception reporting	Required vacations Signature cards
Protection/ correction	Sprinklers Halon Surge suppressors	Software and data backup Retransmission	Termination of disgruntled employees Training
Accountability	Access logs Picture IDs	User identifiers Terminal identifier	Change logs Signature lists

ensure details do not fall through the cracks—to be the glue that holds the team and investigations together. He or she must ensure colleagues communicate through team meetings. The team might get together daily or weekly, depending on the investigation, to talk about its progress. The coordinator also represents the team before top management and law enforcement officials.

Investigator: Depending again on the company's organization as well as its resources, the coordinator may be the investigator. Outside investigators may also be used. In any case, the investigator conducts interviews, interrogates suspects, sets up surveillance, and conducts background investigations on key suspects. He or she also provides investigative support to the other team members.

Information systems specialist: The information systems specialist should be knowledgeable, objective, able to maintain confidentiality, able to operate through procedures and under direction, and be suitable as an expert witness.

Attorney: The attorney must develop an educational relationship with the other team members—the coordinator, the investigator, and the information systems specialist. The attorney must school the other members of the team in the legalities of conducting suspect interviews and in finding and acquiring the right evidence to make a successful case. Forty-seven states have some form of computer crime law. The laws range from the very simple to the most complex. Whether it is a state court or a federal court, the attorney has to know what the appropriate statute is and what evidence is needed for a successful prosecution.[12]

The student can now appreciate that the computer is both a blessing and a curse for industry. Similar to the splitting of the atom, and its resulting use for peace and war, the computer can be used for criminal purposes as effectively as it can be used for its intended purposes. This is one of the most challenging fields for the law enforcement or security professional, and the student who wants to be a leader in one of those fields in the twenty-first century *must* become as expert as possible in the uses and abuses of computers. Those who do so will surely be the best prepared for the challenges of both a new generation of computers and new generations of computer-literate criminals.

Fire Prevention and Safety

A major problem that faces every company is the role of fire and safety officer. Depending on the size and organization of a company, the fire prevention and safety task might be a separate operation or combined with security. In any case, the security department can help by being the eyes and ears twenty-four hours a day for prevention of fires and removal or identification of safety hazards. Although many security colleagues may consider the tasks of fire prevention and safety outside the realm of security and loss prevention, we suggest you regard them as an integral part of the security and loss prevention mission.

Any company or institution must provide a system of fire prevention and control through the use of efficient fire protection services and equipment, implementation of effective fire drills, use of appropriate fire safety codes, and regular monitoring to ensure the safety of employees, customers, and the public. This system should include the following:

- An adequate fire protection service.
- Fire inspections and testing of equipment at least once each quarter by local or state fire officials or other persons qualified to perform fire inspections.
- An annual inspection by qualified outside fire inspectors.
- Placement of adequate fire protection equipment throughout the facility.
- Use of an automatic fire alarm system, certified effective by an independent outside source. The system must be designed to provide early warning of the presence of fire or smoke.
- A written facilitywide fire evacuation plan. This plan should include:
    Floor plan layout
    Location of exits and escape routes
    Location of the fire plan
    Quarterly fire drills, including the total evacuation of all persons from an area
    Special procedure drills for the evacuation and control of special areas
    Plans and procedures for the immediate release of access controls to locked areas
    Plans to provide security during the fire evacuation process

Fire drills are practice sessions designed to teach participants the best means of escape in case of fire. The most difficult areas for proper fire drill procedures are laboratory facilities and those areas where highly classified or restricted information is kept. Drills for these areas, though especially important, must be conducted carefully and with adequate security supervision.

FIRE PREVENTION

The most important aspect of an effective fire protection program is *fire prevention*. All employees, especially security officers, should be constantly on the lookout for fire hazards such as altered electrical outlets, overloaded electrical units, out-of-date or expended fire extinguishers, and improper trash storage. A facility fire not only can cause the company or institution tremendous financial losses, but also can threaten lives when the fire occurs in occupied shop or office areas. It is essential, therefore,

---

SECURITY BRIEF 6–4

Addressable vs. Analog

When specifying a fire alarm system, make sure you are getting what you requested.

Many specifications come out for bid that specify an "addressable" system. Then, when it is installed, the client finds they do not have what they thought they had requested.

Addressable systems are excellent systems, but they do not accomplish what an "analog" system does. "Addressable" systems can identify the device, supervise it fully and tell you only that it is in alarm or trouble. In contrast, analog systems actually read varying levels, or degrees, of conditions and automatically respond to those conditions.

Confusion on this issue became such a problem in bidding large fire alarm systems that the National Fire Protection Association (NFPA) chose to put a definition into the 72 Code this last cycle. It can be found on page 72-11, section 1-4 under Definitions.

So remember, when you are choosing a fire alarm system, if you want the ability to not only address an individual detector by name or number, but also to

see the varying conditions and/or status of that device, as well as to control how the panel operates on those conditions, then you must use the word "analog" in your specification.

An analog detector allows you to adjust for night/day sensitivities and to customize your system to respond in different ways, according to the environment that the detector is mounted in.

A typical use of this feature is in an office environment where smoking is allowed. During the day when people are in the office, you can move the sensitivity of the detectors to a more tolerant level. Then, when the office workers go home, you can have the panel automatically bring the sensitivity up to its highest level. This not only keeps down false alarms, but it also allows for the best use of the intelligent detectors.

Remember, "addressable" only allows you the ability to have a discrete identification. "Analog" allows for actually monitoring the varying conditions, as well as giving you a discrete ID of the device.

Source: Bob Ruyle. *Security* (Cahners Publishing, Des Plaines, Il., 1997) Vol. 34, No. 2, p. 49.

that security personnel, and all other employees, make fire prevention a basic part of their daily activities by detecting, reporting, and correcting all fire hazards.

All employees should be attentive to maintaining good housekeeping standards to augment fire safety, including:

- Proper storage of combustible material
- Prevention of hazardous electrical situations
- Training for employees in fire safety procedures
- Fire drills
- Fire hazards reported to security
- Fire control equipment checked regularly

Following the annual inspection and report of the state fire prevention inspector, every effort should be made to correct all deficiencies noted in the report. When corrections are complete, the security department should notify the state fire prevention inspector, who will reinspect the facility.

FIREFIGHTING EQUIPMENT

Firefighting equipment available within the company or institution should consist of:

- Fire extinguishers located in the work areas, public areas, offices, lounges, kitchens, and all dining rooms.
- Sprinkler systems located in all units.
- Fire alert systems consisting of a dual chamber, ionization-type detector designed to sense both visible and invisible products of combustion. These units are located in all patient wards, offices, public areas, and other congested areas.
- Stand pipes for fire hydrants (local area supervisors should list specific locations for security).
- Fire extinguishers (local area supervisors should list specific locations for security).
- Carbon dioxide extinguishers (local area supervisors should list specific locations for security).

FIRE DRILLS

Fire drills should be conducted at the direction of the security department or the designated fire and safety officer as follows:

1. Drills should be conducted at least once each quarter, and cover all areas of the company on a rotating basis so as to hit each area once annually.

2. The security department should schedule the drills and notify the local fire department and the fire and safety officer of the scheduling. Prior notification of the drill should be limited so as to increase drill effectiveness.

3. The security supervisor and the designated fire and safety officer should monitor drill operation.

4. The drill should begin when the "mock fire" location is established and be considered complete when all personnel assigned to the location are evacuated and the first fire apparatus arrives at the scene.

5. Security officers should be positioned at vehicle and pedestrian entrances and in the parking lots to offer radio accessibility and assistance to the local fire department.

6. Traffic through all entrances should be cleared immediately to facilitate fire apparatus access.

7. When the designated areas are cleared, immediately following the drill, a count of customers, visitors, and employees should be conducted to determine accountability. The drill should not be considered complete until all customers, visitors, and staff signed into or assigned to the specific areas are identified and accounted for.

POST-FIRE INVESTIGATION

A security department investigator should be assigned for all major fires. The investigator should be responsible for conducting a thorough investigation of the incident and providing recommendations regarding accountability. This investigation should be conducted jointly by the local fire department officer on the scene, the state fire marshall, and the security department investigator.

SAFETY INSPECTIONS AND MAINTENANCE

To protect the customers, staff, and visitors to a facility, the security department acts as the eyes and ears of the maintenance and grounds departments to prevent hazards and hazardous conditions to occur. Security officers will report serious maintenance problems and log them in the appropriate daily log. These services should be developed through a written cooperative plan for preventive maintenance of all physical plants with provisions for inventory of, emergency repairs of, or replacement of property, conditions, and equipment that can create serious security and safety problems. This plan should be reviewed annually and updated as needed.

PROGRAM RESPONSIBILITY

Every corporate or institutional facility requires proper maintenance procedures for all its equipment and property. The security department staff is always on the grounds and should be trained to be alert for maintenance and environmental safety matters. To accomplish this, the security department should:

1. Create preventive maintenance routines for critical items of building systems and equipment to minimize out-of-service time due to failures as well as reduce costly breakdown repairs that can create security and safety problems.

2. Detect maintenance deficiencies in their early stages of development and take prompt corrective actions.

SECURITY BRIEF 6 – 5

Simple Safeguards That Work!

Scott Ramsey, national director of information security, Ernst & Young suggests common sense steps:

- All employees, vendors and contractors should be required to sign a confidentiality statement.
- All laptops should be backed up on a regular basis.
- Policies and procedures should exist for the use and downloading of information to laptops.
- Users should not be allowed to script their user IDs and passwords on laptops for remote access.
- Boot level passwords should be mandatory for all users.

- All data should be classified as to importance and access.
- All laptops, desktops and peripherals should be physically and logically secured after business hours.
- Internet access should be limited to those who have a business purpose.

INFORMATION SECURITY: PRODUCT BUYING PLANS

Most Likely Purchases This Year:

1. Lock-downs, Alarms
2. Physical Equipment Tagging
3. Shredders
4. Computer Access Control, Passwords
5. Fiber Optic Cabling
6. Disaster Planning Software

Source: Editors. "Cybercrime: Lock-downs Lock Out Computer Theft." *Security* (Cahers Publishing Company, Newton, MA, 1997), Vol. 34, No. 10, pp. 14–15.

3. Plan and schedule resulting maintenance work to provide a reasonably controlled workflow, thus enabling better use of labor and materials.
4. Detect and reduce overmaintenance and identify problem areas.

INVENTORY OF PLANT EQUIPMENT AND FACILITIES

An inventory of all items on grounds and in buildings should be the foundation for any sound security, safety, and preventive maintenance system. Some of the information may be found in plans, plant records, and property records. An identification number should be assigned to each item or unit of equipment and affixed by a nonremovable tag or other means to the unit. When identifying equipment in a large-scale operation, group numbers according to equipment and function, and always allow for inventory growth. To be useful, the inventory must be current and accurate.

INVENTORY RECORDS

The inventory record will be used to record the facilities and equipment under the overall protective responsibility of the security department. The appointed foreperson of the facilities department should be provided with survey information, updating these records as additions, deletions, and replacement of facilities and equipment are made. Inventory records are very important to the preventive maintenance and loss prevention programs, indicating what is to be inspected, complete with details concerning the make, model, serial number, and so on. Such information assists those providing estimates for replacement and helps prevent possible thefts.

Inventory records should include:

1. Buildings and other property listed on the record sheets in numerical order
2. Installed equipment within each building listed under that building entry
3. Distribution systems, pavements, grounds, and so on, recorded on the record sheet in like groups
4. A remarks column on the record sheet used to record the log book number to which the facility or equipment is assigned

INSPECTION SCHEDULE

The preventive maintenance inspection and record schedule should contain the following information:

1. Type and frequency of the inspection schedule
2. Identification numbers of the facilities or equipment listed in the order of inspection
3. Location of the equipment
4. Description of the equipment, including make, model, and serial number
5. Checklist numbers or codes that apply to each facility or item of equipment
6. Standard time for servicing or inspecting each facility or item of equipment

INSPECTION CHECKLISTS

The preventive maintenance inspection checklist should:

1. Contain a description of the servicing, checks, or adjustments that must be performed during the inspections.
2. Be based on manufacturers' service manuals and other local factors.
3. Be developed and promulgated as various types of equipment and systems become available. Some sources of information are:

   Manufacturers' service manuals. These are valuable guides on how a piece of equipment should be installed, operated, and maintained. They also provide data regarding adjustments, servicing, parts replacements, overhauls, and so on.

Operators. The operators of equipment systems can often provide information on maintenance problems.

CORRECTIVE ACTION

Daily security officer reports should provide a basis for initiation of immediate corrective maintenance and repair work, as well as probable maintenance work. The urgency for maintenance and repair work varies and is divided into four categories: security-related flash, urgent, essential, and projected.

1. *Security-related flash:* This is a situation that creates a serious security or safety threat that could result in harm to customers, visitors, or staff of the corporation, or litigation resulting from such hazards. These requests should be responded to by maintenance within eight hours. Failure to respond will impose vicarious liability on the maintenance staff.

2. *Urgent:* This is a detected situation that might result in an inability to perform the mission of a specific operational activity at the hospital. These requests must be responded to within twenty-four hours of the report.

3. *Essential:* This indicates that some essential process in the company may be threatened by the loss of some equipment or service. These situations will be given the highest priority in the regular scheduling of maintenance and repair, but responded to at least within one week.

4. *Projected:* This indicates that the situation is not critical now, but will become so within a short period (thirty to sixty days). These problems will be dealt with in accordance with regular maintenance and repair scheduling.

WORK REQUESTS

Work requests for defects revealed by security patrols or inspections should be reported to facilities and services and entered into the daily administrative log (unless it is a security-threatening issue). Then a work request will be prepared by the security officers or inspectors and submitted to the appropriate maintenance office. This should be reviewed and necessary work orders issued to correct the defect indicated. Maintenance demands should be grouped according to location or trade and, where possible, preestimated.

PROGRAM EVALUATION

Program evaluation should be a joint activity conducted by plant operations and the security department. Review should include the following evaluations related to the preventive maintenance program:

- Operator inspection reports
- Shop inspection reports
- Yearly inspection reports

- Inventory records
- Maintenance schedule
- Work requests
- Work order completion
- Security and safety concerns
- Loss prevention concerns

Substance Abuse and Other Issues

Substance abuse is estimated to cost U.S. businesses $50 billion a year in lost time, accidents, theft to support the habit, and litigation. The problems with drug abuse are monumental, but it is best to consult with the human resources department to determine the company's or institution's policy on a case-by-case basis. The security professional must know how to identify common symptoms of possible drug abuse by employees and take action according to company policy.

Other specialties that may be of interest to the student of security and that have general applications are terrorism and terrorist activity, white-collar crime (other than computer crime), executive and VIP security, and protecting classified and proprietary information.

SECURITY BYTE 6–4

Popular E-mail Has Dark Side

Just as the personal computer has redefined the workplace in recent years, advancements in electronic communications is the next major innovation.

Thirty-eight percent of senior executives named improved electronic communications as the technology that will have the greatest impact on their firm's productivity over the next three years. The survey was by Menlo Park, Calif.-based RHI Consulting, a specialized staffing service placing contract information technology professionals.

"To remain competitive, businesses continually seek faster and more efficient ways to communicate both internally and externally," says Greg Scileppi, executive director of RHI Consulting.

The downside: *e-mail is an emerging security threat*. Proprietary information can leak through e-mail. Damaging comments can pop out of e-mail. And, in rare cases, outsiders can enter and damage information and instructions through poorly designed e-mail ports.

Source: Zalud Report. "Popular E-mail Has Dark Side," *Security* (Cahners Publishing Company, Newton, MA, 1995), Vol. 32, No. 8, p. 86.

Summary

This chapter has discussed some of the areas of security specialization that cover almost every industry that has need of security. Three were covered in some depth, and a few others received a passing mention. Dozens of others are left for the student to discover in other parts of the text. The purpose of this review was to show how so many functions are common to whatever industry or institution is examined. Crisis planning is essential in all cases if one is to be able to prevent disasters or restore operations for the company following one. Transportation of goods in a large industrial nation like the United States is key to its continuing economic growth. Shrinkage in transit, storage, and during loading is a major problem for security providers, whether proprietary or contracted.

Fire and safety are seen as tasks that are universal to all corporate and institutional activities, but they have been somewhat artificially separated from the similar goals of security and loss prevention. Since the liability for inadequate safety or inadequate fire prevention is such a prevalent issue, it behooves the security provider to do as much as possible to help provide these services as well.

REVIEW QUESTIONS

1. Describe the main steps to take in forming a crisis management team.
2. What is meant by "intermodal transportation systems"?
3. What are four key elements for combatting computer crime?
4. Name at least three kinds of man-made disasters and three natural disasters.
5. Where are the most vulnerable points in transportation security?

TERMS TO REMEMBER

crisis

man-made disasters

disaster

vulnerability

transportation

falsification of documents

intermodal cargo containers

break bulk

infrastructure

internal computer crimes

phreaking

computer security environment

fire drill

ENDNOTES

1. Mayer Nudell and Norman Antokol, "Before the Going Gets Rough," *Security Management*, Vol. 32, No. 3 (March 1988), pp. 49–50.
2. Jonathan Bernstein, "The 10 Steps of Crisis Management," *Security Management*, Vol. 34, No. 3 (March 1990), pp. 75–76.

3. *Disaster Recovery Planning Methodology* (Chicago: Chi/Cor Information Management, 1990), p. 2.1.

4. Michael Hackler, "One by Land, Two by Air," Special Supplement, *Security Management*, Vol. 36, No. 3 (June 1992), p. 31a.

5. Gion Green and Robert Fischer, *Introduction to Security*, 4th ed. (Boston: Butterworth, 1987), p. 308.

6. *Computer Crime: The New Crime Scene* (Washington, D.C.: NIJ, U.S. Govt. Printing Office, January to February 1990), p. 3.

7. Ibid., p. 3.

8. Ibid., p. 3.

9. Ibid., p. 3.

10. Ibid., p. 7.

11. Office of Technical Assistance, *Information Technology Installation Security* (Washington, D.C.: U.S. General Services Administration, December 1988), p. 29.

12. Robert F. Littlejohn, "Teaming Up to Fight Computer Crime," *Security Management*, Vol. 32, No. 7 (March 1988), pp. 37–38.

7

The Organizational Role for Security

A Search for Identity and Respect

As a formal analytical point of reference, primacy of orientation to the attainment of a specific goal is used as the defining characteristic of an organization which distinguishes it from other types of social systems.

—Talcott Parsons

Overview

According to *Hallcrest II*, $57 billion was expended by the security industry in 1990.[1] This reflects a 100 percent increase for security in the period between 1980 and 1990.[2] At the end of the 1990s, this figure may approach $93 billion. Security can now be considered a truly big business, whether in terms of costs, resources, personnel, or payroll. The quality and ethics of those persons who secure these corporate assets and huge sums of money, the kinds of efficient and effective organizational techniques they employ, and the ways in which they try to improve the security "system" will probably in large part determine whether security will move forward as we pass through the 1990s and into the twenty-first century, or revert to past practices that have already proved to be guidelines for frustration and failure.

This chapter is devoted to an overview of security management, the proper organizational role for security managers, and offers a brief examination of organizational and management theory as it has been (or has not been) applied to the problem of security. Perhaps it is in this arena that the security professional can best show to the organizational "bottom liners" that security can be made cost effective and, if it cannot always prevent every loss, at least it can keep things from becoming even worse.

Security and the Development of a Science of Management

As security has evolved and changed, producing new styles of management and proliferating new environments for administrators, so also have there been pervasive changes in theories of formal organization and in concepts related to administration leadership and behavior. The evolution of security and loss prevention management has moved along pathways that run generally parallel to that larger movement.

Conceptions of formal organizations and the roles of all managers have changed radically in the past half-century. Frederick Taylor's **scientific management** movement portrayed the administrator as a highly skilled technician who ensured the smooth operation of such organizational processes as planning, organizing, staffing, directing, coordinating, reporting, and budgeting.[3] Seen from that vantage point, the ideal executive is a rational individual who manipulates the levers of a human machine, correcting deficiencies by rearranging the span of control, the line of command, or the interrelationships of the structural components. Taylor's emphasis was on the anatomy of the system as symbolized by the organizational chart. The basic human tendency not to conform to official specification was ignored, a fact that contributed greatly to the early demise of the scientific management movement.

The so-called human relations movement that followed proclaimed somewhat pompously (as it now seems) that the needs and predilections of the human participants within formal organizations exert a powerful influence, and management would do well to recognize and accommodate them.[4] It was argued that the workers' need to find rewarding social satisfactions in their relationships with one another operates as a strong determinant of morale and, therefore, of production. Research findings soon reinforced that position.[5]

One contribution of that school of thought was an elaboration of the idea of **informal organization** that takes into account how the actual dynamics of status and influence differ from the static lines and boxes on an organizational chart. The boss's secretary, it was pointed out, may exercise great influence, though he or she has little formal status, because he or she can control the access of people and information to his or her superior. In the security environment, the security manager may often relate better to shift lieutenants or line staff than to company management or other nonsecurity staff even though the latter may be higher ranked in the formal organizational structure.

RECENT DEVELOPMENTS

In recent years, more sophisticated theories and research methodologies have been brought to bear on the informal side of organization life. Just as companies came to be conceived of as social systems, generic theories of organization began to define all the systems within which workers join to accomplish work goals as "complex" and "open."[6]

Concern for the psychological and social ingredients of organization life emphasized the responsibility of management to create conditions under which participants could use their capacities fully and creatively.[7] Attention was given to the dilemma of satisfying concurrently the legitimate requirements of the individual and the organization.[8] In contrast with the former preoccupation with hierarchy and the downward flow of authority, modern theorists argue that organizations should be seen as composites of problem-solving groups in which the leaders are primarily concerned with generating wide participation among the members and in which the decision-making power is shared with the members.[9]

Some recent formulations concerning management techniques seem especially applicable to developments in the field of security and therefore help provide a context for much research. Schein pointed out that the work styles of managers reflect the assumptions that they make about people.[10] He set forth four views or assumptions about the nature of humankind that seem to have been operative in security management:

The first view sees people as rational and economic in nature, primarily motivated by materialistic rewards, requiring from management a firm structure of incentives and controls in order to carry out predetermined tasks.

The second view sees the worker as social, primarily motivated by a need for meaningful relationships with others, requiring from management a concern for personal feelings and a structuring of work to bring about satisfying human interactions and group experiences.

The third view sees humankind as potentially self-actualizing. After satisfying lower-level needs, such as survival, self-esteem, and autonomy, people respond to internal forces in seeking a sense of achievement and meaning in their work. The function of management, under this view, is to facilitate the efforts of security staff members to use their energies in creative and productive ways.

The fourth view sees the worker as complex and, though capable of self-actualization, highly varied in responding to different situations. This view challenges management to develop diagnostic skills and wide flexibility in meeting the needs, and thereby maximizing the contribution, of different organization members under constantly changing circumstances.[11]

Certain aspects of those views can be found in both historical and contemporary security administration. The staffs of large, routinized operations have generally been treated by management as **rational-economic**. Smaller operations (especially those for small companies) and community-based security programs have moved toward the view that employees are motivated by social as well as economic satisfactions. Such operations often have given the security staff many opportunities for self-actualization. And some managers do view their staff as complex and seek to use varied skills and methods in working with them, along the lines suggested by Schein.

A BALANCING ACT FOR SECURITY MANAGERS

We must remember, of course, that security managers have managerial relationships not only with security staff but also with all other managers. Indeed, it is the balancing and harmonizing of the two sets of relationships that create some of the most difficult problems, perhaps because security managers (consciously or unconsciously) adopt one view of people when dealing with security staff and another when dealing with other management. Consider, for example, the dynamics that might occur in a company in which the security management treated staff as motivated by social and economic needs, while viewing other management as capable of responding only to their own needs for power.[12]

The historical and contemporary picture of security management's view of other managers seems even more varied than its view of security staff. Many managers have been, and still are, viewed as responding only to the bottom line. Both the time-honored management by objectives work programs, which offer opportunities for small rewards on a sliding scale, and the practice of giving productivity bonuses for conforming behavior stem from a rational-economic view of employees.

One of the most significant developments in security management—the use of small-group process to bring about **consensus** decisions with **synergism**—seems to rest on the concept that security staff, after all, are social humans. Other innovations, such as self-scheduling, have overtones of both the self-actualization and the complex views of security staff. Our position is that security management will be most effective if it is generally consistent in its view of all participants, whether security staff or other management and staff, and if it seeks to develop approaches to them based on the assumption that, though complex, they are capable of self-actualization.

Another formulation from management theory that seems useful in assessing trends in security administration is the typology of organization and management styles suggested by Likert. Distinguishing basically between authoritative and participative organizations, Likert posited four approaches to management, each with specified consequences for the motivation of participants, their job satisfaction, communication, decision making, production, and other variables. The four types, which Likert viewed as stages of development, from ineffective and pathological to effective and healthy management, are as follows (see Figure 7-1):

- Exploitive-authoritative
- Benevolent-authoritative
- Participative-consultative
- Participative-group[13]

It appears that aspects of all four approaches are found in contemporary security organizations. The general trend, however, has been away from type 1, which is illustrated by the traditional security "guard" style, with its dependence on coercive uses of authority, and into type 3 through a mixture of benevolently applied authority and limited democratization of the management process. The use of staff advisory counsels,

Participative-consultative 3	**Benevolent-authoritative** 2
Participative-group 4	**Explotive-authoritative** 1

FIGURE 7-1   *Likert's Four Stages of Development*

the delegation of more authority to security officers, and the involvement of junior staff in long-range planning are examples of the participative–consultative practices adopted in many security operations, particularly those based in or closely tied to the community. The general pattern in security, however, seems closer to Likert's benevolent–authoritative type 2 than to any of the other three.

Some progressive security programs operate along lines similar to Likert's type 4, participative-group. Though differing from one another in many ways, these and similar experimental ventures distribute influence and decisional power widely among the security staff involved and use the group process extensively in guiding program operation.

Security administrators should seek to develop participation at all levels within their organizations. It should be recognized, however, that much empirical research is needed (both in security administration and in generic management processes) to refine understanding of how participative techniques may be employed successfully and how they may be adapted to the realities of particular programs.[14] As we have noted, precipitous efforts to democratize security organizations not only tend to be dangerous but also are usually destined to fail. The introduction of participative methods into programs that are oriented toward the goals of law and order requires great sensitivity to the forces at work in the organization and in its environment.

Security Management Models

Above all, security and security operations are a product of the management's will, backed by policy and action, to resolve a perceived problem in the organization. The early security operations had no problem with the "get tough" wishes of their organizational environments. Through the twentieth century, however, we have been struggling to determine just what we really want to do with, to, or for our organizations. This **model muddle** continues to be a problem for the security administrator. As a manager, the security leader must contend with a staff that is bifurcated into those who are mainly concerned with security and order, and those who are concerned with programs and personnel relations. As we approach the twenty-first century, we need to understand the problems faced by security administrators who are required to accomplish *both* while dealing with turnover, budget cuts, a changing social climate, and the myriad other issues facing them in the last decade of the century. We first discuss control.

BUREAUCRATIC CONTROL

The prevailing management climate for security organizations is bureaucratic control, especially in proprietary operations. In most organizations, the security operation is usually controlled by a combination of coercive rules that prohibit certain kinds of behavior and punishments that are meted out when the rules are broken. Bureaucratic organization is insulated by rules, and violations are punished in the name of equity.

In large corporations that employ thousands of personnel, each with personal problems, the bureaucratic style[15] seems to be the only functional way to cope with control: The process takes precedence over the individual, and employees and even customers become faceless commodities to be routed, worked, secured, protected, and recycled. This nineteenth-century model stresses *process* over *output*. Any social interaction is incidental, a welcome but low-priority byproduct, because the bureaucratic style clearly conflicts with any emphasis on interaction. The separate functions of rigid and formalized organizations create an impoverished climate for behavioral change.[16]

SECURITY OFFICERS

Whether called security guards, turnkeys, watchmen, hacks, security officers, rent-a-cops, or security staff, the general reference is to the persons charged with control, movement management, and observation of the employees, customers, and visitors in U.S. companies. As noted earlier, there are more than 1.6 million line-level security staff in America, only a small percentage of whom are women.

Little research has been conducted about security officers who are not supervisory staff. Few criminological studies have been conducted. That is further compounded by the relatively high turnover rates among security officers, as high as 40 to 60 percent in some contract guard organizations. Much remains to be learned about why some people are attracted to security work, how long they remain employed, their salaries, and why they choose to leave. Those questions are important because security officers form the backbone of organizational efforts to serve and protect those persons working in U.S. corporations and companies.

SECURITY OFFICERS AND THE MILITARY MODEL

The need for an organized and effective control force in security has instilled a paramilitary flavor as a model for most security officers. The adoption of militaristic organizational structures and procedures has made it easier to train a force with limited background, training, or education to do a specific job. The paramilitary approach is seen in the uniforms, titles, and procedures of security personnel. Training is directed to the mission of security, and there is little if any emphasis on

While the military style uniform is the most popular, others are used to "soften" the look of security.

Photos courtesy of Intapol Industries.

interaction with employees and customers. The model of the aloof but efficient guard has emerged, and the hiring of security personnel is more often based on height and weight than on the applicant's ability to work with people. To a great extent, security hiring practices bar those people who can best fulfill the newer mission of security with social interaction. The seniority system used in many security organizations may further discourage the infusion of security personnel with behavioral science backgrounds.

In order to provide the best entry-level personnel and to maintain a level of quality and growth in their staff, many security organizations have established rigid training standards along the lines of police academies. Such requirements will ensure that all staff are eventually exposed to methods that are not simply "more of the same." A current management saying is, "One sure sign of insanity is doing the same thing, over and over, and expecting different results."

To reflect the population in their corporate organization and local community, security personnel should actively recruit from minority groups, women, young persons, and prospective indigenous workers. Employment announcements must reach those groups and the general public.

It is useful to conduct, from time to time, a task analysis of each security position (to be updated periodically) to determine the precise tasks, skills, and qualities needed. Testing based solely on relevant features in a "hands-on" manner, to assure that proper qualifications are considered for each position, helps the administrator know what is needed in training. Those procedures will lead to an open system of selection in which any testing device is related to a specific job and is a practical test of a person's ability to perform, at an acceptable standard, the tasks identified for that specific job.

These are a few of the steps that might help span the presently large communication gap between those who are doing the securing and those being secured. Security officers spend more time, and in more places, than anyone in the general management population than does anyone else in the organization. They should relate well to others since they can be the most positive agents for positive security awareness in that company. They can also destroy any efforts toward change that are attempted if they are an indifferent staff that tries to bypass nonsecurity managers. A move away from the military or police image to the helpful security officer image is critical to bringing about change in the corporate setting.

UPGRADING SECURITY PERSONNEL

The most important social interaction tool is the action between one person and another. Thus, a primary goal for the security manager is the recruitment, training, and retention of employees who are able—physically, emotionally, educationally, and motivationally—to work as a team.

In the security environment, it is often hard to hire or keep qualified personnel. But there is really no good reason for the security officer to "poor mouth" about salaries in the field. The national average entry-level starting pay is not bad when one considers the current minimum qualifications for the applicants.

But even during the early 1990s, when national unemployment rates reached Depression-type highs, some security jobs went begging. Security officer turnover rates in some states are so high that some security administrators openly confess that it is almost impossible to run their operations with consistent policies. Over the past two years that situation has stabilized, with lower unemployment rates and low-priced, high-tech jobs competing with good security operations and losing. Turnover rates do remain high, however, due to burnout and low wages. Some security managers note that it is not unusual for them to lose at least half of their new officers in the first year.

For most security managers and personnel directors, however, the human resource dilemma is shortage, not surplus. Because of the persistent problem of unfilled slots on most shifts, supervisors ask security officers on duty to work another shift ("work doubles"). That situation leads to tired staff and high overtime budgets, but management is seldom willing to increase expenditures for staff, fearing that security officers are just padding the rolls. The concept of audits for "minimum critical staffing" has been tried many times in other parts of the criminal justice system, but budget needs still seem to override attempts at rationalizing staffing patterns.[17]

Although most consider salaries in security to be too low, they are improving. Ranging from $6.50 to up to $10.00 per hour, beginning wages are starting to compare with those of many other entry-level industries.

Perhaps more important than wages is the line-level security employees' sense of public rejection, reinforced in some organizations by the belief that the administrators do not consult them, treat them fairly, or care what they think.[18] Although this specific example is drawn from the field of corrections, the same new channels of communication must be opened between security administrators and security employees, as well as between security employees and other staff. Security administrators should meet with staff to discuss employee problems; security and other staff should also meet together.[19] Those meetings should be regularly scheduled and formally integrated into the organizational procedures.

After two or three weeks of basic orientation, new security staff members usually learn the "ropes" of the security operations by working with one or more officers in a modified on-the-job apprenticeship program, which can too often simply institutionalize and perpetuate the bad habits of the past. Security officers spend twenty-four hours a day with the facilities and staff of the organization. The security officers' actions, words, training, and skills make the difference for nonsecurity staff between a hostile and destructive environment and one that is constructive and humane. Security personnel too often demonstrate behavior that is punitive, contemptuous, and degrading, reflecting a suspicion of employees and others that may lead to a self-defeating game of "cops and robbers." It is in that adversarial relationship that social interaction breaks down. This removes access to the hundreds of extra eyes and ears that could have been useful to the security mission. Perhaps the best way to sum up the most desired atmosphere for a security organization in the twenty-first century is an attitude of "have a good day," not, "make my day."

Evolution of the Management Function in Security

The history of security management as an organizational role can be perhaps best summarized by suggesting that it has passed through three stages, each characterized by a particular emphasis in the handling of the security and loss prevention function: first, **assets protection**, with a heavy emphasis on guards and physical security; second, **loss prevention**, with emphasis on a combination of physical and operational security; and finally, **security management**, with the concept of security as a part of the overall operational roles and financial plans of the organization. Security managers in the past have always tried to mirror these changing emphases and many presently reflect increasing commitment of the system to a fourth goal, that of **integrated partnership** with the overall corporate management team, in which security is recognized as a critical contributor to the organizational goals.

SECURITY BRIEF 7–1

D.A.R.E® Program: A Success

Prevention programs have proliferated in response to concern about substance abuse,* particularly among young people. An understanding of the effects of these programs is only beginning to emerge, however. One such program is the school-based Drug Abuse Resistance Education Program (D.A.R.E.)®. D.A.R.E.® is distinctive for a number of reasons, among them: its widespread adoption throughout the country; its use of trained, uniformed police officers in the classroom; and its combination of local control and centralized coordination.

A recent study, conducted by the Research Triangle Institute (RTI) and sponsored by the National Institute of Justice, confirmed the prevalence and popularity of D.A.R.E.®; revealed that its appeal cuts across racial, ethnic, and socioeconomic lines; and indicated considerable support for expansion of the program.

Created in 1983 by the Los Angeles Police Department and the Los Angeles Unified School District as a substance abuse prevention program for grades K-12, D.A.R.E.® uses a core curriculum consisting of 17 hour-long weekly lessons taught to fifth- and sixth-graders. Since it was founded, D.A.R.E.® has expanded to encompass programs for middle and high school students, conflict resolution, gang prevention, parent education, and after-school recreation and learning. The curriculum has also been revised over the years as a result of research findings and is now more interactive; that is, it promotes active participation by students. D.A.R.E.® has also established a Scientific Advisory Board to aid in self-evaluation and recommend program changes.

The RTI evaluation was two-fold. In the first part the researchers looked at program structure and operations, how the program is perceived by program coordinators at the school-district level, and factors that make for effective implementation. The second part of the study used "meta-analysis," a method of analysis involving synthesis of previous studies, to examine the short-term effectiveness of D.A.R.E.®'s core curriculum. The researchers also compared the effectiveness of D.A.R.E.® to other school-based substance abuse prevention programs.

*For the purposes of this study, substance abuse was defined as use of marijuana, alcohol, and tobacco by school-age children. D.A.R.E.® targets multiple drugs, including alcohol and tobacco.

The full report, *Past and Future Directions of the D.A.R.E.® Program: An Evaluation Review*, by Christoper L. Ringwalt et al., is available from the National Criminal Justice Reference Service, at 800-851-3420.

Source: Editors. CJ the Americas (Office of International Justice, University of Illinois at Chicago, 1995). Vol. 8, No. 1, February–March 1995, p. 15.

We must recognize, however, that each new emphasis has been superimposed upon and added to the earlier ones. Thus, the present network of services can become a bewildering combination of all the functions mentioned. The nature of the "mix" in security management modalities has varied greatly by type of organization. Figures 7–2 and 7–3 describe some of the major tendencies for placing the security function within the hierarchy of an organization.

How the role of security is seen in an organization is often determined by where this function is placed on the organization chart. How deeply the security program is buried below the level of policy making can determine the impact security can have on the operations (and profits) of the company. The security manager should strive to place the function at a level that has as much access to the presidential or vice presidential level as possible. In most companies, however, the security function is placed at one of three levels, as shown in Figure 7–2:

1. *Departmental level*, with direct access to the top policy-making levels of the company. This is the most preferred level for security since it gives the security function a high profile and professional status.

2. *Division level*, with the security manager reporting to a functional director. This is a common model, but very dependent on which functional department security reports to.

3. *Any level below divisional*, which seriously impairs the security function's ability to make any real impact on company policy. This is the least preferred positioning for security.[20]

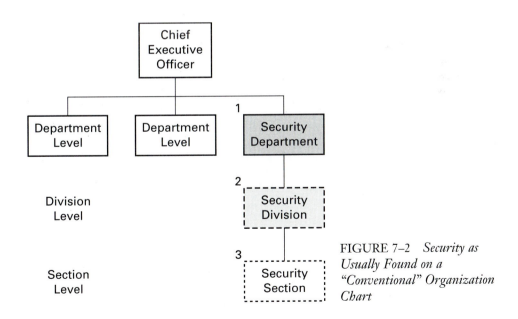

FIGURE 7–2 *Security as Usually Found on a "Conventional" Organization Chart*

FIGURE 7–3 *Contract Security on a "Conventional" Organization Chart*

As shown by Figure 7–3, the same kind of logic should be applied to the contract security organizational placement as well. These are shown in the standard "wiring diagram" type of organization chart, which finds their basis in the concept of a fixed bureaucracy with discrete levels of power and authority. There are, however, interesting contradictions and reversals of these tendencies, along with possible variations to these rigid positionings, which we will discuss later in this chapter.

INFLUENCE OF THE ORGANIZATIONAL ENVIRONMENT

The traditional nineteenth century factory (the archetype of all early business organizations) was a total autocracy. Its single purpose was to produce their product. To accomplish this, it developed a rigid and highly stratified hierarchy along the lines of a military organization. This lead to the rigid, bureaucratic models for organizing described earlier. Authority and status for any security guard operation (proprietary or contract) were related to the lowest levels in the organizations and were usually military style rank, from the captain, to the lieutenant, to the sergeant, to the guard. Each separate security operation became its own small kingdom, and the captain became the king.

Staff tend to be highly protective of this structure, holding to the closely defined prerequisites and prerogatives attached by custom to the various positions and levels. Power was entrenched in those who contributed to the production of the goods or services that described the main purpose of the corporate entity. Changes in emphases, as well as reorganization of many businesses and other corporations within the last few decades, have added another kind of hierarchy, the nonoperational personnel, to the framework of business organizations. A department director for accounting, for example, with a battery of professional and specialized services, has often been given formal authority and position equal to those of the operational department heads. The special authority connected with worker function and specialization was fitted into the structure alongside the traditional authority of rank and seniority held by operational personnel. These trends led to major redistributions of power and authority in the formal organization and resulted stresses and adjustments in the informal organization when resource distribution was related to peripheral duties—such as security.

In addition, these developments have tended to confuse and compound the expanded number of environments in which to make decisions and restrict choices that would be made by other administrators. This environment has changed drastically for security organizations as they have evolved from the traditional forms and structures to a more responsible role in the overall corporate mission.

In the authoritarian organization, all significant decisions were made at, or very near, the top of the hierarchy. Moreover, these decisions were made according to simple and well-understood **standard operating procedures** (SOPs). Such values as good control, safety, and security began to have a concrete quality unlike vague prescriptions such as "just increase efficiency and the company will prosper."

One effect of adding more complex and nebulous criteria to the administrator's decision-making matrix has been to force the actual making of decisions downward toward the lowest level of functional operations. The more difficulty that administrators have encountered in harmonizing operational and support values into statements of policy and procedure, the more they have left to their subordinates the responsibility for making significant decisions.

Characteristics of Security Management

Three pervasive themes have run through security management. First, the goals of physical security and protection have helped keep the vision of the security guard as another form of military or police tactical operation, different from the rest of the organization. In this viewpoint, orders were given to the security captain, and it was expected that the "chain of command" in the security operation would take the appropriate actions to do the job. This developed into an attribute, earned or unearned, of the security manager as a small cog in the big wheel of the corporate mission, one that simply did what it was told and had no input into the process. This we could call the "night watchman" theme.

A second persistent attribute of security management has been a gradualist approach to program development and change. This approach has been characterized by a somewhat frivolous subscription to "new" ideas and generally nonrigorous, non-scientific rules of thumb for determining what to delete from the old system and what to add to it. The predominant conservatism of security system managers has militated against deviations from familiar ways and has led to tokenism in the launching of new technologies and management styles for the "old guard."

Security administrators are not so much responsible for this condition as they are victims of two realities: (1) society's uncertainty about the causes and solutions of the crime problem, and (2) the present inability of social science and research to provide a solid frame of reference for considering alternative courses of action and estimating their consequences. Nevertheless, in any effort to understand how security managers might be more effective innovators, it is necessary to confront the difficulties and frustration that currently surround the process of change.

Incrementalism as an organizational goal can be described as the problem with navigation of two different ships. It is clear that a very long ship (say, a 1000-foot supertanker) can be turned around 180 degrees only very slowly, whereas a short boat (such as a 16-foot speedboat) can be turned almost in its own length. If one tries to turn a supertanker too quickly in a channel, it can easily be run up on the rocks, as happened to the *Exxon Valdez* in Alaska's Prince William Sound. An organization with a long history of autocratic methods is like the long supertanker; it must change its course in short and carefully planned steps and stay on each of those new courses long enough to see if they are effective.

Numerous small-scale examples of change in security organization and programming do run counter to the general pattern we have described. Some experimental programs have been firmly supported by theoretical premises and have been evaluated objectively. Some security administrators and consultants have tried to make change additive rather than fragmentary. Some executives in the system have attempted to move toward change along relatively rational lines while still coping skillfully with a plethora of "irrational" forces in their environments. It is this growing edge of innovation, of improved dissemination of knowledge, and of close connection between discovery and implementation of technique that offers hope for gains in the future. We could refer to this as the theme of "incremental change."

The third and final theme, which has its roots in the "security culture" of the past and still runs through security management today, is the syndrome of isolationism and withdrawal. This condition has helped conceal from other parts of the corporate organization, and the public, the realities of security roles and missions and has thus acted to perpetuate stereotypes and myths. Security forces and operations were, after all, designed and implemented to prevent criminals from attacking the persons, places, and things of both public and private entities. Security administrators found it expedient to honor that mandate. Whereas the police tend to publicize aggressively their views of crime and punishment, the leaders of security tend to avoid public debate, particularly debate centering on controversial issues.

This tendency has had serious consequences. The security field has had limited success in developing corporate or public understanding and support for needed changes. Simplistic or erroneous conceptions of the nature of crime and its prevention have flourished, partly because there have not been effective spokespeople for more sophisticated interpretations, especially at times of "opportunity" when conflict or crisis has awakened the interest of an otherwise apathetic public. This theme we can refer to as the "turtle syndrome," in which security managers keep their heads inside their shells to keep from getting criticized or losing what little they already have.

PRESSURES TOWARD INTEGRATION OF SERVICES

One of the most important developments in American security over the past three decades has been a movement toward the centralization and **integration of services**, along with enhanced public–private cooperation, in some of the more progressive systems. The concept of a coordinated security system possessing a variety of innovative services was in direct contradiction to the historical pattern in which the head of each sector reigned almost as a monarch, typically under the large umbrella of security and crime prevention.

Generally, most of the significant innovations in security practice have occurred within professional, centralized administrative systems whose parts were related through a coherent framework of policy and whose programs were implemented through planning, research, and varied staff services. The field of security needs more unification.

Yet, although centralization of security services within organizations has been a major trend, the security services of the nation as a whole remain balkanized. Different levels of organizations operate the same services. There are schisms between organizational facilities and locations for individualized programs. The security field is still undecided whether a single administrator can provide more effective management for security systems and programs. It is still uncertain, for example, whether the administration of field services should be controlled by the managers that make security decisions or by the departmental structures that administer operational services. We suggest that there are alternative ways to look at security services that not only give security a greater status in the organization but are more effective. Figure 7–4 looks at security in regard to representative activities that affect every aspect and program in the company.

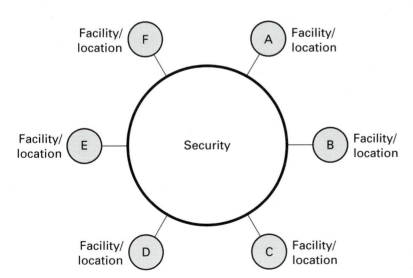

FIGURE 7–4 *Security as a Facility/Location Model*

In a large company, these may be accomplished by different sections of the security program; in a small company, they may all be accomplished by the same person. The important thing to remember is that all these activities affect all departments and facilities/locations in any size or kind of company. It is much more logical to centralize all these activities under a single security program than to spread such activities throughout the company and the resulting duplication and inefficiency.

This simple concept is yet another way to show the overlapping that occurs when you view security as a central factor rather than a peripheral area in a company's operations and activities. Explored as a total team effort for the company, security becomes a vital part of all facilities, departments, and activities. Further evolution of this concept will be shown later in the chapter. First, we must look at the role of evolving management science in security.

SECURITY AND THE DEVELOPMENT OF A SCIENCE OF MANAGEMENT

As security has evolved and changed, producing new styles of management and proliferating new environments for administrators, so also have there been pervasive changes in theories of formal organization and in concepts related to administration leadership and behavior. The evolution of security management has moved along pathways that run generally parallel to this larger movement.

The organizational structure of the contract and proprietary security operations across the United States is quite varied, as might be imagined. There are some common characteristics, however. Because most security operations are managed by former law enforcement or military officers, with the major emphasis generally on *enforcement* rather than on *prevention*, these former officers impose their own background and personal orientation on the treatment of staff and offenders; more often than not, their approach is at odds with advanced organizational philosophy.

Modern management techniques have had a hard time gaining acceptance in a security system that was a closed and total autocracy for more than 100 years. It is not hard to understand that security directors of the 1950s would seldom have the desire or characteristics to become the security managers of the 1990s if they had to give up the absolute control they had held in the past. Systems in transition have made it difficult for these leaders, many of whom came up through the ranks of security staff, to change easily. The complexities of the modern security management mission, with a broad range of security staff that is often better educated and more attuned to the needs of a complex organization, are a major difficulty for the "new" *security manager* role. Budgets, accountability, planning, personnel issues, legal issues, and many other knotty problems make the job hard to deal with.

In an era of shrinking treasuries and rapidly growing security risks, the major problem for the security administrator seems to be able to do more and more with less and less. The educational needs for the upper-level management in security continue to grow. It will not be long before the security administrator will find himself or herself having to complete an MBA or an MPA degree in order to deal with these increasingly complex issues. When even a relatively small business puts a multimillion-dollar budget

While robotics are helping security do the job—the human element will always need management and leadership.

Photo courtesy Cybermotion

in the hands of the security manager, it seems essential that the profession rethink the needs of staff at all levels, but especially those of the security manager.

A New Way to Look at Security's Role in the Organization

We have seen that security has been relegated to a number of roles and placements in most organizations. We now examine some new ways to view security's role, a role that takes place in reality but is seldom described it such terms. As shown in Figure 7–5, security can be looked upon as the hub around which the organization revolves. Every facility or location is touched by the spokes of security. It is very important to view security as a "central" part of an organization rather than as a "box" buried deep in some unrelated department. If management thinks of the security program as another major **profit center**, one that affects every facility and functional location in the company—by prevention of losses, recovery and protection of assets, and safety of personnel—they develop a much different appreciation of the security task. In the

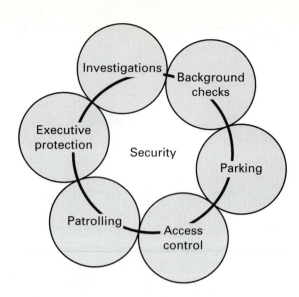

FIGURE 7–5 *Security as Seen in*
Regard to Activities

model shown in Figure 7–5, it is easy to see that security is a constant factor at all locations and facilities of the enlightened corporate entity.

Figure 7–6 shows the ultimate evolution of viewing security's function in any corporate structure—as a departmental partner. Security is the single function that affects every departmental function in an organization. Whether the company is a large multinational giant or a small local business, the various departments have vulnerabilities and risks that can be properly assessed and addressed only by the security function. This applies to the one-person security program or a massive force of personnel and equipment. Once management is able to see that security programs and

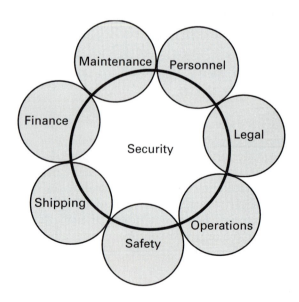

FIGURE 7–6 *Security as a*
Departmental Partner

their personnel can touch every department in the company, security's role can be easily enhanced and enlarged to handle many of the departmental concerns that cannot be addressed by their 9-to-5 staff and employees.

This simple concept is shown by several overlapping areas in a typical company that can be explored as a total team effort:

- *Maintenance* needs to know where to find potential problems, such as system failures, damaged equipment, and breakdowns. These become partnership missions that can be accomplished only by trained security staff.

- *Shipping* needs to be on the lookout for theft, fraud, and waste that can become another partnership mission for security.

- *Personnel* needs help to do preemployment screening and follow-up, investigation of allegations of theft or drug abuse, and other partnership missions to ensure the quality of company personnel.

- *Safety* needs to have all the eyes and ears it can find to protect the personnel and facilities from injury, damage, and litigation. This is not only a function that works well for a partnership mission, but a function that has been moving under the control of security in many companies.

All the other departments (in addition to the brief sample in Figure 7–6) of the company should find clear *value* in the security task if they are shown how it can be

---

S E C U R I T Y   B Y T E   7 – 1

Crime Costs Victims $450 Billion Annually

Crime, according to a federal agency's guesswork, costs the U.S. about $450 billion annually, when counting tangibles such as lost wages, medical expenses and property loss and intangibles such as pain and suffering.

According to the National Institute of Justice, *crime costs about $425 per man, woman and child in the United States, or a total of about $105 billion in lost wages, medical expenses and property losses.* When the values of emotional pain, suffering and the risk of death to victims are factored in, crime costs victims an additional $345 billion each year.

"These findings add substantially to our knowledge about crime victimization, particularly the heavy price victims pay," says NIJ Director Jeremy Travis.

In arriving at their estimates of the number of crimes, the researchers used data from the FBI's Uniform Crime Reports (UCR) and the Bureau of Justice Statistics's National Criminal Victimization Survey (NCVS). Intangible costs were translated into dollar figures by using a method commonly employed in civil damage lawsuits.

Source: O'Toole-Zalud Report. "Crime Costs Victims $450 Billion Annually," *Security* (Cahners Publishing Company. Newton, MA, 1996), Vol. 33, No. 5, p. 84.

achieved. This is a preferred way to describe the security function to management, regardless of the type of company or its size. All potential security managers need to use this description to show that security can be a profit center that is considered so not by what it makes for the company, but for what it prevents or recovers for every department in the company.

Summary

Security administrators will face a series of challenging tasks at the end of the twentieth century, and into the twenty-first. It is clear that the kinds of activities for which they must provide security and loss prevention have changed drastically, both in the level of violent behavior and in the response to it. The security administrator has also been alerted to certain threats and vulnerabilities and countermeasures for them. It sometimes appears that every step forward is counteracted by two steps back.

Modern management techniques have had a hard time gaining acceptance in a system that has been a somewhat closed and autocratic, military-style system for several centuries. It is not hard to understand why the "guard captains" of the 1950s would seldom want to become the "security managers" of the 1990s if they had to give up the absolute control they had held in the past. Systems in transition have made it difficult for these leaders to change easily, many of whom came up through the ranks of the security guard. The complexities of the modern technology of security, such as dealing with a broad range of nonsecurity staff who are often better educated and more attuned to the needs of a complex organization, are major difficulties for the "new" role of security manager. Budgets, accountability, planning, personnel issues, legal issues, and many other knotty problems also make this new role hard for the "old-timer" to deal with.

Despite these problems facing the security manager, there are hopeful signs of progress. Administration's disenchantment with the police-type security "guard" ("Make my day!") as a solution to the problems of security and loss prevention has caused a general movement toward the "security officer" approach ("Have a nice day!"). This in turn has stimulated a general upgrading of security personnel, accompanied by a movement toward professionalism and collective action by both security and other staffs such as fire prevention, safety, risk management, and facilities.

REVIEW QUESTIONS

1. Who was the "father" of scientific management, and what were his main points?
2. Explain the characteristics of a participative-consultative manager.
3. Explain the difference between assets protection and loss prevention.
4. How does incrementalism apply to the development of security management?
5. What can a security manager do to show that security can be considered a profit center?

TERMS TO REMEMBER

scientific management

informal organization

rational-economic

consensus

synergism

exploitive-authoritative

benevolent-authoritative

participative-consultative

participative-group

model muddle

assets protection

loss prevention

security management

integrated partnership

standard operating
procedures

incrementalism

integration of services

profit center

ENDNOTES

1. William C. Cunningham, John J. Strauchs, and Clifford W. Van Meter, *Private Security Trends: 1970 to 2000: The Hallcrest Report II* (Boston: Butterworth-Heinemann, 1990), p 175.

2. Ibid., p 175.

3. Frederick W. Taylor, *The Principles of Scientific Management* (New York: Harper, 1911).

4. For a series of papers illustrating and testifying to this point of view, see Robert Dubin, *Human Relations in Administration* (Englewood Cliffs, N.J.: Prentice-Hall, 1951).

5. Fritz J. Roethliesberger and William J. Dickson, *Management and the Worker* (Cambridge, Mass.: Harvard University Press, 1939).

6. Daniel Katz and Robert L. Kahn, *The Social Psychology of Organizations* (New York: John Wiley, 1966).

7. Douglas McGregor, *The Human Side of Enterprise* (New York: McGraw-Hill, 1960).

8. Chris Argyris, *Integrating the Individual and the Organization* (New York: John Wiley, 1964).

9. Rensis Likert, *New Patterns of Management* (New York: McGraw-Hill, 1961).

10. Edgar H. Schein, *Organizational Psychology* (Englewood Cliffs, N.J.: Prentice-Hall, 1965).

11. Abraham H. Maslow, *Motivation and Personality* (New York: Harper & Row, 1954).

12. Likert, pp. 223–234.

13. Ibid., p. 234.

14. Office of Development, Testing and Dissemination, *Putting Research to Work: Tools for the Criminal Justice Professional* (Washington, D.C.: U.S. Department of Justice, 1984).

15. Eric Poole and Robert Regoli, "Professionalism, Role Conflict, Work Alienation and Anomia," *Social Science Journal* (San Francisco, CA.: Sage, 1989), pp. 323–340.

16. John Shuiteman, "Playing the Numbers Game: Analysis Can Help Determine Manpower Requirements," *Corrections Today*, Vol. 49 (1987), pp. 40–42.

17. Frances Cheek and Marie Di Stefano Miller, "Reducing Staff and Inmate Stress," *Corrections Today*, Vol. 44 (1982), pp. 72–76, 78.

18. American Correctional Association, "After Atlanta and Oakdale: ACA Pays Tribute to Federal Officials, Staff," *Corrections Today*, Vol. 50 (1988), pp. 26, 64.

19. Ibid., p. 66.

20. C. Simonsen, *Building a More Successful Security Program* (Vancouver, B.C.: STA Publications, 1992), p. ix.

8

Risk Analysis

THE HEART AND SOUL OF SECURITY AND LOSS PREVENTION

> *The concept of relative foreseeability reflects the standard practice among private security professionals of conducting 'risk assessments' on everything from rare events like terrorism to common events like employee theft. The goal of such risk assessments is to produce a precise estimate of the risks of a certain type of crime to an organization or individual in specified places and time periods.*
>
> —Lawrence W. Sherman

Overview

There is an old saying in the security of nuclear weapon sites that states "99% security is *no* security." Although very few industrial, manufacturing, or retail operations require the levels of security employed at nuclear weapon sites, the principle is still the same. The *risk* to targets or assets (operations, personnel, and products) of a given operation is determined by the presence of a known threat that is difficult to predict in its timing or impact. One of the most important roles of the security manager is to identify the level of risk and then design ways to counteract the probable threats. This is not simply a physical security approach, but an integrated approach that examines the physical, operational, and managerial methods that create risk and can also be used to counteract them.

Crime and natural disasters are considered to fall into the category of *pure risks*, those that seem to have great loss potential and seldom any benefits. Liability from failure to protect customers, visitors, and others who may visit the premises of a facility is another form of pure risk, perhaps the most costly of all risks in most cases. On the other hand, both losses and benefits might accrue from certain management decisions that calculate the potential losses and provide the acceptable level of security that seems to offer more benefit than cost. These kinds of risks are generally called *dynamic risks* since the amount of loss depends upon the kinds of decisions made by the management team. Both types of risk must be approached in a logical and systematic manner that addresses the roles of administration and personnel, as well as the physical actions required.

What Is Risk Assessment?

Risk assessment lies at the heart of any viable and effective security operation. Without a clear picture of what it is you wish to protect and the impact on the organization from its loss, you cannot develop a program of safeguards that gives you some assurance of its workability. **Risk**, as shown by Figure 8–1, is the sum of the interaction of *probability*, *vulnerability*, and *threat*. Each of these must be considered in your evaluation of a security program.

The first step in **risk assessment** is to observe the conduct of operations, policies and procedures, physical security, traffic flow, and other activities over several periods and at different times of the day and night. This will provide a basis of understanding for later surveys, without any possible attempts at creating "protective smokescreens" to cover up problems by expecting the team to arrive. These initial observations would not be covert, simply unannounced. These observations and detailed surveys and examination of records allow one to conduct a reasonable risk assessment comprising the following four elements:

1. *Risk:* What are the assets that can be damaged, stolen, or lost? For example, there is little risk of someone stealing a mainframe computer, but perhaps it could be seriously and expensively damaged if access to its location is not properly controlled.

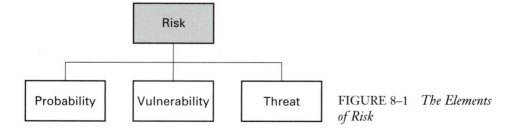

FIGURE 8–1   *The Elements of Risk*

A personal computer may not be very expensive, but if it is the only one available to the activity using it, the impact from its loss may be high. All the risks must be balanced against the second factor, vulnerability.

2. *Vulnerability:* How difficult is it to get to the assets of high risk identified by the survey? If your parking areas are unlighted at night, customers, visitors, and corporate personnel are vulnerable to robbery and sexual assault. Conversely, if high-cost retail items, such as diamonds, are stored in a vault inside a limited-access room of the facility, it lowers their vulnerability and may require little or no corrective action. Even vulnerability, however, must be weighed against the third factor, probability.

3. *Probability:* What are the chances that an attack on personnel or other assets will ever happen? This will be determined by an examination of frequency patterns of various incidents as reported by the police, and others. Clearly, it is not necessary to develop an emergency plan for flooding if the facility is atop a well-drained hill that is 200 feet above the deepest flood ever recorded. However, if there are reports of damages and break-in losses three or four times a week in your parking areas, greater security is probably called for. In an extreme example, if a serial killer has been assaulting and killing young women in the area, it would be prudent to develop procedures to better protect your female customers, visitors, and staff. How you deal with the risk–vulnerability–probability triad results in cost-effective decisions. This allows you to develop effective countermeasures, actions that are balanced against the threat.

4. *Countermeasures:* These are the ultimate reason for all the risk assessment activity and determine what you can do given the resources available. **Countermeasures**

are based on the interrelationship of the preceding factors, as well as management decisions, operational necessity, cost, and common sense. In one example, where unauthorized persons are taking goods from a retail facility, you could initiate an extensive screening and access system that delays each person twenty minutes before entering a shop—and customers will leave in frustration while waiting for access. The thefts will stop, but the retail business will fold. On the other hand, if items such as jewelry or guns are kept in a less-than-secure area, you do not simply put up a sign that says "Valuable Goods Inside—Stay Out." The selected countermeasures should be affordable, simple, and balanced against an identified *threat*, which is a combination of all these factors.

Risk analysis allows you to design countermeasures that are effective but do not interfere with the operations of the business. Examination of all these factors allows management to make decisions that balance cost versus the level of protection, as shown by the analysis done in Figure 8–2.

As noted by Gion Green, one has to consider that "The dollar loss is not simply the cost of the items, but also includes: (1) replacement cost, (2) temporary replacement, (3) downtime, (4) discounted cash, and (5) insurance rate changes."[1] Examples of these categories highlight the *criticality* of each item in your security planning:

1. Replacement cost: In most cases, the product or material needed to replace the item will cost more to replace than the item that was lost, so you have the loss of the item *plus* the increased cost of present value. (For example, widgets that were bought in the spring for sale in the summer and were stolen from the store now cost 15 percent more from the supplier.)

FIGURE 8–2 *Cost Versus Level of Protection*

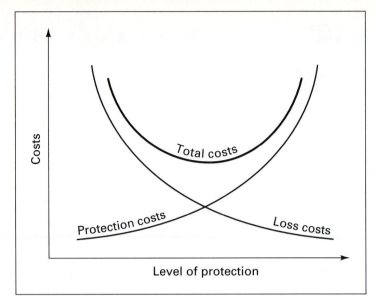

Source: Adapted from Statsföretag AB, Skandia Insurance Co. and Skandia Risk Management Ltd., Stockholm, Sweden.

2. Temporary replacement: If a critical piece of equipment or system is vandalized and is unusable until repaired, the cost of the repairs must be added to the cost of the leased or rented equipment. (For example, if a computer system is down for several weeks, the system must be replaced by a rental while the old system is being repaired.) This can also apply to key personnel who are injured or lost through criminal acts, a very costly replacement.

3. Downtime: A critical item that is damaged, lost, or destroyed may be the very item that can shut your operation down completely. The downtime can result in not only the cost of repair or replacement but also the loss of business during that period, and even payment of staff with no return. (For example, a shipping company has a large vessel that has been tied up at the dock for three weeks, with a full crew on board, because the boilers were sabotaged by a disgruntled employee.)

4. Discounted cash: Because it is essential to get back into operation or production as soon as possible, the company may have to borrow short-term money at much higher rates than normal. (For example, a specialized manufacturer must have a piece of equipment that was lost by theft replaced as soon as possible and must pay a premium on loaned dollars in order to expedite the process.) The lender does a risk assessment, too.

5. Insurance rate changes: If a company has similar losses over time, and fails to take the necessary action to correct this, most insurance carriers would consider the policyholder a bad risk. (For example, a store has been robbed several times, but has taken no action to do a risk analysis and initiate some reasonable countermeasures to harden the target.) The potential for negligence suits also increases and could result in even larger losses from litigation.

EXAMINATION OF LOSSES/INCIDENTS

A proper risk analysis covers a systematic examination of information and activities that can be used to develop countermeasures. The first thing that needs to be determined is what has been happening in the past. If the present countermeasures seem to be doing the job, you might leave well enough alone. However, if current countermeasures do not seem to be doing the job, through an examination of loss and incident reports, shift records, investigations, police files, and news reports, combined with informational interviews with personnel at all levels, you can develop a broad picture of what is really happening and infer some correlations that may identify patterns not otherwise apparent.

ENTRANCE CONTROL AND ACCESS SYSTEMS

How do you enter and exit the areas that may need to be secured? Traffic data about pedestrian and vehicular movement must be collected for analysis and development of a clear picture of where access controls might be modified to better match what is actually happening in each area. Combined with the previous actions, a more rational set of strategies can be developed to develop intelligent routing and monitoring of traffic to reduce probabilities of incidents and losses or easy escape routes. Key and lock controls, placement of high-security locking devices, electronic access cards to track personnel and record access (if needed), and designation of areas restricted to those with actual need to be there can be determined by this type of traffic survey.

SECURITY STRUCTURE AND NETWORKING

The way a security force is organized and equipped can have a favorable or drastically negative impact upon the cost and effectiveness of its operations. Personnel costs constitute the major share of any security budget, and these costly assets must be as efficiently and effectively as possible. The age, training, salary, and experience of the security personnel must also be considered because adequately paid and well-trained security staff can do much more with fewer people. Determining the correct staffing will require a detailed review of the survey results and consultation with the parties concerned. How this force networks with the local law enforcement agencies, and with the rest of the organization, can greatly enhance the effectiveness.

POLICIES AND PROCEDURES

The Achilles' heel of most security operations is the lack of a formal and current **policy and procedure** manual. Many security operations operate with little or no overall *policy* guidance from either the security provider or the client's administration. This causes actions to become merely reactive and seldom proactive. With clear policy statements from the corporate administration, proprietary or contract security providers can develop, publish, and revise a strong set of *procedures* to implement predetermined guidelines. A number of software programs are available that will help security managers develop their own policy and procedure manual. Security policy is usually extracted from overall administrative policies that are already in writing, or derived

The Do's, Don'ts, Dollars and Demands For Security Consulting

Outsourcing. Downsizing. Rightsizing and reengineering.

To keep pace with a dynamic workforce, security decision makers must maximize manpower—and that includes smart use of security consultants.

Some 50 percent of major U.S. corporations cut jobs last year, says the New York-based American Management Association, but many are creating new, technical or market-driven jobs that are often redefined: temporary full-time positions, flex-time, independently contracted. The U.S. Labor Department estimates that about 13 percent of the workforce today is in some form of contingent, contracted or temporary job.

Such a contracted workforce isn't exactly new to security, where 60 percent of job positions are contracted out, according to U.S. Labor Department figures. What is new is the broadening scope, the detailed range of specialties and the higher-level role that contracted consultants are continuing to play. Experts agree: security consulting can be a valuable management asset to draw upon as you need specific expertise or geographic representation.

Background Check

Security consulting services generally fall into three areas: expert litigation, auditing and general management. Some experts cut across all areas.

As premises liability grows into a hefty chunk of tort law, security auditing and management consultants often join the ranks of forensic expert witnesses.

The larger audit and review body of consultants is schooled in physical security issues. A subset—design and technical specialists—

engineers, designs or reviews systems, bridging the gap between audits and protection. A smaller group is more management focused, developing programs, reorganizing departments or serving in lieu of a full time security director.

Some investigators may bill themselves as investigative consultants, which allows them to skirt state licensing required for private investigators. Licensed or not, they delivery everything from background checks to due diligence searches in a merger.

Security Outsourcing Grows Up

Research shows that businesses most often hire security consultants for specialized expertise. But the market is changing and consultants are joining forces to deliver one-stop shopping of a broad range of services.

California-based Pinkerton Security Services is a good example. After its 1988 acquisition by CPP, Pinkerton committed to expand quality and service beyond its bread-and-butter business of contracted officers. The near billion-dollar company's strategic partnering with Whirlpool Corp., Benton Harbor, Mich., shows the concept of comprehensive consulting and services at work.

"Whirlpool has gone through massive expansion in just a few years," says corporate security director Lynn mattice. "We've expanded rapidly with new ventures in Latin America and Europe, and in 1995 grew from 900 to more than 11,000 employees in Asia alone. I have tremendous global security requirements and I need to leverage them."

A long-term strategic partnership with Pinkerton is helping Whirlpool gain that leverage, allowing it to benefit from Pinkerton's global presence and expansion into technical, investigative and management consulting.

The Do's, Don'ts, Dollars and Demands For Security Consulting

"They're reviewing our entire North American operations, matrixing my technical requirements, assessing hardware and software on the market and recommending a consolidated system," Mattice says.

Overall, he estimates the approach will cost about $2 million, including systems—an investment that will pay for itself in less than a year from reduced guard and third-party alarm monitoring costs.

"Consulting has always been an element at Pinkerton," says Jerry Guibord, Pinkerton's senior manager of consulting and design ser-

Workforce Reduction Rationale: Where Consultants Can Make a Difference

Business down	73%
Improved staff utilization	34%
Transfer of work or production	10%
Merger/ acquisition	9%
Automation/new technology	8%
Plant or office obsolescence	4%

Source: American Management Association

Constant shifts and cuts in the labor force put pressure on managers to do more with less—contracting security consultants can help.

vices. "It's become more formalized in recent years with a long-term and proactive vision."

But the bulk of businesses don't have Whirlpool's muscle to leverage single-source supply. In an unpublished study of Bay Area businesses conducted at California State University at Haywood, only companies with upwards of $900 million in assets and revenues have formalized, developed, full-time security departments, programs and staffing. Businesses around $500 million begin to get those programs underway. And those between $50 million and $250 million register growing loss prevention concerns, but haven't pushed a full-scale security initiative.

For such companies, independent security consultants are joining forces to net big-business benefits. The Strategic Consortium International, for example, is a recently formed multi-disciplined association of consultants providing a one-stop network of both general management and highly specialized expertise. And the continued collaborations of the International Association of Professional Security Consultants further encourages networked supply.

"We're moving to a world of the virtual company. We already have fewer hierarchical structures in business. Teams are at the core and outsourced services play on the team," Guibord says.

If we are in fact approaching a seamless, "virtual corporation," few of us will be left commuting to the office anyway. Making better use of consultants is more timely than ever.

Source: Kerry Lydon. "The Do's, Don'ts, Dollars and Demands for Security Consulting." *Security* (Cahners Publishing Company. Newton, MA, 1996), Vol. 33, No. 7, special insert—pp. 1–2.

through interviews and observation. Also needed in this process is a survey of the laws, regulations, and rules that apply to particular activities at the state and local levels.

PHYSICAL SECURITY

The purpose of physical security devices and procedures is to **deter, detect, divert, delay**, or **deny** (the "five Ds") access to sensitive areas of the secured operations and facilities. A physical security survey will determine which of these results are accomplished by current physical barriers and methods, then recommend a more effective use of these physical methods or suggest others. Physical barriers include fences, traffic barriers, exterior doors, and so on, and are generally aimed at reducing the use of costly manned posts.

MONITORING, COMMUNICATIONS, COMPUTERS, SURVEILLANCE

Use of monitoring of specific areas through roving patrols, towers, or closed circuit television (CCTV) is aimed at detecting and preventing criminal activity or other threats before they can occur. Communications are critical to any operation and especially those that are widely dispersed. Communications should be geared for both internal transmissions and coordination with outside agencies or key personnel. Communications can also involve ways for personnel in identified high-risk areas to communicate distress, duress, or emergency conditions back to a security central location. Computers and other critical equipment must also be secured and protected (as well as the data), and security personnel must know how to secure the hardware and software. Surveillance can let security determine what is really occurring in the facility and take action to develop appropriate countermeasures.

PERSONNEL SCREENING

This involves the hiring process for the entire operation, as well as the security department itself. The security department can become a valuable aid to the personnel department by developing methods of verifying critical issues that would preclude an individual's employment (drug abuse, criminal record, and so on) or result in his or her dismissal. As mentioned before, standards for security personnel should be very high and far above the average. Paper and pencil tests for detecting dishonesty and drug use are now available and effective as screening devices. Close coordination with law enforcement agencies can result in excellent ways to find out about individual criminal records as well as ongoing problems.

ALARM SYSTEMS

An analysis of threats to personnel and properties could result in recommending alarm systems for specified areas and monitoring for procedures and responses. The use of alarms must be carefully identified by the outcomes of the risk analysis of each facility. Alarms are of little benefit if there is no clear method for rapid and appropriate response to them.

SECURITY HARDWARE

This involves an analysis of all equipment that can be logically identified and classified as specific for security operations. The effectiveness of such equipment can be maximized only if security personnel are trained in their use and the equipment is appropriate to the threat.

EMERGENCY PLANS AND OPERATIONS

It is essential that the security department become involved with the prioritization and production of emergency plans. These plans should be based on the probability of occurrence of such emergencies as fire, disorder or civil disturbance, major accidents, natural disasters, or criminal activities. Emergency plans should have clear notification chains, lines of authority, and coordination checklists for outside agencies. They should also involve regular practice alerts. Many other threats may be determined that depend on identified levels of crime and violence in the area.

DECISION MAKING BASED ON A COMPLETED RISK ASSESSMENT

Once the necessary surveys have been conducted, the security manager and the management team have a number of options available that are based on the cost-benefit for general and specific countermeasures. These alternatives are affected by overall management policies, available funds, and whether the risk in some cases must be considered a part of the cost of doing business (see Figure 8–3).

ACCEPTANCE

It must be recognized that not all risks can be eliminated completely, nor should all risks be countered by measures that may be more costly than the items being secured. Careful cost–benefit analysis will allow some risks to be accepted as too remote to be worth the cost or effort to protect it.

AVOIDANCE

In this solution, the target that is at risk is either eliminated or removed, or the responsibility is transferred to another facility or operation. In this last case, the risk can be high or low, but it no longer matters because the target of the threat has been eliminated completely. (If the company is using a highly toxic substance in its manufacturing process, one that presents great exposure to liability, it may be best to seek a different process and eliminate such a high-risk operation.)

DIFFUSION

This takes the target of the risk and, where possible, spreads the risk by locating the target at more than one site so that loss of one does not result in loss of all. (If your company has all its computing equipment in one spot, and loss would paralyze the company, it would be wise to have several smaller computer centers that are networked.)

FIGURE 8–3 *The Risk Cycle*

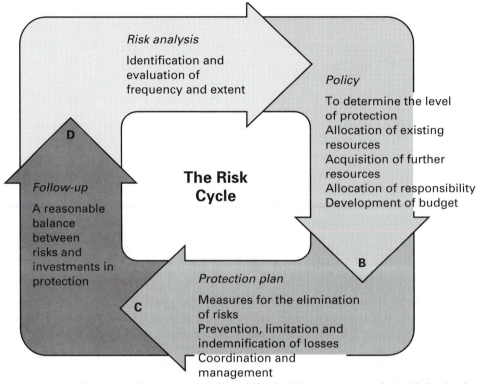

Risk analysis
Identification and evaluation of frequency and extent

Policy
To determine the level of protection
Allocation of existing resources
Acquisition of further resources
Allocation of responsibility
Development of budget

D

The Risk Cycle

Follow-up
A reasonable balance between risks and investments in protection

B

Protection plan
Measures for the elimination of risks
Prevention, limitation and indemnification of losses
Coordination and management

C

Adapted from Statsföretag AB, Skandia Insurance Co. and Skandia Risk Management Ltd., Stockholm, Sweden.

TRANSFER

This generally means to make the cost of loss assumed by another entity, generally an insurance company. Although this provides a certain amount of comfort in marginal cases, the better way to handle risk is elimination wherever possible. Insurance can become very expensive and subject to cancellation if appropriate protective steps are not taken. On the other hand, a professional risk assessment followed by adoption of appropriate countermeasures can provide reduced premiums in most cases. (If the cost of insurance is too high, the company may want to consider self-assumption of the risk to loss of the target by placing an appropriate sum aside for such emergencies.)

REDUCTION

This is the basic reason for risk analysis and security surveys. Risk is reduced by providing the appropriate countermeasures, whether operational or physical, to make it more difficult to threaten the item in risk. Operational policies can change the way things are done to make the risk less probable. Physical methods, combined with valid procedures, can harden the target and accomplish adequate security for the risk. (An access control survey discloses that too many doors are left open to the public and channeling of traffic would be useful.)

The cost effectiveness of security seems always to be in dispute. The difficulty of trying to measure something that never happened (**deterrence**) is much more difficult than measuring the amount of material or product recovered following apprehension of a perpetrator. For this reason, it is essential that risk analysis activity be carefully organized and administered in a professional manner.

Justifying Risk Analysis

When the overall risk assessment has been completed and the supplemental surveys conducted, the results must be carefully reviewed and presented to management. The reasons for the risk assessment should be reviewed and explained in terms of what consequences may incur from ignoring the results and identified risks. As noted by Golsby:

> After all, far more money can be saved by a comprehensive security review [risk assessment] than is spent on its conduct.

But other compelling reasons exist for a company to be subject to a security review. They include the following reasons:

- Obligation to protect personnel and visitors
- Necessity to protect property
- Necessity to protect information
- Legal obligations
- Contractual obligations
- Threat of litigation
- Threat of industrial disputation
- Insurance company requirements
- Moral obligations
- Professional integrity

In the cases listed above, almost all can be reduced to one reason: financial expense. This can take many forms, including the following:

- Replacement cost of equipment
- Repair cost to equipment
- Repair cost to buildings
- Cost of rebuilding
- Loss of revenue due to loss of market edge as a result of information or data loss
- Loss of contracts
- Awarding of damages
- Cost of loss of company time due to industrial disputation
- Increased insurance costs
- Damage to professional reputation or loss of accreditation

When human life is at risk, financial considerations obviously should not take precedence. Therefore, where security has not been reviewed comprehensively, it must not be assumed that the physical well-being of personnel is ensured.[2]

Self-assessment or assessment by an outside consultant can make the security program that it is aimed at provide optimum protection of persons, facilities, and operations and provides great value to the company. How the assessment is presented can determine whether or not management implements its conclusions and recommendations. In some cases, the decision is based on statutory or legislative mandates. In the case of Department of Defense (DOD) contractors, the ***Industrial Security Manual*** (ISM) is clear in regard to self-inspection. In Chapter One, Section Two, Paragraph (1-2068), it states:

> Contractors shall establish a self-inspection program for the purpose of evaluating all security procedures applicable to the facility's operations. Contractors shall review their security system on a continuous basis and shall also conduct a formal self-inspection to occur between inspections conducted by the Defense Investigative Services (DIS), Cognizant Security Office (CSO). At the discretion of Management, the inspection may be conducted by a security representative(s) of the facility or by a home office facility, principal management facility, or cleared parent representative(s). In any event, management shall establish, at an appropriate organizational level, a procedure for evaluating the effectiveness of the self-inspection program. Self-inspection shall consist of an audit of all the facility's operations in light of its Standard Practice Procedures and the requirements of the *ISM*.

> Deficiencies identified as a result of self-inspection shall be corrected promptly. If difficulty is encountered in resolving a deficiency, the DIS will provide assistance on request. A record of the date(s) of the self-inspection shall be maintained until the next formal inspection by the DIS.[3]

This type of *mandatory* direction in regard to a continuing process of risk analysis has a lot of merit in terms of seeing that the process is done and corrections are made. Though the stringent requirements for government security may seem excessive to the normal business or industry, the principles could and should be applied to any security operation. The self-inspection process in a security program can too become easily just another coverup unless management sets high standards and then supports the attainment of them. As Skurecki states: "The old philosophy of not hanging out the dirty linen to view has no place in a sound, self-inspection security program. Security awareness doesn't only include the do's and dont's of quality security practices. It must go beyond compliance to include a well-organized, informative, honest, sincere, and complete security program."[4]

Whether it is called a security review, security assessment, protective security risk review, security audit, or security survey, the *process* of examining the crucial elements of a security program remains the same. These have been amply described by Golbsy:

The **security review** consists of the following four stages:

1. Resource appreciation
2. Threat assessment

3. Risk analysis

4. Identification of weaknesses and recommended solutions

The first stage in conducting a security review—resource appreciation—is to determine exactly what is to be protected. It is pointless to try to improve security without knowing what requires protecting.

The second stage of the security review is the threat assessment. This is a judgment of the probability of an event taking place that could adversely affect an organization's resources, assets, or activities.... Threats can be criminal, such as theft, arson, assault, robbery, or sabotage; terrorist, such as politically motivated attacks; commercial, such as industrial espionage, theft of trade secrets or other proprietary information, or adverse media publicity; or natural disaster, such as fire, flood, wind, or earthquake. The nature and range of the threat to a particular organization also depend on the type of activities and work force the organization engages and its location.

The third stage in the security review is the risk analysis. In this stage, a judgment is reached on the existing security arrangements being able to resist threats identified by the threat assessment. During the site surveys and interviews, information gained concerning the current security arrangements is analyzed together with the threat assessment. This is also a time-consuming process that is best undertaken by appropriately trained personnel and it should identify all the vulnerabilities of an organization.... Risk can be described by the following formula: risk = intention + capability + opportunity.

The final stage in the security review is to identify weaknesses and recommended solutions. This can only be done by trained personnel after the three previous stages have been completed. During the final stage of a security review the assessor can rate the risks and prioritize the threats in descending order of importance. This rating is particularly important, since it indicates where limited resources should be directed to do the most good and assists the assessor in making a judgment whether to accept or transfer the risk or to recommend that resources are assigned to provide protection.[5]

Clearly, there must be some systematic and structured manner to conduct this process in order to ensure that all the bases have been touched. Although there are literally hundreds of checklists and formats for security surveys, we next present a sort of generic format to follow in that process.

THE PHYSICAL SECURITY SURVEY: A QUALITATIVE GENERIC FORMAT

This section provides a framework for a competent and complete security survey that contains and covers all the elements we outlined earlier. This methodology will determine the level of protection required for the various aspects of the operations being surveyed. This is a systematic examination of assets, threats, and vulnerabilities that establishes the probabilities of threats occurring, the cost of losses if they do occur, and the value of the safeguards or countermeasures designed to reduce the threats and vulnerabilities to the operations. This methodology prioritizes the various risk elements in subjective terms and against a baseline of acceptability.

Step one is to develop a survey *plan*, the most important element of any successful venture. This phase should include a strong commitment from the management of the organization to support a professional job, both administratively and financially. During the development of a survey plan, the security manager should (1) select properly qualified and competent persons to become members of the survey team (even if it is necessary to employ consultants in some areas, it is essential to cover all the disciplines involved with the activity being surveyed); (2) develop a team statement about the objectives of the survey and see that it is documented and disseminated; and (3) collect as much background information as possible about the facilities, activities, and operations *before* starting the survey process.

Step two requires determining what elements of the corporate operation are most important to organizational survival. It is essential to determine which ones are vital so that resources can be concentrated on those activities to examine them in the greatest detail. First, a list must be developed that identifies those operations or processes that produce the most benefit to the organization. (Pareto's law states that 20 percent of an organization's operations are responsible for 80 percent of the production. It is this 20 percent that must be identified.) Next, another list must be developed that delineates those activities that are considered most vital to the company's operation, including those that could result in major losses from:

- Fraud, theft, or illegal gain
- Misuse of data or programs resulting in large financial losses
- Miscalculation of payments, benefits, or inventories
- Failure to produce critical items on schedule
- Adverse effects on ongoing operations or life-threatening situations

The last action in this step would be to consolidate the two lists into one *prioritized* list of operations deemed to be the most important to the organization.

Step three identifies, inventories, and evaluates the assets (targets), as defined by the management of the company, that need to be protected in some manner. Such assets would include facilities, machinery, personnel, administrative records, raw materials, products in storage or shipment, computer software and hardware, communications, transportation, and many other targets unique to that company. Replacement cost of these items should be calculated and documented for use in later analyses.

Step four is to identify those threats that might cause the most harm to the facilities, personnel, or operations being surveyed. These threats should be developed from a large number of sources and listed on some type of threat sheet. A sample threat sheet is shown in Figure 8–4.

Step five involves estimating a numerical assessment of associated losses by the impact of that loss if the threat should occur. This is determined by each of the threats

FIGURE 8–4   *Threat Sheet*

Asset/ threat	Impact score	Probability score	Criticality placement
1_____/_____			
2_____/_____			
3_____/_____			

listed, using an impact scale that employs a low-to-high matrix shown in Figure 8–5. This will provide the team with a subjective, but comparable, set of numbers for each threat regarding the impact on the company if that threat occurs.

Step six is to evaluate all the threats listed in terms of the *probability of their occurrence*. Teamwork is essential in this step in order to come up with a useful, synergistic consensus of the probability by rating each threat from low to high probability. After each member of the team assigns a number to each threat from the frequency ranges, the numbers are averaged and assigned an impact score, as shown in Figure 8–6.

FIGURE 8–5   *Loss Evaluation Scale*

Low	Low to medium	Medium	Medium to high	High
1	**2**	**3**	**4**	**5**

FIGURE 8–6   *Impact Scores*

Asset/ threat	Impact score	Probability score	Criticality placement
1. Computers/flood	**1.5**		
2. Computers/theft	**2.3**		
3. Computers/fire	**4.5**		

FIGURE 8–7   *Probability Scores/Criticality*

Asset/ threat	Impact score	Probability score	Criticality placement
1. Computers/flood	1.5	1.7	Low/low (green)
2. Computers/theft	2.3	4.5	Low/high (amber)
3. Computers/fire	4.5	5.0	High/high (red)

These subjective, but synergistic, numbers are then used to plot criticality on the impact–threat axes of the grid shown in Figure 8–7. This process will show graphically where each threat falls by projecting each point from its axis to a point in one of the four sectors of the grid, from low/low to high/high. These impact–threat scores can then be entered on the form as to their numerical values and positioned on the grid, as shown in Figure 8–8.

FIGURE 8–8   *Impact–Probability Matrix*

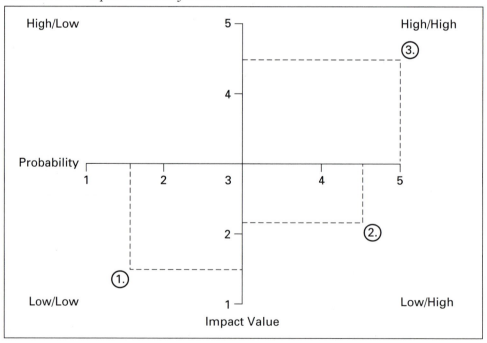

The point at which each threat is plotted can also be placed on a **risk factor determination barometer**, which shows by color zone which threat has the highest priority for detailed and in-depth surveying. Although it is not necessary to use this chart (shown in Figure 8–9), it is a handy graphic for easily explaining survey priorities and actions to the staff.

In *step seven*, the survey team will analyze weaknesses or points of susceptibility in the facilities, operation, and activities. The team will search for weaknesses in administrative, technical, and physical controls that relate to the goals of deterrence, detection, diversion, delay, and denial.

Step eight is the identification of safeguards and countermeasures for each threat considered and the costs associated with their procurement and maintenance. Possible safeguards and countermeasures and their costs can be listed in two columns of a worksheet, as shown in Figure 8–10.

It is possible to list several safeguards or countermeasures for a single threat. Also a single safeguard or countermeasure can reduce the risk to more than one threat. Generally speaking,

FIGURE 8–9   *Risk Factor Determination Barometer*

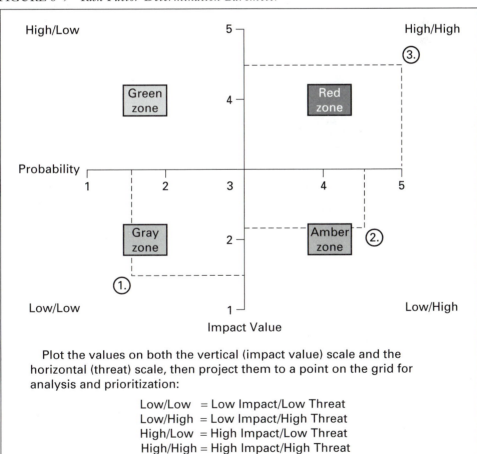

FIGURE 8–10   *Cost Analysis*

Asset/ threat	Criticality placement	Safeguard	Safeguard costs
1. Computers/flood	Low/low (green)	X	$X,000
2. Computers/theft	Low/high (amber)	Y	$XX,000
3. Computers/fire	High/high (red)	Z	$XXX,000

the survey team should first concentrate on those threats that come out in the red or amber zone on the risk factor determination barometer.

In *step nine*, the team conducts a cost–benefit analysis of the safeguards and countermeasures listed in step eight. This analysis needs to be very thorough and must ensure that those safeguards recommended for implementation are cost effective. The overall cost should be considerably less than the possible loss if these safeguards and countermeasures are not implemented. Those selected should offer the maximum protection at the minimum cost.

Step ten ranks the safeguards and countermeasures in an order of priority for selection by the approving executive. It is now necessary for management to decide the acceptable level of risk and if it is within the resources available to implement additional safeguards or countermeasures.

SURVEY REPORT FORMAT

When these ten steps have been completed, the survey team will compile the results in a written report to management. A suggested outline for this report is as follows:

1. Introduction
    a. Background for the survey
    b. Scope of the survey
    c. General methodology and approach
2. Impact priority identification
3. Threat probability identification
4. Risk factor determination
5. Vulnerability analysis
6. Safeguard or countermeasure identification
7. Cost–benefit analysis

SECURITY BRIEF 8-2

Movie Studios Lose $250 Million a Year to Piracy

America's major film studios lose more than $250 million a year in revenue to movie pirating.

The usual scenario is for fake copies of movies to be released just as legitimate copies are about to hit video stores according to the Motion Picture Association of America (MPAA). The MPAA has headquarters in Washington, D.C. with an office in Encino, Calif.

Phony distributors, street vendors, and flea market dealers offer pirated videos at less than half a legitimate store's price. A fake video dealer may appear legitimate by selling mail order at a significantly lower cost.

Fakes are very inferior in quality. But on some sophisticated fakes "we have to use electronics to evaluate them," says Marisa Pica, media representative for MPAA's Anti-Piracy Operation. "We have a lab in Encino to do it. It can measure if this copy is the third or fourth generation or whatever generation it is. Only first generation copies are available in legitimate stores."

With new technology, especially with digital, it will be easier to make copies. "But we are working on a way to prevent digital copying," she says.

Global Problem

Inside the U.S., New York City is the leader in producing pirated videos. Outside the U.S., China and Russia take the lead.

"China allows only a dozen U.S. movies to be imported a year to protect its own industry," says picar. "In Russia we need an enforcement and strengthening of copyright laws and legitimate distributors."

The MPAA has offices in 78 countries working to stop piracy, fight quotas and open legitimate lines of distribution.

MOVIE VIDEO PIRACY		
	1995	**1994**
Civil Seizures	384	357
Criminal Seizures	832	554
Voluntary Seizures	291	255
TOTAL SEIZURES	**1,507**	**1,166**
Videos Seized—Civil	134,358	127,356
Videos Seized—Criminal	389,130	269,060
Videos Forfeited Voluntarily	29,001	29,480
TOTAL VIDEOS SEIZED	**552,499**	**425,896**
TOTAL VCRs SEIZED	**3,842**	**2,352**
Persons Charged Criminally	733	279
Persons Convicted	253	244
Persons Sentenced	249	212
Investigations Initiated	2,209	1,906
Restitution Awarded ($)	$604,997	$412,959

Source: Motion Picture Association of America

Nearly $200,000 more in restitution was collected from movie video pirates in 1995 compared with 1994. Total number of movie videos seized increased by more than 100,000 compared with 1994.

8. Conclusions and recommendations

Appendix A: Team members

Appendix B: Priority operations and activities

Appendix C: Assets inventory and costing

Appendix D: Safeguard or countermeasure costs

Even though no process can list all the aspects of an operation or activity, the procedures listed here can ensure that the subjective aspect of security surveys can made into ordinal data for comparative analysis. The checklists used for a number of security operations can be found in many texts and security agency manuals. Some of these sources are listed in Appendix A.[6]

Summary

This chapter has discussed the complexity of trying to assess the risk to a company's assets in some kind of systematic and logical fashion. The tendency in the security industry over the years has too often been to "shoot from the hip" when trying to (1) determine the most probable targets in a company, (2) determine the most logical threats to those targets, (3) determine the vulnerability of those targets to specific threats, (4) determine the probability of those threats occurring, (5) relate the cost of securing those targets as compared to their value to the company, and (6) conduct any kind of cost–benefit analysis of their actions in the name of security.

The processes and actions described in this chapter require more intense scrutiny of the problem than has been possible in the past. Most businesspersons today are "bottom liners" who must balance company needs against available resources on a whole company basis. Security departments must be prepared to show the cost and benefit of all of their operations, or they will be overpowered by other departments that have more skill in showing the value of their requests. A simple checklist of what is and what is not being done for security at various parts of the company is no longer enough to sell the need for countermeasures. The methodology described in this chapter is not complicated, but it does take some effort to show that security *can* be a cost-beneficial part of the company's overall efforts to protect the bottom line. Security reviews and surveys should not have to be mandated as they are in the *Industrial Security Manual*, but should be a normal process that is fought for and treasured as one of the security manager's most valuable tools.

REVIEW QUESTIONS

1. Describe the three elements that result in risk.
2. What are the advantages of well-written policies and procedures?
3. List and describe the five Ds and their role in a risk assessment.
4. What is the general outline for a report of a risk assessment?
5. Why is it useful to plot the appropriate numbers on a risk factor determination barometer?

TERMS TO REMEMBER

risk	*five D's*	*security review*
risk assessment	*deterrence*	*risk factor determination barometer*
countermeasures	Industrial Security Manual	
policy and procedure		

ENDNOTES

1. Gion Green, *Introduction to Security*, 4th ed. (Boston: Butterworth, 1987), p. 117.
2. Mark Golsby, "Four Steps to Success," *Security Management*, Vol. 36, No. 8 (August 1992), p 57.
3. Michael H. Skurecki, "The Service of Surveys," *Security Management*, Vol. 36, No. 8 (August 1992), p 57.
4. Ibid., p. 64.
5. Golsby, "Four Steps to Success," *Security Management*, pp. 53–57.
6. The author is grateful to the General Services Administration for much of the material contained in this section.

9

Litigation

THE BIGGEST THREAT TO CORPORATE ASSETS

Civil liability cannot be totally avoided, yet jury awards or settlements can be reduced, or won, if businesses take a more proactive security posture.

—Robert J. Meadows

Overview

It is sad, but true, that the United States has become the most litigious country in the world. This distressing situation is the result of a large number of factors, but the major cause is the lack of proper action taken *before* a serious problem occurs and deteriorates to a point that results in a lawsuit. When those who have the responsibility to provide reasonable care over persons, property, and places fail to do so, they risk being sued for the consequences. This chapter aims to make the student aware of, and understand, the importance of liability to a security operation. We have discussed the bottom line as a part of the security operation's mission. Perhaps nothing short of a war can have more potential impact on the company's bottom line than major litigation that results in gigantic awards in the millions of dollars, often because they failed to provide adequate security for their customers and personnel. And because the security manager failed to elicit support from the administration of the industry or institution. The student must first understand the basic elements of liability.

What Is Liability?

The basic points to consider in determining whether or not **liability** has occurred are:

1. Did the defendant owe a duty to protect and provide reasonable security to the plaintiff?
2. Did the defendant fail to provide reasonable security and breach this duty?
3. Was lack of such security by the defendant the *proximate* cause in fact?
4. Was the failure of security the *foreseeable* cause?
5. Did injury or harm to the plaintiff result?

These critical items are necessary to provide a reasonable set of grounds for finding against the defendant. These are best described and outlined by Spain, as follows:

Duty owed: Plaintiff may argue defendant owed a **duty to provide reasonable security** based upon one or a combination of the following factors:

1. Business invitee, and*
   a. Special relationships (i.e., patient in hospital)
   b. Special facts and circumstances (i.e., foreseeability)
2. Voluntary assumption of duty
3. Statutory duty
4. Contract
5. Warranty of habitability

*(Note: A few states, in moving away from the business invitee classification scheme, have taken a more complex look at duty and stated duty is based not only upon the status of the victim and the foreseeability of harm, but also upon the severity of the risk to be avoided, the cost of avoidance, and relevant public policy considerations.)

Breach of duty: Plaintiff may argue defendant breached its duty to provide security based upon its failure to:

1. Comply with a statutory law
2. Meet professional standards
3. Meet industry practices/standards
4. Meet local community standards
5. Meet advertised standards
6. Meet contract/voluntary/assumed standards
7. Provide adequate warning
8. Conduct/follow security survey/assessment

9. Develop/follow security policies and procedures

10. Retain qualified security manager and staff
    a. Background checks
    b. Appropriate experience/education
    c. Competitive salary and benefits to retain

11. Train security and non-security staffs
    a. Proper documentation
    b. Programs for new/experienced employees
    c. Programs for managers
    d. Professional memberships
    e. Professional literature

12. Retain sufficient staff for risk

13. Properly equip officers (i.e., radios)

14. Properly patrol facility

15. Use/maintain appropriate security hardware
    a. Lights
    b. Locks and key control
    c. Fences
    d. CCTV
    e. Bullet resistant glass

16. Maintain landscaping/shrubbery

Cause in fact: In order to determine if defendant's failure to provide reasonable security was the **cause in fact** (i.e., *actual fact*), of plaintiff's injuries, the courts use either the:

1. "But for" test or
2. "Substantial factor" test

"But for" defendant's failure to provide reasonable security, would plaintiff have been injured at that time and place?

—or—

Was defendant's failure to provide reasonable security a "substantial factor" in causing plaintiff's injuries?

Foreseeable cause: In order to determine if plaintiff's injuries were **foreseeable** by the defendant, the courts use either the:

1. "Prior similar rule" test
    a. Type of prior criminal activity
        (1) Crime against property
        (2) Crime against persons

    b. Frequency of prior criminal activity (usually 3–5 years)

    c. Date of prior criminal activity

    d. Location of prior criminal activity

2. "Totality of the circumstances" test*

    a. Prior similar crimes not essential

    b. All relevant information admissible

      (1) Prior crimes

      (2) Local crime statistics

      (3) Industry crime statistics

      (4) Company crime statistics (even other locations)

      (5) Type of neighborhood

      (6) Proximity of major roads

      (7) Employee complaints (very damaging)

      (8) Use of security officers

      (9) Employee crime awareness program

*(Note: Evidence listed under the totality of the circumstances test may be admissible under the prior similar rule provided plaintiff first introduces evidence of prior similar crimes on the premises.)

3. Imminent danger

    a. Specific person is dangerous at time/place

    b. Specific person is in danger at time/place

Injury: The **injury** to the plaintiff was a direct result of the factors listed above.[1]

THE COST OF LITIGATION

The statistics in regard to suits involving inadequate security show some chilling trends. In a recent study that examined national reporter systems and selected legal journals from 1978 to 1987, it was found that the number of cases per year grew from an average of only 27 in the first two years to more than 110 in the last two years of the study. More significant, the average judgment or settlement grew from just under $100,000 to more than $800,000 in that short time span, with plaintiffs receiving settlements or judgments in more than 50 percent of the reported cases.[2] Since that time, the amount of awards in most cases have exceeded $1 million.

    Although these are startling statistics, keep in mind that inadequate security lawsuits are a situational risk that varies significantly from state to state, even from community to community. Based on a review of American Trial Lawyer Association documents from 1984 to 1988, the four most active states were found to be (in descending order) California, Texas, Florida, and New York.[3] Many states have tried to initiate "caps" to litigation awards, but this has not significantly reduced the number of lawsuits claiming negligent security, negligent supervision, negligent training, and negligent hiring that continue to drain the treasuries of U.S. businesses and institutions. In fact, the cost of litigation is probably the most serious threat to most businesses and institutions in America today.

The cost of litigation is not just the settlements or judgments that result from negligent security, but also the cost to defend against such actions. Even a successful defense can run into a huge bill. In descending order, most cases of inadequate security involved apartments (20 percent), hotels (17 percent), restaurants (17 percent), retail (13 percent), schools (6 percent), hospitals (4 percent), parking lots (3 percent), gas stations (2 percent), and other (18 percent).[4] Sherman and Klein reported primary defendants were residential landlords (29 percent), motel owners (16 percent), retailers (15 percent), and common carriers (6 percent).[5] Obviously, the best way to defend against such litigation is to not have it happen in the first place. Proactive security and management support is the best answer.

Why is all this necessary? In the healthcare industry, for example, a recent survey of the 21,000-member Emergency Nurses Association revealed that security is a nurse's biggest concern. The number of security-related lawsuits grew by 29 percent between 1987 and 1989.[6] According to *The Lippman Report*, a widely respected monthly newsgram:

> …if present hospital litigation trends continue, one-half of all hospitals will have faced one or more security-related suits by the end of 1992. Recent court rulings indicate that, increasingly, hospitals are being found liable for damages when crimes that occur on their premises are judged to result from inadequate security. In such cases, a jury may award compensatory damages to the plaintiff to cover medical and related expenses, lost wages, and pain and suffering. But that may not be the end of the story. Sometimes a jury finds that a hospital's inadequate security is the result of *gross negligence*. In such instances, the jury may grant the plaintiff punitive as well as compensatory damages. *Punitive* awards are particularly significant because they tend to be larger than compensatory awards, because they have no upward cap, and because they are not insurable. Nor is liability necessarily limited to the institutions themselves. *Directors*, managers, and even members of hospital boards could be held personally liable for crimes that occur on hospital property if such crimes are judged to have resulted from breach of duty. [Emphasis added][7]

Any one can be subject to a lawsuit at some time in his or her security career. The responsible security professional will have prepared his or her employer and staff for this to lessen the validity of any claim and, thereby, negative financial exposure.

EXAMINING THE DUTY TO PROTECT

Certain conditions within a businessperson's control facilitate the commission of a crime and, in some cases, are foreseeable and preventable. Crimes are seldom committed at random. Criminals prefer to operate in locations where they will not be

SECURITY BRIEF 9–1

Knor v. Parking Co. of Am.

The plaintiff had chosen to park her vehicle in the defendant's parking garage while she was at work. She had selected that particular garage due to its proximity to her place of employment and because in her opinion it was the safest lot in the area. A major factor in that determination was a sign posted which stated that a security guard was on duty from 6:00 a.m. until 6:00 p.m., Monday through Friday.

Upon returning to her car at 5:15 p.m. one evening, she was kidnapped by two escaped convicts who locked her in the trunk of her vehicle. They held her for thirteen hours, raping her repeatedly and threatening to kill her. As a result, the plaintiff suffered post-traumatic stress, depression, and a loss of memory of the attack. She became unable to relate to men and sexually dysfunctional. She also developed an eating disorder and agoraphobia.

The plaintiff's suit alleged inadequate security which resulted in the breach of an implied contract and failure to foresee the probability of her attack. Plaintiff proved that the burned-out bunker located next to the lot was a haven for vagrants and other undesirable individuals. Two criminal assaults had previously occurred at the garage. In addition, one of the plaintiff's assailants testified that the two had spent the night preceding the attack in the bunker and had on four occasions checked the lot for an unlocked vehicle.

Plaintiff also provided evidence that the guard, who was a retired truck driver, aged 67, had no experience and was not trained. He was also unarmed and had been told to stay in the guard's shack and not to patrol the area. The guard stated that he had informed management of the situation with the bunker. No action had been taken.

The plaintiff had requested $600,000 but was offered $50,000 by the defendant. The jury awarded the plaintiff $2 million.

Source: Hamilton County Court of Common Pleas, OH, No. A85-09133 (July 14, 1989)

identified or captured. They therefore select sites that offer opportunity without risk. The criminal's decision to strike at a particular location can be made on impulse, or it can be the result of a long-term plan. Regardless, the reason the criminal has chosen a particular location is his or her perception of the likelihood of success.

Criminals are motivated to commit crimes when their surroundings suggest they can get away with it. Causes of action are based on the premise that when businesses operate sites that attract or encourage criminal activity, they will be found negligent and liable to the victims of attacks if they owed a duty to the victim and knew, or should have known, that factors within their control increased the likelihood of criminal attacks.[8]

As a rule, a private person does not have a **duty to protect** another from criminal acts by third persons.[9] However, cases have established that owners or occupiers of business premises owe their customers and prospective customers a duty to use reasonable care to protect them from foreseeable criminal acts.[10]

In *Tucker* v. *Sandlin*,[11] Phyliss Tucker was raped in a parking ramp. The Michigan Court of Appeals held: "An act or omission may be negligent if the actor realizes or should realize an unreasonable risk of harm to another through the conduct of a third person which is intended to cause harm, even though such conduct is criminal."[12]

The issue of third-party liability as a consequence of a criminal act is one of current interest because of increased litigation and the efforts of businesses to shield themselves from exorbitant civil judgments.

Courts now reject the argument that personal security of individuals is solely a police function and hold, as the New Jersey Supreme Court did in *Butler* v. *Acme Market*,[13] that merchants have a duty to provide adequate protection to their customers.[14]

In an effort to provide adequate protection, businesses are lighting their parking lots, warning employees and customers about dangerous conditions, and making private security one of the largest growth industries in the country. With businesses spending more than $20 billion each year and employing more than 1.1 million people in private security, it is obvious that the prudent businessperson is listening to what the courts are saying.[15] The message is clear: Provide a reasonably secure environment for customers, or compensate the victims of foreseeable criminal attacks. By simply conducting a cost–benefit analysis, businesses are being persuaded to take precautions in lieu of paying huge jury awards.

Business owners, customers, employees, and the community as a whole are the benefactors. A safe environment for living, shopping, and conducting business is achieved when responsibility for crime prevention is delegated to those who are in a position to effect it.

Duty is a question of whether the relationship between the actor and the injured person gives rise to a legal obligation on the actor's part for the benefit of the injured person. The responsibility of business is determined by the status of the individual coming onto the premises, the duty of care owed under traditional tort rules, and what the businessperson knew or should have known about the likelihood of criminal attack.

THE IMPORTANCE OF THE STATUS OF THE PLAINTIFF

Status should be the first consideration in analyzing a duty relationship. The **status of the plaintiff** is a question of law to which different legal duties are attached.[16] Most jurisdictions continue to differentiate the duties owed to the plaintiff depending on his or her status as a trespasser, licensee, or invitee. As stated in *Duarte* v. *State of California University*,[17] the "indispensable factor to liability founded upon negligence is the existence of a duty of care owed by the alleged wrongdoer to the person injured or to a class of which he is a member."[18]

A trespasser is a person who comes on the premises or land without permission.[19] Usually, the duty to a trespasser is only to refrain from willful, wanton, or reckless disregard for the trespasser's safety. Exceptions to the trespasser rule include children and continuous and known trespassers.[20] Although considerable agreement exists that general negligence standards should be applied to all persons invited or permitted on the premises, there is less accord on how trespassers should be handled.

A licensee is a person who has permission from a competent authority to do an act that without permission would be illegal or constitute a trespass or a tort.[21] This is usually the person who comes on the property with express or implied permission. The occupier of the premises is required to warn the licensee of unreasonably dangerous hidden conditions known by him or her but unappreciated by the licensee.[22]

An invitee, on the other hand, is a person on the land of another who enters by invitation, express or implied; whose entry is connected with the owner's business or with the activity that the owner conducts or permits to be conducted on his or her land; and whose presence represents a mutual benefit to the owner.[23]

The leading British case of *Indermann* v. *Domes*[24] holds that those who enter business premises that concern the occupier will enjoy the occupier's affirmative duty to protect them not only against dangers of which the occupier knows but also against that which with reasonable care he or she might discover. Therefore, the duty of reasonable care owed to an invitee is greater than that owed to a licensee.

Armstrong v. *Sundance Entertainment Inc.*[25] exemplifies the importance of status designation. In Armstrong, the plaintiff was shot while sitting inside his car outside a closed nightclub.[26] The grounds for liability turned on whether persons who were earlier patrons should be considered licensees or invitees once business closes.

The court ruled that "one who uses the premises of a merchant at a time beyond which the implied invitation extends is a mere licensee."[27] In denying liability, the court ruled:

> To determine whether a person is an invitee or a mere licensee the nature of his relation or contact with the owner or occupier of the premises must be determined. The test is whether the injured person at the time of the injury had present business relations with the owner of the premises which would render his presence on the premises was for his own convenience.[28]

The view in *Restatement of the Law, Second, Torts* agrees with *Armstrong*. Section 314A makes it clear that a possessor of land has no duty of reasonable care to one who has ceased to be an invitee. Therefore, a defendant may be negligent but not civilly liable if the plaintiff's status fails to establish a duty that the defendant's actions breached.[29]

A minority of jurisdictions, however, follow the rule of *Rowland* v. *Christian*,[30] in which the California Supreme Court eliminated the status distinction and created a simple negligence test. The status of the plaintiff is an important first step in this type of lawsuit, but the student should be mostly concerned with cases that involve invitees or follow the *Rowland* v. *Christian* rule.

TRADITIONAL TORT RULES

Originally, businesspersons had no recognized legal duties toward those who chose to come to their premises. Such persons took the premises as they found them, including the physical hazards known to the occupier. The injustice of such a policy forced courts to carve out exceptions to nonliability. For one of the exceptions to arise and create a duty, there must be a special relationship between the holder of the duty and the one to whom the duty is owed. According to *Restatement of the Law, Second, Torts*, specific relationships imposing duties have been found as follows:

- A common carrier is under a duty to its passengers to take reasonable action to protect them against unreasonable risk of physical harm and to give them first aid after it knows or has reason to know they are ill or injured and to care for them until such time as they can be cared for by others.

- An innkeeper is under a similar duty to his or her guests.

- A possessor of land who holds it open to the public is under a similar duty to persons who enter in response to his or her invitation.

- One who is required by law to take or voluntarily takes the custody of another under circumstances that deprive the other of his or her normal opportunities for protection is under similar duty.[31]

The ***Restatement of the Law, Second, Torts*** in a caveat expressed no opinion on whether other relations may impose a similar duty. However, it states in a later comment that "the law appears to be working slowly toward a recognition of the duty to aid or protect in any relation of dependence or of mutual dependence."[32] The prediction appears to be accurate since the trend has been to find a duty based on the dependence between businesses and customers.

In 1970, in *Kline* v. *1500 Massachusetts Ave. Apartment Corp.*,[33] Sarah B. Kline was assaulted and robbed in a common hallway of her apartment building. The U.S. Court of Appeals reviewed the issue of "whether a duty should be placed on a landlord to take steps to protect tenants from foreseeable criminal acts committed by third parties." The District Court was reversed and the appellate court found, as a matter of law, there was such a duty.[34]

The landlord is no insurer of his or her tenant's safety, but he or she certainly is no bystander. And when, as here, the landlord (1) has notice of repeated criminal assaults and robberies, (2) has notice that these crimes occurred on the premises exclusively within his or her control, (3) has every reason to expect like crimes to happen again, and (4) has the exclusive power to take preventive action, it is fair to place on the landlord a duty to take steps within his or her power to minimize the predictable risk to his or her tenants.[35]

By holding that a landlord is not an insurer, the court clearly rejected the imposition of strict liability. Likewise, no strict liability is imposed on businesses to provide absolute safety for customers. Any such liability is based on negligence. Although *Kline* held the landlord responsible for the common areas of a building, a more recent case, *Laz* v. *Dworman*,[36] held that a renter should be protected from foreseeable criminal acts inside a rented apartment.[37]

The renter had complained about a defective lock on her sliding glass door. Despite these complaints, the lock was not repaired, and she was later raped. The plaintiff also established that other rapes had occurred in the complex that the owners knew about. Although previous Oklahoma cases dealt only with liability for crimes committed within common areas, *Laz* broadened an owner's duty to protect tenants from foreseeable crimes in the rented premises when reasonably prudent steps could prevent such occurrences.

Duty is not only imposed on landlords. Illustrative of this line of cases is a 1986 case in which the California Supreme Court ruled a condominium association could be liable to a victim of a crime.

In *Frances T. v. Village Green Owners' Association*,[38] the plaintiff asked the association to install lights in her courtyard because her condominium had been burglarized. When the board of directors voted not to install lights, she installed her own. Later she was ordered to turn them off because they violated association rules. She complied with the order and was raped that night.

The court ruled that an association has the same duty of care as a landlord because it has authority to regulate security.[39] The court also ruled that individual directors could be found liable if they "specifically authorized, directed, or participated" in the negligent acts or did not act to prevent injury.[40] Liability for the assault was premised on the factual finding that the association had knowledge of existing crime. In addition to the broadening of the owners' duties, there is a trend to hold others in positions of authority liable for their negligent business decisions.

Many business–customer relationships fall into this special relationship category as discussed in section 314A of the *Restatement of the Law, Second, Torts*, but as the court on *Duarte v. State of California*[41] stated,

> …the list and the concept (special relationship) has a general elasticity, charac-
> teristic of tort law principles.…in keeping with this growth process, the
> California courts have determined that the entrepreneurial land occupier has the
> duty to exercise reasonable care to protect invitees, patrons on the premises,
> from unlawful acts of third persons.[42]

The growth process discussed in *Duarte* gives plaintiffs a better opportunity to survive motions for summary disposition and get to the jury, even if they do not fall specifically within the narrower requirements of Section 314A. This is done by applying traditional tort rules and Section 344 of the *Restatement of the Law, Second, Torts*.[43]

For the student of security and loss prevention, this means that careful understanding of the status of persons who might become victims of third-party crimes must be clearly understood and conveyed to management and staff to protect from liability.[44]

KEY FACTORS IN NEGLIGENT SECURITY LITIGATION

In order to protect the assets of the business or institution, the security manager must be aware of the kinds of factors that weigh the heaviest in negligent security cases. In addition to the normal rules used by the court in such litigation, a number of key factors can be crucial in defending against such charges. All security programs should be examined in terms of the six factors listed here. This list is neither comprehensive nor exhaustive, but can be a good beginning to providing the security manager a way to assess his or her security program in the incredibly expensive area of litigation. This list, as prepared by Bates, is the top six factors to consider, regardless of the kind of business or institution being protected:

1. *Prior crime activity:* Although some states like Massachusetts and California have done away with the requirement that prior crime be shown, it is still strongly persuasive to show an unsafe environment. Prior similar crime, if close in time and type, may have a devastating effect on the defense of a case. Prior dissimilar crime is also effective to show generally unsafe conditions. One type of crime often leads to another. For example, conditions that allow for property crime may also allow for violent crime. A landowner's knowledge of prior similar crime and subsequent failure to warn of the risk is frequently cited in inadequate security cases. Complaints about problematic tenants, guests, customers, or visitors have been used as evidence of notice to unsafe conditions. Similarly, the failure to evict or otherwise remove such undesirable people can lead to liability.

2. *Security operations:* Staff size is a relative issue because there are no industry standards for what would be the appropriate number of security personnel to employ in a given location or business. The security practitioner must do what the expert or consultant would do—compare the immediate property to other similar properties, allowing for differences in size, crime rate, location, and demographics. This approach is referred to as the "community standard," which the courts will usually accept as representative of the practices of a particular industry.

3. *Employment practices:* Hiring practices, training, and supervision fall under this category. Hiring or screening problems become evident when a security officer or other employee is hired without adequate screening and commits a crime or tort. In states where it is expressly forbidden for a security contract agency to hire a convicted felon, a record check is essential. The level of the background check required will vary depending upon the potential risk posed by the employee. For example, employees given master keys or access to vulnerable members of the population (such as children or elderly) should be investigated more extensively. Training issues are raised when the employee is unable to perform the functions of the job because of inadequate training. Supervision problems include the failure to discipline and the retention of personnel who show a tendency toward violence.

4. *Physical security measures:* Quality and quantity of hardware are both factors in many inadequate security cases. Questions are raised not only about the sufficiency of certain hardware, such as locks, CCTV cameras, keys, lighting, and barriers, but also about whether the equipment was properly maintained and can be shown to have been in working order when the crime occurred.

5. *Environmental conditions:* An external or outdoor factor can be shown to have contributed to the crime if it created an environment conducive to the activity. The nature of the facility (such as an all-women's college), overgrown shrubbery that gives an assailant a place to hide, and the accessibility of the facility (in an urban

setting or next to a wooded area) have all been cited as relevant factors leading to liability in security issues.

6. *Management-related issues:* Such factors as falsely advertising that an apartment building has 24-hour security or promoting a facility as a family motel have been successfully argued as directly relating to harm suffered by a plaintiff. Additionally, oral statements by the sales staff, information contained in brochures, or the misleading appearance of security (an alarm panel disconnected but not removed) have led to so-called "reliance" theories of liability that numerous plaintiffs have succeeded in proving.[45]

Liability for inadequate security can take on a seemingly endless number of factors. The limit to the attacks on the security manager's programs is bounded only by the creativity of the plaintiff's attorney and the willingness of a judge or jury to accept them, and to grant large awards to plaintiffs. Security professionals must keep up with the trends in case law and how these cases might affect their industry or institution. They must then incorporate the necessary countermeasures before a lawsuit faces them and their employer, often with devastating consequences.

WHAT ARE THE DAMAGES?

As we have noted, many types of businesses are in serious threat from litigation—litigation that can result in millions of dollars being awarded to a plaintiff, and that can, and does, put companies out of business. In the late 1980s and the beginning of the 1990s, the amount of the awards had risen even more dramatically than previous studies have shown. In Atlanta, five verdicts in personal injury and death cases have exceeded $10 million—and three of them exceeded $20 million.[46] In the past, if a worker committed a negligent act, a plaintiff might bring suit using the legal theory of *respondeat superior*. This simple concept meant that the worker was acting on the behalf of the employer (master), and therefore the rule was to "let the master respond" (*respondeat superior*). This early rule simply held the employer liable for any acts of negligence by its employees, and the fault or lack of fault of the employer was not relevant. This began to make employers a bit more cautious about the quality of their employees.

As we saw before, the first key to a negligence action is whether the defendant owed a duty of protection from harm to the plaintiff. Foreseeability as to the conduct of employees acting for their employer, or acting independent of directions, has created a major industry in the security business or screening and backgrounding of security staff. A dangerous employee, acting under the concept of *respondeat superior*, and without the employer's actions to check them out before placing them on duty, can cause major damage to the company's image and treasury. These damages can be both compensatory and, even more damaging, punitive.

Compensatory damages and punitive damages represent two categories of awards for which injured persons can sue. Compensatory awards are designed to compensate the injured party for the loss caused by the wrong or injury and may include reimbursement for medical bills, lost wages, pain and suffering, emotional injuries, and physical impairments. Punitive or exemplary damages are damages other than compensatory that may be awarded to punish the defendant for outrageous conduct and to deter similar malfeasance in the future. Following the common-law tradition, most courts in the United States recognize and allow punitive damages to be imposed as a means of punishment and deterrence. In recent years, U.S. courts have encouraged a more liberal use of punitive damages than have other common-law countries.

This increase in punitive damage awards may be attributed in part to a decrease in the legal standards plaintiffs are required to satisfy to qualify for such damages. In early years, punitive damages were recoverable only if fraud, malice, or oppression were proved. As part of a trend in making punitive damages easier to obtain, the highest courts in Indiana, Oregon, and Arizona have ruled that the proof of gross negligence will justify the imposition of punitive damages.

As a matter of public policy, a number of states totally bar insurance companies paying for punitive damages levied against their insured; other jurisdictions' coverage for punitive damages arises solely out of vicarious liability. Seven states prohibit insurance coverage for punitive damages in all circumstances: California, Colorado, Kansas, Minnesota, New York, North Dakota, and Ohio. Six states limit insurance coverage of punitive awards to defendants vicariously liable for the acts of others: Florida, Illinois, Indiana, New Jersey, Oklahoma, and Pennsylvania.

Twenty-two jurisdictions recognize the right of insurance companies to provide coverage for punitive damages without restriction: Alabama, Arizona, Arkansas, Connecticut, Delaware, District of Columbia, Georgia, Idaho, Iowa, Kentucky, Maryland, Mississippi, New Hampshire, New Mexico, Oregon, Rhode Island, South Carolina, Tennessee, Texas, Vermont, West Virginia, and Wisconsin. Nine states have not yet formulated on the insurability of punitive damages: Alaska, Hawaii, Missouri, Montana, Nevada, North Carolina, South Dakota, Utah and Wyoming. Seven jurisdictions do not recognize exemplary damages as a form of recovery: Louisiana, Massachusetts, Michigan, Nebraska, Puerto Rico, Virginia, and Washington.

States interdicting insurance payments for punitive awards do so to inflict maximum punishment on the offending party and to deter such conduct in the future. These jurisdictions reason that the economic pain of being deprived of insurance coverage for a punitive verdict would be relieved and the deterrence element eliminated if an insurance carrier were authorized to pay the defendant's fine.

In a major case involving the insurance coverage of punitive damages, which declared that it is a violation of public policy,[47] the court held "that the burden would ultimately come to rest not on the insurance companies but on the public, since the added liability to insurance companies would be passed along to the premium payers. Society would be punishing itself for the wrong committed by the insured." Punitive damages generally exceed the amount of a compensatory award; often, the punitive damages represent a multiple of the compensatory remedy. Juries and judges are required by law to consider the defendant's financial condition when determining the size of a punitive damage award since courts set the amount based on the defendant's wealth. Because these awards are expressly designed to inflict monetary pain, a minimal fine against a wealthy defendant will likely fail to achieve the punishment aims of exemplary damages.[48]

It is clear that the security professional must be very aware of the status of various types of compensatory and punitive damages that can affect their business or

Metal Detectors: Not Just For Airports Anymore

We're used to seeing metal detectors in airports. It is expected that in order to get on a plane we will encounter at least one metal detector, and be required to deposit keys and other metal objects in a separate basket before we go through.

But the new generation of metal detectors is smarter, more efficient, and likely to be found in more places than the usual.

"I think the primary need for metal detectors was obviously the airports," says Floyd Twight, president of Tectron Engineering. "Today, most airports are equpped with metal detectors. With all the other problems in society, where weapons are more and more prevalent, there are new applications opening up. We're seeing needs at federal buildings, hospitals, sporting events and even manufacturing settings."

Better Detection

Concurrent with new applications, is better, more reliable technology. For example, Tectron currently is working on developing a completely uniform field inside the detector, Twight says. "One aspect of metal detection is that the placement of the weapon on the body can affect detecting. A lot of companies have spent a fair amount of effort trying to minimize this, and there has been quite a bit of succes. But there is still a lot further to go."

Another problem with metal detectors often is their inability to distinguish a gun from a belt buckle when set at higher levels of security. This also is changing, says Bob Madden, executive vice president of Crown Technical Systems, Cleveland, Ohio.

Crown is the exclusive U.S. distributor for the Italian company, CEIA, based in Arezzo, Italy. "These detectors are able to discriminate against different types of metals to pick out the metal common in threat objects like guns and knives," Madden says.

The newer metal detectors are computer based, he adds. They are smarter, and able to give more information, such as the count of people who went through the detector and up-to-the-minute flow rates.

New Applications

Another advancement in metal detection comes not from what they can do, but how they are used.

Companies such as Tectron and others are starting to combine the detectors with other systems, such as turnstiles, or portals. This concept allows people access to areas—provided they are free of weapons.

"I think as this catches on, it will be an attractive alternative for applications with multiple entrances," Twight says. "It would be a simple matter for one security officer to handle two and maybe three entrances at one time. If someone trips the alarm while the officer is occupied at another unit, they can't just walk through and run."

Madden sees many applications for these scenarios. "We see them being used more frequently in commercial applications such as banks, 24-hour convenience stores, fast food chains, even industrial plants. Employers are getting very concerned about employees bringing weapons into the workplace."

Source: Editor. "Metal Detectors: Not Just for Airports Anymore," *Security* (Cahners Publishing Company. Newton, MA, 1995), Vol. 32, No. 8, pp. 20–21.

institution in the jurisdiction in which they are located. It is also clear that the security manager must be careful in the selection, retention, and promotion of personnel charged with security duties. Failure to screen them properly, train them to industry standards, and provide them with guidance on what to do is a dark cloud of danger to litigation. One way to moderate that problem is to provide clear policies and procedures for the security operations.

POLICIES AND PROCEDURES: A SUIT-PROOF VEST?

As noted, negligent or inadequate security has become the grounds for litigation and a source of huge settlements against businesses and institutions. There are still some "soft" spots in providing adequate security. Policies and procedures present an opportunity to show either strength or a soft underbelly in regard to lawsuits alleging negligent security. Security managers should consider the following "six Ps" for guidance in developing their own policies.

Policy: A **policy** describes a management decision on a specific issue or concept. Well-written, clear policy eliminates having to redecide issues already resolved and gives employees a guide for correct response and action in similar situations as they occur.

Procedure: Procedures list what steps an individual or team should take to complete an action following a specific policy decision. Procedures should have a specific starting and ending point. They also include the reports and paperwork needed to complete the action. There is a saying, "If it ain't documented, it didn't happen." It is essential to leave a documented trail to protect the actions taken because any *undocumented* actions are sure to come back to haunt the security manager.

Practice: No set of policies or procedures is valid if **practices** in the field do not correspond to what has been written. Tasks done incorrectly or illegally because correct procedures have not been written down and followed are just as bad as not doing what is written down. One does not make policies and procedures about a specific action if it is clear that there is neither the personnel, financial resources, nor administrative support resources available to follow them. Instead, one must document these shortcomings to superiors and keep on pushing for the resources in documented form. If certain practices are neither needed nor required, they should be eliminated. Then resources can be better used for what is essential to protect the corporate or institutional assets from litigation.

Production: Policies and procedures can often be so dry and unreadable that the average staff member or security officer either will not read them or cannot understand them. These critical documents must be written in clear, concise, and readable language. They must also have a format that breaks them down to the smallest possible units of information (one policy per topic, one procedure per policy), and that is uniform so that readers know exactly where to look to find answers to questions they may have about their duties.

Post orders: Every assignment must have a set of post orders that covers the duties, responsibilities, and expectations of a specific job or post. To have the greatest value, however, post orders must be developed in conjunction and cooperation with

Statistics and Trends in Security Litigation

After reviewing 250 cases from 1983 to 1991, the following data and trends were observed:

Sixty-five percent of all security-related cases involve inadequate security, 57 percent of all plaintiffs are female, and 43 percent are male.

Most Common Types of Defendants Sued	Percent
Residential landlords/ condominium associations	31.5
Hotels/motels	19
Retail stores/shopping malls	14.5
Restaurants/bars	8
Hospitals	5
Schools/universities	2.5
Commercial properties/ office buildings	6

Most Common Crimes Committed	Percent
Sexual assault*	28
Assault and battery	25
Wrongful death	20
Assault and battery and rape	7
Assault and battery and robbery	5

*Note: In some states, such as Florida and Nevada, sexual assault is considered rape.

Specific Locations of Crimes	Percent
Apartment unit	21
Parking lot or garage	15
Hotel room	14
Retail store	13
Restaurant/bar/casino	9
Elevator	2
Hallway	2
Office	2
Hospital room	3

Fifty-one percent of all cases were settled, 40 percent went to juries and had verdicts returned, and 9 percent went unreported.

The average settlement amount is $600,000, and the average jury award is $1.3 million.

Source: Liability Consultants, Inc.

the people who work the posts. Simply to prepare a "laundry list" of tasks for a post is useless if they cannot be accomplished by the person to whom they are assigned. The post order is one of the best tools for justifying staffing levels if it clearly describes what *must* be done and compares this with what *can* be done with existing resources.

Perseverance: Policies, procedures, practice, production, and post orders are valid only if they are part of a living **document**. Once the effort has been expended to write them down, it is foolish not to review them regularly and revise them when conditions change. If this is done, as it is in far too many cases, the business is not protected, and even has yet another basis for litigation. Reviewing and rewriting are not only smart activities, they are essential. If one does not have the resources to produce and update a valid set of policies and procedures, some way of doing so must be found.

Following a simple list of the six Ps allows the security manager to analyze needs for a reasonably suit-proof policy and procedure manual. One courts disaster, however, when trying to run the security operation with a gigantic set of policies and procedures that cannot possibly be followed by using the resources available. Big policy manuals are nice to show to someone one is trying to impress, but *substance* is what the attorney for the plaintiff is searching for.

It is equally dangerous to operate with ancient and inadequate policies and procedures that only remotely describe what is actually being done with available resources. Carefully coordinated (with those who must do them) and drafted policies and procedures that reflect actual practice, contain solid post orders, can be read and understood, are kept current, and are capable of being done by existing resources reflect sound management principles, as well as less costly insurance.

In addition to negligent or inadequate security, personal damage suits and civil rights actions are costing companies and institutions millions of dollars each year. The first items that attorneys usually request in discovery are the policies and procedures manuals of the company or department. When policies and procedures are outdated, poorly constructed, and clearly unused, attorneys usually decide to go ahead and bring suit. On the other hand, if they find organized, complete, correct, current policies and procedures that match up with current practice, they may back off and look for easier prey.

Responsible security managers take the time to analyze their present policies and procedures and then find the time, personnel, hardware and software to develop them properly. The cost of the entire process is much less than even the smallest out-of-court settlement. A good solid set of policies and procedures is the same as a good protective vest for a police officer—the protection is well worth the cost.

VICARIOUS LIABILITY: YOU CAN'T BURY YOUR HEAD IN THE SAND

The concept of **vicarious liability** is one that has had great impact in the security field. As we mentioned in Chapter Seven, too often the security operations are delegated to a very low rung on the corporate ladder. Vicarious liability essentially means that one becomes responsible (and liable) for the actions or inactions of others that result in injury or harm to a plaintiff. This is usually in the supervisory or management chain and is seldom understood by those above the security manager. For example, the security manager conducts (or contracts a consultant to conduct) a major risk assessment and security survey that results in a lot of deficiencies that need to be corrected. The security manager does what he or she can do to correct them with present resources and requests more support through the chain of command. Say a major problem is found in outside lighting near the parking lot. Management decides that such lighting is not affordable at this time and rejects the request. If an employee becomes a victim of crime because of the poor lighting, the vicarious liability moves to those who had the ability to act but did not do so. This kind of negligence is just what a plaintiff's attorney wants to find.

The security manager must make management aware that the recommendations of experts (whether in-house experts or consultants) are powerful tools for them to respond to in the best way possible. To ignore recommendations for security measures is simply to document for the plaintiff the basis for not only compensatory damages, but probably (where possible) punitive damages as well since the courts tend to view failure to act on known dangers as gross negligence.

Summary

That the security professional must be part attorney to do the job effectively seems to go with the job as we enter the twenty-first century. Have we gone too far in our attempts to reduce liability exposure? It is sometimes true that we experience "paralysis by analysis" when we weigh every move in terms of liability? Canton does a good job of addressing this issue:

> We seem to have forgotten that risk analysis is an inherent part of our job and that to be effective we must determine acceptable levels of risk, not just eliminate all liability exposure. It is easy to justify inaction because of possible exposure and cost. It is not easy to justify spending time and money to protect against possible exposure.

> This flawed reasoning is not really so uncommon and can be very subtle. Let's look at several examples:

> Because of the tremendous risk present when security personnel are armed, many companies prefer unarmed officers and have reaffirmed officers' traditional and limited duties to observe and report. Considering our industry's track record with armed officers, this is not unreasonable. However, we have again let a good idea take us too far by placing all weapons and restraint devices in the same class as firearms.

> …we have systematically stripped them of any means of protection. Many security officers are forbidden to carry chemical agents on duty even though they have the right to do so as private citizens. Officers are not allowed to use the batons, even where state certification programs exist, because "they might hit somebody." Officers do not carry handcuffs because "they do not make arrests." Even basic unarmed defense training is frowned upon as too aggressive. Officer safety has been subordinated to appearance. We have forgotten that self-defense does not automatically mean the use of lethal force.

> At the same time, our clients and employers are demanding more aggressive performance from our personnel. This demand is partly to justify the high

expense of security officers and partly because, with public resources strained or unresponsive, they have no one else to turn to. How often have we heard "I called security, and they didn't do anything" or "Your guard just stood there the whole time and did nothing?" Our excuse is that the risk is just too great if officers go beyond observing and reporting. But we have to look at the message we are sending to our clients, employees, and security officers. What we are really saying is, "I don't trust you and I don't trust your level of training."[49]

The recurring theme is that we do not need to be afraid to do our jobs if we select good people, train them well, keep on top of current threats to liability, then document everything we do. It doesn't happen by itself. Everyone must be aware of the litigation threat and the costs if we lose control. As I was taking a course on tort law in graduate school, one of the third-year law students reeled off a set of facts: then he asked the professor if, under those facts, he could sue. The professor, a judge of some twenty-five years, stroked his chin and answered, "Of course you can sue, you fool! The question is *can you win?*" We need to understand that we will be sued for many things during our security careers. What we do beforehand will make it more difficult for the plaintiff to win, or award the plaintiff less money if he or she should win.

REVIEW QUESTIONS

1. Why is duty to provide reasonable security such an important concept for security managers?

2. Explain what is meant by a "tort."

3. How can vicarious liability affect a corporation's bottom line?

4. What is the difference between compensatory and punitive damages?

5. What is the importance of matching policy and practice?

TERMS TO REMEMBER

liability	*duty to protect*	*policy*
duty to provide reasonable security	*status of the plaintiff*	*practices*
cause in fact	*Restatement of the Law, Second, Torts*	*document*
foreseeable injury	*vicarious liability*	

ENDNOTES

1. Norman M. Spain, *The Law of Inadequate Security* (Paper presented at American Society for Industrial Security, 37th Annual Seminar and Exhibits, September 1991, Orlando, Florida [unpublished]), pp. 3–5.

2. Robert Figlio and Susan Adams, *Premises Litigation Award Study: 1978–1987* (King of Prussia, Pa.: CAP Index, Inc., 1988), p. 3.

3. Robert Meadows, "The Likelihood of Liability," *Security Management*, Vol. 35, No. 7 (July 1991), pp. 60–66.

4. Figlio and Adams, *Premises Litigation*, p. 123.

5. Sherman and Klein, *Major Lawsuits Over Crime and Security: Trends and Patterns, 1958–1982* (Washington, D.C.: Crime Control Research Corporation, 1984).

6. Tom Kramer. "Crime in Hospitals 1988, 1989—the latest IAHSS Surveys," *Journal of Healthcare and Protection Management*, Vol. 7, No. 2 (Summer 1991), pp. 1–29.

7. "Hospital Security," *The Lippman Report* (May 15, 1992), pp. 1–4.

8. *Isaacs* v. *Huntington Memorial Hospital*, 38 Cal. 3d at 130.

9. *Kline* v. *1500 Massachusetts Ave., Apartment Corp.*, 141 US App. DC 370, 439 F.2d. 477 (1970).

10. *Lopez* v. *McDonald's*, 238 Cal. Rptr. 436, 438 (Cal. App. 4 Dist. 1987) at 444.

11. 126 Mich. App. at 701, 337 NW 2d at 637 (1983).

12. 126 Mich. App. at 704, 337 NW 2d at 639-40.

13. 89 NJ at 270 (1982).

14. 89 NJ at 274.

15. William C. Cunningham and Todd H. Taylor, *Private Security and Police in America* (Portland, Oreg.; Chancellor Press, 1985).

16. *Rodis* v. *Herman Kiefer Hosp.* 142 Mich. App. at 425, 370 NW 2d 458 (1985).

17. *Duarte* v. *State of California*, 151 Cal. Rptr. 727 (1979).

18. *Duarte* v. *State of California* at 731.

19. *Restatement of the law, Second, Torts*, sec. 339 (Philadelphia: American Law Institute, 1977).

20. *Restatement of the Law, Second, Torts* (setting out the criteria where a child trespasser would be barred from recovery).

21. James R. Nolan et al., *Black's Law Dictionary*, ed. Henry C. Black, 5th ed. (St. Paul, Minn.: West Publishing Co., 1985), p. 829.

22. *Restatement of the Law, Second, Torts*, sec 342.

23. *Black's Law Dictionary*, 5th ed., p. 742.

24. *Black's Law Dictionary*, p. 100.

25. *Armstrong* v. *Sundance Entertainment Inc.*, 347 SE.2d. 292 (GA. App. 1986).

26. *Armstrong* v. *Sundance Entertainment Inc.* at 293. (Armstrong left the nightclub before it closed and remained in parking lot.)

27. *Armstrong* v. *Sundance Entertainment Inc.* at 296.

28. *Armstrong* v. *Sundance Entertainment Inc.* at 297.

29. *Restatement of the Law, Second, Torts*, sec. 314A, comment b (1977).

30. William L. Prosser, et al., *Torts, Cases & Materials On*, 7th ed. (Mineola, N.Y., Foundation Press, 1977), p. 144.

31. *Rowland* v. *Christian*, 69 Cal. 2d. 108, 70 Cal. Rptr. 97, 443 P.2d. 561 (1968).

32. *Restatement of the Law, Second, Torts*, sec. 314A (1977).

33. *Restatement of the Law, Second, Torts*, sec. 314A, comment b (1977).

34. 141 US App. DC 370, 439 F.2d. 577 (1970).

35. 141 US App. DC at 485.

36. US App. DC.

37. 732 P.2d. 455 (Okla. 1986).

38. 732 P.2d. at 458.

39. 42 Cal.3d. at 490 (Cal. 1986).

40. 42 Cal.3d. at 493.

41. 42 Cal.3d. at 494.

42. 151 Cal. Rptr. 727 (1979).

43. I am especially thankful for the use of the materials on the topics on duty, status, and traditional tort rules in the preceding section. It has been extracted from a wonderful article by James Kohl, CPP, "Foreseeing One's Duty to Protect," *Security Management*, Vol. 33, No. 9 (September 1989), pp. 133–139.

44. Norman Bates, "Litigation: A Loss to Prevent," *Security Management*, Vol. 32, No. 4 (April, 1988), pp. 95–97.

45. Patrick A. Dunn, "Your Rights to References," *Security Management*, Vol. 35, No. 7 (July 1991), pp. 67–68.

46. *Northwestern National Casualty Co.* v. *McNulty*, 302 F.2d. 432 (1962).

47. Most of the material for this section was extracted from Andrew J. Anthony and Frederick F. Thornburg, "Liability Lessons: Security on Trial," *Security Management*, Vol. 33, No. 4 (February 1989), pp. 41–46.

48. Lucien G. Canton, "Limiting Liability Exposure: Have We Gone Too Far?" *Security Management*, Vol. 34, No. 1 (January 1990), pp. 71–72.

10

Physical Security and Access Control

THE WONDERS OF TECHNOLOGY

The least an organization should expect from an installed [entrance control] system is that it keep out unauthorized personnel but let in authorized users.

— Stephen M. Rogers

Overview

The goal of all human beings since we came together in social groups has been to feel secure and safe in our personal and group environment. Starting out with spears, rocks, and bramble-bush fences, we have developed much more sophisticated devices to protect ourselves and our belongings in the couple of thousand millennia that have passed. Although considerably different in the use of modern technology, the same basic principles and techniques are used today. Ranging from electronic warning devices to nuclear weapons, the basic means of protection have remained using the same physical security concepts and principles to keep the "bad guys" out of our personal and collective space. This chapter will explore the basics of physical security and access control as it is practiced within every security program at some level.

At the core of every criminal effort are some specific assets (as discussed in Chapter 8) that have become the target. Any criminal effort looks for the easiest path to the assets. Every security manager needs to make that path more difficult, both to find and to traverse. This chapter explores the means and methods for providing physical security as a part of the integrated security plan.

The Concept of the Five Ds

The use of physical security is based on what is sometimes referred to as the **five Ds**, which outline the primary purpose of each physical device or other security measure used. The five Ds, as used in this chapter, are deter, detect, delay, deny, and destroy:

- *Deter:* Often the intruder can be deterred by the very presence of physical security methods. The sight of a strong, high, well-posted fence that protects the perimeter may just be enough to deter the intruder from attempting entry. Poorly built and poorly maintained fencing, gates, lighting, or other security systems send a message to the potential intruder that no one really cares about security at that facility.

- *Detect:* This is done by *diverting* the intruders and channeling them into areas where they can be seen (visual detection) or where they will activate alarms or monitors tht will pinpoint their location (remote detection). It is crucial to provide for detection as soon as or, better yet, before the intruder has breached the perimeter of the facility.

- *Delay:* Even after the intruder decides to attempt entry and once inside the perimeter, the way barriers are planned and arranged can cause enough delay for special devices or the security alert force to respond and thwart penetration, or effect capture as soon as possible after penetration. Making the scaling of a wall more difficult by angled overhead barriers, topping a fence with razor wire, or creating a series of barriers between the perimeter and the next area can slow the intruder down and make apprehension or retreat more likely.

- *Deny:* This is a major objective of any security, to deny the intruder access to the specific assets being secured. Denying the intruder is generally accomplished by a greater "hardening" of security nearer to the assets location, either by making the barriers much more difficult closer to the asset or by providing a series of barriers that will allow the backup security force to arrive in time to apprehend the subjects.

- *Destroy:* Though not always the objective of security methods, in some cases, the last possible response may require the destruction of the intruder, or the destruction of the asset (for example, a file on a computer that would compromise national security, or some deadly substance in a research laboratory). Destructive force, against (for instance, armed terrorists) may also be required as a response to protect the lives of personnel. Another meaning of destruction is the complete frustrating of the planned criminal activity by physical security means.

At every point in the planning process for physical security, the security manager must consider these purposes and work them into each device or procedure.

The Concentric Rings of Security

The need for security begins at the boundary of personal or community space. If that space is not clearly defined, or some method of definition and security warning is not provided at that point, the task of the invader of that space is made easy. In the interpersonal world of one-on-one human interaction, a simple step back or raised hand can define the borders of one's personal space. Nations and states have clear border points, usually defined by some natural boundary (for example, an ocean, river, or mountain range). But smaller pieces of personal property or commercial "turf" are often more difficult to delineate. This is where the role of physical security, and the purposes of different types of such security, help not only define the boundaries of the enterprise but also provide security and access control.

LINE-OF-PROTECTION IN PHYSICAL SECURITY

As shown by Figure 10–1, one way to look at security is from a **line-of-protection** viewpoint. The line from entry point to the asset itself is interdicted by a series of physical barriers that seem to be like the layers of an onion or the circles on a target, with the asset as the bull's-eye. Each layer has a specific way to provide physical security for protection of the heart of the onion, the asset being protected. We now examine these line-of-protection layers.

THE OUTER PERIMETER

The **outer perimeter** is most generally defined as the point at which the controlling entity has ownership of or responsibility for the property, physical assets, and personnel within that boundary. The first lines of defense at the outer perimeter are **protective barriers**. The most common type of barrier for the outer perimeter is some kind of fence. Natural barriers, such as sheer cliffs or river frontage, can also be integrated into a fencing plan. The decision about what kind of fence to use is based on the criticality to the asset being secured if the fence is breached at any point, the size of the area to be fenced, and the cost-benefit of the fencing strategy. For example, a property that covers many acres could have its critical assets in a building that is miles inside the perimeter. This remote boundary may be surrounded by a simple two- or three-strand barbed wire fence and posted with no trespassing signs at regular intervals. A second fence, hardened and providing better security, might then be placed in closer proximity to the critical assets being secured. A low security and remote perimeter fence might also be patrolled by a vehicle on a random pattern to determine when or if it has been breached.

FIGURE 10–1 *Line-of-Protection Concept*

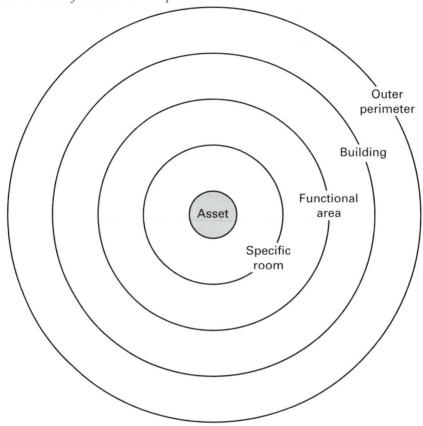

SECURITY LIGHTING: THE BEST KIND OF DEFENSE

The use of lighting at every point in the line-of-protection concept is the most cost-effective and useful physical measure that can be employed. Lighting at the perimeter is usually accomplished by floodlights placed high above the fence and pointing outward to produce glare in the eyes of the intruder and visibility for the security force within. Inside the perimeter, lighting can be paced out to provide constant illumination or can be activated by the intruders when they trip devices to light up the immediate areas. Light standards should be placed close enough together to provide the amount of illumination that would allow for the reading of headlines on a newspaper.

The electrical wires for perimeter and interior light standards should be buried and protected from being cut by intruders. All lighting should have backup generation capability, triggered by any power interruption, in order to provide a constant source of illumination. Even the best lighting is ineffective if the areas being lighted provide cover for the intruder. **Clear zones**, at least 20 feet wide on either side of the fence, should be made by removing all brush, shrubbery, and trash that could provide possible hiding areas. This not only provides a neat appearance, but allows for motorized and foot patrols around the perimeter in a more expeditious manner.

Lighting should be used at entry points and in parking lots to assist in providing better security. Guard houses at gates should be lighted more brightly on the outside than in the interior to allow the guard to see out clearly, but so that those entering cannot see in. (One-way glass can also help in this regard.) Because parking facilities are very high-risk areas, care must be taken to provide adequate lighting; furthermore, unnecessary bushes and shrubbery that could provide places for intruders or criminals to hide should be removed. The basic principle of good lighting is to combine barriers with effective illumination in order to detect intrusion as soon as possible. Lighting is an effective deterrent to criminal activity since most criminals would prefer stealth and darkness for their efforts.

FENCES: THE FIRST LINE OF DEFENSE

The choice of fence type is part of the risk analysis and should always be cost effective for the assets to be secured. Fences can be further enhanced by the use of a number of physical or electronic devices to detect actual or attempted entry.

Intrusion detection devices are ways in which new or existing fences can be made more effective, especially in installations that involve high-security assets and large areas of fence to secure. The devices can be made to trigger alarms for immediate response, or alert and redirect closed circuit television monitors to cover the point of intrusion. The Vietnam war saw the development of many kinds of perimeter detection devices, and the development and implementation of fiber optics have made them more practical and reliable.

Gates and guardhouses are used to direct and check vehicular and pedestrian traffic through specific points along the outer perimeter. Gates can be manned, unmanned, or with entry controlled by access cards or keys. Gates are usually placed at all critical routes to the inner facility and can employ a number of security measures to divert, delay, or deter intruders. Some types of gate controls are as follows, in descending order of security level:

- Armed gate guards using a "sally port" to check out the entry and exit of vehicles and pedestrians.
- Unarmed guards using identification cards and signing in all visitors and vehicles. Could include liftable and lowerable "tire rippers" to stop vehicular traffic.
- Unmanned gates with oversight by CCTV and manual release for entry and exit. Could also employ tire rippers to control vehicular traffic, lockable turnstile for pedestrians, control from monitor site.
- Automated gates controlled from a monitoring center that lifts or lowers, or slides back, the portal devices. These could also be "hardened" further by using tire rippers and locking turnstiles.
- Automated gates controlled by keys or electronic card readers, combined with control from a monitoring center for visitors and vendors.

- Designated employee entrances and exits, controlled by keys or electronic card readers. Visitors and vendors would be routed to specific gates and controlled by one of the methods listed.

- Gates that are opened only during working hours and controlled (based on criticality) by one or more of the methods listed.

- Open access through specific gates only at certain times of the day or days of the week. Stronger access control at building(s).

- No gates, but traffic funneled and directed along certain routes by signs and physical barriers.

As can be seen, simply selecting the kinds of gates or gate controls can be difficult. The security level of the facility and the need to continue to have normal commerce through gates can determine the **throughput** (how long it takes to process entry or exit) needed to minimize dead time for employees, customers, and suppliers. Should the intruder get past the outer perimeter, the next line-of-protection point usually begins at the building exterior.

THE BUILDING EXTERIOR

Not all facilities have the luxury of a fenced and protected outer perimeter. The perimeter of many facilities might begin at the exterior of a building or building complex. This kind of first line of defense is sometimes called the **building envelope** by those who provide security planning through architectural design. In planning for security on a building exterior, the security professional needs to consider at all times that this is a three-dimensional object that must be protected from the sides, top, and below.

Windows tend to be the most vulnerable entries, followed by doors, rooftop entry points (skylights, vents, elevator shafts), and more unusual entry points such as tunnels underneath the floors or underground power ditches. It must be considered that the easiest way to penetrate the building is to cut right through the walls, which might be only wood and plasterboard, even though high-security doors and windows might be installed.

A general rule of thumb on windows or other openings on the exterior of a building is that if they are larger than 96 square inches and less than 18 feet from the ground they must be hardened in some manner to prevent entry. This can be accomplished in a number of ways, depending upon the building materials, the need to keep the appearance of the building intact, and the assets to be protected inside. These can range from installation of bars to the replacement of glass with modern security glass or other unbreakable materials.

Doors are most vulnerable at the locks, hinges, frame, and panel materials. The first line of security for doors (and windows) is the use of lighting above them. Lighting, combined with a hard-wired alarm system integrated into their frames, along with warning signs, can deter a thief from attempting entry. Hardening of the door can include being sure that the hinges are inside, the pins are welded to the hinge, the door frame is made of heavy wood or metal, and the panels to the doors are solid and reinforced with sheet steel if required.

The number of doors should be kept to a minimum in order to be able to secure the building most effectively. Doors used for heavy traffic can have special hardware installed to make them less of a burden for the operations of the business or institution. Seldom used doors can be secured by devices that are more secure, even if they tend to be slower in operational terms. Doors that must be used for emergency exits can be equipped with locking devices called "crash bars," which can be easily opened by pushing on the bar from the inside, while remaining securely locked on the exterior. To prevent these doors from being wedged open for the convenience of staff, who may want to go outside to smoke or even assist in an unauthorized entry, such doors should be individually alarmed and posted.

One must not forget the floor of a building as a possible entry point. In some cities, the utilities and sewers are underground and provide possible entry points for a determined intruder. In many cases, the building has been carefully secured at the

SECURITY BYTE 10 – 2

Get Real on Terrorism

For most buildings in America, the best way to counter terrorism is to do the same things you would to counter ordinary crime—and little more.

Security system countermeasures that combat ordinary criminal activity generally combat terrorism. Setting aside structural engineering issues, risks unique to terrorism, such as truck bombs, should simply be accepted—in most cases.

Why?

Truly effective countermeasures, such as closing public streets, are out of the reach of most security and facility managers.

Since such attacks are highly unlikely, learning to live with the risk should not be difficult. Any American driving on the highway has already intuitively learned the concept of "acceptable risk."

In terms of death and injury, a terrorist attack has a far, far lower probability than dying or being hurt in a traffic accident.

Of course, expenditures to specifically counter terrorism are valid if:

- your facility or organization is a target of persons or groups known to commit terroristic acts;

- if it has national or international notoriety or symbolic significance; or

- if your interests are threatened by perceptions of vulnerability to terroristic acts. One example: tenants will leave your building unless security is visibly enhanced.

    If your facility fits any of those criteria, do as much of the following as you can:

- Conduct a fresh, dispassionate risk assessment.

- Don't react to hysteria or paranoia or fixate on a single source of threat.

- Instead, develop countermeasures on the basis of total risk—not just a popularized threat, such as fertilizer truck bombs or pipe bombs.

- Segregate or screen vehicles; restrict indoor parking to trusted persons.

- Establish setbacks; slow or stop vehicles.

- Harden the facility.

- Establish an effective access control system for people, vehicles and objects.

- Introduce psychological deterrents into building design; displace incidents to some other target.

- Provide conspicuous, high-resolution, time-lapsed video recording of high-risk areas to assist in investigations and deter wrongdoers.

Source: John Strauchs. "Get Real on Terrorism," *Security* (Cahners Publishing Company. Newton, MA, 1996), Vol. 33, No. 9, p. 18.

doors, windows, and rooftops, but the floors are easily breached by tunneling or use of existing openings for various purposes. The financial institutions that have been breached by tunnels are warnings to the security planner to not only look out and up, but also *down* to provide complete protection.

Lighting should be used on rooftops if they are vulnerable to unauthorized entry. Lighting should also be placed at the corners of, and on the walls of, the buildings to provide security illumination. Loading areas, alleys, dumpsters, and other places where intruders could be hidden should be lighted as well. If required, these areas can also be monitored by CCTV. Patrol activity by roving security officers enhances the security in areas where little activity takes place and where intruders might find places to hide. In some larger complexes, a security officer may be placed at a designated entry for control of access and exit of personnel. This post might also monitor CCTV and alarm devices. If the smart criminal has managed to breach the outer perimeter and the building envelope, the next line-of-protection is the functional area.

ALARMS

The use of alarms, either independently or in conjunction with other forms of monitoring, is an important adjunct to a good physical security plan. Alarms must have three basic components: (1) a triggering device, (2) an enunciator that alerts some kind of recognition of penetration, and (3) a response of some kind. It is clear that no alarm is effective as anything but an irritant to an intruder unless there can be some response by guards or others. An alarm can be used to frighten away an intruder if it is loud and perhaps includes a spoken message. Some alarms are silent but do alert a guard force or some other deterrent device to act to capture or destroy the intruder.

Alarms are often tied into other devices, such as those that can lock the intruder into an area, turn on lights, or activate CCTV monitors while the guard response force gets to the scene. The kind of sensor can vary greatly, based on the area to be secured and the value of the asset being secured.

One of the major problems with alarm systems is that they tend to have a high ratio of false alarms. This creates a number of problems, either with the local police (if they are tied into the system) or with the security response force. It has been reported that as many as 90 percent of alarms are found to be false, which results in negative attitudes to alarm systems. This has been greatly improved in the recent past, and alarm systems are becoming more reliable and useful. In any case, most of the false alarm problems are *people* problems, often precipitated by employees who have failed to follow procedures and set off alarms accidentally. Despite their faults, alarm systems do prevent forced entry, and the burglary rates for companies with alarm systems were significantly lower than those without them.

FUNCTIONAL WORK AREA

If the building interior security has been planned properly, the various parts of the activity will be divided into functional areas that have been designated by their level of risk and vulnerability. In a computer complex, the area might be divided up into security zones, as shown in Figure 10–2. This same principle can be applied to any type of operation, providing either **nested** or **independent security zones** based on a risk analysis of the operations of the company or institution.

Physical security measures in the functional work areas include alarms, key or card access controls, and checkpoints manned by security officers at high-security operations. Compartmentalization of functions into discreet functions (administration, word processing, copying, assembly, and so on) greatly assists in the security of the functional areas. Badges and access cards then make the task of controlling personnel much easier. This allows the narrowing down of the line-of-protection concept to the specific room in which the most critical assets are contained. Again, it should be emphasized that no alarms are effective without someone to monitor and respond to them.

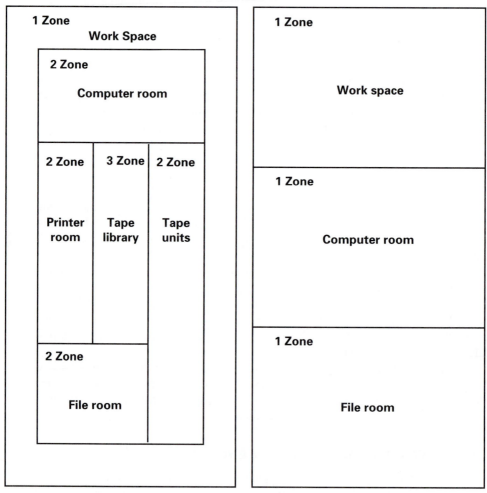

FIGURE 10–2 *Examples of Security Zones*

THE SPECIFIC ROOM AND THE ASSET ITSELF

As one gets down to this final stage, there is a number of ways to harden the target. This room can be specially constructed for maximum security (as in a bank vault), or it can employ a number of physical security devices to ensure that it is especially difficult to penetrate this inner circle. These include the use of biometric entry control devices that have almost no failure rate in identification of authorized personnel. (We cover these in detail in Chapters 12 and 13.) Another valuable physical security device is the use of special entry portals that utilize the sally port (sometimes called a mantrap) concept combined with high-level identification devices. The person desiring entry goes through one door and then is locked in the portal until he or she can pass the next identification test and then be passed on into the specific room. If the test is failed, the alarms are sounded and the doors locked until a security officer can arrive and clarify the situation. Additional security controls include CCTV monitoring or security guard posts or both, depending on the level of security required. Once the person has entered this ring of the onion, the next access is usually to the asset itself.

The type of physical security used at this point depends largely on the assets being secured. These can include alarm devices on the assets themselves, safes or locked filing cabinets, personal body alarms (for personnel), self-destruct devices on the equipment or objects, and special dispensers of gases or other agents aimed at destruction of the intruder. If the security professional has done his or her job thoroughly in the previous stages of planning, the need for drastic devices may not be great.

As you have seen, the line-of-protection concept lets a security professional analyze how to deal with the physical security needs of a business or institution. Another way to look at this kind of security planning is to use a combination of physical measures, administrative measures, personnel subsystems, and specific system countermeasures. This is generally referred to as the *layered* approach to security.

THE LAYERED APPROACH TO SECURITY

This approach to security planning is more oriented to the systems that are in place to secure assets than toward the specific techniques used by the security system. In addition to the physical countermeasures discussed earlier, the security manager may employ a number of other such measures, including guard and attack dogs, signs, mirrors, lock-down devices for equipment, marking of tools and equipment, paper shredders, metal detectors at entrances, electronic price tags at retail outlets, and computerized telephone lines and other electronic controls. Layering as a concept is shown in Figure 10–3.

ADMINISTRATIVE COUNTERMEASURES

The second layer, **administrative countermeasures**, deals with how the business is run to provide maximum security through administrative procedures. This is sometimes refereed to as operational security (OPSEC). The administrative countermeasures tend to provide ways in which to complement the physical measures with procedural

FIGURE 10–3 *The Layered Approach to Security*

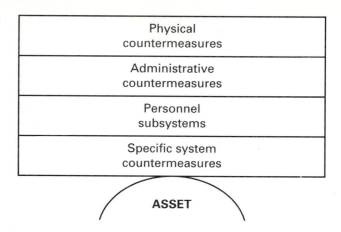

controls to implement security. Some of the most important aspects involve security awareness, policies and procedures involving security by nonsecurity staff, and arrangement of operations to make loss prevention more effective.

In the first case, the business has an obligation to provide security awareness training to all the personnel in the company and developing a team approach to security and loss prevention. Leaving the job of security to just security personnel is a major mistake made by many employers. In most cases, employees in every department are aware of vulnerabilities and risks that can affect their employer's assets, but have not been given an opportunity or channel to apply this knowledge. This can be corrected by actively involving the employees in the security staff meetings, using suggestion boxes, and employing other formal methods to convey comments and observations. To fail to provide education at all levels about the impact of both external and internal theft is to demonstrate indifference to such behavior. To fail to get input from everyone in the business about these issues is even worse.

As we mentioned in Chapter 9, policies and procedures are a positive and effective way for administration to deal with almost any issue. Security policies and procedures are usually for the security staff and seldom seen by other departments. The administration must work with security to see that security awareness is included in the policies and procedures for every department, with assistance from security staff in their development and production. The procedures developed will help ensure that the operations in each department are invested with a commitment to security and loss prevention. Security procedural controls can be as simple as the way that areas are monitored to more complex devices such as searches of persons and vehicles. Often the authorization of legal search and seizure procedures will deter a great amount of internal theft.

The last step is for the security professional to conduct a security analysis of the physical placement of various procedures and operations that may expose assets to criminal behavior. This can be as simple as moving the cash register toward the back of a convenience store to prevent what the police call "stop and rob" activity. It can also include crime prevention through architectural design in the construction phase of a company facility that provides for nested or independent security zones and other security aspects for minimizing risks to the assets. (We cover this topic in detail in Chapter 13.)

PERSONNEL SUBSYSTEMS

Personnel subsystems can help reduce the risk to the company assets by improving the quality of the persons hired, including security personnel screening before hiring. Kuhn points out that this process has a lot going against it:

- A shrinking pool of qualified workers
- Diminished employee loyalty
- Tougher legislation surrounding employee selection practices
- Defamation of character suits brought against employers who provide references to ex-employees
- Increasing workplace theft and drug use
- A growing number of vicarious liability and negligent hiring suits[1]

Selecting personnel should include a background check that verifies the information provided by the applicant in regard to previous employment, education records, and (when necessary) prior criminal records. An employment interview should be conducted that is specifically job related, nonaccusatory, and nondiscriminatory, but gives the interviewer a chance to get face-to-face reactions to critical questions. Paper-and-pencil tests to determine potential for future criminal or antisocial behavior are being used widely. The best of these have been thoroughly tested and have developed national norms. Careful investigation of these tests should be made before using them. The polygraph test has been severely restricted in its use for employment screening. The decisions of the Texas Supreme Court,[2] in 1987 were followed by the Employee Polygraph Protection Act in 1988.[3] This act precluded polygraph usage in preemployment processing, with a few exceptions for prospective employees of private armored car, security alarm, and security firms. This is not a blanket exception, however, and it does not apply to proprietary security departments that supply security for the company on an exclusive basis.

The growth of computer banks that hold information about all of us has given birth to a whole new industry in the security field. Companies (usually associated with a private investigation agency) now offer computerized background checks that provide a quick, reasonably accurate, thorough set of data that is usually accompanied by an analysis of the potential of the applicant. These searches include public records of criminal activity, workers' compensation records, driving records, credit records, verified education records, and even medical and military records. With all this at their disposal, it becomes more difficult for companies to defend cases of negligent hiring on the basis of not knowing the applicant was lying.

SPECIFIC SYSTEM COUNTERMEASURES

The last layer deals with **specific system countermeasures**, which are specialized to the particular asset at the core of the program. These countermeasures have a range as large as the items being protected. These can be special access systems for computers, safes and vaults for valuables, or electronic tags for merchandise. Many of these countermeasures involve access control to specific areas, the topic of our next section.

ENTRANCE CONTROL: A CRITICAL ELEMENT

No other segment of the security industry has enjoyed more research and development than access control. This has resulted in a frenzy of new systems, user identification methods, integration of alarm point monitoring, control functions, and features that only a decade ago were thought of as science fiction. Largely responsible for this development is, as in many other industries, the computer. Using computers, manufacturers of access control devices are now able to create system, of tremendous power and flexibility. As a result, the security office has been transferred into a high-tech area with vital information instantly available to the security staff.

CARD-BASED SYSTEMS

In a **card-based system**, the card reader reads the data on the card, transforms this data into a number, and sends it to a control unit access control panel (ACP). The panel analyzes the number and verifies that all conditions to grant access are satisfied before the door is released.

If a printer is connected to the ACP, a message is printed stating who was granted access to the protected area and the time and date he or she was allowed to enter. If access is denied, the message includes who attempted to gain access and why the request was denied (wrong time, day, or door).

This information can also be transferred to a computer (host). In this case, the host did not play an essential part in the access cycle because the ACP had all the necessary information with which to operate, and the host was simply used as a logging, presentation, and programming device, thus making this a computer-enhanced or distributed processing system.

Some manufacturers use the host as a processing unit in which all verification and access decisions are made. In such systems, the only verification done in the ACP is the verification of the facility code, or system code as it is sometimes called. If the facility code is correct, the ACP sends the sequential number of the card to the host. The host finds the card number in the database; checks the time and day of the week; and if the card is authorized at the access point, sends a command to the ACP to release the door. Messages are presented on the screen or printer that an access request was granted or denied.

Explosives Detection Choices: Myth vs. Reality

If someone told you they had a detector that could find minute traces of drugs AND explosives on the body, in a suitcase or in a package, would you believe them?

The fact is that such devices to exist. However, as one recent incident demonstrated, fradulent claims can be easy to make and to believe. A South Carolina company was barred temporarily from making or selling a unit that amounted to little more than a hollow plastic box with a paper "chip" inside. Yet, the company managed to sell about 1,000 of the devices before they were caught.

"Those incidents do our business a lot of harm," says Tony Jenkins, president of Ion Track Instruments, Wilimington, Mass. "We are in the business of finding things that nobody else can see." Ion Track uses a chemical trace detection method called Ion Trap Mobility Spectrometry to successfully locate explosives or drugs on people or in suitcases or packages—very similar to what the fraudulent company claimed.

Choose Carefully

Jenkins has some advice for companies or agencies looking for bomb detection equipment: "I would suggest that anybody looking to purchase equipment in this field get an opinion from an authority that has been heavily involved in this." In the narcotics detection arena, Customs or the Army are good authorities, he says. And the FAA is good for explosives detection.

Other manufacturers concur. "Check references," says Dennis Cunningham, national sales director for Control Screening, Greensburg, Pa., an X-ray manufacturer. "See a demonstration of this product."

Kristoph Krug, director of research and development for Vivid Technologies, Waltham, Mass., strongly suggests testing the unit yourself with real materials. There are other things to be aware of, as well.

"Most of the 'new technology' (in explosives detection) has been around in one form or another for a long time, often in the medical or military environments," Krug says.

Another consideration, Cunningham points out, is to be sure of what you need. "Sometimes people are buying things they don't really need for that application."

Technology Options

"Where you have environments with multiple, mixed materials, such as an airline passenger's suitcase with toiletry items, cameras, laptop computers and other items all mixed together, many of the newer technologies are good," Cunningham says. "They are designed to help separate out multiple choices. But in an instance such as mail bombs, you are for the most part still at the basic level for screening, where density is the most important thing."

Control Screening has a conveyorized unit specifically designed to screen mail. Portable, the unit can also be used as a purse or package scanner.

A step beyond X-ray, Vivid Technologies' unit works on the principle of dual energy X-ray, Krug says. Unlike regular X-ray, the machine measures individual materials and looks for specific characteristics. It can look for drugs, explosives, and even U.S. currency, Krug says. "It's good at finding materials that are always made of the same stuff."

Depending on what you're looking for, trace detection can be useful in screening the

Explosives Detection Choices: Myth vs. Reality

person as well as the bag, Jenkins says. "We do configure detection systems into both portable units and walk through units which will grab samples from around the body and detect explosive vapors." The walk through units are frequently used in conjunction with X-ray, he says, because they can determine if the person has been handling explosives.

With national and international bombing incidents, increasing at an alarming rate, new devices are likely to continue to come to market.

One positive trend Jenkins sees is that the detection is getting more specific. "From equipment five years ago, which could detct but not identify, we are now capable of identifying the specific material."

Source: Editor. "Exposives Detection Choices: Myth Vs. Reality," *Security* (Cahners Publishing Company. Newton, MA, 1996), Vol. 33, No. 5, p. 22.

WHICH KIND OF SYSTEM?

Arguments can be made for both types of systems. The distributed processing system makes faster access decisions and, therefore, can process more people through an area in a given amount of time. Until recently, it was necessary to program each ACP individually, but software developments for hosts in this system have made it possible to program, from the host, several ACPs at the same time.

These systems also benefit from the fact that there is no reduction in security if the communication line between the ACP and the host is down since all the decisions and verifications are done by the ACP, not the host. Most ACPs of this type are able to store access transactions in a buffer in case of host failure or communication line. Once the problem is corrected, the ACP can upload the information to the host for storage on the hard disk.

The drawback with a card-based system of this type is that there is generally little flexibility and few features. Capabilities such as disabling (masking) of alarm points and activation of multiple relays are seldom found. After all, a card is just a means of carrying a number, and the ACP will have a given instruction for that number (verify and grant access). In some of these systems, the instruction can vary when the card is at a different reader, but it is still relatively limited. Functions such as sending a duress alarm if the cardholder is under threat are not practical.

INCREASING THE SECURITY LEVEL

To increase the security level and flexibility of such systems, many manufacturers are adding a keypad to the card reader. This means that the user who is requesting access will use both a card and a code. Most systems use a specific code for a specific card, but some systems recognize only one code that remains the same for all cards.

The addition of the keypad to the card reader serves several purposes, one being the increased flexibility now that the system can offer the user the capability of sending a silent duress alarm to the ACP or host. Card-based systems incorporating alarm-monitoring circuits (intrusion detection) and control functions (output relays to control various devices) are usually computer driven.

SYSTEM CODING

Figure 10–4 is a simplified system with one host, two ACPs, and one intrusion detection station (IDS). The IDS has alarm input points (control points). The host in this example has only one communication port; therefore, it is not necessary to identify each port on which the messages are received. To illustrate this concept, we will identify the communication port.

Connected to the communication line are ACPs (ACP1 and ACP2), each having four access points. A message from door two of ACP1 will look like this: 1,1,2,XXX (communication port 1, ACP1, door 2, card number XXX). The host then finds on the hard disk the conditions and name for that cardholder and the parameters for access point 1,1,2. These parameters can be the location for the ACP and the physical location of the door itself, described in English as a stockroom door, panel in west wing.

The fourth door on the second ACP will be identified by the host as 1.2.4—meaning communications port 1, ACP2, door 4. This number sequence is then used as an index to store additional information, such as door location.

The same concept is applied when the system is identifying alarm points and for storing additional data at each alarm point, as shown in Figure 10–5. If, for example, the third alarm panel circuit of IDS1 on communication line 1 is violated, the message (index) would be 1,1,3. The host, of course, has a way to differentiate an IDS from an ACP, and this may be done in several different ways, such as having all IDSs send a character like an *, along with the IDS address, which would then read 1, *1, 3, or addressing them differently from the ACPs. Whatever the method, the concept is the same and repeats itself once more for the control (relay) points.

Again, the system must have a way to differentiate control (relay) points from alarm points. For relay 5 of IDS1 on communication port 1, the message would be 1, *1, C5, where C stands for a control relay.

ALARMS AND CODES BY CATEGORIES

Let's look at some instructions that can now be filed under the index number of an alarm port. In some systems, alarms are separated by categories, and each category can be assigned a priority level. This means that in large systems with heavy traffic, several alarms may be lined up. A new alarm of high priority is then processed and presented before other lower priority messages are processed. In this case, the category is included in the alarm point information.

Examples of categories are fire, intrusion, duress, no-alarm monitor point, and test. Examples of transmission, processing and presentation priorities, assigned to categories, are the following:

FIGURE 10–4 *A System with One Host, Two ACPs, and One IDS*

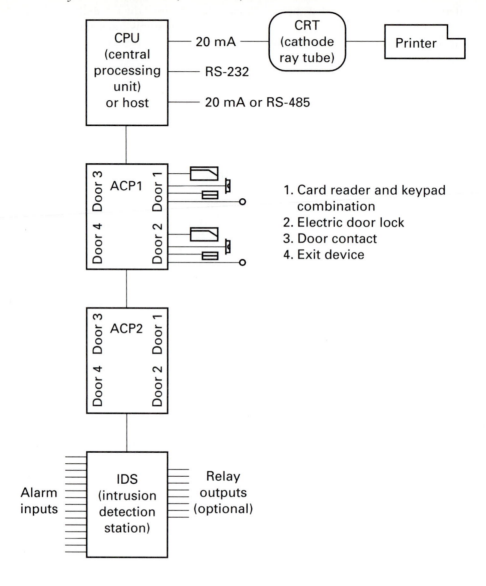

1. Card reader and keypad combination
2. Electric door lock
3. Door contact
4. Exit device

- Priority 1:   Fire
- Priority 2:   Intrusion
- Priority 3:   Duress
- Priority 4:   Monitor point

- Priority 5:   Trouble conditions
- Priority 6:   Test point
- Priority 7:   Return to normal (alarm)
- Priority 8:   Trouble, return to normal

FIGURE 10–5   *Identifying Alarm Points*

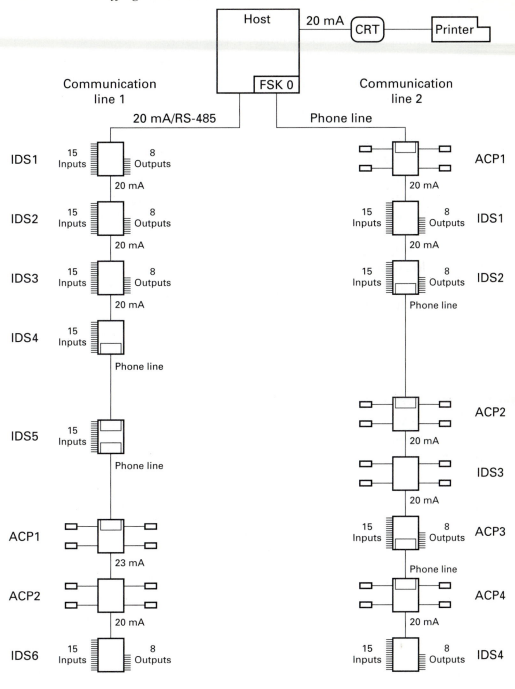

The following is an example of alarm information given the message 1, *1, 3.

- Category: Intrusion.
- Route alarm message to printer 1, terminal 2.
- Description (English text—motion detector in west hallway of warehouse 2).
- Normal status of the input (open or closed).
- Masked (ignored) during time zone.
- Active relay or relays 1.
- Mask other alarm points.
- Display instructions to guard.
- Require acknowledgment from a guard.
- Display a floor plan of the area in which the alarm is activated.
- Let persons on the security staff write a comment of their action (such as working overtime, accidentally walked into the field of a motion sensor while on way to vending machine).
- Route this alarm report to the following devices: printer 1, terminal 2.
- Similar information is stored under the access point index number—access point 1,2,1—such as basic entry point and description: west lobby door.

In more powerful systems, additional data can be entered, such as the following:

- Access request messages routed to printer 2, terminal 3.
- Antipassback entry or exit.
- Elevator control access point (will activate multiple relays).
- Guard tour point.
- Alarm masking access point.
- Two-person control access point.
- Area loading access point (minimum, maximum).
- Authority presence required.
- Enable second authenticator.
- Time/attendance point.

The explanation of these items is sometimes, but not always, obvious. In some systems, several terminals and printers may be remotely located. In that case, alarm messages and access messages from those areas can be routed to printers or terminals located in that specific area.

ANTIPASSBACK ENTRY OR EXIT

Antipassback (APB) prevents a user from passing back the card to allow a second person to enter. Access is also denied to someone attempting to follow (tailgate) the user into an APB area without using his or her own card or code.

A few powerful systems even have an internal access point. This means that if a user tailgates himself or herself into an APB area, access is denied to all access points within the APB area since the system did see the person enter the area.

ELEVATOR ACCESS POINT

Elevator access point means that this access point triggers additional relays to enable travel to restricted floors. This access point is linked to cardholder information so that the system knows which relays (floors) this specific user is authorized to travel to. Some systems also log which floor the elevator traveled to and then return the elevator car to the lobby.

GUARD TOUR ACCESS POINT

A guard tour access point differs from one manufacturer to another depending on how the manufacturer perceives the concept. In most cases, the simple form of guard tour is sufficient. Under that concept, an access point is defined only as an access point, and the guard has a separate card that records only that the guard was on location at the specified time. This is very straightforward and does not require special software.

The next step is systems with the capability of defining a number of access points of the system in a sequence that the guard follows during a tour and of defining the amount of time it should take to move from one point to the next. In this case, it is also necessary to allow some tolerance to adjust for the guard being a little early or late. For example, if it should normally take a guard five minutes to go from point 4 to point 5, you may want to allow for a window of plus or minus thirty seconds at point 5. If the guard is too early, it could mean that he or she is cheating somehow, and this will create a message at the host.

If the guard runs past the maximum time allowed, it may mean something has happened to the guard. At that point, the system would generate the message, "guard too late at point 5." The control room officer may then want to call the patrol officer on the radio. If the guard is simply delayed in reaching the checkpoint, the report will log the actual elapsed time from the previous point. The system will then allot the normal time to go from point 5 to point 6 on the tour.

For added flexibility, some systems will include a keypad. This arrangement allows the guard to use the card if everything is normal and on time. If the guard knows that he or she will be late to the next checkpoint, the guard can enter a code giving a time while reporting the delay to the next checkpoint, or he or she can enter a duress code alerting the control room officer of trouble.

ALARM MASKING ACCESS POINT

An alarm masking access point could be one located at the entry of an area secured with volumetric protection. Before a user is granted access to the area, one or more alarm points may have to be masked. The capability to do so is assigned to an access point, and the sensors to be masked are assigned with the user's card.

In simple terms, a card can cause a masking operation. One or several alarm points may be grouped into, for example, masking operation 19, the research and development lab on the third floor. Alarm points assigned to this masking operation are masked until the masking operation is reversed (the user leaves the area) or until a specified masking time is up.

To prevent accidentally trapping the user in an area by removing the mask from a motion sensor in the hallway, alarm points may be a part of several masking operations that can be applied and removed independently from each other.

TWO-PERSON CONTROL POINT

A two-person control point is the access point leading into an area in which at least two people have to be present. For this to operate properly, antipassback has to be in effect at all access points to the protected area since the system must count the number of users entering or leaving the area. If the number of users within the protected area is zero, then two users are required to enter their cards or codes within the time span of a few seconds to be allowed access. Of course, both users have to be authorized to be in the area.

If the user count within the area is two or more, only one card or code may be required. To enter such an area, the system must verify several items: the first card or code entered is valid at that area, the APB status of the user is correct, the time and day of the week are valid, and the number of users within the area is two or more. If any of these parameters is not satisfied, the system denies access. A few keypad and card readers are equipped with a message display that lets the person seeking access know if access was granted or denied, and if denied, the reason why. If the user count within the area is fewer than two, the system lets the user know that access will be granted if a second valid user enters his or her code or card.

To leave the area, a user must go through the same process in reverse. The system checks all parameters of the card or code and checks the user count in the area. If the user count is three or higher, exit is granted. If the user count is only two (which means if the user leaves there will be only one left in the area), exit is denied unless both enter their cards or codes to leave the area together.

AREA LOADING ACCESS POINT

An area loading access point also requires an entry–exit authenticator. In this case, however, it may not be necessary to use the same level of identification verification on the exit side. For example, a card or code may be required to enter the area, but a card may be the only identification required to exit.

For an area monitored for loading (occupancy level) with a maximum number of occupants set at ten, the system counts every entry and exit, tabulates the number of occupants presently in the area, and grants access as long as the current number of occupants is fewer than ten. The eleventh person will not be granted access until someone leaves the area.

AUTHORIZED PRESENCE REQUIRED

Authorized presence required is a restriction placed on an access point going into an area in which a person responsible for the area must be present before the system grants access to anyone. The prerequisite is, of course, an entry–exit authenticator so that the system is able to detect when the person with the authoritative responsibility leaves the area and then not grant access until he or she returns.

ENABLE SECOND AUTHENTICATOR

The enabling of a second authenticator is a feature found in only one system. However, this particular user has several such access points. In this case, the access point is an entrapment portal, often referred to as a mantrap.

There are many ways to configure and operate mantraps. As described under physical security, both doors are normally closed and locked. A user pushes a button, and one door is unlocked. The user steps into the module (sally port) and presents a card to the reader. As the system verifies the facility code of the card, a message "enter PIN code" (PIN stands for personal identification number) appears, and a scrambling keypad is activated. The user enters the PIN, and when the host verifies that the code matches the code associated with that particular card, a message appears on the display prompting the user to use a second authenticator (a retinal scanner).

After the retinal pattern has been verified as the pattern for this user, another message appears on the display informing the user that the weight sensors are now measuring the total weight of the entire mantrap module and the contents (user and anything carried in or out). This weight is then compared with the weight measured at the last passage (in or out) of the particular user. Any mismatch of these parameters causes an alarm within the security control center, and voice communications can be established with the person in the module. Entry will not be allowed beyond the module until the discrepancies are resolved.

TIME AND ATTENDANCE ACCESS POINT

Time and attendance access points vary greatly from one system to another (offered at all). One simple way to provide such a service is to dedicate a card reader or keypad to recording employee entry to the facility, and exit at time of departure. Several software packages available from the non-security industry take into consideration such variables as pay methods, overtime calculations, and compensatory time due. Time and attendance is an office function, not a security task, and should be kept out of security systems.

The following list shows examples of access point and alarm point assignments. Of course, an access point with a special assignment (such as an alarm masking point) will not perform its special function for every user who enters a card or code. These are just functions that the system performs from the specified access points when a card and/or code with matching assignments in the cardholder database is entered to tell the system such information as which points to match.

Function-related card assignments for an access control system are as follows:

- Time assignment
- Day assignment
- Access point assignment
- Activation of additional relay or relays (always)
- Activation of additional relay or relays (during time zone)
- Guard tour
- Masking of alarm point or points
- One- or two-person control
- Visitor
- Visitor escort privileges
- Authority (such as area supervisor)

The first three function-related card assignments are very basic and determine when and where a user is allowed.

The assignment "activation of additional relay or relays" is used, for example, when elevator control is required. When used at an access point defined as an elevator control access point, the card or code tells the system to activate certain relays so that the system knows the floors that the person is allowed to go to (which relays to energize). It may only be necessary to activate several relays during certain hours—for instance, afterwork hours in the evening.

A card or code defined as a guard lets the system know that when this card or code is entered at an access point defined as a guard tour access point, it may not have to open the door but just log the guard as having reached the location. It will also know which tour this guard is patrolling and may anticipate the arrival of a different guard patrolling a different tour when the same point is used in several guard tours (like the control center).

When a mask alarm card or code is entered as an access point defined as an alarm masking point, the system knows which alarm points to mask and for how long. For instance, this allows a guard to cross an area protected with volumetric devices and an employee to work after hours in his or her area while the rest of the building is secure.

A card or code can be defined as one that must be used in conjunction with someone else's card or code when entered at an access point defined as two-person control. This second person can be anyone else, a specific person, or a member of a specific group of persons. The system checks if two persons are always required to enter together or only if the current area occupancy is fewer than two.

Visitor and visitor escort are variations of the same concept. The operator of the control center can determine who has the authority to escort a visitor. A visitor status is assigned to a card or code not allowing the visitor to enter into secured areas alone. A visitor is allowed entry only after the system has granted access to a person who has a card or code assigned with visitor escort authorization. If several visitors are escorted by the same person, the escort is granted access first and then holds the door open as the visitors enter their cards one at a time.

Authority is a multilevel feature that can be assigned to a card or code. In a way, the visitor or escort is a combination of two-person control and authority. The authority can be an area supervisor. When this person is present in his or her area, other users with access privileges may enter.

If the supervisor leaves, no other person will be allowed into the area. This can be elaborated on by having several levels of authority (or priority) in the same system, the higher levels overriding the lower so that, for instance, the owner of the company can enter the area even if the supervisor is not present.

Applying the Principles

Now that we have a foundation of knowledge about access control systems, let's examine a fictitious building, as shown in Figure 10–6. This shows a building with ten access points connected to three ACPs. The ACPs report on one common communication line to the host.

ACP1, access point 1, is the door into an office; access point 2 is an entry–exit reader from APB area 1; access point 3 is an entry–exit reader into APB area 2 from outside the building; and access point 4 is another entry–exit reader into APB area 1.

ACP2, access point 2, is an entry–exit reader into APB area 3 and an access point with an area loading and authority presence requirement. Access point 2 is an entry–exit reader into APB area 2; access point 3 is a normal access point with a request-to-exit pushbutton, and access point 4 is unused at this time.

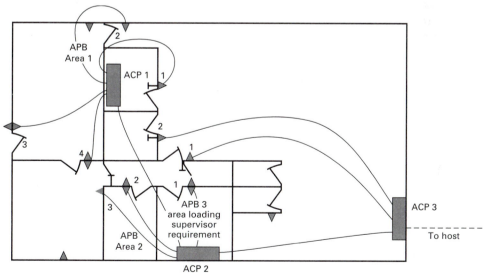

FIGURE 10–6 *Access System Configuration*

ACP3, access point 3, has two access points, both just standard access points with request-to-exit pushbuttons.

As shown in Figure 10–7, the ACPs are inside the area with the highest security level controlled by the ACP. We now add a safe and a filing cabinet, and a guard tour to check on the area. We have added two more access points to the system, one to the filing cabinet (ACP3, access point 3) and one to the safe (ACP4, access point 4).

We determine that we want the guard to walk the area, as shown in Figure 10–7. Since the first station of a tour is usually the control center, we start at the entry point as the number 2 station of the tour. So, we configure ACP1, access point 3, and a guard tour point 2 of tour number XXX.

In this example, the guard is allowed to enter the area, so the system unlocks the door. The guard enters and walks to the exit reader/keypad of the area, which is not necessarily a guard tour station. Then the guard walks over to the reader/keypad at the filing cabinet (ACP3, access point 3). This is guard tour station number 3, and the elapsed time should be, let's say, thirty seconds (plus or minus ten seconds from station number 2). The guard then walks to the reader at ACP1, access point 1 (guard tour station number 4). The system will not release the door here since the guard is not allowed into this office. All that is needed is to check that the door is locked. The guard will then go to guard tour station number 5 at the safe before leaving the building.

If we now add alarm monitoring to the system by an IDS—and have the alarm points masked during normal working hours, allowing personnel to move without violating any alarm sensor—this would mean that when the guard enters his or her card or code at the entry, the alarm points must be masked. So, now we made ACP1,

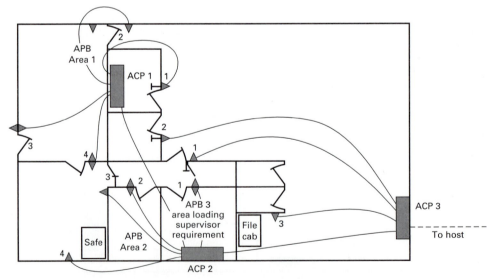

FIGURE 10–7 *Access System Configuration with Guard Tour Points*

access point 3, an entry-exit and guard tour station. We must also make it mask alarm point 1,2,3 of IDS1: (*1, 1) (*1, 2) (*1, 3).

This example shows the concepts and applications of the various assignments that can be made to access points, cards or codes, and alarm points. There are, of course, many ways to arrive at the same result. In this particular example, one communication line connects the ACPs and the IDSs to a host computer.

The host in this example makes all the decisions, sends commands to the ACPs and IDSs, grants access, makes alarm points, and so on. It is, however, becoming more common for the various ACPs and IDSs to communicate and send commands to one another without the host having to make any verification and decisions. It is the direction our future systems will most likely take—toward more powerful controllers, more intelligence, and more decision making at the local level. This will reduce the dependence on communication lines and host computers, as well as increase the speed of each transaction and decision.

The host computer will increasingly be used as a presentation enhancer with features like color graphic displays and extensive data on each alarm or access point, including messages that prompt guards to take certain actions. The capability of the host to generate various types of reports and statistics will develop as more sophisticated and interactive software becomes available.

Some manufacturers use a distributed processing database system, where several smaller hosts (PCs) are connected to form a network of their own. Each host communicates with a larger central computer. In large-scale systems, this approach minimizes the dependence on communication lines while the system can still be operated and programmed from either the central host or a local station.

In the case of smaller, decentralized systems, look for more features as processing power and memory increase, allowing each local panel to increase the database of users, access and alarm points, and, of course, instructions (software). There will also be more flexibility, allowing card technologies of different designs to work in systems that use codes or various biometric devices.[4]

Summary

In this chapter, we have briefly covered the roles of physical security and access control for the integrated security systems of the present and future. The basic activities in all these systems are developed in the careful planning and conduct of a risk assessment (as outlined in Chapter 8). The physical security survey can be used as an appendix to that document to develop physical, administrative, personnel, and system-specific countermeasures. The access control systems are also generated from the risk assessment and should be developed in concert with the latest versions of access control technology and computerized systems. This kind of technology is the future of security, and serious students need to learn how to apply such systems, even if they are not experts in their design and development. Chapter 12 will examine much of the latest technology in security equipment and how vendors develop and present them for use by the security industry.

REVIEW QUESTIONS

1. What kinds of outer perimeter protective barriers are the most common and useful?

2. Describe the differences between nested security zones and independent security zones.

3. What are the main reasons for the growth in use of computers in the security field?

4. What is meant by "line of protection" in security planning?

5. List some major considerations for selecting access control systems.

TERMS TO REMEMBER

five Ds

line of protection

outer perimeter

protective barriers

clear zones

intrusion detection devices

throughput

building envelope

nested (independent)
  security zones

personnel subsystems

specific system counter-
  measures

ENDNOTES

1. Ryan A. Kuhn, "The Psychological Test," *Security Management: Special Supplement—The Ways and Means of Screening* (March 1990), p. 21.

2. *Texas State Employment Union* v. *Texas Department of Mental Health*, 1987.

3. *The Employment Polygraph Protection Act (EPPA)*, US Code 10, 1988.

4. Again, I express my gratitude for the use of the material written by Lars R. Suneborne in a special supplement on access control called "Access to Utopia," *Security Management: Special Supplement—What's the Latest Word in Access Control?* (July 1989), pp. 8A–14A, 58A–64A.

11

Crime Prevention

A MAJOR ELEMENT OF SECURITY AND LOSS PREVENTION—ROLES AND PRACTICES

> *Crime prevention is an elegantly simple and direct approach that protects the potential victim from criminal attack by anticipating the possibility of attack and eliminating or reducing the opportunity for it to occur—and the possibility for personal harm or property loss should it occur.*
>
> —National Crime Prevention Institute

Overview

Crime in America is a "boom" industry, one that has flourished over the years, and though it has had periods of decline in recent years, it continues to prosper. It seems clear that any action that can be taken to prevent a crime is an action that is in the best interests of society. But with the country under siege by crime, drugs, and violence, it is difficult to expect police to be able to focus on preventing the next crime when so many remain unsolved. In this chapter, we discuss crime and its origins as well as efforts being taken to prevent crime before it occurs.

Common-Law Origins of Crime

Most crimes fall into one of two categories: **felonies** or **misdemeanors**. Felonies are a group of offenses considered in most societies serious enough to deserve severe punishment or even death. Although they vary somewhat in their specific names, the major felony crimes are remarkably similar for all jurisdictions. In the United States, we have come to define most common-law crimes as felonies because we inherited many of their designations from the English common-law statutes. Under the common law, which developed by history and precedent, there were three categories of crime: treason, felony, and misdemeanor.[1] Treason was always considered to be a crime for which death was the punishment. Originally, the distinction between felonies and misdemeanors was based on the premise that all felonies were capital offenses, also involving forfeiture of all lands and property of the perpetrator. On the other hand, misdemeanors called for lesser penalties. Even though the United States, as a British colony, adopted many aspects of **English common law**, the severity of felony punishment was modified to reflect the American way of life. From a practical standpoint, to execute every colonist convicted of the many crimes that fell into the "felony" category would have severely thinned the ranks of colonial laborers and explorers.

The distinction between a felony and a misdemeanor in modern America is generally based either on the type of institution in which the offender would be incarcerated or on the length of the sentence imposed. Most felony convictions require a sentence of more than one year, to be served in a state prison. This guideline is not universally applied, but it serves as a good rule of thumb in determining which crimes are generally considered felonies. Most legal agencies tend to lump the various kinds of felonies into categories that pertain to the social harm involved: offenses against the person, offenses against property, offenses against morality and decency, and so on. We now examine those categories and the correctional clients they produce.

CRIMES AGAINST THE PERSON

Four of the eight major or "index" offenses cited in the Federal Bureau of Investigation's Uniform Crime Reports are usually **crimes against the person**.[2] These four crime categories (murder and nonnegligent manslaughter, aggravated assault, forcible rape, and robbery) are the "headline crimes" that attract the media and create public fear, promoting attitudes and support for "get tough" laws and more aggressive law enforcement. Despite their shock effect, the four offenses accounted for only 12.5 percent of the index crimes reported in 1991 (1.8 million of 14.5 million).[3] The emphasis placed on those crimes is demonstrated by the higher percentage of them that are cleared by arrest—which is hardly a surprise since it is only logical that the principal resources of our law enforcement agencies should be marshaled to solve those crimes that the public fears most. An average of 52.3 percent of the crimes in

SECURITY BYTE 11-1

Felony

A criminal offense punishable by death or by incarceration in a state or federal confinement for a period, typically one year or more, of which the lower limit is prescribed by statute in a given jurisdiction.

these four categories are cleared by arrest, compared with only 18.3 percent in crimes against property. Murder and nonnegligent manslaughter lead with a clearance rate of 68.2 percent, aggravated assault follows with 60.6 percent, forcible rape has a 52.5 percent rate of clearance, and robbery has only a 28.7 percent rate.[4]

CRIMES AGAINST PROPERTY

Of the estimated 3.8 million individuals who are under correctional supervision in America each day (2.1 percent of all American adults), the majority are placed there for offenses against property. Even with the low clearance by arrest percentages, the sheer volume of the property crimes tends to keep our prisons full. Reported incidents of burglary, for example, totaled more than 3 million in 1990,[5] and the clearance by arrest rate for burglary was 14.4 percent. Similar figures apply to both larceny (17.7 percent) and auto theft (17.2 percent), with convictions for all three offenses totaling more than 1 million clients for the correctional system.

The offender against property is usually young. The number of auto theft cases alone is a major percentage of the total for those offenses. It is estimated that an automobile is stolen in the United States every twenty seconds. Persons under eighteen accounted for 33 percent of the reported burglaries cleared by arrest.[6] Crimes against the person may account for the longer sentences, but crimes against property contribute most to the volume in the correctional pipeline.

Burglary is usually considered a crime against the habitation and is the most common crime reported in the crime index. More than 3 million burglaries were reported in 1990. Because 66 percent of burglaries are committed in dwellings, it is a crime that alarms the citizens. That fear prevails even though trends since 1985 show decreases in residential burglary both during the day and during the night. In fact, the only type of burglary that has shown constant increases since 1985 is nonresidential burglary in the daytime, caused in great part because of families in which both parents are at work all day. There is a great amount of fear, sometimes resulting in the victim's overreaction, that forcible entry into one's home necessarily implies violence against one's person. The homeowner's zeal for self-preservation results in a number of tragic accidental shootings each year, even though burglary offenders are seldom aggressive. It has been estimated that property worth billions of dollars each year is taken to obtain money for drugs. Because the crime of burglary requires stealth and cunning, offenders are seldom caught at the scene: more often, they are caught when they

---

SECURITY BYTE 11 – 4

Crimes Against Property

A summary term used by UCR, both as a subclass of the Part I offenses and as a subclass of Crime Index Offenses, but with different meanings.

As a subset of Part I offenses:

> Robbery
> Burglary
> Larceny and theft
> Motor vehicle theft

As a subset of Crime Index offenses:

> Burglary
> Larceny and theft
> Motor vehicle theft

---

attempt to sell the stolen goods. Although the clearance by arrest rate was less than 12% in 1990, the figures can be deceptive. Some burglaries are perpetrated by more than one offender, but in other cases, one person may be responsible for numerous offenses.

CRIMES AGAINST MORALITY AND DECENCY

Crimes that may get even more publicity than murder are those that have a sexual connotation. Child molesters, for example, excite widespread public alarm and high media interest. Such individuals also assume the lowest position in the inmate social system in most prisons. Many of the so-called **acts between consenting adults** are being removed from the criminal codes, leaving only the forcible assaultive sexual predators and assaultive homosexuals to be sent to prison. This aggravates an already growing problem of controlling violent crime—and presents potential litigation problems for security managers.

OTHER REPORTED CRIME

Although the four serious index crimes against the person, which are regularly reported to the FBI, are important indicators of crime in America, many other crimes are listed that affect private security more than some of these. The other crimes that are in reported in the FBI's **Uniform Crime Reports**, though they do not produce such exciting headlines, make up 87.5 percent of the crimes reported to the police (an average of more than 12 million crimes per year.) And this does not include the vast number of crimes that are not reported to the police, but are often handled within a family, neighborhood, or business or institution. The sheer volume of crime in the United States seems to say that crime prevention has been fighting a losing battle. Lest we despair, however, we need to look at more details and especially the potential impact on the private security sector.

Impact on Business and Institutions

The impact of crime on the business and institutional sectors has many aspects beyond the obvious. *The Hallcrest Report I* reported the indirect costs of economic and other crime against business, government, and the public:

EFFECTS ON BUSINESS
- Increased costs of insurance and security protection
- Costs of internal audit activities to detect crime
- Costs of investigation and prosecution of subjects measured in terms of lost time of security and management personnel
- Reduced profits
- Increased selling prices and weakened competitive standing
- Loss of productivity
- Loss of business reputation
- Deterioration in quality of service
- Threat to the survival of small business

EFFECTS ON GOVERNMENT

- Costs of investigation and prosecution of suspects
- Increased costs of prosecuting sophisticated (e.g., embezzlement) and technology-related (e.g., computer) crimes
- Costs of correctional programs to deal with economic crime offenders
- Costs of crime prevention programs
- Costs of crime reporting and mandated security programs
- Loss of revenue (e.g., loss of sales tax, untaxed income of perpetrator, and tax deductions allowed businesses for crime-related losses)

EFFECTS ON THE PUBLIC

- Increased costs of consumer goods and services to offset crime losses
- Loss of investor equity
- Increased taxes
- Reduced employment due to business failures

Note: These effects are concerned only with nonviolent business crime, but if the total crime environment of institutions (schools, hospitals, museums, etc.) were also considered, the effects on institutions would include the following:

- Declining enrollment, attendance, or occupancy due to crime-related incidents
- Employee turnover and recruitment costs due to fear of crime incidents
- Increased costs of services
- Increased costs of insurance and security protection[7]

Crime prevention in law enforcement agencies has not always gotten the support or recognition it might deserve. Often this is from the entrenched attitude by law enforcement that **crime prevention** is not really "police work." Although concerned with crime prevention, the rising street-crime rates place police in a crime-response mode and unable to devote the resources to perform this mission for policing. Because of the growing tidal wave of street crime and the failure of reactive policing in recent years, police administrators finally have begun to get law enforcement to explore alliances with private security professionals in an effort to find the community roots of crime and truly begin to prevent it.

It is difficult to get support for an activity that is almost impossible to measure. How do you measure what hasn't yet or didn't happen? With the advent of community-based and value-oriented policing (discussed in Chapter 4), crime prevention practitioners are finally beginning to get some of the support and respect they deserve. They have begun to expand the role of crime prevention in police agencies beyond that of giving lectures and passing out pamphlets. These activities are important adjuncts to crime prevention, but working in the communities as a full partner with other community resources seems to be the wave of the future. Some crimes, however, lend themselves to the most concern by private security agencies. These are the crimes that more directly affect the bottom line. They are beginning to require more help from private security, especially as police resources continue to shrink.

The main offenses and offenders are larceny and theft, burglary, robbery, trespassing, vandalism, assault, arson, white-collar crime (check fraud, credit card fraud, embezzlement, computer crime) and drugs in the workplace. The nature of these offenses requires coordination with local law enforcement, full administration support from employers, and efforts by all security staff and general employees to prevent their occurrence.

LARCENY AND THEFT

Many types of crimes fall under this broad category, including both external and internal larceny and theft, shoplifting, employee pilferage, cargo theft, theft of negotiable documents and cash, and illegal use of services where no violence occurs and the item stolen does not belong to the person taking it. As we mentioned in Chapter 2, when does taking home pencils for the kids graduate into taking other valuables? A series of thefts from purses stored in desk drawers can decimate the morale of an office staff. The private security manager must combat this kind of theft by providing security awareness training for staff that is specific to these crimes. Other methods of combating theft are limiting access to areas where theft is easy, frequent audits and inventories, marking company property, and being vigilant on security rounds.

Management must help in the crime prevention effort by taking firm and decisive action against those who chose to steal from the company or from their fellow employees and are caught. It must be shown that petty theft will not be tolerated and the company will take swift and certain disciplinary action, including dismissal. For theft that reaches criminal levels, management should support the security manager in pressing for police prosecution. These actions will make clear to potential offenders that such behavior will not be tolerated and possibly deter them from considering such actions.

BURGLARY

The techniques outlined in Chapter 10, in regard to physical security and access control, are the main crime prevention techniques for burglary at a business. Strict

SECURITY BYTE 11–5

Larceny and Theft

The unlawful taking of the personal goods or property of another with the intent to permanently deprive the owner of the property or goods. Grand larceny and petty larceny are determined by a value above or below a statutory amount.

procedures for the locking of doors (many burglars simply walk in an unlocked door), good exterior lighting, protected windows, and a reliable alarm system are the best ways to prevent industrial burglary. A strong adjunct to these procedures is to lock most valuable items in hardened cabinets or safes, making it all the more difficult for the burglar. In large companies, access control and ID badges help employees identify and challenge strangers who are trespassers and burglars.

Residential burglary also extends to tenants in managed rentals, guests at hotels and motels, and resort areas. The same principles apply in these cases as to one's own home:

MAKE IT LOOK AND SOUND OCCUPIED

- Leave the lights and the radio or television on when you leave the room.
- See that there are good locks, and then use them.
- Deadbolts are usually provided and should always be used when in the room, and when you leave.
- Use the one-way peephole before you let anyone into the room, then open the door while still on the chain.
- Let the front desk know when you will be gone for a long time so that they can have security check your area.

DON'T REWARD THE BURGLAR WHO DOES GET IN

- Place your valuables in the front desk safe deposit box (especially cash, jewelry, and cameras).
- Be a good neighbor.
- If you observe anything suspicious, report it to security or the front desk.

Burglary in the lodging industry is a crime that security professionals definitely want to prevent. First, the loss will probably be charged off against insurance, resulting in increased rates; second, too often burglaries turn into rape, robbery, or murder.

SECURITY BYTE 11 – 6

Burglary

The entering of a structure without the owner's consent with the intent to commit a crime. Commercial burglary refers to the same act at a place of business. Residential burglary refers to this crime when committed at a dwelling, whether occupied or empty. (The penalties for burglary of an unoccupied dwelling are generally much more severe.)

ROBBERY

Robbery is a crime that is always just around the corner for any kind of business. This is especially true for financial institutions, or businesses that process a lot of cash (supermarkets, department stores, large restaurants, race tracks, and so on). Employees should react to a robbery by staying as calm as possible and letting the robber have the money. The employee's life is not worth any amount of money.

The robber of the late 1990s is probably an amateur and could be of any age or either sex, though most are male. The robber is probably nervous, intoxicated, and possibly high on drugs or hurting for a fix. Any robber should be considered dangerous, even if no weapon has been displayed. Employees and security staff should follow these rules:

- As hard as it might be, try to be calm and treat the robber in a normal, polite way.
- Listen to the robber. Do exactly what you are told to do.
- Observe the robber, without obvious staring, and mentally record any distinguishing features, clothing, language and accents, weapon, and so on.
- Avoid any comment or action (such as a sudden movement) that might upset or surprise the robber.
- If you have to do anything extra to comply with the robber's wishes, explain what you need to do before you do it (like reaching under the counter for a key).

The robber probably does not want trouble. By being courteous and cooperative, you can help assure that he or she will leave without anyone being hurt.

After getting what he or she cme for, the robber will leave, so don't get involved with trying to delay the robber. After the robber leaves, staff should have been trained to:

- Activate an alarm, if there is one, and call security or 911.
- Lock all the doors, if possible, so that the robber cannot reenter.
- Without going outside, try to identify the getaway method. If a vehicle, try to get its color, model, and license number, and the direction the robber headed.

SECURITY BYTE 11-7

Robbery

The unlawful taking of personal property from a person or in the person's presence, against the person's will, by force or threat of force. In many jurisdictions, the use of a weapon in a robbery will add significant mandatory time to the offender's sentence.

- Preserve all evidence, and block off all areas that the robber may have touched.
- Take any victims aside and allow them a chance to recover from the trauma.
- As soon as possible, have the victims fill out a suspect description form similar to the example shown in Figure 11–1.
- Try to get all other witnesses to stay until the police arrive. Ask them each, privately and without talking to the others, to fill out a suspect description form.

Once the police arrive, the security manager should meet with them. After the police arrive, the following procedures should apply:

- Only officials with proper credentials should be allowed to enter the crime scene.
- Employees should not talk to *anyone* about the details of the robbery, the amount taken, or the security policies of the company.
- News reporters should be referred to management or the police.
- Wait until the investigation is under control and the police tell you may reopen the business or area of the crime.

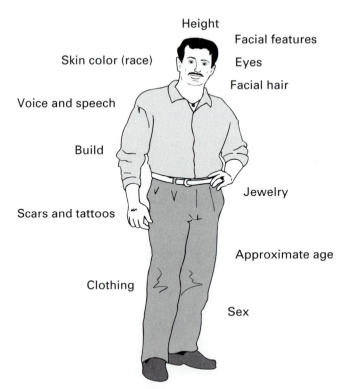

FIGURE 11–1   *Suspect Description Form*

A robbery is always a traumatic event. When a weapon is used, it is often against someone who may not know a pistol from a cannon. In this case, a gun sheet can be used, as shown in Figure 11–2, to help the victim identify the weapon. Robbery not only affects the company's bottom line, but the publicity can also hurt future business. This crime needs to be prepared for and handled carefully when it occurs.

TRESPASSING

A **trespasser** may be trying to find shelter or food, to do drugs, or to commit another crime. Trespassers pose a problem in crime prevention for the security manager, as well as a liability concern. The best way to prevent trespassing is to carefully post the areas that are not to be entered without proper authorization, and include pertinent laws and statutes, with penalties listed. This helps protect the company for liability

Unless you are quite familiar with weapons, it may not be practical to try to learn and remember all the variations. However, the three major categories are depicted here. If you can remember the type of information shown here, it will be helpful to the investigation.

Revolver
The cylinder holds the bullets and revolves to put them in position.

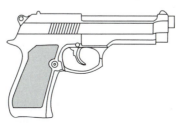

Automatic or Semiautomatic
These are flat-sided and generally have a "squared-off" appearance. The bullets are in the clip in the handle grip.

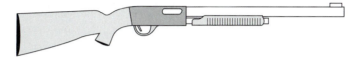

Shotguns—Regular and Sawed-Off
These are either single-barreled or double-barreled. The sawed-off versions are obviously short and blunt looking.

FIGURE 11–2   *A Gun Sheet*

from "accidental trespass." Another way to keep from causing further potential criminal acts, or liability to clients, staff, and visitors, is to train all personnel on how to deal with the issue. Depending on the jurisdiction, it may be reasonable to issue **trespass citations** to those who are first-time offenders. Repeat offenses will eventually result in a report to the police of criminal trespass, and offenders can be arrested (usually a misdemeanor or a restraint order). Depending on the kind of business enterprise, trespassers can become a serious problem if they are not warned properly. Exterior lighting is another way to keep trespassers to a minimum. Trespassers should always be handled politely and professionally, so as not to incite them to other criminal acts such as assault, vandalism, or arson.

VANDALISM

As mentioned, vandalism can be committed by trespassers who become enraged over being removed. After dealing with trespassers, staff should be especially alert for such acts of retribution. A major type of vandalism today is the writing of graffiti on walls, fences, trucks, signs, and other surfaces. Most of this graffiti is done by gang members, or gang **wannabees**, who generally have no respect for anyone's property. To prevent and discourage this activity, the security manager should work with the local police gang units, and get maintenance to paint over the graffiti as soon as possible after it is discovered

Vandalism is a serious problem in business areas where large percentages of the property are closed down. Vandals, for a number of reasons, seem to feel that these vacant shops or factory buildings are fair game for vandalism. The best way to protect such properties is to have some kind of activity moved there, arrange for more patrols by police, or hire security personnel. The use of lighting may be the cheapest and most effective way to deter vandals at such sites.

ASSAULT

The crime of assault is often used as the basis for major litigation that asserts assault has occurred, with negligent security as the proximate cause. Many cases of battery or sexual assault occur in unlighted parking lots, or during unescorted trips by staff to the parking garage at night. These suits often result in multimillion-dollar awards or settlements. Assaults and robberies are the topic of many suits in the lodging industry. Although not all such acts can be prevented, especially if they result from spur-of-the-moment decisions by the perpetrator, some crime prevention tactics can be applied to try to:

1. Reduce the potential for occurrence
2. Train all staff in security awareness and techniques to avoid crime
3. Be sure that all areas where clients, customers, visitors, and staff may have to travel are well lighted and in good working order
4. Keep all shrubbery areas lighted, trimmed, and free from places where potential assaulters may hide
5. Be sure that escort services (grouped or individual) are provided when requested

Assault, whether sexual or physical, is a terrible thing for anyone to experience. Failure to seek out ways to prevent this crime from occurring, or reduce its possibility, is sure to result in litigation when it does occur. Close coordination with law enforcement crime prevention experts will make the job that much easier for the security manager and develop a sense of concerned teamwork.

ARSON

An arson fire is one of the most frightening types of crimes. It is clear that there are a number of motives for arson, but in western Washington State, in late 1992, a string

Arson

The willful, malicious burning of property. It can be committed for financial gain, to hide other crimes, for revenge, or just for personal gratification.

of apparently motiveless instances of arson held the populace in terror. Many of these fires put small and medium-sized businesses into receivership and lots of people out of work. The range of motives and behavioral characteristics for arson are pointed out by Inciari and Binder:

Revenge arsonists, the most prevalent type, are persons who, as a result of arguments or feelings of jealousy or hatred, seek revenge by fire. The victims are typically family members and relatives, employers, or lovers. In retaliation for real or imaginary wrongs, revenge arsonists set ablaze their victim's property or the premises in which they reside. These arsonists appear to be the most potentially dangerous of all types. They set occupied dwellings afire with little thought as to the safety of those within, thinking only of the revenge they must have on their specific victims. Furthermore, they are often intoxicated at the time of the offense. No elaborate incendiary devices are employed, typically only matches and gasoline. Although their crimes are premeditated, they take few steps to conceal their identities and are thus easily detected by alert investigators.

Vandalism arsonists include teenagers who willfully destroy property solely for the purpose of fun and sport, although at times revenge motives may be partially present. As opposed to other arsonists, who work alone, vandalism arsonists usually have at least one accomplice. They tend to set fires at night in churches, school buildings, and vacant structures.

Crime-concealment arsonists set fire to premises where they have committed other offenses. The crime is usually burglary but sometimes murder, and arson in an attempt to cover the traces of the criminal or obliterate the proof that another crime has taken place. Such fires are usually set at night in unoccupied dwellings or places of business.

Insurance-claim arsonists include insolvent property owners, small-business owners, small-business operators, and other individuals who, because of extreme financial pressure, incinerate their own property to collect the insurance on what has been destroyed. As a rule they do not set fire to occupied dwellings, and their offenses generally take place in the daytime.

Excitement arsonists set buildings ablaze for the thrill connected with fires. Some like setting or watching fires, whereas others enjoy viewing the operations of fire fighters and fire equipment. (Occasionally a volunteer firefighter is found among them.) Their offenses take place at night, they rarely set ablaze anything but uninhabited buildings, and they are usually intoxicated at the time of the offense.

Pyromaniacs are pathological fire setters. They seem to have no practical reason for setting the fires and receive no material profit from them. Their only motive seems to be some sort of sensual satisfaction, and the classic "irresistible impulse" is often a factor.[8]

It is reported by the FBI that arson is one of the fastest-growing crimes in the United States, with 89,912 cases reported in 1990.[9] Crime prevention in the case of arson has a number of aspects for the security manager to consider:

1. Keep all outside areas clear of combustible materials, especially those that can be used as *ignitors* (gasoline, shredded paper, oily rags, and so on).

2. Coordinate with human resources to find whether a discharged employee might seek revenge.

3. Coordinate with local fire and police agencies to be aware of potential arson activity in the area.

4. Conduct arson awareness training to all personnel, and practice fire evacuation regularly.

5. See that empty buildings are clean and free of combustibles, and are patrolled regularly.

WHITE-COLLAR CRIME

A major area of growing public concern about crime involves white-collar offenses: crimes that are committed by persons acting in their legitimate roles in business or government. Such offenders include elected officials, businesspersons, dentists and other medical professionals, automobile mechanics, corporate polluters of the environment, embezzlers, persons who accept bribes and excessive gratuities, those who sell power or influence, tax evaders, those who make false insurance claims, persons of the cloth who take funds donated by their congregations for personal gain, stockbrokers who use inside information for profit, and many others who commit such crimes of greed and immoral behavior. Recent offenders in those categories include Reverend

SECURITY BYTE 11–12

White-Collar Crime

Illegal acts characterized by guile, deceit, and concealment, committed by persons acting in legitimate roles in business or government.

Jim Bakker, baseball great Pete Rose, former Speaker of the House James Wright, stockbroker and inside trader Ivan Boesky, Congressman David Durenburg, and hotel tycoon Leona Helmsley.

Most **white-collar offenders** have positive self-concepts and do not regard their actions as crime or themselves as criminals. Rather, they tend to rationalize their acts as "sharp business practices" or as claiming money they feel due to them and not received for their substantial efforts. Such offenses are seldom detected, much less prosecuted. There is no reliable estimate of the financial damage from white-collar and corporate crime, although the total may well exceed $200 billion per year.

Marshall Clinard, one of the foremost students of corporate crime, argues that the auto, defense, and pharmaceutical corporate giants have abused the public's trust, defied democratic principles and subverted the democratic process, endangered the public and the environment, and engaged in widespread bribery of elected officials at home and abroad.[10] Clinard argues further that self-regulation and the regulatory machinery are ineffective in controlling corporate abuses of this nature.

Clinard advocates stiffer penalties, heavy fines for abusers' corporate executives, and fines and imprisonment for top corporate managers. Finally, he calls for widespread publication of offenders' names and crimes and cancellation of a corporation's license to do business (in essence, a "corporate death penalty") if further violations occur.

Imprisonment for white-collar criminals, when it does occur, is most likely to be for short periods in low-security federal facilities. The infrequency of incarceration as a sanction for white-collar offenders does not, however, mean that they go unpunished.[11] Civil and regulatory agencies often impose huge fines and remove critical licenses needed to continue operating, resulting in humiliation, bankruptcy, and loss of the means to make a living in such a position of trust. James Inciadri argues that white-collar criminals are increasingly being punished, despite earlier research findings.[12] There is some evidence that the likelihood of incarceration can have a deterrent effect on at least some types of white-collar criminals.[13] Such offenders will likely become clients of probation, alternative sanctions, and parole agencies in the future.

Prevention of these white-collar crimes is difficult because they involve breach of trust, stealth, and adequate means (in most cases) to cover up or delay their discovery for long periods. The examples we discuss next cost U.S. businesses multibillions of dollars each year, much more than burglary and robbery combined.

CHECK FRAUD

Check fraud and bad checks can create havoc for any business, but especially for a small business. In the flat economy of the early 1990s, many small businesses were willing to take a chance on a check rather than pay the fees required by the major credit card companies. It is essential for the merchant to prevent such losses by following strict identification procedures (such as asking for two pieces of photo identification) and writing down all the information if they have doubts. Depending on the business, the merchant should call, or have security call, for verification on checks over a baseline amount.

The differences between a bad check and forgery are sometimes blurred, but forgery can be reduced if the merchant carefully checks signatures on the secondary identification. A few seconds might save hundreds, or even thousands, of dollars.

Not all criminals are involved with street crime. White-collar criminals usually violate our trust. Clockwise from top left:
Ivan Boesky (Photo by E. Peterson, courtesy of UP/Bettman Newsphotos)
Charles Keating (Photo by Sam Jones, courtesy of AP/Wide World Photos)
Michael Milken (Photo by Mark Peterson, courtesy of AP/Wide World Photos)
Pete Rose (Photo by Mark Lyons, courtesy of AP/Wide World Photos)
Leona Helmsley (Photo by David Cantor, courtesy of AP/Wide World Photos)

Another deterrent for check writers who are writing checks for more than is in their accounts is the setting of a substantial penalty for bad checks (10 to 25 percent of the check's face value, for example). And this needs to be followed up, by a collection agency if necessary. Although crime prevention techniques are helpful, lists of bad accounts to check against are another way to prevent that "rubber check" from finding its way into the till.

CREDIT CARD FRAUD

The same techniques are used to prevent taking charges on an expired, overcommitted, or stolen credit card. It is even more critical because of the fees and rates of interest often charged by the issuing banks. Strict procedures for identification and verification also need to be used here. Lists of stolen credit cards are available and should be checked if there are any doubts. This kind of vigilance not only can stop a thief, and save the merchant a lot of money and pain, but also can prevent the unauthorized or illegal user of such cards from messing up the credit of the card owner. The latest developments in the prevention of credit card fraud include holographic images, which are very difficult to counterfeit.

EMBEZZLEMENT

This is the kind of crime that can be stopped only by preventive measures that cause the handling of funds to be buffered by layers of stringent controls. It is a sad commentary

---

SECURITY BYTE 11–13

Federal Government Agencies Privatize Background Checks

A private firm, but one that's employee-owned, has acquired the Investigative Services business of the Office of Personnel Management, the background checking service for the Executive Branch of the Federal government.

The new firm, US Investigations Service, Inc., will become the U.S. leading provider of background investigations. It is unclear how aggressively the new firm will go after other background investigation business or if the firm will partner with others.

It's also unclear the level of access to Federal government files the private firm will have for its Federal government clients—or the cost of access to that data.

The move by President Bill Clinton furthers the Administration's privatization efforts. The core business: background investigations for most Federal agencies including the Department of Justice, the Treasury Department, the Veterans Administration and the Department of Energy.

Source: Editor. "Federal Government Agencies Privatize Background Checks," *Security* (Cahners Publishing Company. Newton, MA, 1996), Vol. 33, No. 9, p. 114.

that most embezzlers work their way into positions of trust, *then* they begin their methods for stripping the treasury. Crime prevention measures can include frequent external audits to be sure no leaks are in the fiscal system. The lifestyles of key members in the fiscal chain should be reviewed regularly, and occasional paper-and-pencil honesty testing should be a condition of the position.

The security manager can be a big help in this effort by becoming aware of how funds are handled and suggesting ways to protect these assets. In small to medium-sized businesses, it pays to have outside consultants or certified fraud examiners review accounting and other procedures, especially if the profits seem to be shrinking unaccountably (in these companies, the funds are often handled by a single person). It should be preventive policy that all checks must be signed by more than one person, and no one should sign blank checks just to make it easier for the other signatory. Embezzlement is a crime that is not often prosecuted. A crime prevention (deterrent) technique that includes prosecution of the offender is not only just, but good business.

The embezzler is usually a trusted employee who is taking advantage of the employer's confidence. In many cases, the embezzler has been given more authority than the position calls for. Methods of embezzling are limited only by the imagination.

In the simplest situation, where transactions are often made with cash, the money is received and the employee merely pockets it without recording the transaction. A theft of this type is difficult to prevent or detect since the transaction is a cash sale and no subsequent entry is necessary in receipt or accounts receivable records. To reduce temptation, prenumbered sales invoices or cash register receipts should be used for all sales regardless of the amount or method of payment. Spot checks and other monitoring procedures can also assure that cash sales are being recorded.

A somewhat complicated type of embezzlement is called **lapping**. This involves the temporary withholding of receipts such as payments on accounts receivable. Lapping is a continuing scheme that usually starts at a small amount but can run into thousands of dollars before it is detected. For example, take an employee who opens mail or otherwise receives cash and checks as payment on open accounts. The employee holds out a $100 cash payment made by customer A on March 1. To avoid arousing A's suspicion, $100 is then taken from a $200 payment made by customer B on March 5. This is sent on, together with the necessary documentation, for processing and crediting to A's account. The embezzler pockets the remaining $100, which increases the shortage to $200.

As this "borrowing" procedure continues, the employee makes away with increasingly larger amounts of money involving more and more accounts. A fraud of this nature can run for years. Of course, it requires detailed record keeping by the embezzler in order to keep track of the shortage and transferring it from one account to another to avoid suspicion. Any indication that an employee is keeping personal records of business transactions outside the regular books of account should be immediately investigated and policy established to forbid such practice.

Sometimes an embezzler who is carrying on a lapping scheme also has access to accounts receivable records and statements. In this case, he or she is in a position to alter the statements mailed out to customers. Thus the fraud may continue undetected over a long period, until something unusual happens. A customer complaint may spotlight the situation. Or the matter may surface through audit procedures such as confirmation of accounts receivable. One embezzler who also handled customer complaints was able to avoid detection for many years. The amount of the shortage reached such proportions and covered so many accounts that he dared not take a vacation. He also ate lunch at his desk every day lest some other employee receive an inquiry from a customer concerning a discrepancy in a statement. The owner-manager for whom he worked admired his diligence and loyalty. Fellow workers marveled that his apparent frugality enabled him to enjoy a rather high standard of living. But the inevitable finally happened. This employee was hospitalized with a serious ailment and, during his absence, his fraudulent scheme came to light. One reason many firms require that employees must take their vacation time is to keep some "indispensable person" from dispensing company funds to themselves illegally.

Sometimes company bank accounts are used for **check-kiting**. In fact, losses from some large check-kiting schemes have been found that were great enough to cause a company to go broke. In the usual scheme, the person kiting the checks must be in the position to write checks on and make deposits in two or more bank accounts. One account could be the embezzler's personal account and the other a business checking account. If the embezzler has an accomplice in another business, two business accounts may be used. If a company has more than one checking account at different banks, these accounts may be used to carry out the fraud.

The check-kiter is taking advantage of the "float," or number of days between deposit of a check and collection of funds. There may be several days between the date when a kited check drawn on bank A is deposited in bank B and the date the check is presented to bank A for payment. Assuming that it takes three business days for checks to clear, a simple kite between two banks could go as follows: On December 1, a check in the amount of $5000 drawn on bank A is deposited in bank B. On December 2, the check-kiter cashes a $5000 check payable to cash and drawn on bank B, with a teller at bank B. Since the original kited check will be presented to bank A on December 4, the check-kiter (on or before that date) will deposit a $6000 check drawn on bank B, in bank A, not only to insure payment of the original kited check but to increase the amount of the kite. As the process is repeated, the kited checks become larger, more cash is withdrawn, and the scheme can continue until the shortage is covered—or until the kite "breaks" when one of the banks refuses to honor a kited check because the funds on deposit are uncollected.

A temporary kite may be used by a dishonest employee to conceal a cash shortage at the end of a period by depositing a kited check into the company account. This brings the bank balance into agreement with the books. CPAs will request "cut-off" bank statements to detect fraud of this type.

Dishonest employees can figure out any number of ways to defraud their employers. Purchasing agents can accept kickbacks from suppliers for purchasing goods at inflated prices. Salespeople can pad their expense or travel accounts. Personal items can be bought and charged to the company. Cashiers in retail companies can undercharge relatives or friends for merchandise. False vouchers can be prepared to conceal thefts from petty cash funds (not so "petty" in many cases). Overtime can be falsely recorded. Moreover, quite substantial amounts of money may be lost through the cumulative effect of such seemingly minor abuses as personal use of company postage stamps, supplies, and equipment as well as charging personal long-distance phone calls to the business. The list goes on. Some large companies even have annual "amnesty days," where employees are allowed to turn in supplies, materials, tools, and equipment without any action being taken. In a very large company, just pens, pencils, and other office supplies can run into many thousands of dollars saved.

The first and most important thing an owner, manager, or security manager should do is set a good example. Employees watch what management does and are likely to imitate good habits—and bad ones. An employer who dips into petty cash for a golf game, fudges on the expense account, uses company funds for personal items, or sets other examples of loose business behavior should not be surprised when employees think, "If it's good enough for the boss, it's good enough for me."

COMPUTER CRIME REVISITED

We covered many aspects of computer crime in Chapter 6, but a few comments here as a crime prevention tactic may help. The estimated losses through computer crime are more than $50 billion per year. This is an amazing figure when one considers that this is only the computer crime we know about, which most agree is probably less than 10 percent of actual losses. Computer crime is almost impossible to stop completely. Any system has to have some way to get into it, or repairs could not be conducted. It is essential that those who have access to computers in business have a thorough background check before being hired. Outside audits should also be conducted randomly to determine if the user has been attempting to use the system for embezzlement or illegal use of data.

To protect a corporation, bank, or other electronically dependent business from outside "hackers" is a never-ending job that requires the tightest discipline and adequate access control (biometrics, conformational codes, and so on). The best way to prevent computer crime is by using the same five Ds we talked about in Chapter 10. *Deter* the hacker by logs and audits that recover phone numbers and trace them to the offender. *Detect* the hacker by tracing devices that are built into the system. *Delay* the hacker with a series of difficult "hoops" to go through before logging on is allowed, including biometrics identification. *Deny* access if any of the procedures are not cleared. And *destroy* the purpose of the computer criminal by making the system totally off-line and inaccessible.

A wide range of techniques are employed in computer-related crimes. The choice of technique is largely determined by the knowledge and skills of the perpetrator, coupled with the opportunity to apply this to effectuating the crime. The technique can be highly sophisticated, requiring considerable technical expertise, or quite mundane, requiring little or no technical knowledge. The following descriptions are of the more commonly employed techniques:

> *Data diddling:* This is the simplest, safest, and most common method used in computer-related crime. It involves changing data before or during their input to computers. The changing can be done by anyone associated with or having access to the processes of creating, recording, transporting, encoding, examining, checking, converting, and transforming data that untimely enter a computer. Examples are forging or counterfeiting documents; exchanging valid computer

tapes, cards, or disks with prepared replacements; source entry violations; and neutralizing or avoiding manual controls.

Trojan horse: The Trojan horse method is the covert placement of computer instructions in a program so that the computer will perform the unauthorized functions but will still usually allow the program to perform its intended purpose. This is the most common method in computer program–based frauds and sabotage. Instructions may be placed in production computer programs so that they will be executed in the restricted or protected domain of the program and have access to all the data files that are assigned for exclusive use of the program. Programs are usually loosely constructed enough to allow space to be found or created to insert the illegal or unauthorized instructions.

Salami slicing: An automated form of crime involving the theft of small amounts of assets from a large number of sources is identified as the salami technique (taking small slices without noticeably reducing the size of the whole). For example, in a banking system, the demand deposit accounting system for checking accounts could be changed (using Trojan horse methods) to randomly reduce a few hundred accounts by 10–15 cents by transferring the money to a favored account where it can be withdrawn by normal procedures. No controls are violated because the money is not removed from the system of accounts. Instead a small fraction of it is merely rearranged. The success of this kind of fraud is based on the idea that each checking account customer loses so little that it is of no consequence. Many variations are possible. The assets may be an inventory of products or services as well as money.

Logic bombs: A logic bomb is a computer program executed at appropriate or periodic times in a computer system that determines conditions or states of the computer that initiate the perpetration of an authorized, malicious act (usually the start-up of a computer virus). A logic bomb can be programmed to trigger an act based on any specific condition that may occur or be introduced. Logic bombs are usually placed into the computer system using the Trojan horse technique.

Scavenging: This is a method of obtaining information that may be left in or around a computer system after execution of a job. Simple physical scavenging could be the searching of trash barrels for copies of discarded computer listings or carbon paper from multiple-part forms. More technical and sophisticated methods of scavenging can be done by searching for residual data left in the computer after completion of a job. For example, a computer operating system may not properly erase buffer storage areas for the temporary storage of input or output data. Some operating systems do not erase magnetic disk or magnetic tape storage media because of excessive computer time to do it. Therefore, new data are written over the old data. It may be possible for the next job to be executed to read the old data before they are replaced with the new data—data that were stored from the previous job.[14]

The average amount stolen in a bank robbery is about $6000, whereas the average amount stolen in a bank computer fraud (at least those known about) is about

$600,000. With no fingerprints to find, no footprints, and no witnesses, the computer crime *must* be prevented before it occurs. Crime prevention units that specialize in these crimes will, of necessity, be made up of police and private security experts in the twenty-first century.

DRUGS IN THE WORKPLACE

Drugs in the workplace cost U.S. businesses more than $500 billion yearly from lost time, stolen goods to support habits, industrial insurance, accidents, lost time, low-quality products, and many other factors. The drug epidemic accelerated rapidly in the mid-1980s, with the development and marketing of crack cocaine. This does not mean other drugs of choice have waned, however. The amount of total drugs seized by law enforcement has grown to massive numbers. In 1988, 1841 pounds of heroin were seized. In 1989, 181,511 pounds of cocaine were seized. In 1990, 143,864,195 dosage units of stimulants (methamphetamine and other variations) were seized. Heron has made a resurgence, and 2464 pounds were seized in 1991.

Even though the quantities seized are enough to get the whole nation high, these numbers are but a small percentage of the tidal wave of drugs entering the United States. Drugs are a $500 billion business, and the "supply side" always seems to be able to expand to meet demand.

The only sure method of detecting and preventing drug use (along with drug sale) in industry and institutions is drug testing. Kuest, a drug expert, notes what drug testing is and why it is used:

> *What is it?* Chemical testing is not a security or personnel tool. It *is* a piece of medical data to be used by medical personnel. We need to get the urine out of the human resources office or this piece of useful information will be barred from use.
>
> *Why is it used?* Chemical testing is helpful in assessing applicants and current employees. The interpretations and misinterpretations of the results are what concern many civil libertarians. When urine is examined for drugs during a pre-employment physical, the findings only indicate *potential high risk behavior*. The information is no different from data received from a back examination or a psychological examination. If a drug commonly associated with substance abuse is found in the urine of a job applicant and that potential employee offers no acceptable explanation for its presence other than by abuse, the employer may want to define that as potential high risk behavior not suitable for the workplace. And, instead, may offer employment to another qualified candidate who does not display high risk behaviors.[15]

Therefore, the only real crime prevention techniques against drugs in the workplace involve good employee screening, awareness training for all staff, policies that provide for severe measures if drug abuse is found, and an employee assistance plan for first timers. Security staff and supervisors must be on the lookout at all times for signs of abuse.

Summary

Crime prevention is a law enforcement and private security task whose time has finally come. It has been around for many years, buried in the police departments of America, but often as work for other than "real cops." The crime prevention person of past decades was likely a police officer who was disabled or near retirement, or a female employee given the job as a gesture. This has all changed, and the role of crime prevention has been given a new look. Considering the magnitude of the crime problem in America, along with the reduced budgets and shrinking police forces, prevention must be given a major role.

At the same time, the increased professionalism of security managers and rapidly growing size of the private security industry has begun to penetrate the formerly exclusive turf of law enforcement—more and more through cooperative invitation. The direction of this trend is still not clear, but the twenty-first century appears to have great need and potential for a more realistic use of resources for "social protection" as a new approach to solving the problems of crime, security, and loss prevention. A more efficient and effective use of *all* the community resources in this new campaign in the war on crime may be the only way to ever stop the increase in crime that now sees almost 300 of every 100,000 Americans locked up in prison at a cost of more than $20,000 apiece per year. The private security industry, with its long history of crime prevention as an applied science, should become the leadership partner in this battle and encourage mutual assistance and cooperation with its police counterparts.

REVIEW QUESTIONS

1. What are the major differences between felonies and misdemeanors?
2. What agency in the government produces the Uniform Crime Reports?
3. How are assets allocated for the various types of crime? Is it based on logic?
4. List the crimes against the person in the UCR.
5. Explain the differences between lapping and kiting in check fraud.

TERMS TO REMEMBER

felonies	*Uniform Crime Reports*	*white-collar offenders*
misdemeanors	*crime prevention*	*lapping*
English common law	*trespasser*	*check-kiting*
crimes against the person	*trespass citations*	
acts between consenting adults	*wannabee's*	

ENDNOTES

1. Rollin M. Perkins, *Criminal Law and Procedure*, 4th ed. (Mineola, N.Y.: Foundation Press, 1972), p. 4.

2. T. J. Flanagan and K. Maguire (eds.), *Sourcebook of Criminal Justice Statistics—1991*. (Washington, D.C.: Bureau of Justice Statistics, 1992), p. 372.

3. Ibid.

4. Ibid.

5. Ibid.

6. Ibid., p. 439.

7. William C. Cunningham, and Todd H. Taylor, *Private Security and Police in America: The Hallcrest Report I* (Boston: Butterworth-Heinemann, 1985), pp. 4–5.

8. J. A. Inciardi and D. Binder, "Arson," in *Encyclopedia of Crime and Justice* (Chicago, Ill.: The Free Press, 1983), pp. 76–82.

9. Flanagan and Maguire, *Sourcebook of Criminal Justice Statistics–1991*, p. 427.

10. Marshall Clinard, *Corporate Corruption: The Abuse of Power* (Westport, Conn.: Praeger, 1990).

11. Mark Cohen, "Corporate Crime and Punishment: A Study of Social Harm and Sentencing Practices in Federal Courts, 1984-1987," *American Criminal Law Review*, Vol. 25 (1989), pp. 605–660. See also Pamela Busy, "Fraud by Fright: White Collar Crime by Health Care Providers," *North Carolina Law Review*, Vol. 7 (1989), pp. 426–550.

12. James Inciardi, *Criminal Justice* (New York: Harcourt Brace Jovanovich, 1990), p. 99.

13. Steve Klepper and Daniel Nagin, "The Deterrent Effect of Perceived Certainty and Severity of Punishment Revisited," *Criminology*, Vol. 27 (November 1989), pp. 721–743.

14. U.S. Department of Justice, *Basic Considerations in Investigating and Proving Computer-Related Federal Crimes*. (Washington, D.C.: U.S. Government Printing Office, 1988), pp. 2-1–2-4.

15. R. D. Kuest, *Drug Testing in the Workplace*. Unpublished paper presented to the Puget Sound Chapter, ASIS, Seattle, Washington, 1989.

12

Security Products, Consultants, and Vendors

The Technological and Services Sector of Private Security

History reveals that the growth of the United States from an agrarian country to a powerful industrial nation was facilitated by advancing technology and labor-saving devices it produced. Where we used technology we prospered; where we ignored it, we have done so at our own peril.

—Richard H. Cantor

Overview

Security has been, historically, a labor-intensive industry. The classical security "guard" was usually an older person on some kind of retirement pay. Even the extremely low pay was sufficient to attract enough people to provide minimal security for a minimum of cost. When U.S. industry evolved into the highly technological and equipment-conscious levels of the 1990s, the security of these expensive devices became increasingly critical. Internal and external theft became technological challenges, with inventory done by computers, assembly done by computers, and transactions conducted on electronic media. As we discussed in Chapter 11, crimes and criminals have changed dramatically. This has required that the persons and equipment for protecting these new technologies grow and advance along parallel tracks. The need developed for security "officers," persons who possessed skills equivalent to those of the well-trained police officer in the public sector and who were knowledgeable about what they were protecting. This chapter discusses the current products that vendors have developed specifically for security, or have brought to security through technology transfer from other sciences and operations. This chapter examines these many technologies, the roles of the vendors, and the roles of those who provide technical consulting to an industry that is heading toward the year 2000 at warp speed.

Downsizing and Upgrading in Security

As businesses and institutions downsized workforces to keep down the huge payrolls of the past several decades, security has had to try to find ways to increase personnel capabilities while still reducing overall personnel costs. As the movement toward legislative standards for the security industry accelerates, it is essential that it keep pace with the techno-revolution or price itself out of business. Personnel costs have already caused a growing shift away from proprietary security to contract security. And this trend does not seem to be slowing down. As shown in Table 12–1, the proprietary segment of the security industry will actually *shrink* by the year 2000, and the contract service and manufacturing side could almost *double* by the turn of the century.

The products, services, and systems sectors of the security industry have done a fine job of keeping up with the pace of change and providing the technology, research, and planning needed to stay current with the rest of industry. This segment of the security field has been roughly divided into technology and products for the following functions:

- Access control
- Closed circuit television (CCTV)
- Integrated systems
- Identification

TABLE 12–1

PRIVATE SECURITY INDUSTRY
HALLCREST PROJECTION OF NUMBER OF EMPLOYEES (To the year 2000)

Year	Contract Service and Manufacturing Employees	Average Annual Growth Rate	Proprietary Security Organization Employees	Average Annual Growth Rate	Total Private Security Employment	Total Average Annual Growth Rate
1980	556,000	N/A	420,000	N/A	976,000	N/A
1990	965,000	6%	528,000	2%	1,493,000	4%
2000	1,473,000	4%	410,000	-2%	1,883,000	2%

Source: William C. Cunningham, John J. Strauch, and Clifford W. Van Meter. *The Hallcrest Report II: Private Security Trends 1990–2000* (Butterworth-Heinemann, Hallcrest Systems Inc., 1990) p. 176.

- Intrusion detection
- Communications security
- Hardware
- Security officers

Several publications deal with these issues and inform the industry on the latest developments and devices. Among the leaders is the magazine *Security*.

ACCESS CONTROL

We discussed access control principles and applications in Chapter 10. Since the dawn of time, humans have tried to devise ways to control entry and exit to their property and facilities. Early developments resulted in the concept of locking devices. From the first crude keys to the electronic marvels of today, access control has grown into a real science, with new techniques being developed by engineers and applications designers almost daily.

The two most common types of access controls that are at the edge of technology today are **card reader access devices** that (1) require passing through, pushing into, or inserting a card manually into the reader or keypad and (2) are placed or passed by in the **proximity** of the reader. The common **Wiegand** access card, which uses coded, twisted wires that convert magnetic energy to electric energy at the reader, has been used for access control devices since the late 1979. These cards are now making a resurgence with new systems protocols, which hold promise of finally making it possible to integrate separate systems and products into one network. As noted by Lydon:

> What's changing about Wiegand cards is really a change for all card access systems—the introduction of standard communications language or protocol that will simplify how we put systems together. For Wiegand card users, the introduction of the protocol, dubbed SPAN, opens new doors.
>
> SPAN will allow myriad devices from different manufacturers to share data and operate on a single network. For Wiegand card users, systems will more easily integrate with facility management and other security systems. This flexibility will help Wiegand match the utility of magnetic stripe or bar code cards, the omnipresent technologies that are finding multiple applications in a single system—as ID-access-debit-meal service applications prove.
>
> In typical systems today, wire pulling costs can be as much or more than the system itself. But because a networked system runs on a single pair of wires, users will be able to identify a tremendous savings on installation.[1]

The simple diagram in Figure 12–1 shows how the power of this new idea can make multiple systems finally able to work as an integrated whole.

Eight basic card-encoding technologies are on the access control market today: Wiegand, **magnetic stripe**, proximity, barium ferrite, infrared, bar code, smart cards,

FIGURE 12–1 *Access System Structure: Before and After SPAN*

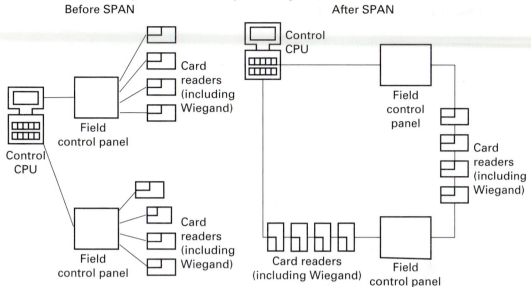

Source: Editors. "Access Control." *Security* (Cahners Publishing, Des Plaines, IL, 1996), Vol. 33, No. 8, p. 19.

and Hollerith. Of these technologies, Wiegand, magnetic stripe, and proximity are estimated to share, about equally, 85 to 90 percent of the market. Magnetic stripe has been in use the longest; Wiegand was introduced in the late 1970s; and proximity has been gaining in use over the past five years.[2]

Proximity cards offer the major advantage of "hands-free" operation. All proximity cards send an activate code into the reader device by simply being brought close to it. Most range about 6 inches, but designers are increasing that with better antennae and new circuit designs. Proximity cards are somewhat limited by their relatively high cost, but since they are not passed or inserted through or into a reader, they can be incorporated into badges or placed on vehicles and other flexible options. They offer good resistance to moisture and temperature and are durable. Readers are somewhat subject to interference but, if properly installed, work well. In situations of high-volume traffic and relatively low security, these cards are very handy. As new developments make proximity cards more secure (about 98 percent reliable at this time), they are sure to gain even more favor from users.

Today, upwards of 125 manufacturers or systems designers offer access control systems. These range from small, standalone units designed to protect a single door, to systems capable of handling hundreds of doors and thousands of individual cardholders. The technologies vary from a simple admit or deny decision to complex systems capable of tracking each time the card is used and storing information about when and even by whom it was used. Some systems incorporate other functions such as time and attendance.[3]

CLOSED CIRCUIT TELEVISION

Closed circuit television (CCTV) for security has been around almost as long as television itself. It was not difficult for security professionals (and television manufacturers) to see the potential cost savings in personnel by having the capability to observe areas of the facility without having to leave the control room until something alerts the observer. From that early concept has come the latest technologies in CCTV that seem to present a new development each month, including the use of CCTV on robots that perform roving patrols. The concept of using television as an adjunct to security operations makes the security director somewhat like a Hollywood director—with a miniproduction every day. The difference is the players are real, and the people who watch the monitors must keep there attention riveted on them—even if there are long, boring stretches in the story. As shown in Table 12–2, over $23 million will be spent on each item per year by 2000 A.D.

The latest important developments in CCTV are with the smaller integrated circuits, improved low-light level lenses, and solid-state cameras. The solid-state camera has proved to be more cost effective and much superior to the older tube-type cameras. Until just a few years ago, tube cameras were used at most security sites. Rapid technological development of the charge-coupled device (CCD) has made the solid-state camera the clear future for CCTV. These advanced-technology cameras have many advantages:

- Ease of operation
- Long-term reliability
- A wide range of applications
- Equal or better visibility in low light
- Better image quality
- Less power to operate
- Less susceptible to vibrations
- Less susceptible to magnetic fields
- Better cost and application value

CCD cameras are being made smaller and smaller through miniaturization. This has allowed for more creative applications in areas that were not possible with the older, more bulky tube cameras. (They are even being installed in the eyes of mannequins at high-priced department stores.) An important use of these miniature marvels is for company camera surveillance:

Over the past 20 years covert camera surveillance has come of age, becoming a widely accepted practice used by many companies. Security directors see covert video surveillance as one of the most cost-effective and simple solutions to many basic security violations.

When companies first introduced off-the-shelf hidden camera systems two decades ago, the only other alternative was a do-it-yourself approach that frustrated security

TABLE 12 – 2

GROSS ANNUAL EQUIPMENT SALES REVENUES, 2000

Category*	Annual Revenues (shipments**)	Average Annual Rate of Growth	Change in Annual Rate of Growth from 1990	Market Share	Change in Market Share from 1990	Change in Market Share from 1980
Access control	$1,700,000,000	13%	-26%	7%	+3%	+7%
Closed-circuit television (CCTV)	$755,000,000	11%	-5%	3%	+1%	+2%
Alarms	$1,650,000,000	8%	0%	7%	0%	-1%
Bomb detection and X-ray equipment	$190,000,000	11%	+1%	1%	0%	0%
Metal detection	$84,000,000	11%	+1%	0.4%	0%	0%
Electronic article surveillance	$1,100,000,000	14%	-11%	5%	+2%	+4%
Computer security and shielding	$650,000,000	13%	-4%	3%	+1%	+2%
Telephone security	$85,000,000	5%	-12%	0.4%	0%	0%
Security lighting	$1,737,000,000	8%	0%	7%	0%	-1%
Security fencing	$6,000,000,000	4%	-1%	25%	-9%	-27%
Safes, vaults, and security storage	$731,000,000	6%	-9%	3%	-1%	+1%
Locks	$3,541,000,000	7%	-5%	15%	0%	+2%
Other	$5,500,000,000	8%	-7%	23%	+2%	+9%
Total	$23,723,000,000	7%	-3%			

*Includes all ancillary products and materials.
**U.S. sales (shipments) only.

Source: William C. Cunningham, John J. Strauch, and Clifford W. Van Meter. *The Hallcrest Report II: Private Security Trends 1990–2000* (Butterworth-Heinemann, Hallcrest Systems Inc., 1990) p. 205.

people. The cameras used super 8mm film that would take a picture at adjustable intervals. Although efficient, portable, and cost-effective, these cameras had many limitations.

Light level was critical since the cameras could not see in poorly lit areas. They could not be used for employee theft since the film had to be developed, making immediate viewing impossible. In addition security staff had to change film cartridges at least once a day, which was not only a nuisance but could jeopardize the integrity of the surveillance.

With all these drawbacks, why were these cameras a success? Compared with the alternative, a staffed surveillance, the cameras were tremendously cost-effective. Here was a piece of equipment that would give a security director an extra pair of eyes for pennies a day. It did not sleep, eat or take breaks. It told its story quickly and objectively, and it would retell it the same way every time.[4]

The latest benefit is from CCTV monitoring systems is the growing use of color monitors at the central stations. This has shown a number of benefits, not the least of which is the monitoring officers feeling less bored. Tests have shown that an almost catatonic state sets in if the operator is left on station too long. In this state, a small army could march across the gray mass of the monochromatic monitors and be ignored. Color monitors, especially in areas of high security, can certainly help this fatigue factor. The extra benefits for identification purposes were discussed by the security director for the Jamaica Hospital in Jamaica, New York: "The need for security in hospitals has grown dramatically in the past few years and color monitors helped greatly. The results were rather dramatic; we went from no security to a management system that gives us a better idea of people in it. You can see what color clothes people are wearing, what color packages they are holding."[5]

Alarms that are connected to motion sensors can also silently activate or switch screens, or at least make them blink to alert the hypnotized observer. It does not seem too far-fetched to visualize belt or wrist monitors, activated by sensors in remote areas, that will allow a single security officer to effectively be in two or three places at the same.

CCTV is here to stay, but there have been attacks on its use, based on violations of employee privacy. Although the era of "Big Brother" has long since arrived, most security professionals are very careful in using the new technologies that make that frightening world possible.

SECURITY BYTE 12-1

Video's Operational Requirements

1. Users should be able to call up any camera on any monitor.
2. Any camera within an alarmed area should automatically switch to a large monitor and record the event.
3. Area detection is important to allow time for video recording of incidents.
4. Parking areas require both general area coverage and a method to sense an alarm.
5. Design should offer the operator the most information from the field with the least amount of effort. Video multiplexers, time lapse records, and integrated security video and audio can help.

INTEGRATED SYSTEMS

Now, more than ever, security systems are facilities tools, and software is the key. Chicago-based Morton Internal knows this well as it moved to larger facilities. It was able to use applications that went beyond security and develop a total, integrated approach designed by a **systems integration** engineer. This is the cost-cutting wave of future security (and integrated) systems.

In this case, the access control and monitoring software also controls the radio–telephone interconnection system. Security personnel can answer the phone via radio. The system also connects a remote paging system. Security personnel receive a thirty-six-character readout of alarms while away from the central monitor. The security supervisor lauds the integrated systems cost savings: "We were paying our data processing people $30–40,000 a year to run our time and attendance/access control programs. Now we can run it all on the same DEC computer that runs access control and alarm monitoring, and prints out reports on laser printers we already had."[6]

This kind of use of existing and new equipment is typical of the motivation that is taking security toward systems integration. Investments in hardware are seen, especially with the greater capacity of most PC systems today, as opportunities to do more with the existing equipment or tie it to something else. It is not even necessary for users to design new software (a very expensive operation) but, simply, to modify the software on hand or buy off-the-shelf versions that are compatible. This changes the security from one that has been traditionally hardware driven, to one that is software driven. With hardware on site, the security manager can now negotiate with software companies to give them something that uses the equipment's full capacity.

As it becomes increasingly expensive and complicated to install system after system of readers, alarms, monitors, and so on, the wise decision is to use the talents of systems engineers and software programmers to integrate all systems. As shown in Figure 12–2, this process is underway in many cases, and it is a trend that seems to be gaining popularity in the industry. If security managers become the driving force behind these moves, security will achieve a better position on the corporate ladder and be able to demonstrate that the cost savings gained can be shown as bottom-line enhancers.

FIGURE 12–2 *Percent of Users with Integrated Systems*

Connections Between	Percent
Security, life safety	40
Access control, CCTV	30
Access, CCTV, intrusion	27
Security, human resources	27
Security, facilities management	19
Access, photo ID or video ID	17
Access, time and attendance	15
Multi-tasking exists	9
Access, transaction processing	5
Access, process contol	2

Source: Editors. "Integrated Systems" *Security* (Cahners Publishing, Des Plaines, IL, 1997), Vol. 34, No. 4, p. 15.

IDENTIFICATION

Identification (ID) of people, products, and equipment has grown with the technological revolution at the same hyperpace as the rest of the basic tools of security. The earliest form of ID for people was simply to recognize the person on sight. The tools and equipment in early times were hand-made, and distinguishing one from another was easy. In today's mobile society, it is impossible to tell one person from another without methods that can make a positive identification certain. Tools and equipment are now made by mass production, and one screwdriver or typewriter looks exactly like another. From this vexing problem, an entire industry and technology has grown.

The identification of persons has had a varied history, and now ID systems include everything from picture ID cards to retinal scanners. In the next several paragraphs, we attempt to describe some of these systems in brief. This technology changes so rapidly that it is difficult to find the latest developments anywhere but in the latest journals and magazines.

The most basic ID system for most persons is the **picture ID**, generally, a simple head shot of the user that is laminated in plastic, as in a driver's license or military ID. These cards usually require a signature as well, for a second comparison point. From this simple badge, the industry has developed high-tech, computer-driven ID systems that can take a picture, print the necessary information, and laminate the card all in one sitting. They are now often done on plastic cards that have Wiegand or magnetic strips, even bar codes, built in to act as further ID points and use as access control cards as well. Enhancement of these simple cards can be done by using fingerprints or other biometrics systems, either on the card or as a response to a prompt by security officers or readers.

Cards now can be self-expiring or disappearing (for short-time visitors or at temporary facilities) and can contain vast amounts of information on laser discs that have been implanted. It is also possible to create specialized ID cards on the computer for a specific purpose. The number of variations and possibilities for ID badges has only begun to be explored.

Biometrics systems require three steps to provide the most positive kind of identification: (1) enrollment of the person by the particular system (for example, rolled fingerprints on file or in a computer bank, or voiceprint on file and ready to compare); (2) entry into the biometrics device or scanner; and (3) acceptance or rejection of request for ID, based upon technical comparison with enrolled data. **Biometrics** systems are the current rage in the development of high-security sites and include the following:

1. *Fingerprinting:* This is one of the oldest biometrics methods of identification of persons. Biometrics systems scan and analyze the whorls and ridges on the fingertips and make a comparison with an enrolled print. This process is made more reliable with the comparison of more than one print.

2. *Voiceprint:* This technology compares the wave patterns on the fluctuations in the human voice. It has some problems with persons who have a cold but is very reliable for most ID applications.

3. *Hand geometry:* This looks at the length of the hand and relationships to fingers. The scanning device measures hundreds of points of reference. It can be enhanced by reading the palm prints as well.

4. *Palm prints:* This is a comparison of the patterns of whorls and ridges on the palm. It can also include the fingers in the analysis to make it more reliable.

5. *Signature dynamics:* This employs a special pad that not only compares the signature, but analyzes the pressure on the pad as the writing is done. It can be either a signature or a phrase that uses more of the alphabet.

6. *Keyboard rhythms:* This requires the user to type a phrase into the access computer keyboard and then compares the rate pressure and pauses that define that person's dynamics. It is good for computer access.

7. *Retinal scans:* This is probably the most secure system. It measures the pattern of blood vessels on the back of the eye with a low-level infrared scan of 320 points along a 450 degree scan. It can scan through contacts, but not glasses, and can be as reliable as .0001 percent for rejection of impostors.

Identification of things runs from engraving on the item (as in "Operation Identification" at police stations) to hidden microdots that can carry up to fifteen lines of information about ownership. The most common system used today is the bar code that is read by a reader and confirms the information contained in the bars. Everyone who shops has come into contact with bar codes. Combinations of ID tags are becoming popular in the security and retail industry. The security tags are also used as price tags and work with detection systems to prevent removal of items from the store. An interesting new development is one that combines electronic bar code technology that identifies objects, even at long range, or when obscured by dirt or ice. It operates via a portable hand-held reader. Efforts in this area of ID are sure to become more sophisticated in the future. Combined with signage that warns property stolen will be traced to the thief, this technology helps deter shoplifting.

INTRUSION DETECTION

We discussed the use of sensors and other methods of detection for intruders in some detail in Chapter 10, but some highly sophisticated applications of integration of other technologies are finding there way into intrusion control. The biggest news is in regard to the projected use of **fiber optics** in outdoor protection. Lydon points out the development:

> The fiber optic boom that's hit everything from cameras to phones may add new appeal to outdoor protection. As an alternative to buried coaxial and electromagnetic sensor cables, fiber optic sensor cables have advantages. They aren't affected by electromagnetic or radio frequency interference that can cause false alarms.

> And as an alternative to above-ground fence sensors, fiber optics isn't impeded by snow, fog or rain. Buried fiber optic sensing systems respond to pressure,

movement and sound, or any combination of these, depending on system configuration and adjusted sensitivity.

Two concerns about fiber optics, cost and slicing difficulty, are important considerations for outdoor systems.[7]

One of the oldest forms of intrusion protection, fences, is amid a technological revolution as well. Although security fencing is the perceived norm, many of them use motion detectors and enhanced technology.

COMMUNICATIONS SECURITY

The problem of communicating securely and effectively has always been the bane of security and law enforcement. With the advent of digitized communications, satellite receivers and transmitters, and telephones that now go anywhere, it seems that problems with communications have finally been solved. Right? Wrong. Consider the amount of cross-currents and interference that is floating around the planet. As an example, the London Stock Exchange recently had some mysterious interference with their computer transmissions (not good if you are giving out bids for millions). They finally traced the problem to the radar on a ship on the Thames.

This incident led to the development of a new type of glass that acts as a screening filter for electronic emanations that can interfere with communications systems. The result will be a rush by high-security buildings, banks, and industries to protect computer and computer-operated systems from interference. This was a crossover by a product that was originally developed to protect against electronic surveillance. It seems that technology breakthroughs seem to rattle around until someone "discovers" a use for them in some other application.

A major communications security issue is the theft of long-distance services by fraud, now approaching a billion-dollar annual problem for carriers. All the major long-distance carriers are working on the problem, and the federal government is now forming task forces to seek out offenders and prosecute them. A spokesperson for AT&T points out the issue, "Long distance fraud is a serious criminal problem. We should stand squarely with our customers against people who steal their service."[8]

The battle over radio, telephone, cellular, or some new communications system on the horizon continues. This spurs competition and has improved communications as a whole by large factors in the past decade. Television on telephone lines makes it feasible to provide such services to a security program in the near future. Whichever technology wins the race to reliable and effective communications, the security industry will be the ultimate winner. Secure communications, whether through multichannel scrambling or by hardened land lines, are essential to security. The place to watch development is the major telephone companies and the military. Developments there will presage the next step in communications.

SECURITY BYTE 12 – 2

Smart Buyer's Checklist

Security technology has a lot to offer—if it is chosen and used right. When your organization prepares to make a major security system purchase, make sure to ask yourself these questions first:

- Have you analyzed your security needs comprehensively and quantitatively?
- Do you know specifically what risks you are expecting the system to deter, deny, detect, respond to and recover from?
- Can the system meet your actual security requirements?
- Are the system's goals achievable and sustainable?
- Will your staff be able to efficiently operate it?
- Under legal scrutiny, will the system be considered standard security practice in response to reasonably predictable risks?
- Will the system grow with your organization's needs?
- Is it compatible with emerging technology?
- Is it more system that you will ever need?
- Is the system state-of-the-art or a remake of old and tired technology?
- Do you understand the difference between a fully integrated system and a hardware-interactive system?
- How much operational overhead will be needed to support administration of the system, compared to your current costs?
- Have you performed a value-added analysis of the system?
- Will it provide a net present value to your organization?
- Can you use the system to generate revenue?
- Will the vendor support you in marketing to tenants or other prospective customers?
- Is your organization obscuring security management strategies by focusing entirely on physical security systems?
- Is there an unrealistic expectation of what the system can accomplish?

A careful examination of these questions will always lead to a wiser, more effective purchase.

Source: Ira Somerson. "Smart Buyer's Checklist," Security (Cahners Publishing Company. Newton, MA, 1996), Vol. 33, No. 12, p. 44.

Access the Future: Smarter, Integrated, Value-Added

The "information superhighway" is a reality in today's access control market.

Forget about the Internet and CD-ROMs and interactive game playing.

Electronic access control advances put security squarely on the information highway right now.

That's the message from manufacturers and end users alike.

"In today's security departments, there are fewer people using more technology in smarter ways," says George Campbell, president of Fidelity Security Services, a division of Fidelity Investments. "The key is communications networks and how to use them effectively."

The current security industry is a different one than even a few years ago, David Schuldt, president and CEO of Casi-Rusco, Boca Raton, Fla., told a recent conference of end users and his firm's business partners. This new industry relies on "converged security solutions." And access control will play a vital role.

Business Sense

One way security has changed within the corporate environment: It's no longer an "island," with its own budget, computer systems and databases, says Casi-Rusco's vice president of marketing, Jim Spencer. "Security directors are no longer the only person who decides security: It's the MIS director, the facility manager, and in some cases the communications manager."

Moreover, security is increasingly viewed by business organizations in financial terms— ROI or Return on Investment justification, not just systems features and benefits.

Robert Magedoff, marketing manager, commercial/industrial division for Sensormatic, Deerfield Beach, Fla., sees the access control of the future as a management tool as well as a security vehicle. "Security access control will be part of an MIS solution. Access control is really information flow: It's about who's allowed in and who gets in."

When security departments start using their strengths as management tools, that will make things more effective for the business as a whole, Magedoff adds. "When you combine functions such as access control with time and attendance, you are able to meet that ROI quotient."

Integration/Strategic Alliances

The way security manufacturers meet today's demands of end users and businesses is with integration, alliances, and acquisitions.

"There is a clear trend in access control toward making systems value-added, one-card systems," Campbell says. These systems integrate access with a variety of other functions, including ID, video, monitoring and time and attendance. "It's not access control and intrusion and CCTV anymore. It's total asset protection."

"If you're thinking of a system as segmented into these different areas, you're losing protection, because that kind of thinking doesn't capitalize on the strengths of certain subsystems," contends Campbell.

George Temidis, manager of security systems at IBM, agrees with Campbell about the direction of security and access control.

His access control vision: a computer-delivered service that stresses automation.

"We are heading towards very large, networked systems. We will be providing access control like a service to your various locations, and automating as much as we can."

Many manufacturers offer "integrated solutions," says Jim Hunter, director of security product marketing for Simplex, Gardner, Mass. The next step is single platform solutions, whether that's achieved by strategic

Access the Future: Smarter, Integrated, Value-Added

alliance, acquisitions or mergers. "When you take a look at a technology such as video imaging, it's really only three years old. What many end users have is a stand-alone solution, with separate databases for access control and video imaging that is no longer acceptable."

In fact, some end users want to take it even a step further and "integrate" their "integrated system" with the entire corporate network.

"There is a tremendous change that is going to take place in the marketplace," says Ed Chandler, consultant and president of Security by Design, Concord, Calif., a consulting and design engineering firm. "Most large corporations are doing things with Wide Area Networks. We have the potential to be connected across the world, all over the world. Yet very few security departments take advantage of WANs."

Using the building administration structure that's already in existence means fewer entries of redundant information, Chandler says.

"It's a cost issue," Campbell explains. "You can tear wire and use a separate lease line, or you can use the methods that are there already."

Hardware/Software

All this networking and integrating means that "software is the access control of the future," Magedoff says. "Customers are demanding open architecture, and it's software that will make the difference between systems.

Magedoff, for one, predicts that Microsoft Windows NT will likely become the industry standard for software. "You have 85 percent of the world on Windows-based systems. Networks are running through Windows." Hunter agrees. Simplex's new

NT3400 is an "integral" system that runs on the Microsoft Windows NT operating system.

Other respected vendors have products running on, and see a similar future for, OS/2 and UNIX platforms.

Cards and readers of the future? Many predict the smart card will take off in the U.S. by the end of this century. The one card scenario we're seeing on college campuses today will eventually incorporate smart cards," Magedoff says.

Yet even the smart cards will likely be "multi-tech." According to Casi-Rusco's Barry Clarke, manager of the engineering group designing products, proximity will dominate access control cards, yet some customers will want to use a smart card as their access control system. "You have two solutions: either read the smart card, or present a single card solution with perhaps a prox assembly, mag stripe and chip all on one card."

Readers will be wireless and multitech, Magedoff says. "Multi-reader technology will solve the problem of recarding, because the software can read anything it wants," he says.

Access control is heading at full speed towards the "converging" of multiple technologies and applications. And while there will probably always be an "access control" industry, particularly for small to medium-sized applications, at the higher end "there will not be an industry as we know it today," Hunder contends.

"I don't believe at that (bigger) end of the spectrum there will be just an access control supplier anymore," Hunter adds. Instead, there will be a number of large security system manuacturers that offer integrated security and business solutions.

Source: Karyn Hodgson. "Access the Future: Smarter, Integrated, Value-Added." *Security* (Cahner Publishing Company. Newton, MA, 1995), Vol. 32, No. 6, pp. 19–22.

HARDWARE

All the aforementioned technologies contribute to the almost daily parade of new hardware for the security industry. The American Society for Industrial Security (ASIS) had almost 900 exhibitors at their annual Seminar and Exhibits in 1991. The only limitation to those who want to show their wares to the security managers of the ASIS seems to be a place big enough to house this hall of miracles. If you liked to go through hardware stores as a kid, the exhibits at these meetings are your dreams come true.

The vendors sector of the security industry is growing faster than any other. The dazzling number of new "toys" can boggle the strongest minds. It seems impossible to list the hardware that is on sale for the security professional, so we list only a few of these new products:

- A random number generator teamed up with a combination lock on the entry door. This is possible because of the miniaturization and processing capability in new access systems.
- A bar code system for stationary posts to log in employees and allow access to special areas by reading the bar code on the employee's badge.
- A wireless art and object protection system that provides protection by monitoring specific objects.
- A wireless sound system for use by up to 200 people.
- A new generation of portable FM radios.
- Fraud detection software designed to assist financial and general businesses by providing a method for combating the fraudulent use of personal data.
- Security robots using digital sonar to navigate miles of paths through extensive office and laboratory facilities.
- A new paper shredder that cuts up sensitive documents to 1/32-by-1/2-inch particles, impossible to reassemble.
- An infrared gas detection system that reads concentrations by linking hundreds of detector points.
- A low-light video camera that can provide videos under starlight conditions of 0.00005 lux.
- Self-destructing hang-tags for parking and visitor controls that allow the word *expired* to come up as the day progresses.

As you can see, from just a brief review of a few of the hundreds of items now available, the growth of the hardware business bodes great things in the years ahead for gadget junkies and serious security professionals as well.

SECURITY OFFICERS AND TECHNOLOGY

Let's not forget the most important element in the person–technology interface, the security officer. It should be understood that training, education, and national standards for security personnel are strongly espoused by planners, lobbyists, and consultants in security.

Key points of the Martinez legislation included:

1. States would adopt licensing regulations for private security firms and employees.

2. Companies would have direct access to the FBI files to expedite background checks. The bureaucracy currently in place prohibits such immediate access, delaying FBI screening by up to six months.

Some of the bill's training requirements:

1. Eight hours of classroom study, plus four hours of on-the-job training for unarmed officers prior to duty assignment.

2. Additional fifteen hours of training and passing of marksmanship test for armed officers.

3. Annual refresher courses for all officers.

Part of this process will almost certainly involve polishing the tarnished image attached to the security industry.[9]

The person/machine interface recognizes that high-tech security requires high-tech employees who are screened, trained, and educated. Only security officers of that caliber will be able to do more with fewer people, by maximizing technology and non-conventional ways to provide security services. This push for national standards may have some negative impact on the smaller contract security companies, but it is supported strongly by most of the large national contract security guard companies. The president and CEO of Borg-Warner, the parent company of both Burns International and Wells Fargo, stated:

> The public has a right to expect that someone called a security officer—even though unarmed—has been properly screened and trained in his or her duties. Our industry has been urging individual states to adopt training and background check requirements for years, but the progress has been slow.[10]

It is well for the serious security professional to follow this trend carefully in national involvement for security standards. It may be difficult at first for security contract companies to meet even these minimal standards, but the client will soon see the advantages from higher quality personnel and become a supporter for even more stringent standards in time. Police officers have been able to enforce the standards they enjoy only over the past twenty-five years or so. Corrections officers now have much higher standards, which also have become mandatory only in the past fifteen years or so in many states.

Security officers have been helped by technology in many ways, including more effective shift planning by computer-assisted monitoring of hours. It is not just a matter of working fewer billed hours, but using the right people in those hours. The vice president of Command Security Corporation puts it like this:

The easiest way to staff an assignment is to get the guy who always goes where you want him to go. But that might not be best. At the end of the week, you might have six employees on a site. Five of them have worked 32 hours apiece, and one 90 hours. Your costs just went through the roof.

About 60 to 70 percent of each hour of officer services goes toward the officer's base wages. Tax and mandatories (worker's compensation, FICA, unemployment) run between 19 percent in New York to nearly 24 percent in Florida. Add that to uniforms and vacations and things get pretty tight, considering that the hourly billing rate is approximately $10.00.

Take that same officer and work him overtime, and his base wage has gone to a minimum of $9.00 an hour. Add taxes and mandatories for another $2.10 and you're suddenly in the hole $1.10—before overheads.[11]

On large operations for security, at multiple sites and at varying hours, it is no longer practical to do scheduling without a solid computer program. This kind of program, which tells when to cut off hours and reduce overtime to provide the same service at less expense to the contractor, is currently available and continues to improve. Before such a program was installed at Command Security Corporation, the overtime rate ran 6.5 percent (that is 6.5 percent at a rate of at least $1.10 per billed hour). Since the program has been used, the overtime billing runs less than 2 percent. Here is a case where technology from other industries and helpful technicians can really improve both security effectiveness and the bottom line for the client.

Upgrading security officers can also be done by extensive first aid training and certification. About half of all security officers will respond to a medical emergency. "A security staff trained and certified in first aid and CPR can be a real plus for proprietary and contract organizations. Certification also helps compliance with OSHA requirements."[12] It is not difficult to implement a first aid and CPR training program, and much can be gotten for no cost. To make it attractive and useful (and a very good countermeasure for certain litigation), the following might be tried:

- Use certification as part of a horizontal or vertical promotion scheme.
- Host first aid and CPR classes on site.
- Certify instructors within your organization.
- Provide tuition reimbursement to officers who seek certification on their own.[13]

Just like the development of multiuse computers, or electronic alarms that perform dual duties and augment other systems, the security officer (the most costly system to maintain) must become multipurpose and able to expand capabilities. This can be done by training, but also by augmenting the person part of the person–machine interface with nonhuman capabilities.

The use of weapons and vehicles has long been the easiest way to augment the power and range of response by security officers. Technology has broadened that range of choices by providing specialized forms of transportation, night vision devices that can see in almost absolute darkness, listening devices that can pick up conversations at great distance, pinhole cameras to conduct surveillance without being seen, and a host of other technical wonders. There are now even robots that can augment a security force and patrol areas ahead of officers, or go places that security officers cannot go.

Long a topic of science fiction, the robot and robotics devices for augmenting security are here, today. Some efforts are somewhat small scale, but other developers of "robo-guards" are pushing the technological envelope. The developers of a high-tech labor saver called Spimaster, states:

> "...it is not meant to replace human officers. Granted, our vehicle can do some things an officer can't do, but it allows the officer to concentrate on the things he's better at....In a lot of ways you could compare the robot to the tractor, which farmers thought would ruin their economy. In the end, though, it took a lot of grunt work away from them."[14]

For routine patrol and repetitive or dangerous observation tasks, the robot also can work twenty-four hours a day, and it doesn't need coffee breaks, lunch, or overtime pay (see Figure 12–3).

There is also a trend today, because of the high risk of liability from use of armed officers, to find less lethal ways for officers to respond to assaultive behavior. Chemical agents that have fewer side effects and are able to incapacitate the

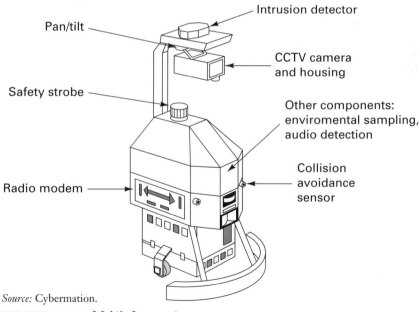

Pan/tilt

Intrusion detector

CCTV camera and housing

Safety strobe

Other components: enviromental sampling, audio detection

Radio modem

Collision avoidance sensor

Source: Cybermation.

FIGURE 12–3 *Mobile Integration*

offender quickly are presently on the shelf, or under development. Another recent trend is the return to the use of humankind's oldest friend—the dog. Guard dogs to augment the human force have been very effective in reducing security incidents. At Butterworth Hospital in Grand Rapids, Michigan, they have been able to reduce security incidents by 75 percent. The concept is new, and may be somewhat controversial because of recent problems with attack dogs used by police agencies, but the users say:

> It's just like when you're hiring a regular officer. You want to make sure he has proper training. We put the dog through several situations for high stress, check their disposition and do follow-up work with them even after they are assigned....We wanted to do something before we had a [security] problem. Dogs just make more sense."[15]

In all cases, however, there must still be a human intelligence—whether mechanical or animal—behind the technology or augmentation, a human that is better trained, better paid, and provides better security with all means available must respond in some manner.

SECURITY BYTE 12–3

Consulting Checklist

- Use referrals and network with peers and counterparts to find quality consultants. It's not a Yellow-Pages decision.

- Look for professional accreditations and affiliations. Find out about screening processes behind them.

- Define project parameters, objectives and deliverables up front.

- Understand the consultant's process and fees.

- Define a project schedule. Monitor progress.

- When you don't know where to start with security, buy or negotiate a consultant's review time to equip you with a to-do list.

- Don't ask a management generalist to specify an integrated system—it's time to tap design and engineering expertise.

- Sell management on the need for independent advice by translating it into measurable business criteria: return on investment, project savings, quality, value and cost control.

Source: Editor. "Experts on Trial: Proving Opinions." *Security* (Cahners Publishing Company. Newton, MA, 1996), Vol. 33, No. 7, Special insert, p. 4.

Consultants: Saviors or Scammers?

The **security consultant** has grown in stature since the days when he or she had less than shining credentials and was usually a former police officer or military person with little other than some experience in law enforcement. A consultant can be a great asset to security managers who are trying to determine what they need to do to reach excellence and protect their employers. Keller describes the kinds of consulting usually found in the security industry:

> Within the field of security consulting, practitioners also specialize in management, technical training and forensic consulting. Management consultants who specialize in security are the most common. These consultants evaluate a security operation and provide advice on how it can be managed better. Most also provide preventive physical security and management advice to commercial and institutional clients. The advice includes recommendations for improving security by upgrading locks, alarms, procedures, staffing, or training. Management consultants also write reports for the client's management and include suggestions for saving money by redeploying security resources.

> Technical security consultants provide more detailed advice on locks, alarms, CCTV, access control systems, and other technical security matters. These technical consultants often work directly for architects or engineers and sometimes produce bid documents, specifications, blueprint system designs, and other high-tech documentation.

> Technical security consultants conduct value surveys to ascertain whether clients are getting their money's worth from service contracts. They usually specify products and equipment by name—an acceptable practice if the recommendations can be justified and if no conflict of interest is present. However, the consultants are not affiliated with the product and never accept compensation in any form for naming a certain product. The interest of their client is the primary objective.

> Security training consultants and educators comprise a small segment of the profession. These professionals write security programs or training materials, conduct seminars, teach in universities, and also conduct research.

> The final major segment of the profession is represented by forensic consultants or expert witnesses. These individuals serve as expert consultants to the court or to attorneys on matters that involve security legislation. To recognize you as an expert witness, the court must find that you are considered a leader and expert in the industry by your peers. Forensic consultants conduct research and analysis and provide extensive, and highly technical, advice to lawyers.

> The depth of knowledge in forensics is impressive, and adopting this specialty, while highly attractive to many security professionals, is the best way to get blown out of the water as a consultant. Forensic consulting is not for the faint

of heart, and is only for true experts. One major mistake and your career is down the drain. One white lie and you become the defendant in a perjury trial. In short, if you aren't qualified for this consulting specialty, have enough common sense to stay out of it.[16]

Keller's advice on **security experts** is sound. The qualifications that are looked at by the court for presenting expert testimony to the jury are quite structured and specific. This makes the attorney (defense or plaintiff) comfortable that the expert, as Keller puts it, is not "shot out of the water by the judge before ever seeing the jury." The basic qualifications to look for in an expert witness (and actually for any consultant) are as follows:

1. *Experience:* Does the expert have experience in the specific type of security issue that is at the core of the litigation? How much experience? Where? At what level (security officer or corporate director of security)? How many times has the expert testified as an expert? In what matters? In this specific kind of issue?

2. *Education and training:* Does the expert's background come from academic education? In what field of study or academic discipline is the education? Security or criminal justice? Any education in the specific issue at hand? What degrees does the expert hold? Bachelor's? Master's? Ph.D.? Any specialized training that has been taken in the security industry? Military? Has the expert taught the applicable and relevant subjects at a college or university? In training seminars?

3. *Leadership roles in the security field:* Has the expert been recognized by his or her peers by election to leadership roles? Has the expert received awards and recognition by recognized professional groups for security expertise? How recently was this leadership demonstrated? What level of management can the expert demonstrate? Security manager? CEO?

4. *Professional membership and certifications:* Does the expert belong to and is he or she an active member in organizations like the American Society for Industrial Security (ASIS), the International Association of Health Security and Safety (IAHSS), or similar organizations? For how long? Is the expert a Certified Protection Professional (CPP), Certified Fraud Examiner (CFE), or some other designation awarded by peer examination?

5. *Contributions to the profession:* Has the expert written articles for security journals? Written books on security topics? Published textbooks or academic articles in academic or professional journals? Had speaking engagements for security professional groups or service organizations? Written anything on the specific topic at hand?

6. *How many times has the expert testified and been qualified as an expert?* For the plaintiff? For the defense? If the expert is seen as having testified exclusively (or mostly) for just one side or the other, he or she may be painted as a "hired gun," who will testify on any topic for a fee. What is the expert's fee schedule? Are any fees contingent on your side winning the case?

Although the qualifications to be a consultant are stringent, that is to the advantage of the user. It is also cost effective to pay for this high level of expertise only when

Know What You Need When Planning for Systems Integration

If front-end integration is required to provide functions that are not performed in the sub-systems, then you are really not talking about simple system integration. You are instead dealing with added functionality or system ehancement.

In most cases you are still better off using the phased approach for the installation.

The phased approach, by providing the opportunity for an accurate and fully-detailed integration design, reduces development cost to its lowest level.

Without the phased approach, the fact that added functionality is needed in the front-end system may not be discovered until after installation. Here are some things to watch for:

1. Last-Minute Design Changes

Design and development of the front-end integration should include allowances for last-minute design changes. They always happen; so why not plan for them in advance?

After Phase One installation, and before finalizing the front-end design, your security department's hands-on personnel can help the dealer or integrator make last-minute changes only once.

2. Meet in the Middle

When the sub-system manufacturer does not provide a front-end integration package, ensure that the manufacturer is not opposed to the use of a third party front-end with their product. There may be hidden complications involved where the manufacturer expresses opposition to the idea of front-end integration.

3. Measure Twice, Develop Once

This is the software development version of the carpenter's "Measure twice, cut once."

The same principle applies to custom systems design, whether the system is larger or small.

In this case the best "measurement" to take is a review of the set of installed sub-systems, after they have been fine-tuned to your requirements.

The most accurate design "measurements" can be taken from observation of the installed sub-systems in action, and from the list of requirements that are provided by you, the now-knowledgeable customer operating the sub-systems in your facility.

Debugging Time

Remember to allow a period of time for debugging the installed front-end system equivalent to 10-20 percent of the development calendar time.

For example, if the installed system took 25 weeks to develop, you should allow 21/2 to 5 weeks for debugging time.

As changes are made to the specifications and design documents, make sure your vendors update and reissue the written documents to all parties.

Graphical examples should be included to document or clarify design intent. "Screen shots" (printouts of system display screens) from example installations should be included where such systems are referenced in the specifications or design documents.

Define Technical Terms

A glossary of technical terms used in specifications and design documents, where terms are explained in plain English, will go a long way to expediting the design and approval process.

Source: Ray Bernard. "Knowing What You Need When Planning for Systems Integration." *Security* (Cahners Publishing Company, Newton, MA, 1995), Vol. 32, No. 10, p. 43.

you need it, not as a person on full-time payroll. The advantage of using a consultant to analyze the user's security programs and security issues from an objective "arms-length" status gives more credibility to the recommendations and findings. Security managers may be the least objective persons to analyze their own problems. A good, qualified, unbiased, and articulate consultant can be a big help.

Summary

The security industry needs to have help from others to provide services and products to improve the way security is done, to discern how much it costs, and to analyze its effectiveness. Security consultants can suggest the technology or management controls needed to improve the operations; security engineers and planners can design the systems that are needed to accomplish the change; and manufacturers and vendors will develop the products that can do it the best. It is up to security managers to train their personnel to make it work.

The trend in security is toward the use of technology to accomplish more, with greater effectiveness and with fewer people. People are the most expensive part of the cost of security, so industry is going full speed to find ways to assist, augment, or even replace humans in as many security tasks as possible. Remember that the person–machine interface must be retained if security is not to become a purely mechanical effort. All the technological miracles in the world will not replace the *judgment* of a single human mind. Humans must view CCTV monitors and be ready to respond to incidents, access controls need human decision makers ready to override the rare mistake, and humans must operate the computers that run on programs developed by humans. Humans are the most expensive tool for security, but they are also the most important. If they are carefully screened, thoroughly trained, and given the tools to do the job, they will not soon be replaced by cameras and robots.

REVIEW QUESTIONS

1. List the types of card reader devices that assist in access control.
2. What are the advantages to system integration in security planning?
3. Name several kinds of biometrics systems and their advantages.
4. What are some of the positive aspects of using a security consultant?
5. List the important qualifications of a security "expert."

TERMS TO REMEMBER

card reader access devices	*closed circuit television (CCTV)*	*biometrics*
proximity		*fiber optics*
Wiegand	*systems integration*	*security consultant*
magnetic stripe	*picture ID*	*security experts*

ENDNOTES

1. Kerry Lydon, "Wiegand's Re-energized, Thanks to SPAN Protocol," *Security*, Vol. 29, No. 5. (May 1992), p. 17.

2. Richard L. Mourey, "It's in the Cards," *Security Management: Special Supplement—What's the Latest Word in Access Control?* (July 1989), p. 17A.

3. Ibid., p. 20A.

4. David Hersh and Carol Hersh, "I Spy," *Lights! Camera! Action!: A CCTV Supplement to Security Management* (March 1990), p. 6A.

5. "Color Video Gives More Security Data," *Security*, Vol. 29, No. 3 (March 1992), p. 27.

6. Kerry Lydon, "True Integration: It's in the Software," *Security*, Vol. 29, No. 2 (February 1992), p. 31.

7. ——. "Hot Fiber Optics Systems Move Into Perimeter Uses," *Security*, Vol. 29, No. 4 (April 1992), p. 45.

8. Stephen C. George, "Long-Distance Fraud Spurs Phone Company Protection," *Security*, Vol. 29, No. 7 (July 1992), p. 37.

9. ——. "New Officer Bill Sets Standards for Both Armed and Unarmed," *Security*, Vol. 29, No. 10 (October 1992), pp. 53–54.

10. Ibid.

11. Ibid.

12. "Command Security's Computer Helper," *Security*, Vol. 29, No. 7 (July 1992), pp. 11–12.

13. "CPR, First Aid Help Meet OSHA, Other Requirements," *Security*, Vol. 29, No. 6 (June 1992), p. 70.

14. "Robots Make Rounds, Augment Officer Force," *Security*, Vol. 29, No. 2 (February 1992), p. 53.

15. Stephen C. George, "Canine Patrol: Firearms Alternative," *Security*, Vol. 29, No. 5 (May 1992), p. 71.

16. Steven R. Keller, CPP, "So You Want to be a Consultant..." *Security Management*, Vol. 35, No. 2 (February 1991), pp. 28–29.

13

Security and Loss Prevention Systems Integration

The Security Design and Integration process applies equally to the security owner/manager as the system user and the architect/engineer as a system designer. This approach will assure the proper selection and combination of manpower, procedures, information, facilities and equipment into a fully responsive and operationally effective system based upon expected risks at reasonable cost.

—Richard P. Grassie, CPP

Overview

The process of security design involves the selection and incorporation of various security strategies into a unified system according to a plan initially outlined by the owner/manager and architect/engineer. Integration, on the other hand, is the seamless combination of security countermeasures that emanates from the design process and results in an interoperable security system that controls risks and protects the critical assets of an organization. In fact, security design and integration is more than just the creation of three-dimensional safe and secure spaces. It is a combination of art (countermeasure selection) and science (design and integration) that reflects and documents the culture in which the space was created. Building owners and security managers need to understand these basic concepts before they can successfully design and integrate control systems that are cost effective and responsive to a particular building's needs. The process of design and integration referred to in this chapter is depicted in Figure 13–1.

These same building owners and managers have been traditionally confronted with the ultimate building control dilemma: how to cost effectively and efficiently

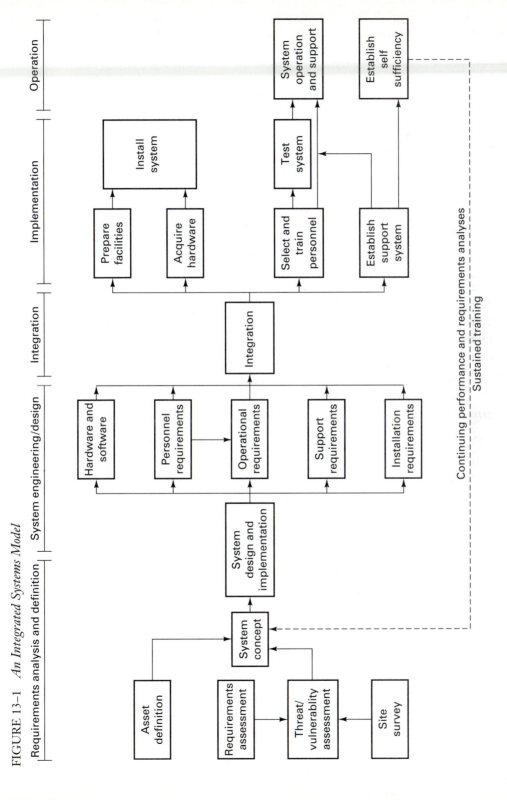

FIGURE 13-1 *An Integrated Systems Model*

procure one single building monitoring system that integrates security, access control, fire monitoring, and energy management. In the last decade and beyond, commercial firms and government agencies have been inclined to purchase individual building control systems to serve these four functions. The result was a virtual monitoring and display nightmare aggravated by the proliferation of unrelated systems and recurring multiple expenses, equivalent training of staff, and maintenance of separate systems.

Today, building owners and security managers are able to procure from a single source one integrated building control system that eliminates the technological fragmentation of the past while saving considerable expense and increasing building control efficiency. Now, faced with the multiplicity of threats and facility control requirements, owners can rely upon one integrated system uniquely designed to facilitate complete building security management for multiple tenants.

Unfortunately, many building owners and managers have been reluctant to procure fully integrated building control systems out of the fear that these systems involve considerable expense and a wide assortment of sophisticated and specialized equipment. This reluctance is not necessarily justified. A number of affordable strategies lead to successful security system integration with state-of-the-art technologies.

The Advent of Systems Integration

A decade ago, the security manager's portfolio of technology was limited to relatively simple sensors, expensive closed circuit television, archaic photo-ID systems, unidimensional access control systems relying more on manpower than technology, and nondistributed processing systems that had limited applications and required major capital expenditure approvals to purchase. Today, however, the security industry offers a wide assortment of capable technologies and integrated systems at affordable prices.

The principal issue building owners and managers face when considering integrated building control systems is how to establish the appropriate priorities for certain alarms, particularly security and safety alarms that could involve life-threatening situations. Although some contend that security should always be separated from all other building control functions, the advent of systems integration and the increased compartmented processing power of computers allow the owner and manager to set priorities and effectively manage a wide array of alarms.

Integrated security systems are also used to reduce the cost of providing essential security services. Integrated systems permit more economical and efficient use of manpower usually assigned to building patrols and fixed guard posts. Integrated intrusion detection and access control systems have become electronic extensions of the security organization by permitting remote monitoring of critical locations at a lower initial equipment cost versus continuing manpower expenditures. In addition, security technology can be used in place of other physical security measures that cannot be employed because of safety regulations, operational requirements, appearance, layout, cost, or other reasons. Security technology can provide additional protective measures at critical entry points or within a building's high-security or sensitive areas. Technology can also provide increased in-depth protection, where the use of multiple protective measures for increased system reliability is considered essential by the owner.

Two Technologies Are Better Than One In Bomb Detection

Events in recent months have put an unfortunate focus on bomb detection. While the Unabomber and Oklahoma City are the most publicized, incidents in the U.S. have continued to rise in the last few years.

Several technologies exist to thwart bombs, from large airport-sized systems such as those available from American Science and Engineering (AS&E), Cambridge, Mass., and InVision Technologies, Foster City, Calif., to bomb and drug "sniffing" equipment from Thermedics, Chelmsford, Mass., Ion Trak Instruments, Wilmington, Mass. and Barringer Instruments, New Providence, N.J.

We've seen much more interest in exposive detection in the wake of Oklahoma City," says Ken Wood, president of Barringer. "Everyone now realizes that these are not isolated incidents. It's probably going to get worse."

All of these technologies offer improvements over the traditional X-ray, which rely on operators to spot potential threats. But they can be expensive, cumbersome, and many facilities—particularly airports—have already invested in X-ray systems.

Bomb Detection Retrofit

As of next month, a different kind of solution will be available. X-ray company EG&G Astrophysics, Long Beach, Calif., and bomb detection manufacturer Quantum Magnetics, San Diego, will introduce a combined system.

The Quantum Magnetics technology, Quadropole Resonance (a form of the MRI technology used in the medical field), works by using low-intensity radio waves to momentarily disturb certain atoms. As the atoms return to their preferred positions, they produce a distinct signal that is analyzed by the computer. The technology works for both explosives and drugs, and takes an average of five seconds.

Available as a complete unit, or as a retrofit to existing EG&G X-ray units, the system will provide two levels of screening.

Screening Process

"We think it's going to revolutionize explosive detection technology," says Rebecca West, manager of public relations for Quantum Magnetics. "It's the first system that combines two advanced technologies together."

The procedure for using the new systems will begin with the Quadrupole Resonance scanner. Bags will be placed in the unit to be scanned, then passed through the X-ray. If anything is found by the QR, the operator will be alerted by a message, or a red light.

Joint Strengths

"The QR has a better than 99 percent detection rate for very small amounts of explosives," says Christina Phan, marketing manager for EG&G Astrophysics. "QR can detect explosives anywhere in a bag, no matter what its orientation. With X-ray, however, the operator might miss seeing small amounts, or sheet explosives."

On the QR side, the technology is not designed to see metal or detect certain weapons the way X-ray is, West says. "As far as the agreement goes, it's ideal for both, because each technology covers the weaknesses of the other," she adds. "They are two good technologies, and we hope that by combining them, we will have as close to a fool-proof system as you can get," Phan says.

Source: Karyn Hodgson. "Two Technologies Are Better Than One In Bomb Detection," *Security* (Cahners Publishing Company. Newton, MA, 1995) Vol. 32, No. 9, p. 23.

Integrated building protective measures may include detection sensors, automated access control elements, closed circuit television, fiber optic or some other type of communication and transmission lines, and multiplexed control and display equipment to tie all the various elements together into one central location. This chapter explores the various generic security technologies available for selection by the owner and security manager in the formulation of a truly integrated building security system. The student will be able to put the pieces covered in past chapters together into a integrated whole and see how it can apply to real-world security issues.

Initial Building Security Considerations

Integrated security needs for a building must be determined early in the design phase as part of the project programming and definition process. Burglary, industrial espionage, assault, robbery, rape and murder are crimes that imperil lives; these and employee theft all tend to increase the cost of doing business. As crime increases, building owners as well as their architects and engineers, are being called upon to address security problems by incorporating security into the design and construction of all building types.

Designing a facility without security in mind can lead to unsafe and insecure environments, eventual lawsuits, and potential employee injuries. Retrofitting a facility with needed protection equipment plus additional security personnel can be a very expensive undertaking. If not properly planned for and installed, that equipment can distort important building design functions, add to security personnel costs, and result in exposed unsightly alarm systems or blocked doors and windows.

Security concerns need to be defined by the owner and security manager at the beginning of the facility design phase. Subsequent assistance in formulating system objectives and design details can be provided by a security consultant or an architect or engineer. The proliferation of security devices we have on the market today, coupled with rapid advances in system technology, requires security planning specialists with a working knowledge not only of the devices themselves but also of the various integration possibilities for joining discrete systems for increased facility monitoring effectiveness. Electronic intrusion detection, perimeter protection, surveillance and access control techniques must be elements considered in a total security system and design approach. Each technique has distinct technological and operational characteristics, and environmental reactions, along with differing requirements for installation and maintenance.

TECHNOLOGY DESIGN CONSIDERATIONS

The design of integrated systems incorporating the latest security technology is borne out of the realization that certain assets at risk as well as operational requirements for control of personnel and facilities must be factored into the design. The owner must consider the range of events (threat assessment) potentially confronting the asset(s) to be protected, the probability that a potential loss event will become an actual loss event expressed in quantitative terms (risk assessment), the relative exposure of assets given the potential threats and risks (vulnerability assessment), the consequences of information compromise, possible loss of life or equipment, and the degree of disruption to normal operations. These considerations provide a planning baseline to establish technology systems objectives to detect, assess, and respond to the unauthorized entry of a secured area. The response time required by the security force to arrive at the secured area after a verified alarm is a key factor in selecting various complementary technologies, establishing the required in-depth protection, the penetration delay capabilities for specific barriers, and other operational protective measures.

The specific functions of integrated security systems that drive the security design process are listed here. A total security program considers a wide range of countermeasure options and combinations to perform each of these functions.

- Deter
- Delay
- Deny
- Control
- Detect
- Communicate
- Assess
- Surveil
- Display
- Monitor
- Command
- Respond
- Intervene
- Investigate

The **security technology design** process is a key element in the overall building project development plan and is typically based upon the functions listed. The integration of electronic intrusion detection, assessment and surveillance, and access control subsystems into proposed building requirements for barrier or delay elements, response force availability, and owner operational requirements all place specific constraints on the building security design process. Therefore, it is imperative that these functional requirements for integrated building security systems be incorporated at concept development and flow progressively to the more detailed phases of engineering and installation planning management. Their inclusion as a basis of design throughout the entire process can lead to avoiding the costly and disruptive consideration of security requirements at prefinal design and occupancy phases of major design and construction projects.

INTRUSION DETECTION TECHNOLOGIES

Detection technologies provide electronic sensing and reporting of man, machine, and contraband items moving across, over, under, or through restricted areas of a building and perimeters or through control points. Detection technologies can increase control over specific points or spaces within a protected area by electronically sensing one or more types of phenomena and reporting the outputs to the security control station. Exterior sensors can be deployed either singularly or in an overlapping configuration to maximize the probability of detection (P_d) around an area or along a facility perimeter. Exterior sensors also may be attached to a barrier or installed above or below the ground. They use a variety of phenomena to sense intrusion and require careful analysis, site engineering, and installation to ensure adequate performance.

Interior sensors can be used to provide an alarm upon detecting entry to facilities or access to critical areas or assets within a facility while minimizing the need for manned security posts. Point sensors can be used to protect doors, windows, and other openings, as well as critical assets such as containers and high-value items, high-value manufacturing equipment and cargo, or other standalone special assets. Volumetric sensors placed strategically along the corridors of a building can provide an alarm on detecting the presence or movement of an intruder inside a confined space of a facility.

Recent advances in sensor technology have witnessed the introduction of sensors that combine two complementary technologies, such as infrared and microwave or ultrasonic devices, within a single sensor housing to provide for enhanced protection in more difficult environments and less likelihood of defeat by a more sophisticated intruder. In addition, current advancements in sensor processing technology have resulted in the recent introduction of smart sensors that actually contain a processing capability that responds more accurately to valid intrusion stimuli and effectively filters out common sources of nuisance alarms.

The increasing effectiveness of contraband detection technologies has provided the ability to detect such items as plastic weapons, plastics explosives, radioactive materials, and other unauthorized items entering or leaving an area. Considering the terrorist threat posed by a concealed cache of plastic explosive in a portable radio, similar to the device that detonated Pan American World Airways flight 103 over Scotland, the airport security community is currently being equipped with the technology to detect and respond to such previously undetectable threats.

ASSESSMENT AND SURVEILLANCE TECHNOLOGIES

The annunciation of remotely dispersed intrusion detection devices throughout large buildings, along with the monitoring of facility access, creates a need for the security force to be aware of the validity, severity, and nature of the event that triggered the alarm. This requires, in part, the strategic placement of closed circuit television, manned patrols, and guard posts to provide continuous surveillance of sensitive areas and assessment of alarmed areas. The effective employment of CCTV accelerates the evaluation process, fills informational gaps, and helps security managers expedite the decision-making process. Properly located and controlled CCTV equipment can provide both the command/control and the response to the threat. The integration of assessment elements such as lighting and CCTV are often critical to security force confidence and safety, and have a direct bearing on the overall integrated building system cost. Furthermore, CCTV monitoring requirements need to be carefully configured at the central display location to accommodate manpower and structural limitations.

Video assessment may be employed to provide the control and display operator with the capability to visually assess alarm zone activities, such as intrusions through the boundary and perimeter of an area or within a critical facility. When integrated with exterior or interior sensors, CCTV allows the operator to view alarm zone intrusions for an adequate period before initiating a response. The use of CCTV for assessment increases the efficiency and effectiveness of operator and security response personnel to alarm events. It is a significant, cost-effective alternative to human assessment and has demonstrated a return value by facilitating security upgrades without expensive manpower authorization increases.

The use of CCTV, particularly when installed to be activated in conjunction with a sensor or access alarms, significantly enhances the safety and response effectiveness of the security force and reduces the need for expensive and fixed security posts. What's more, sensors with unique processing characteristics can provide a discrimination capability to detect specific targets. This special assessment capability could be included in the overall security system design to ensure CCTV system performance and provide for a positive assessment capability for the response force.

State-of-the-art CCTV devices can also be used to detect intruders by processing video frames and transmitting intruder information to the operator who performs surveillance of an area using the CCTV. In this sensing capacity, CCTV is also an element of the detection subsystem. CCTV may also be employed for surveillance of critical access points and high-security areas, and as an activity recording element.

The preferred technique for integrated medium and large CCTV systems is to maintain continuous activation of the entire CCTV system and use a centrally located video switch to scroll and display sequential CCTV cameras on assigned CCTV monitors and a multiplexer to control the display formats. An alarm would automatically display the alarmed video sector camera scene. The use of a video switcher reduces the number of monitors required for display of sector video data if the purpose of the system is assessment of alarmed zone(s) based upon an electronic link between the intrusion detection/access control systems and the CCTV system.

Solid-state charged coupled device (CCD) cameras have replaced tube-type cameras as the preferred camera of choice for all CCTV applications. They use a solid-state array to serve the purpose of the imager. Since the other camera components have used solid-state electronics for some time, the tube has been the inherent CCTV camera reliability weak point. Elimination of this vacuum tube increases reliability as well as minimizing maintenance requirements for the camera's interior components. At present, these cameras cost anywhere from $250 to $800, depending upon whether they are black and white or color. However, since tube replacement is no longer a maintenance cost driver as in the standard tube camera, the life cycle cost of the solid-state camera is significantly less. The solid-state imager is more sensitive to the infrared and near-infrared spectrum.

No single assessment method should operate on a standalone basis. They must all be integrated to focus attention on the need to provide both the command/control and response force with reliable information on the nature and magnitude of an intrusion event. The specific circumstances will determine the appropriate mix and degree of assessment elements to be employed for a particular building.

ACCESS CONTROL TECHNOLOGIES

Access control is a process that serves to permit or deny entry, thus regulating the flow of personnel, vehicles, and material into a building. The criteria for approving access includes the verification of a person's authorization to enter a facility or, in some cases, the additional verification of a person's identity through biometric means. The criteria can be verified through one or more of the elements of security: personnel, equipment, and procedures. The proportional use of these three elements to authorize access involves the analysis of both the specific threat to the protected area or asset and the requirements of operational procedures to assure mission accomplishment. Automated access allows personnel to enter and exit an area without security force intervention unless the system initiates an alarm. When an alarm does occur, the security force can assess the situation and initiate the proper response action.

Automated access control systems permit an electronic device to grant or deny access based upon prior approval of authorization criteria encoded into a badge credential or a keypad. This approval authorization sequence is information that must be communicated to the equipment in a form acceptable to the electronics. This information provides the criteria for access or egress. In general, an automated access control system comprises a central controller, an enrollment console, an event video or hardcopy display, and portals controlled by a coded credential and reader linked to electronic locking devices such as an electric strike or electromagnetic locking device. The primary advantage of these systems is that they are largely pick-proof compared to conventional lock-and-key controls. If the badge is lost, they can be easily voided by deleting identification data from the system. The central processor constantly monitors the condition of remote readers, and all access activities are logged on a permanent record.

The increased popular use of automated access control systems in security environments has been primarily due to potential cost tradeoff more than any other criterion. The use of microprocessor technology and recent advances in coded credentials has led to lower system costs to electronically control access and to perform a host of ancillary functions from a single security control point. Rather than a manned security post, the employee credential, or badge, is now increasingly the access authorization means, and the central processor is providing alarm display, control, and related total system integration functions. With sufficient intelligence, these systems can perform highly sophisticated authorization and reporting functions with the simple insertion of the coded credential and pay for themselves with reduced or redirected manpower costs.

BASIC AUTOMATED ACCESS CONTROL ELEMENTS

Building barrier elements may be integrated into access control elements through the configuration of turnstiles, sally ports, and structural components to channel the flow of people through controlled portals while facilitating entry and egress during high-use periods. Machine-intensive elements electronically perform the entry authorization and verification process using a variety of technologies and preestablished, mostly automated, access criteria. These systems range from small applications providing control over a few portals to large, distributed computer-based networks capable of performing multiple functions. The elements that may be configured with machine-intensive systems include the following:

1. Card-based entry control devices that electronically read preprogrammed data unique to each card and authorize or deny access attempts at specific portals or record departure from the area. Cards may also serve as identification badges with photo identification pictures laminated or sublimated onto the card itself. Reader elements may be employed on both entry and exit as standalone units or in conjunction with positive personnel identification number keypads for a second means of access verification.

2. Positive personnel identification and verification elements in high-security applications where more than one access authorization level is required. These elements may include coded keypads (personal identification number, or PIN), a combination of coded keypads and card readers, CCTV for facial confirmation, or biometrics readers (personal identification verification, or PIV) to key upon the unique features of each authorized individual, such as hand geometry, speech, face, fingerprints, and retinal or signature identifications.

3. Processor or central memory for control units that incorporate various automated access criteria based upon area authorization, time zoning, multiperson access rules, antipassback prohibitions, or other features.

Examples of **secondary verifications** are PINs; physical characteristics; photographic image matchups to personnel files; biometrics systems such as hand geometry, fingerprints, handwriting, speech, and weight. Secondary systems, with the exception of biometrics systems, are less secure than coded credentials. This is due to the easily read identification media and the wide latitude to accommodate variations due to environment, stress, and other data entry errors that may deny access to authorized owners. A personal identification number is the most commonly used secondary verification system because of the relative ease in obtaining an accurate specific data entry and the immunity of this data to environmental influences. The use of a secondary means of access authorization is generally limited to selected high-security applications where throughput rates and cost concerns need to be controlled. Various systems now commercially available have substantially reduced the likelihood of machine error to the point where their use is universally recommended.

PERSONAL IDENTIFICATION NUMBER (PIN)

For card access systems with PIN options, the readers have keypads where the PINs can be entered. In most cases, the PINS are not stored in the central controller's memory but are derived from the credential ID numbers following some encryption algorithms. In this case, the reader itself matches the entered PIN with the calculated number to validate the coded credential before it sends the data to the central controller. The preferred method is a system that either assigns a PIN or allows an owner to select a PIN unrelated to his or her badge ID number. Personal identification numbers are vulnerable to covert discovery by unauthorized personnel through visual observation of keypad entry sequence or poor owner control over his or her code.

VIDEO COMPARATOR SYSTEMS

The use of a video comparator requires a guard to verify an individual's identity based on visual characteristics. By using a graphic user interface module in an access control system, the person seeking authorization for entry into an area can have his or her photo image stored in a separate database linked to the access control system and immediately displayed onto the access control monitoring screen. The electronically stored image is used for comparison with a real-time image of the individual requesting entry. Although video comparators are not positive personnel identity verification systems, they have an advantage over manual picture ID systems in that it is difficult to tamper with the stored image used in the comparator system. Nevertheless, they are categorized as having a low resistance to counterfeiting. In this sense, the video comparator is comparable to the badge exchange system. Enrollment capacity is the maximum number of images that can be stored by the system. The access time is the time elapsed from identification number entry until the stored image is displayed for viewing.

HAND GEOMETRY

The measurement of relative finger length is a unique characteristic used in verifying a person's identity. **Hand geometry** is a distinct measurable human characteristic. These systems have a high to medium resistance to counterfeiting.

HANDWRITING

Signature verification has been used for many years by the banking industry. Automated handwriting verification systems have been developed that use handwriting dynamics such as velocity, acceleration, and pressure as a function of time. Statistical evaluation of these data indicates that an individual's signature is unique and reasonably consistent from one signature to the next. Systems have been developed that use from one to three axes of dynamic measurements. Transducers can be located in either the writing instrument or the tablet. Like hand geometry, signature verification has a high to medium counterfeiting resistance level.

SPEECH

Speech is a useful attribute for identity verification, and it is well suited to automated data processing system entry. Speech measurements useful for speaker discrimination include waveform envelope, voice pitch period, relative amplitude spectrum, and vocal tract resonant frequencies. It has a high resistance to counterfeiting and has been perfected to the point where rejections of authorized individuals when the person has a cold can be minimized.

FINGERPRINTS

Fingerprints have been used as a positive personal identifier for more than one hundred years and are still considered one of the most reliable means of distinguishing one individual from another. The art of processing human fingerprints for identification has been greatly enhanced in recent years by the development of automated systems. These systems, which rely on pattern recognition of either a single finger or several fingers and computerized data processing, have an application in access control. All fingerprint identification systems require accurate finger positioning and pattern measurement for reliable identification. Fingerprint systems possess a high resistance to counterfeiting.

OTHER TECHNIQUES

Other techniques for positive personal identity verification include **retinal scan**, palm prints, weight, facial recognition, or combinational systems. Retinal scan is increasingly receiving interest as a third means of entry verification but has resulted in employee resistance because of possible health concerns. The key to a biometric method's potential universal use is the relative intrusiveness of the device to the individual seeking verification. Tests and evaluation of biometrics personnel verification systems for high-security portals are continuing. Where design requirements mandate a third means of access authorization and verification, issues related to throughput and verification error rates as well as resistance to defeat via counterfeiting will provide design parameters on system selection.

SMART CARDS

A relatively new development in the field of access control is the **smart card**. Smart cards actually contain a tiny microprocessor that identifies the owner or holder by recording practically every unique detail of his or her life. The microprocessor can store a wealth of personal identification information, including a person's biometrics data such as fingerprints or facial shape, that can be unlocked only by the holder for verification. The smart card can store large quantities of information—several thousand to several million pieces—and can create encryption algorithms to generate unique PIN requirements. In use mainly overseas, the smart card is presently prohibitively expensive for general application, although its increased use by the general public is a virtual certainty.

All card access badges are susceptible to alteration, decoding, and duplication or loss. The degree to which the technology and associated procedures resist these threats is important to the integrity of the security system. For more critical access verification requirements, additional verification systems requiring either a code to be entered on a keypad or physical characteristic confirmation may be advisable for backup to card-only access authorization. The second verification is to minimize the vulnerability associated with insider collusion and lost or stolen cards.

Typical locking hardware that is compatible with automated access control systems includes electric strikes, electric bolts, and electromagnetic locks. Each of these devices is available with one of two features termed "fail-safe" and "fail-secure," configured in either alternating or direct current. The design of an automated access control system must consider such variables, which are related to portal use and application of local and national fire and electrical codes. Some electronic locks have a feature where the user can select either fail-safe or fail-secure by moving a latch device located inside the locking device. In the event of loss of power in a building, fail-safe locking devices fail in the open mode. Conversely, fail-secure locking devices remain locked in the event of loss of power. All portals in a building associated with fire or emergency exit should fail-safe in the event of loss of power, whereas access to highly critical assets should remain secure in the event of loss of power.

The standard features of the automated access control system provide enhancement of security operations, particularly where the equipment outperforms the human in repetitive functions. This creates a more secure environment, since the human element is permitted to perform in the area where greater efficiencies are achieved. Definitions of who is permitted access based upon the criteria of area, portal, time zone, holiday schedule, loading, two-man rule areas, and the subsequent recording of the information relative to use can be essential to the mission of security. The automation of electronic alarm processing within the same control center provides a single source of information regarding the facility or activity security. The other software enhancements of automated guard tours and patrols, redundant life safety system monitoring, security trace, data encryption, and centralized control or reporting can improve the versatility of the system. The capabilities of the system to call up electronic commands to address detected events with specific details, telephone numbers, and prioritized sequences reduce further the margin for human error by reducing the requirements for human judgment.

AUTOMATED ACCESS CONTROL INTEGRATION

Automated access control integration needs to be considered early in the design process—where automated access control and intrusion detection, along with other facility control functions, will be used. The typical access control processor provides sufficient software and processing capability to integrate alarm monitoring as a standard feature. The designer needs to consider the acceptability and total requirement for control and display, and to specify according to cost and benefit where both requirements are established.

"Seeing" the Future of ATM Access

In this increasingly complex electronic age, banks have more to worry about than just physical access to their facility. In fact, many bank patrons rarely enter the interior at all, preferring to use a remote ATM. And, sooner than later, the personal computer will also peform those functions.

All this means that securing financial transactions, positively identifying customers and preventing fraud have become prime concerns. One technology banks are turning to for help is iris-based biometrics. Japan's largest manufacturer of ATMs, Oki Electric Industry Co. Ltd., will deploy the IrisIdent product from Sensar, Moorestown, N.J., in all Japanese markets requiring authentication of personal identity.

Closer to home, Citibank will be testing the device through the summer. And other banks are considering the technology as well.

Technology Specifics

Sensar licensed the right to include iris recognition technology from IriScan, Mt. Laurel, N.J., into their image acquisition software system for financial transaction applications.

"From a mathematical perspective, the iris is the most unique feature on the body," says Kelly Gates, marketing manager for IriScan. "The chance of two irises having the same code are one in 10 to the 60th power."

With the Sensar agreement, the technology has gotten even easier to use. "We've spent millions of dollars and 15 man years of time to develop a product that can read the iris from three feet away," says Kevin McQuade, vice president of strategic business development for Sensar.

The Sensar product is actually software and algorithms that use off-the-shelf cameras to automatically focus in on the user's eye and make an access decision within three seconds.

How It Works

The Sensar system will allow a bank customer to step up to an ATM and be recognized. "They don't have to touch anything," McQuade says. "There is no hygiene issue. We automatically do all that with the cameras."

The camera technology is taken from military applications, McQuade explains. Because the product is software based, the cameras already in ATMs could be adapted to this technology, performing two roles at once. "A lot of banks like that we take the patron's picture during the transaction," McQuade says. If a customer disputes a transaction, the bank can even fax them that picture, proving that they were there.

One advantage to positively identifying the customer is to allow them to do larger transactions remotely. These could include wire transfers, bank checks, and higher value transactions.

Another advantage is the ability to do "cardless" transactions. "As the customer is using the ATM and typing in the transaction, the system is making the identification," Gates explains. "And if you forget

"Seeing" the Future of ATM Access

your card, you can go to the ATM within your banking system and still get money out using your iris identification."

Many Applications

While, initially, applications will focus on ATMs, a wide range of banking services could eventually employ this technology.

"We believe that the initial applications will be in the financial community," McQuade says. "There are many billions of dollars being lost to fraud in banking. This is a way to know the customer better."

That will open up the way to applications such as home banking, he adds. "This technology reaches across all areas that banks want to touch their customers.

Computers in the future will have video conferencing technology. Customers will be able to call into their bank's homepage and download this software. That would activate the camera, which would locate their eye, encode and encrypt the information and open up their account.

According to McQuade, customers could start seeing iris recognition in banks within six months. But while this will allow extended transactions and provide higher security to customers, it will not initially replace the PIN. "They will still be able to use their PIN," McQuade says. "But if they have a Citibank account and are at that location, they will be able to get more money and perform other transactions."

Source: Editor. "Seeing the Future of ATM Access," *Security* (Cahners Publishing Company. Newton, MA, 1997) Vol. 34, No. 6, p. 44.

COMMUNICATIONS TECHNOLOGIES

A critical element in an integrated security system is the communication link that transmits information from sensors, access devices, and video components to the security force display and assessment equipment. Two principal considerations for selection of the appropriate communication techniques are the basic economic and technical requirements and the degree of security to be afforded to the communication system. In determining how to transmit information and protect these communication links, the system designer may consider a number of approaches. There is no one best solution for all applications. The specific requirements for each protected asset must be considered and a design solution selected with threat, cost, and other design constraints as parameters. However, several system-level communication considerations should be evaluated in commencing the requirements analysis phase of security systems designs.

Communications in security involves the transmission of sensor, CCTV, status, and access control data. The knowledge of intrusions and intrusion attempts or system compromise or failure must be communicated from the sensor to the monitor in a clear, speedy manner that is resistant to compromise and conducive to rapid fault detection and repair. Hardwire, microwave, radio frequency (RF), and fiber optics communications means may carry the electronic signals, voice, or video communications required for security operations.

Hardwire or landline communication is typically a physical wire connection from point to point. The type of signal transmitted and the susceptibility of that signal to interference or compromise will dictate the need for protection from environmental and human-initiated degradations of the communications link. The communication link between camera and monitor in the simple closed circuit television system is most often on coaxial cable, or fiber optic networks. Recent advances have introduced telephone lease lines as a means of CCTV image communication. The coaxial cable provides shielding and grounding characteristics that are critical for video signal quality. Very long alarm communication wiring can be managed by existing or specially installed telephone company wiring. Connections between buildings and within large facilities often can be cost effectively accommodated by the telephone utility wiring since most security communications needs are conducted via low-voltage wire pairs. Radio frequency communication media may be used for security information transfer. Although most often used for two-way voice communications, significant new developments in the RF alarm transmitter subsystems have occurred within the past ten years. Wireless RF systems work in conjunction with detection sensors to provide transmissions of the detected event from the device location to the monitor location. Microwave transmission provides for high-speed transmission of data, television signals, multiplexed alarm signals, and multiplexed telephone. Microwave is limited to line-of-sight transmitter to receiver and behaves very much the same as light signals.

Fiber optics is a reliable communications media suited for point-to-point, high-speed data transmission. Fiber optics bandwidth is virtually unlimited, and extremely high data transmission rates can be obtained, as well as transmission simultaneously of sensor and control data and back and video data on a single fiber. Transmission of color graphic data requires the use of multiple fibers. For most security applications, fiber optics provides adequate built-in line security protection, and it is often used where external electronic interference is a problem for the data communications media. Fiber optic cable is immune to electrical influences, static electricity, lightning, water, and most other fluids. Cable distances can be unlimited with the addition of repeater units. Protection against compromise is inherent because of the sophistication of techniques required to intercept, monitor, and compromise the signal.

Many of today's security applications, especially video, are implemented in a one-way mode of operation such as the basic video surveillance system. Equipment is available from some manufacturers that will allow the multiplexing of up to thirty-two video signals across a single fiber. These systems simply combine the signal through the fiber, and then split the signal at both ends, and through software controls, allow the receiver to view each signal as required. These applications lend themselves well to large remote CCTV systems such as airports, industrial complexes, or warehouse farms.

CENTRAL CONTROL TECHNOLOGIES

Central control and display technology provides the focal point for communications, display of alarm information, system status, and system support and performance. Integrated alarm reporting, display, access control, and video assessment and surveillance functions elements provide the system operator a network that facilitates effective command, control, and communications for timely response to verified threats to security. Some control and display equipment includes display control processors, map or pictorial displays, control display devices or keyboards, printers, and information storage devices. The equipment may perform its function autonomously or in conjunction with other security equipment. Communications equipment provides for the interconnection of sensors to their respective controls and displays. This equipment may include certain interface electronics, collectors, control units and processors, modems, radios, cabling, and any other equipment used in transmitting signals and information. In the total systems context, communications also involves hardwire and RF voice communications systems essential to command and control of the security organization. This may also include manually or automatically actuated duress alarms that permit personnel to signal a security control center for assistance.

Local control units can be strategically situated throughout a building to collect and communicate to a central control location the alarm and status signal data from access card readers, intrusion detection sensors, and CCTV for assessment. With built-in microprocessors for event processing and on-board memory, these control units or data-gathering panels can operate independently of the central processor authorizing transactions based upon stored tables of authorization for extended periods. Once the central processor comes back online, the control units are automatically polled to send stored transactions (alarm and access) back to the central processor for archival purposes while the control units are refreshed with updated tables of authorization. This data is transmitted to a central console or a control and display device. Much of the state-of-the-art control and display technology currently available has been developed with these centralized control requirements as cost-effective functions.

Control and display elements provide for the continuous monitoring, through cathode ray tube (CRT) displays and the annunciator panel, of all detection and access control subsystem outputs. They also provide a capability for the system operator to provide zone status control. There is an additional option for a monitor and control unit that is microprocessor based with an integral processor assembly, display panel, control keyboard, printer, and an auxiliary power supply. Systems are capable of monitoring, annunciating, controlling, and displaying the status of uniquely identified zones. Other elements provide for the recording and printing of necessary data. They sort user-entered time, date, and installation-related data such as zone numbers, zone descriptors, and transponder addresses, and provide management with a current, valid report of security activities. The system size and related operational factors usually dictate the use of control and display units, which can be complex and sophisticated. The complexity and sophistication of the system depends upon such factors as number of sensors, sensitivity of the restricted area, and the desired performance parameters for the system.

RELATED SYSTEMS

The fully integrated security system must incorporate elements from several other subsystems in addition to those already discussed. These include voice, personnel-

Parking at High Speed? More Security, Less Delay

Bombings, shootings, carjackings and thefts are some of the hazards that can lurk in parking facilities. As the World Trade Center bombing demonstrated, the need for greater access control can be paramount.

Parking garages are often located in remote, unprotected areas, and requiring personnel to roll down a window to gain access can expose them to security risks, not to mention inclement weather. In high traffic areas, delays can also be a problem.

Enter systems that don't require any action from the driver. In fact, he or she may not even have to stop.

Control, No Hassle

From Westinghouse Security Electronics, Santa Clara, Calif., the WSE License Plate Reader incorporates a video camera, infrared strobe, and computer hardware and software. When the driver approaches the parking facility, the camera takes a picture of the vehicle and "reads" the license plate to determine whether to grant or deny access.

"In a parking environment like the World Trade Center, the LPR can also provide video output," says Keith Cahalen, marketing product manager at Westinghouse. "The unit can be set up to tie with the host, so that when a car pulls up to the gate, it has the ability to pull up that video image on a monitor in the guard station."

Sensormatic Electronics Corp., Deerfield Beach, Fla., provides an RFID system that mounts on the dashboard of the car. When the car nears the gate, the transponder is read by an antenna and reader system.

Reading speed ranges from 55 mph (for RFID) to 100 mph (for LPR). But actual use can be slower, depending on whether a gate or parking arm is used. In that case, a driver can enter "as fast as the gate will go up and down," says Terry Price, group vice president for Sensormatic.

Vehicle Tracking

Unlike card or keypad access control, these systems can identify the vehicle, driver, or both—and provide a record of entrances and exits.

"In a corporate parking situation, you often have two goals," Cahalen says. "You want to make sure only employees gain access. But in many areas, the government is starting to require car pooling programs, and proof tht the corporation is complying. The LPR provides absolute proof that a specific car came through."

In other situations, it is important to know not only what car came through, but who was driving. This can be accomplished with the LPR by combining it with a card access system, Cahalen says.

Sensormatic's Sensor•ID technology interfaces directly with the access control system, Price says, so that the transponder ID in the car matches the employee's badge.

Source: Karyn Hodgson. "Parking at High Speed? More Security, Less Delay," *Security* (Cahners Publishing Company. Newton, MA, 1993) Vol. 30, No. 12, p. 9.

Exit Controls Tie to On-demand Cameras

An inventive and practical electronic bridge between delayed egress door controls and a hotel/casino's CCTV system provides security instant surveillance at the point of delayed exit.

The door-to-CCTV design is part of a state-of-the-art security/fire and suppression system in the San Juan (Puerto Rico) Marriott Stellaris Casino that boasts the latest in control and surveillance.

The property, originally the DuPont Plaza Hotel in Puerto Rico, was rebuilt and transformed into the new Marriot. A headline-making fire razed the hotel several years ago. All but the tower is new in the 525-room casino/beachfront hotel.

Perimeter Control

The hotel and casino complex uses Securitron-Magnalock Corp., Sparks, Nev., exit door control systems in both delayed and immediate egress applications on all exit doors. Newer than simple pushbar exit controls, delayed egress systems can program to annunciate locally and/or remotely as well as provide a set period of time before the door can be opened.

Around 18 Magnalock Model 62 electromagneic locks are part

INTEGRATING EXIT CONTROLS
✓ Immediate egress
✓ Delayed egress
✓ Local and remote annunciation
✓ Camera power-up
✓ Exit point video

Hotel and casino exit controls dovetail into a multiplexed video surveillance system.

of the installation, as well as accompanying TBS-3 Touch Sense Bars and one LCP Lock Control Panel. When the exit control system is activated, it annunciates locally and activates a green light at the control center.

Instant camera power-up and identification provides ready surveillance of the indicated area.

Specified into the hotel's CCTV design: Toshiba black and white and color cameras models 536 and 537 and IK627 color as well as Torrance, Calif.-based Javelin's Omni Video System. Recording devices in the casino are real-time; the hotel uses timelapse methods. Multiplexing switching devices are part of the CCTV/monitor systems in the control rooms.

About 100 color CCD 1/2-inch surveillance cameras with pan/tilt and other lens options are positioned around the casino, lending to better identification of chips and cash in money counting areas. Black-and-white 1/2-inch CCD-cameras, about 64, are used in the hotel, including most public areas, lobbies, elevators, all exits and a 92-car parking gararge. Low-light cameras cover parking areas.

Complete Security

The hotel has two separate control rooms, one for the casino and the other for the hotel, according to Pedro Rivera, director of security and surveillance.

Rivera has charge of a staff that includes 13 compliance or security officers for the casino; six surveillance agents with one supervisor; and for the hotel, 55 security officers with another supervisor.

"Our goal is to protect our guests and the property," Rivera says.

related equipment, and most important, the procedures subsystem. The procedures subsystem is perhaps the most critical nonhardware subsystem to the eventual design. This will involve intensive user and security force involvement primarily at early design review stages to ensure that the proposed systems can be supported procedurally by the users.

SYSTEM INTEGRATION

Each of the security subsystems (detection, access control, communications, closed circuit television, and control and display) represents a nonexhaustive inventory of elements that security system designers may find appropriate to their needs. Considered individually, they offer little real protection to an owner's assets. Collectively, a mix of these protective measures keyed specifically to facility and site-unique requirements composes a subsystem-level material list. It remains for the owner and designer to integrate these components into a total system design.

The term *system integration* describes the primary objective of the security system design process: to incorporate these physical elements (barriers, sensors, communications media, control units, CCTV, and so on) with personnel and procedures to result in an integrated approach to asset protection. Each subsystem element needs to be evaluated in terms of both its individual contribution to specific vulnerability reduction and its overall contribution to the total effort. The consideration of one offers tradeoff in terms of cost and benefit to the other. A physical barrier with ten minutes of delay has a cost compared to real-time notification of intrusion via an electronic sensor zone with CCTV assessment.

The selection of which option is more appropriate depends upon several factors, namely, the availability and capability of the security force to respond within a specific time, the value of the asset, the criticality of the mission, the capabilities of the adversary, budgetary constraints, and a host of other factors. Technology integration is the culmination of the choices appropriate to individual asset protection decisions. How do all the selected protective measures and components required for their operation fit together for total system effectiveness? Answers to this question are as applicable to the

---

SECURITY BYTE 13 – 1

Don't Touch That Fence!

The problem with fences is they can be climbed. The problem with many perimeter detection systems is they are subject to many false alarms.

But what about a system that combines perimeter detection with a fence that deters climbers?

The Power Fence from Gallagher Security (Int.) Ltd., Hamilton, New Zealand is a "safe" electric fence that alarms when someone actively tries to climb it.

Animal, People Control

Based on a system originally used for safe animal control, the fence incorporates an energizer that produces high voltage, short duration impulses of up to 8,000 volts every 1.2 seconds. The system complies with all national and international standards including U.L. 69, says Graham Harper, the company's UK general manager.

"Just touching the fense wouldn't make it alarm," Harper says. "But if you try to compromise or climb it, then it alarms." The fence can be attached to existing fences, or used on its own—behind another fence to prevent accidental touching.

Applications

It's currently being used to protect facilities in several countries, including the UK, where British Gas and Ryder Trucks are two users. But, Harper warns, the fence is not intrinsically safe, and should not be used in hazardous areas.

Another British company, the National Grid, is also using the fences—to protect its power generators.

The company found that at many of their electricity substations, the safety earth straps designed to ground the conductor were being vandalized for the solid copper strapping. In addition, each time a fence was compromised to get to the copper, it left a hole that children could easily slip through.

Since installing the fence, Harper says, there have been no further successful copper theft attempts at the National Grid.

Power Fence will come to the U.S. market later this year.

Source: Karyn Hodgson. "Don't Touch That Fence!" *Security* (Cahners Publishing Company. Newton, MA, 1994), Vol. 31, No. 8, pp. 24–25.

protection of a department store or convenience outlet as to a corporate compound with an extensive perimeter and more than one hundred individually protected areas.

Whether the security system designer is working with the design of a relatively small system with detection and control display devices or a large system with multiple elements from all subsystems, all the subsystems must be integrated into a total systems approach. Equipment component selection, then, depends entirely upon the ability of these components to communicate within a complete security system configuration. Thus, the various sensors selected for detection must report to either a control unit or a centrally located collector. For smaller, single-facility applications, this and a central annunciation device may be all that is necessary. Likewise, when used, associated CCTV video assessment signals, synchronized and programmed according to sensor zone or sector alarms, also need to communicate through a central switching device for alarm zone and CCTV camera correlation. Both the video and alarm data or signals need to be transmitted to a central reporting location for assessment and response. The automated access control element, when used, must communicate with a central processor where access authorization memory is maintained.

In a complete security system configuration, all the sensors, CCTV cameras, automated access controls, communication and data transmission lines, and related support equipment link to successfully provide alarm and status information. This information is transmitted to either a single control operator or a combination of operators at a central control and display unit located either on or off the site. When necessary, such items as control/display redundancy and independent power requirements need to be considered. In order to successfully achieve this objective, the security system designer is challenged to select the most effective technologies as well as the most appropriate hardware to communicate security system information to a compatible central control and display unit. Unless the combination of protective measures deters, delays, detects, assesses, and permits effective response, the asset to be protected is vulnerable to penetration.

Summary

Security technology is playing an important operational role in many office, industry, and government buildings. Examples of that important role are with contraband detection, walkthrough metal detectors, explosive detectors, computerized antibomb design (designing to withstand explosions), vehicle barriers, closed circuit television (video monitor and camera and time lapse recording) systems, credential readers, elevator floor and passenger control, security lighting, and security control and information display. Such well-controlled security features are becoming commonplace in newer office buildings. Some new high-rise office towers have elevators with infrared optical readers that after normal business hours will scan a tenant's ID card and go automatically to the authorized floor.

High-tech systems not only offer greater protection, but they can reduce security costs by reducing the need for night guards. Savings can average 25 to 40 percent, with the average payback period being 12 to 24 months. Remember that the best electronic security systems tell you only that there is a problem. The systems do not stop the burglar or rapist; if no one responds to the alarm, there is no protection.

Architects and engineers who know the value and basic functions of electronic intrusion, perimeter protection, and access control devices can be much more effective in producing better and less-troublesome security systems. The complexity of the hardware and technology presents complications for building owners responsible for determining which equipment will best meet their safety and security needs. Stringent security codes across the country necessitate the installation of these elaborate systems, both in older buildings and in new construction.

Security design and technology should be laid out in advance. Although architects and contractors have always been aware of the need for security in buildings, many fail to plan and install the system when it is easiest to do so, before the building shell is complete. The failure to plan can result in potentially significant additional expenses and time, as well as lay the foundation for lawsuits involving failure to provide proper security.

REVIEW QUESTIONS

1. How does the use of hand geometry work to increase security?
2. Why should security design and technology be laid out in advance?
3. Who should the security technology designer work with to maximize security?
4. Can high-tech systems offer greater protection and reduce security costs by reducing the need for night guards? If so, how?
5. How does system integration eliminate technological fragmentation?

TERMS TO REMEMBER

security technology design *hand* *smart card*
secondary verifications *retinal scan*

ENDNOTES

The author is very grateful to Richard P. Grassie, CPP, and Joseph A. Barry, CPP, for their kind permission to use the fine materials in this chapter. As working professionals, and experts in the design and implementation of integrated security systems, they are very familiar with the cutting-edge materials that I wanted to discuss in this text.

14

The Twenty-First Century

Where Next?

"Would you tell me please, which way I ought to go from here?"
"That depends a good deal on where you want to get to," said
the Cat.
"I don't much care where—" said Alice.
"Then it doesn't matter which way you go," said the Cat.

—Lewis Carroll

Security at a Turning Point

Perhaps, like Alice in her Wonderland, we are at a point in the security industry that it doesn't really matter which way we go. On the other hand, while the concept of "if you don't know where you are going, any road will get you there" has been often applied to such a situation, its basic premises are flawed. Actually, even if you *do* know where you are going, you still need to know where you are now and you should have a compass and a map to have any certainty of getting there. This text has made an attempt to find out where we are now, and the efforts of the *Hallcrest Report I* and *II* have provided us with a rough, but well-drawn, map of the future. Now we must use our compasses wisely to try to plot a safe course to that destination. Unfortunately, the course is not over a smooth sea, but a stormy ocean that has many deadly hazards to consider as we sail. Some are already in sight, others lurk just below the surface and wait to sink us.

THE WORKFORCE IN AMERICA: A CHANGING TIDE

As we mentioned in Chapter 12, although technology has made great strides in the security industry, security remains primarily a people task. Unfortunately, the security industry is using more and more technology at a time when the trends among U.S. workers may be going in the opposite direction. What is the pool from which security will draw its personnel in the year 2000? Johnston and Hacker make some interesting points in their *Workforce 2000*:

> In the next decade changes in the economy will be matched by changes in the workforce and the types of jobs that will be performed.
>
> - The population and the workforce will grow more slowly than at any time since the 1930s.
> - The average age of the population and the workforce will rise, and the pool of young workers entering the workforce will shrink.
> - More women will enter the workforce.
> - Minorities will make up a larger share of new entrants to the workforce.
> - Immigrants will represent the largest share of the increase in the population and the workforce since the First World War.[1]

Such a dramatic change in the pool from which the security industry must draw employees, especially the contract security companies who have traditionally supplied entry-level jobs, will have major impacts on how quickly security can enter the age of technology. Kaverman[2] expands on this theme to a great extent. Because of this cooling off of population growth, organizations will find themselves competing for the most qualified prospective employees. The competition will force companies to develop innovative compensation and lucrative benefits packages to attract potential employees.

These individuals, more than ever before, are abandoning the traditional view of employment security in favor of jobs where they can use and be recognized for their individual skills, knowledge, and talents. This phenomenon will have some serious implications in the security industry, where employees are drawn from an entry-level workforce base and where benefits tend to be less generous than in many other industries.

At the end of the 1990s, women are expected to join the workforce in even greater numbers than in the 1980s. If the trend continues, when we enter the twenty-first century, approximately 47 percent of the workforce will be women, and 61 percent of all women will work. In addition, women will have made up approximately three-fifths of the new entrants into the labor force between 1985 and 2000.[3] As a further challenge to security managers, much of the increase in the numbers of women in the workforce has come from increased participation by women with children. Of the 14.6 million married women who joined the labor force between 1960 and 1984, 8 million came from families with children. During the same period, the proportion of married mothers at work grew from 28 to 61 percent, and the share of all children under six whose mothers worked grew from 19 to 52 percent.[4]

By the year 2000, minorities will make up a larger share of the workforce. Nonwhites will make up approximately 29 percent of the net addition to the workforce between 1985 and 2000, and will represent more than 15 percent of the workforce by the turn of the century. Black women will make up the largest share of the increase in the nonwhite labor force.

Another important factor for organizations and security professionals to consider when examining the impact of this data is that by the year 2000 it is thought that black women will outnumber black men in the workforce. This is a significant contrast to the pattern among whites, where men outnumber women by almost three to two.[5] Another relevant factor to consider is the burden of social disadvantage that these future employees will undoubtedly bring with them to the workplace.

This influx of minorities into the workforce has prompted some companies to initiate innovative training programs in pluralism and cultural diversity. These programs are designed to help prepare traditional first-line supervisors and middle managers to deal with tomorrow's new employee whose background and life experience may be worlds apart from their own.

Companies and guard services will be challenged to assimilate these people with diverse and often marginal education and experience in a workplace that is becoming more technology oriented. To function effectively in the twenty-first century, high-tech workplace, these people will need reading, comprehension, and technical skills far above those they currently possess. Obviously, this presents organizations with major training and education challenges. It also challenges vendors to develop more user-friendly technology for this workforce.

PROFESSIONALISM AND PRIVATE SECURITY IN THE 1990S

After taking a look at the forces and developmental patterns of more than 200 specific issues affecting organizations, the American Society of Personnel Administrators (ASPA) identified five fundamental topics where change is occurring most rapidly. At the top of the list was education, the key issues in which were listed as *literacy, employee education and training, management development, plant closing, drop-out prevention, retraining,* [and] *industry obsolescence.*[6]

A major factor in the last half of the 1990s in regard to developing managers in the security field is the entry into this male-dominated realm by women. More and more women are finally reaching levels of the security industry that reflect "responsible charge" and are becoming better prepared to pass through the glass ceiling and into top management. As noted by Allen:

> Women security professionals of the '90s are goal-oriented, have plans, and are committed to being the best at what they do. These women are involved in their communities and professions, have vision, and are not willing to settle for status quo.

> These women are continually fine-tuning their tools, plowing and pruning the risk areas in their field, and cultivating their coworkers to produce a better security-oriented product.

To my surprise, however, only 6.1 of ASIS's [American Society for Industrial Security] membership is comprised of women, and many women do not know about the CPP [Certified Protection Professional] program sponsored by the Society.

As security professionals—male and female—we know many challenges await us in the coming decade. The security professional of the '90s must be astute,

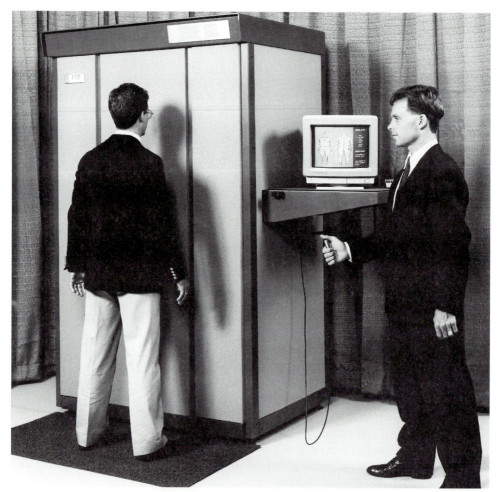

The first production unit of IRT Corporation's SECURE 1000 features an improved scan time, greater ease of use and service, and also maintains the same safe levels of operation as the research prototype. IRT's SECURE 1000 quickly scans a person to detect and locate concealed weapons, explosives, ellicit drugs and other contraband that would no unnoticed by conventional metal detectors. Through use of real-time, computer-aided image processing, SECURE 1000 automatically displays the shape and location of concealed objects.

Photo courtesy of IRT Corporation.

proficient, perceptive, adaptable, dedicated, and above all multi-disciplined to manage effectively.

I believe the '90s offer women the opportunity and the challenge to expand their horizons and to experience the exhilaration of a field that is ready to receive and respond to women security professionals.[7]

It is clear that the security industry must always strive to keep pace with the changing character of the workforce if it is to meet the expected growth in needed security personnel in the twenty-first century.

SEXUAL HARASSMENT IN THE SECURITY WORKPLACE: A NEW CHALLENGE

The aforementioned growth factors of women in the workplace offer a major challenge for the security industry. In the late 1990s, there is a growing awareness of the gender discrimination that takes place in the workplace. The confirmation hearings for Supreme Court Justice Clarence Thomas focused a bright and eye-riveting spotlight on the issue of sexual harassment in a way that kept Americans glued to their television sets for days. Whatever your feelings about the outcome of that hearing, it has caused the issue of sexual harassment to emerge in ways that had before been kept in the dark. In an industry that has traditionally been dominated by males, and is now employing more and more females, it is essential that the security managers and providers become aware of the consequences of such illegal and disruptive behavior.

The legal framework of sexual harassment directs the security manager on how to help management handle complaints with effective security processes, and work with the investigation of those complaints from their employer and other staff. Federal guidelines contained in Section 703 of the Civil Rights Act of 1964, as amended, point out that employers are expected to examine "the record as a whole and the totality of the circumstances such as the nature of the sexual advances and the context in which the alleged incidents occurred." Determination of the legality is always made on the facts, on a case-by-case basis.

"The employer is responsible for acts of sexual harassment in the workplace where the employer (or its agents or supervisory employees) knows or should have known of the conduct unless it can show that it took immediate and appropriate corrective action." Prevention of such activity is the best protection for the employer, and security can help to see that the message gets out to both security and other staff. Federal guidelines suggest five strategies for prevention of sexual (or other) harassment:

1. Raise the subject affirmatively.
2. Express strong disapproval.
3. Develop appropriate sanctions.
4. Inform employees of their right to raise the issue of sexual harassment.
5. Develop methods to sensitize all concerned.

Sexual Harassment at Work

What is sexual harassment?

1. Sexual harassment is any repeated and unwanted verbal, physical, or gestural sexual advances, sexually explicit derogatory statements, or sexually discriminatory remarks made by someone in the workplace which are offensive to the worker involved, which causes the worker to feel threatened, humiliated, patronized, or harassed, or which interfere with the worker's job performance, undermine job security or create a threatening or intimidating work evironment.

2. It is a new name for a problem which is certainly not new. It is not sexual flirtation based on mutual consent. Sexual harassment is frequently a display of power, which is intended to intimidate, coerce, or degrade another worker. It is a form of victimization about which increasing concern is being expressed in the workplace.

3. Sexual harassment encompasses a wide range of unwanted sexual advances including:

   - Unnecessary physical contact, touching or patting
   - Suggestive and unwelcome remarks, jokes, comments about appearance and deliberate verbal abuse
   - Leering and compromising invitations
   - Use of pornographic pictures at the workplace
   - Demands for sexual favors
   - Physical assault

Who are the victims?

4. Women are mainly the victims of sexual harassment. Sexual harassment affects all women regardless of their age, marital status, physical appearance, background or professional status. Studies have revealed some high-risk groups: young women under 30 and unmarried, widowed, divorced, or separated women, especially with dependents.

5. Sexual harassment does not affect women alone. Some men also feel they are victims. However, women are more vulnerable due to their position on the labor market. Despite laws on discrimination, women remain confined in poorly paid, low-skilled, or low-status jobs, while men predominate in better-paid, authoritative positions and supervisory jobs.

6. The continued segregation of women and men in traditional roles at the workplace contributes to the persistence of sexual harassment. Sexual harassment is often the result of an abuse of authority where individuals use their position and power to intimidate or coerce other workers, for example, where there is a clear-cut division of status between male management and female staff. There are many other instances of sexual harassment. Women who work in nontraditional, male-dominated industries and occupations are often victims of sexual harassment. Fellow workers may

Sexual Harassment at Work

use harassment as an intimidation tactic to discourage women applying for and working in traditionally male occupations. Harassment can be used also as a weapon to undermine the authority of women supervisors and managers.

Who are the harassers?

7. Sexual harassment can be perpetrated by colleagues, immediate supervisors, management, or clients. One study found that suggestive remarks and requests for sexual favors are usually made by immediate supervisors or management. Unwanted physical contact usually comes from colleagues as does physical aggression. Clients also harass workers by leering or making compromising invitations.

The effects of sexual harassment

8. Sexual harassment can result in a woman leaving her job rather than facing the harassment. She may be dismissed or lose promotion prospects for failing to comply with the suggestions made to her. It creates a stressful and hostile working environment which can lead to mental and physical illness for the recipient and an uncomfortable atmosphere for other workers. The woman who is harassed is always made to feel at fault.

9. Victims of sexual harassment suffer tension, anger, and anxiety, which often manifest themselves as depression, insomnia, and other stress-related medical problems, such as headaches, skin disorders, digestive problems, cystitis, etc. Especially in developing countries, victims can also suffer loss of face and social ostracization leading to family hardship and even break-up.

10. Sexual harassment interferes with job performance and satisfaction. If the victim reports the incident or refuses to comply, the harasser often has the power to affect her working conditions, training, and promotion opportunities and job security. The victim is often forced to resign, or is even fired. Even after leaving the job, the harasser may jeopardize the victim's future job opportunities by giving her a bad reference. The conditions which contribute to women's vulnerability in the labor force—high unemployment and restricted employment opportunities—make leaving a job to avoid sexual harassment a step most women cannot afford to take.

Since this involves change, often radical change, in the work environment, it is often difficult to get the points across without eventual resort to litigation. If the security industry is to avoid these extreme, and costly, measures to effect change in behavior, it must make use of the stages of the adaptive model suggested by McQueen:

The first stage is *denial:* "I can't believe they are trying to tell us what to do in our private lives. I will date whom I want—it's none of their business. And that is true until the dating/mating behaviors affect the workplace.

The second stage is *anger:* This stage is typically accompanied by rebellious and disobedient behavior. The employee tests the system and your ability to enforce the rules. When inconsistent enforcement occurs, the employee is convinced that the rule is silly. Measures must be taken to stop defiance of authority.

The third stage is *bargaining* or *negotiating:* This is probably just a whisker behind the anger stage because of testing behaviors. Stories (the majority is gossip) will undermine your sincerity unless all managers make it clear that the rules of conduct will be enforced.

The fourth stage is *depression*, which is signaled by a quiet and lethargic period: This stage allows people to adjust their conduct and their workplace (take down posters of scantily clad individuals) and find new ways to interact with coworkers and decorate work spaces. This isn't as hard as it seems, but many employees will consider it grossly unfair.

Then fifth stage is *compliance* or *acceptance:* And this is the goal—voluntary compliance with the terms and conditions of employment, which includes following the rules for safety and security of the work force and workplace. If individual employees find they cannot comply, they are free to resign or accept the disciplinary consequences of noncompliance.[8]

As mentioned, the security industry's source of personnel in the late 1990s will surely reflect the diversity of persons available for such work. More women in the workforce will be reflected in security employees as well. Sexual harassment cannot be

---

SECURITY BYTE 14–1

Soft on White Collar Crimes

Of 500 executives convicted of finance fraud:

- 78% sent to prison
- 13% get 5+ year sentence
- Finance fraud 36.4 months
- Car theft 38 months
- Burglary 55.6 months

Source: University of California, Irvine

Source: Editors. "Reports of Incidents that Impact Asset Protection." *Security* (Cahners Publishing Company. Newton, MA, 1995), Vol. 32, No. 1, p. 9.

tolerated as the mix of men and women changes in this traditionally all-male work-force; neither can other forms of intolerance and harassment be tolerated for the broad diversity of workers that seems to be the future of America. This issue not only can create great friction for security managers, and offer poor role models to other employees, but also can result in very expensive and devastating litigation in both areas.

The Breakout of Peace and Impacts on Security

When the Berlin wall finally came down in 1989, and the Soviet Union and the Eastern Bloc nations began to look to some new forms of government, the world seemed to have become somewhat of a safer place. The hue and cry of a strapped nation became one to find ways to use the so-called savings from the "peace benefit" for other purposes. The nation became complacent about the need for security against terrorists and the protection of classified documents and materials in a rapidly shrinking defense industry. This will be a continuing problem in the twenty-first century as the "new world order" defines itself. Before the world got too relaxed, however, a war in the Gulf took place, while ethnic battles for power broke out in Bosnia, Somalia, Rwanda, and other hot spots throughout the world. The United Nations began to take a stronger role in controlling world crises, but still looked to the United States to carry the majority of the burden for world police work. Security has found itself twisting in the winds of drastic change and uncertainty, going from crisis to crisis with a sense of confusion and trepidation.

In order to find a niche in a world without *military* superpowers to fear, private security in the United States now finds itself in the middle of a war between *economic* superpowers, all trying to get the edge on the others. The economic wars between the European Economic Community, Japan and the Pacific Rim, and the United States are now joined by the former Soviet Republics in the battle for market share of world commerce. A natural adjunct to these "economic armies" has become known as corporate intelligence. Only recently has it become known how intensively companies spy on one another. The stakes are high, and the battles are serious. Hamit gives us a chilling portrait of the problem:

> There is a difference, however, between what actually occurs and the image often portrayed in popular culture. Industrial espionage, like any form of espionage, is a crime and a threat that must always be heeded, especially where electronic eavesdropping is concerned.
>
> A nice little business can be done in reassuring the overly cautious, or perhaps just plain paranoid, that their premises are safe from such intrusions. While some charades may satisfy the impulse of some clients to feel important, they overlook the larger threat of information leaking wholesale to an adversary, through competitive intelligence. Indeed, so many intelligence gathering operations are done that those performing them now have their own trade association, the Society of Competitor Intelligence Professionals (SCIP).
>
> Most [intelligence gathering] techniques are legal and legitimate and do not even breach confidentiality, but such activities neatly replicate the classic intelligence

cycle of collection, evaluation, and counteraction. Competitive intelligence is a threat to be guarded against.

If we place this legitimate need for information into a global context, it is not hard to imagine large multinational corporations formalizing this process and setting up their own intelligence units. Such firms have a legitimate need not only for the kind of information gathered by non-criminal means, but also for political and economic information concerning the nations where they have business operations.

Futurist Alvin Toffler has speculated that multinational corporation security departments may evolve into private armies to protect the companies' far-flung assets where host countries cannot. Indeed, an example is the mercenary soldiers who were hired to protect oil tankers in the Persian Gulf during the Iran–Iraq War.[9]

It is clear that, in a world in which technology is changing daily, the knowledge of the type and timing of change is a powerful weapon in economic warfare. The knowledge of the marketing plans of a company, the release date of a new computer chip, or the pending design of a new car transmission can result in serious corporate trauma to either side of the competitive formula. The emergence of the Russian state as a developer of free-market capitalism for a huge consumer market in almost any kind of Western goods is a real threat for industrial intelligence and can easily raise it to the level of espionage. The networks are already in place, and many of the activities in support of industrial expansion in Russia and the other former Soviet provinces are in the hands of former KGB or GRU officers with the training and skills to collect information easily.

The task for security, in this old threat to new processes, is to make sure that they have in place the countermeasures against such industrial spying and use them effectively. This idea is reinforced with some observations by Bryen:

> Today the world's major industrial powers are locked in a struggle. The struggle is aimed at gaining technological advantage and market share. Clearly, failure to acquire a satisfactory market share—in both internal and export markets—can have a severe, negative impact on a nation.

> The danger of losing market share can be seen in some U.S. communities. Many vital industries are disappearing right before our eyes. The U.S. automobile industry is shrinking, and there is no prospect that it will ever regain the market share it once had. The U.S. semiconductor industry has, for the most part, lost critical segments such as the production of DRAMS (dynamic random access memory systems), which are essential for computers. The machine tool industry has decayed, and many world-famous companies have either pared down their operations or shut down altogether.[10]

This emerging war of the economic powers offers great opportunity for the security professionals that can work to find ways to protect the information, transmissions, and products in a way that uses the technology, making design and production easier to make security easier. The types of proprietary information that must be protected in the twenty-first century are trade secrets about basic manufacturing techniques, design methods and design manuals, operational instructions for enhancing plant operations, training manuals for machine tools and products themselves, data from testing operations or sampling, specifications of raw materials, experimental reports and data, engineering drawings and notebooks, cost and pricing data, profit margins, customer lists and discount policies, plant capacity, and anything else that gives the competition an edge.

Some valid ways to safeguard proprietary information are as follows:

1. Have more than adequate locking devices.
2. Have a receptionist or security post screen every visitor to the facility.

SECURITY BYTE 14 – 2

The Financial Fraud Stick-up

With America's political and social attention on street crime, guns, drugs and youthful offenders, *it's a shock to realize the extent and growth of financial fraud.*

While dollar figures on all types of losses are inherently questionable, *financial fraud probably exceeds losses from theft, robbery, burglary and vandalism.*

Incidents affect huge numbers of businesses and people.

When KPMG's Forensic and Investigtive Services surveyed 501 U.S. companies recently, it found that *75% had one or more financial frauds and 56% had multiple frauds. The cost: $225 million.* A single loss for a false invoice incident exceeded $300,000 for 20% of these companies. A check fraud loss averaged $360,000.

For consumers and small businesses, the numbers are as gloomy. Take bad checks. *In 1993, reports the American Bankers Association, there were 1.3 million of them out of 61.1 billion written.* The cost to banks alone: $815 million. The average bad check: $643.

Even more startling: as many as *19 percent of Florida residents have been the subject of a major consumer scam, swindle or fraud,* according to the results of a new statewide survey. The AT&T Consumer Rights Survey found telemarketing fraud is the fastest growing segment.

Private security and law enforcement are responding. But their resources are already stretched combating street crime and physical security threats. *Financial fraud prevention and incident investigation call for new types of technology and training. And there's a lag as law enforcement and security professionals play catch up.*

Adding its own spin: a growing distaste by federal and state legislators for new laws to fight business crime. *And the Republican majority in Congress and various states are diminishing the ways people can seek damages.*

Source: Zalud Reports "The Financial Fraud Stick-up." *Security* (Cahners Publishing Company. Newton, MA, 1995), Vol. 32, No. 7, p. 60.

3. Use modern access controls to all areas.

4. Limit access to the public to designated areas.

5. Never allow competitors in the plant unescorted.

6. Enforce limited handling of all documents to need-to-know basis.

7. Log out and account for all written materials.

8. Shred all computer printouts and other documentation before it goes to a trash area.

Preventing the loss of national secrets is no different from preventing the loss of corporate secrets in terms of how it should be implemented. Security professionals will find a growing demand for proprietary information security and industrial espionage countermeasures, and must find new and better ways to perform these tasks.

THE FIGHT BY SECURITY TO BE A TEAM PLAYER

One of the most difficult tasks ahead for private security and loss prevention is more a problem of organizational psychology than it is of new technology. As the long recession of the early 1990s deepened, CEOs and their team of executives sought ways to cut or replace services done by persons on payrolls. This has resulted in a broad swing toward the use of contract security, or lowering the role of security management in the hierarchy, or elimination of security persons and replacing them with hardware and technology. This a very disturbing trend and one that is part of the economic cycles that often defy logic. In today's litigious society, that is like driving as fast as you can because the car is low on gas.

This situation is described beautifully in an article by Serpico:

Did you ever get the feeling that you were standing with hat in hand, begging, when trying to gain approval for a security department request?

Well, you're not alone. Many security managers have had that experience. The reasons, especially in these difficult economic times, vary. But one constant among the variables is cost. That is a reality we must all face at one time or another.

In some industries, security is often one of the first to feel the effects of the budget ax. With all departments competing for resources, you may be at a distinct disadvantage because you are not perceived as contributing to the bottom line.

Other reasons for not granting security-related requests are more frustrating. One of them is management's unawareness of the [security] department's value. Some memos can languish in an executive's "hold" box until the edges of the paper turn yellow.[11]

In Chapter 7, we discussed the organizational placement of the security operation and its subsequent ability to influence the course of the company. One security department was reduced to reporting to the plant groundskeeper. This action gave the new security supervisor literally no power to control the department's destiny. Was this a lousy security operation? No. It was a department in which the leadership had little or no interest in the way it was run. The people on the staff were well educated and highly motivated, but they were invisible to the powers that be. The security manager was content with the status quo and did not attempt to show the corporate leadership what they were doing, how well they were doing it, and what that all meant in terms of losses prevented or recovered.

The challenge for the new generation of security professionals is to get the message across to upper management that security can, and does, contribute to the bottom line in many ways. The fine balance of security being seen as a "necessary evil" or "frill" and a productive and cost-effective operation is one that probably creates the greatest challenge to those who enter the security field in the 1990s.

> The aim of any security department should be to provide an environment in which the company's board may plan and execute its corporate strategy without interference from hostile or criminal acts. Every company is exposed to possible disruption of its activity and pecuniary loss by deliberate acts of a person or persons, acting for a wide variety of motives.
>
> The risk may be dealt with in one of five ways:
>
> 1. Accept it (no action)
> 2. Ignore it (pretend it doesn't exist)
> 3. Avoid it (by ceasing operations)
> 4. Transfer it (e.g., with insurance)
> 5. Reduce it (by devising and implementing a security strategy)
>
> If reduction is sought, security must be designed and viewed as a vital part of corporate strategy, one that functions in cooperation with every sector of company operations.[12]

It is essential, not only for the security industry but also for corporate and institutional America, that the message be gotten to decision makers that security can strike that fine balance between alarmism and overreaction and head-in-the-sand inactivity. The proper development of security strategy, involving top leadership at every step, must go through seven critical stages:

1. The delineation, in some detail, of the perceived threat or threats to corporate assets

2. The conceptual outline of security strategies designed to counter, at various levels of effectiveness and cost, the perceived threat or threats

3. Senior management direction to the security department to implement a particular strategy

4. The detailed drawing up of security plans by geographical location, functional area, or other subgrouping

5. The execution of any works or changes necessary to implement the plans in the previous phase

6. The implementation, by departments, of the security plans, monitored and assisted by the security department

7. The continual reassessment and reevaluation of the security strategy and procedures, with modifications as appropriate

Much of this can be achieved with little more than willpower, with existing staff and within budget. However, a dramatically new view of the security function must be taken before a strategy as comprehensive and effective as this can be taken.[13]

It is clear that twenty-first century managers will need to reexamine the ways in which they measure productivity. To survive, security providers and security managers will need to look at team management concepts and self-managing skills in order to maximize productivity for service provision. These management concepts should involve teams comprised of security personnel and all other affected departments. If properly initiated and supported, this concept can have direct measurable results, among which are:

- Productivity increases as workers are given responsibility for their own product or service
- Gains in productivity of 30 percent are not uncommon
- Having teams do the whole job rather than parts of it creates pride in ownership
- Quality increases because team members are responsible for the entire project
- Workers assume responsibility for duties traditionally reserved for management, such as scheduling, inventory control, employee selection, and performance appraisals
- Employees with a broader understanding of operations are better able to move from job to job and develop more skills
- Teamwork makes it possible for each person to do several or all of the tasks necessary to produce one product or a single service[14]

There is no way that such revolutionary techniques can be put into place without a commitment by security managers to share the planning, implementation, and follow-up actions with the security staff team. Regardless of the innovativeness of the manager, and the advanced state of technology, the worker remains the key ingredient in the business changes coming in the next decade.

The corporate security organization seems to be under economic attack as well, with *Hallcrest* predicting reductions in proprietary security forces and dramatic increases in the contract security sector by the year 2000. Most of the rationale behind this movement is based on costs. The mistake in this movement may be that the corporation tends to "throw the baby out with the bath water," not only hiring contract officers, but cutting their in-house security management as well. Some companies have seen that they have lost control of the security philosophy of their industry, one that is clientele specific, and given it over to organizations that provide security to anyone who needs it (for example, a hospital needs a different kind of security philosophy from a manufacturing firm).

A new approach is beginning to be tried, one that is a blend of using contract security for the line officers with using an in-house security manager that provides leadership and liaison between the two components. As long as the cost of personnel and benefits remains as high as they have been, this mix will allow the in-house security manager the flexibility he or she needs to provide security forces where and when needed and to cut them immediately when they are not. This concept is rather new and will need to be examined carefully in the years ahead.

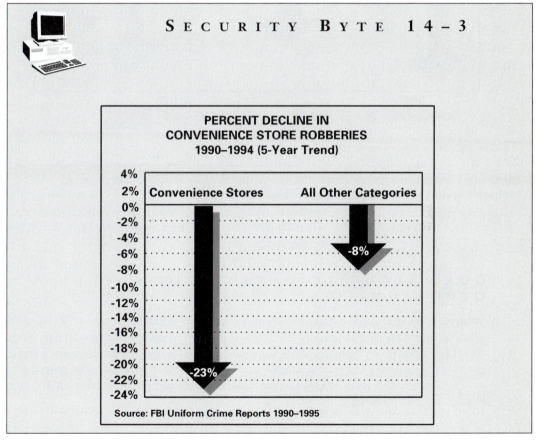

SECURITY BYTE 14 – 3

PERCENT DECLINE IN CONVENIENCE STORE ROBBERIES
1990–1994 (5-Year Trend)

Convenience Stores: -23%
All Other Categories: -8%

Source: FBI Uniform Crime Reports 1990–1995

Source: Chris Baum. "Slashing-Robberies." *Security* (Cahners Publishing Company. Newton, MA, 1996), Vol. 33, No. 3, p. 17.

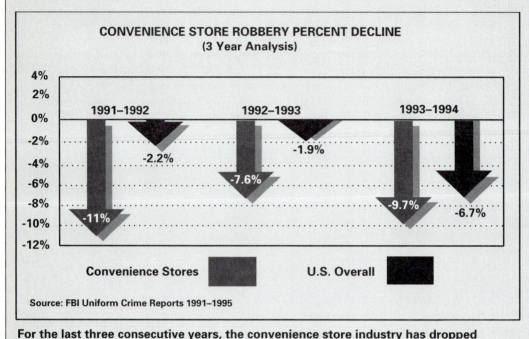

CONVENIENCE STORE ROBBERY PERCENT DECLINE
(3 Year Analysis)

1991–1992 -2.2% -11%
1992–1993 -1.9% -7.6%
1993–1994 -9.7% -6.7%

Convenience Stores   U.S. Overall

Source: FBI Uniform Crime Reports 1991–1995

For the last three consecutive years, the convenience store industry has dropped robbery volumes at a higher rate than the nation.

Source: Chris Baum. "Slashing-Robberies." *Security* (Cahners Publishing Company. Newton, MA, 1996), Vol. 33, No. 3, p. 17.

DOES SECURITY OFFER GOOD OPPORTUNITIES?

Security is often looked upon as just an entry-level job or transient type of work. This may be somewhat true at the line level, but studies are showing that the management level of security is beginning to show some comparability to other professions. Langer gives a composite picture of the security and loss prevention manager who emerges as earning the highest income (salary plus cash bonuses and profit sharing) is the one with direct policy-making authority:

> He or she is located in Dallas/Fort Worth, Tennessee, Pittsburgh, Los Angeles/Long Beach, Houston, Kansas City, New York City, or Chicago [cities and states have been merged into one category].

This composite individual is employed by a conglomerate: a petroleum, coal, or natural gas producer; a chemical, pharmaceutical, plastics, or rubber products manufacturer; a communications service; a security service; or a utility service. His or her company employs 25,000 people or more and has an annual salary budget of $10 million or more.

This theoretical employee has 25 or more years of experience, a graduate degree, and holds the Certified Protection Professional (CPP) designation. Although security directors or managers with policy-making responsibility have an average income of $53,600, a number of individuals in this group earn more than $150,000 per year.[15]

Of course, at the other end of the salary spectrum are the unarmed security officers, whose average annual income is $15,700 per year. Between these two extremes lie the vast bulk of the security personnel in this country at the end of the 1990s.

Education and certification are major factors in determining salary for those companies that require higher standards in these areas. At the top levels, those with a graduate degree earn up to 23 percent more than those with a bachelor's degree and 56 percent more than those with an associate (two-year) degree.[16]

Experience is another major factor in salary and compensation, with those with only one or two years of experience averaging $31,700, whereas those with twenty-five or more years of experience average $67,000 per year.[17] The security director or manager without policy-making authority was found to make an average of 22 percent less than those with this power.

If you wish to make the security industry your choice of career, it is to your advantage to gain experience and education. The CPP status apparently leads to increased income in the security and loss prevention field. The average holder of the CPP who is a security director or manager with policy-making authority has a 26.6 percent higher average income than an individual without the CPP. The average security director or manager with the CPP has the same amount of advantage over those who do not hold CPP certification.[18]

Summary

How does one summarize the future? As we come to the end of this overview of the dynamic field of security, on the cusp of the twenty-first century, we are still left with the question of just what security is. Is it people, technology, physical means, or all of the above? Sutherland has asked this question in a way we all can agree:

> Many people in security have been confronted with the statement, "the company is paying for security, but is not getting it." This statement is usually made after a significant loss has occurred and that organization's senior management is looking for an explanation. Woe to the security manager who does not have an acceptable reason.

The basic problem with this statement is that security, like beauty, is in the eyes of the beholder. Just what is the company paying for when it pays for security? Does security mean no losses of company equipment or money? Does security mean everyone is safe while on company property? Does security mean every risk has been identified and reduced to the lowest level?

If senior management contemplates these questions, it will have already begun to answer the question, "what is security?" Only when security has been defined can a security manager begin to develop a security program that will satisfy company requirements.[19]

This simple statement, and the diagram in Figure 14–1, bring security down to the essentials. We have discussed in this text how important it is for security to become a profession and a field that earns the respect of their employers, the community, and their colleagues in law enforcement. It is hoped that this feeling of worth, partnership, and professionalism will provide a nation in which everyone can feel a little safer. It is for those who choose to enter this fascinating field to take the steps necessary to make security and loss prevention a major force in U.S. corporations, institutions, and communities.

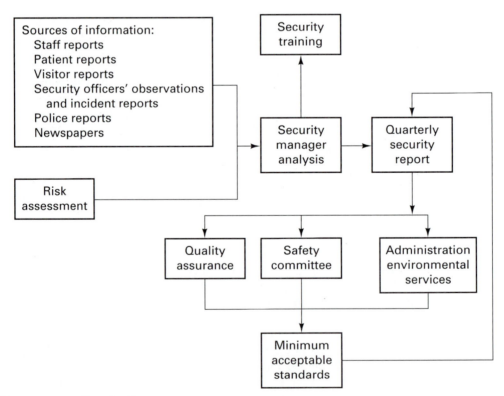

FIGURE 14–1   *Security Program*

REVIEW QUESTION

1. Describe in two pages what the major trends will be in security for the beginning of the twenty-first century and how security managers will cope with them.

ENDNOTES

1. William B. Johnston and Arnold E. Hacker, *Workforce 2000: Work and Workers for the 21st Century* (Indianapolis, Ind.: Hudson Institute, 1987), p. 78.
2. Steven C. Kaverman, "2000 and Beyond," *Security Management*, Vol. 34, No. 9 (September 1990), p. 55.
3. Johnston and Packer, *Workforce 2000*, p. 78.
4. Ibid., p. 87.
5. Ibid., p. 92–93.
6. "Adapting Your Business to Fit the New Employee," *Personnel Administration* (January 1989), p. 41.
7. Catherine I. Allen. "What Do the '90s Hold for Women in Security?" *Security Management* Vol. 36, No. 4 (April 1992), p. 108.
8. Iris McQueen, "Sexual Harassment: Are You Protected?" *Security Management* Vol. 34, No. 12 (December 1990), p. 59.
9. Francis Hamit. "Taking On Corporate Intelligence," *Security Management*, Vol. 35, No. 10 (October 1991), pp. 36–38.
10. Stephen D. Bryen, "The Market for Interception," *Security Management*, Vol. 34, No. 9 (September 1990), pp. 97–98.
11. Philip A. Serpico, "Are We a Part of the Corporate Family?" *Security Management*, Vol. 35, No. 10 (October 1991), p. 104.
12. W. H. Wyllie, "Striking a Fine Balance," *Security Management* Vol. 34, No. 9 (September 1990), p. 73.
13. Ibid.
14. Kaverman, "2000 and Beyond," p. 54.
15. Steven Langer, "Learning About Earnings," *Security Management*, Vol. 36, No. 9 (September 1992), p. 69.
16. Ibid., p. 74.
17. Ibid., p. 74.
18. Steven Langer, "What We Earn." *Security Management* Vol. 34, No. 9 (September 1990), p. 68.
19. Garrell E. Sutherland, "Answering the Question—What is Security?" *Security Management*, Vol. 36, No. 7 (July 1992), p. 59.

Glossary

I am grateful to the Law Enforcement Assistance Administration for the publication of the *Dictionary of Criminal Justice Data Terminology*, from which many of the following terms and definitions have been extracted. It is in the spirit of that effort to standardize criminal justice terminology that we have decided to include this section. We hope that students, especially those new to the field, will take the time to read and absorb the meanings of these tools of the trade. To obtain more detailed information about the terms in this glossary, the student should write to U.S. Department of Justice, National Criminal Reference Service, Washington, DC 20531.

Abscond (corrections) To depart from a geographical area or jurisdiction prescribed by the conditions of one's probation or parole, without authorization.

Abscond (court) To intentionally absent or conceal oneself unlawfully in order to avoid a legal process.

Acquittal A judgment of a court, based either on the verdict of a jury or a judicial officer, that the defendant is not guilty of the offense(s) for which he or she has been tried.

Adjudicated Having been the subject of completed criminal or juvenile proceedings, and convicted, or adjudicated a delinquent, status offender, or dependent.

Adjudication (criminal) The judicial decision terminating a criminal proceeding by a judgment of conviction or acquittal or by a dismissal of the case.

Adjudication (juvenile) The juvenile court decision, terminating an adjudicatory hearing, that the juvenile is a delinquent, status offender, or dependent or that the allegations in the petition are not sustained.

Adjudicatory hearing In juvenile proceedings, the fact-finding process wherein the juvenile court determines whether or not there is sufficient evidence to sustain the allegations in a petition.

Adult A person who is within the original jurisdiction of a criminal, rather than a juvenile, court because his or her age at the time of an alleged criminal act was above a statutorily specified limit.

Alias   Any name used for an official purpose that is different from a person's legal name.

Alternative facility   An alternative place of limited confinement that may be an option for certain kinds of offenders. Such facilities may include treatment settings for drug-dependent offenders, minimum security facilities in the community that provide treatment and services as needed, work/study-release centers, and halfway houses or shelter-type facilities. All of these are less secure than the traditional jail but offer a more stimulating environment for the individual.

Appeal   A request by either the defense or the prosecution that a case be removed from a lower court to a higher court in order for a completed trial to be reviewed by the higher court.

Appearance   The act of coming into a court and submitting to the authority of that court.

Appearance, first (initial appearance)   The first appearance of a juvenile or adult in the court that has jurisdiction over his or her case.

Appellant   A person who initiates an appeal.

Arraignment   The appearance of a person before a court during which the court informs the individual of the accusation(s) against him or her and during which he or she enters a plea.

Arrest   Taking a person into custody by authority of law for the purpose of charging him or her with a criminal offense or initiating juvenile proceedings, terminating with the recording of a specific offense.

Arson   The intentional destruction or attempted destruction, by fire or explosive, of the property of another or of one's own property with the intent to defraud.

Assault   Unlawful intentional inflicting, or attempted or threatened inflicting, of injury upon another.

Assault, aggravated   Unlawful intentional causing of serious bodily injury with or without a deadly weapon or unlawful intentional attempting or threatening of serious bodily injury or death with a deadly weapon.

Assault, simple   Unlawful intentional threatening, attempted inflicting, or inflicting of less than serious bodily injury, in the absence of a deadly weapon.

Assault with a deadly weapon   Unlawful intentional inflicting, or attempted or threatened inflicting, of injury or death with the use of a deadly weapon.

Assault on a law enforcement officer   A simple or aggravated assault, in which the victim is a law enforcement officer engaged in the performance of his or her duties.

Assigned counsel   An attorney, not regularly employed by a government agency, assigned by the court to represent a particular person(s) in a particular criminal proceeding.

Attorney/lawyer/counsel A person trained in the law, admitted to practice before the bar of a given jurisdiction, and authorized to advise, represent, and act for other persons in legal proceedings.

Backlog The number of pending cases that exceeds the court's capacity, in that they cannot be acted upon because the court is occupied in acting upon other cases.

Bombing incident The detonation or attempted detonation of an explosive or incendiary device with the willful disregard of risk to the person or property of another, or for a criminal purpose.

Bondsman-secured bail Security service purchased by the defendant from a bail bondsman. The fee for this service ranges upward from 10 percent and is not refundable. The bail bondsman system, which permits a private entrepreneur to share with the court the decision on pretrial release, has been criticized for many years and is becoming obsolete in more progressive jurisdictions.

Booking A police administrative action officially recording an arrest and identifying the person, the place, the time, the arresting authority, and the reason for the arrest.

Burglary Unlawful entry of a structure, with or without force, with intent to commit a felony or larceny.

Camp/ranch/farm Any of several types of similar confinement facilities, usually in a rural location, which contain adults or juveniles committed after adjudication.

Case At the level of police or prosecutorial investigation, a set of circumstances under investigation involving one or more persons; at subsequent steps in criminal proceedings, a charging document alleging the commission of one or more crimes; a single defendant; in juvenile or correctional proceedings, a person who is the object of agency action.

Case (court) A single charging document under the jurisdiction of a court; a single defendant.

Caseload (corrections) The total number of clients registered with a correctional agency or agent during a specified time period, often divided into active and inactive or supervised and unsupervised, thus distinguishing between clients with whom the agency or agent maintains contact and those with whom it does not.

Caseload (court) The total number of cases filed in a given court or before a given judicial officer during a given period of time.

Caseload, pending The number of cases at any given time that have been filed in a given court, or are before a given judicial officer, but have not reached disposition.

Cash bail A cash payment for situations in which the charge is not serious and the scheduled bail is low. The defendant obtains release by paying in cash the full amount, which is recoverable after the required court appearances are made.

CCH An abbreviation for computerized criminal history.

Charge A formal allegation that a specific person(s) has committed a specific offense(s).

Charging document A formal written accusation, filed in a court, alleging that a specified person(s) has committed a specific offense(s).

Check fraud The issuance or passing of a check, draft, or money order that is legal as a formal document, signed by the legal account holder but with the fore-knowledge that the bank or depository will refuse to honor it because of insufficient funds or closed account.

Chief of police A local law enforcement officer who is the appointed or elected head of a police department.

Child abuse Willful action or actions by a person causing physical harm to a child.

Child neglect Willful failure by the person(s) responsible for a child's well-being to provide for adequate food, clothing, shelter, education, and supervision.

Citation (to appear) A written order issued by a law enforcement officer directing an alleged offender to appear in a specific court at a specified time in order to answer a criminal charge.

Citizen dispute settlement The settlement of interpersonal disputes by a third party or the courts. Charges arising from interpersonal disputes are mediated by a third party in an attempt to avoid prosecution. If an agreement between the parties cannot be reached and the complainant wishes to proceed with criminal processing, the case may be referred to court for settlement.

Commitment The action of a judicial officer ordering that an adjudicated and sentenced adult, or adjudicated delinquent or status offender who has been the subject of a juvenile court disposition hearing, be admitted into a correctional facility.

Community facility (nonconfinement facility, adult or juvenile) A correctional facility from which residents are regularly permitted to depart, unaccompanied by an official, to use daily community resources such as schools or treatment programs, or to seek or hold employment.

Community service A period of service to the community as a substitute for, or in partial satisfaction of, a fine. This disposition is generally a condition of a suspended or partially suspended sentence or of probation. The offender volunteers his or her services to a community agency for a certain number of hours per week over a specified period of time. The total number of hours, often assessed at the legal minimum wage, is determined by the amount of the fine that would have been imposed or that portion of the fine that is suspended.

Complaint A formal written accusation made by any person, often a prosecutor, and filed in a court, alleging that a specified person(s) has committed a specific offense(s).

Complaint denied The decision by a prosecutor to decline a request that he or she seek an indictment or file an information or complaint against a specified person(s) for a specific offense(s).

Complaint granted   The decision by a prosecutor to grant a request that he or she seek an indictment or file an information or complaint against a specified person(s) for a specific offense(s).

Complaint requested (police)   A request by a law enforcement agency that the prosecutor seek an indictment or file a complaint or information against a specified person(s) for a specific offense(s).

Conditional diversion   At the pretrial stage, suspension of prosecution while specific conditions are met. If conditions are not satisfied during a specified time period, the case is referred for continued prosecution.

Conditional release   The release of a defendant who agrees to meet specified conditions in addition to appearing in court. Such conditions may include remaining in a defined geographical area, maintaining steady employment, avoiding contact with the victim or with associates in the alleged crime, avoiding certain activities or places, participating in treatment, or accepting services. Conditional release is often used in conjunction with third-party or supervised release.

Confinement facility   A correctional facility from which the inmates are not regularly permitted to depart each day unaccompanied.

Convict   An adult who has been found guilty of a felony and who is confined in a federal or state confinement facility.

Conviction   A judgment of a court, based either on the verdict of a jury or a judicial officer or on the guilty pleas of the defendant, that the defendant is guilty of the offense(s) for which he or she has been tried.

Correctional agency   A federal, state, or local criminal justice agency, under a single administrative authority, of which the principal functions are the investigation, intake screening, supervision, custody, confinement, or treatment of alleged or adjudicated adult offenders, delinquents, or status offenders.

Correctional day program   A publicly financed and operated nonresidential educational or treatment program for persons required, by a judicial officer, to participate.

Correctional facility   A building or part thereof, set of buildings, or area enclosing a set of buildings or structures operated by a government agency for the custody and/or treatment of adjudicated and committed persons, or persons subject to criminal or juvenile justice proceedings.

Correctional institution   A generic name proposed in this terminology for those long-term adult confinement facilities often called prisons, "federal or state correctional facilities," or "penitentiaries," and juvenile confinement facilities called "training schools," "reformatories," "boys' ranches," and the like.

Correctional institution, adult   A confinement facility having custodial authority over adults sentenced to confinement for more than a year.

Correctional institution, juvenile   A confinement facility having custodial authority over delinquents and status offenders committed to confinement after a juvenile disposition hearing.

Corrections   A generic term that includes all government agencies, facilities, programs, procedures, personnel, and techniques concerned with the investigation, intake, custody, confinement, supervision, or treatment of alleged or adjudicated adult offenders, delinquents, or status offenders.

Count   Each separate offense, attributed to one or more persons, as listed in a complaint, information, or indictment.

Counterfeiting   The manufacture or attempted manufacture of a copy or imitation of a negotiable instrument with value set by law or convention, or the possession of such a copy without authorization, with the intent to defraud by claiming the copy's genuineness.

Court   An agency of the judicial branch of government, authorized or established by statute or constitution, and consisting of one or more judicial officers, which has the authority to decide on controversies in law and disputed matters of fact brought before it.

Court of appellate jurisdiction   A court that does not try criminal cases but that hears appeals.

Court of general jurisdiction   Of criminal courts, a court that has jurisdiction to try all criminal offenses, including all felonies, and that may or may not hear appeals.

Court of limited jurisdiction   Of criminal courts, a court of which the trial jurisdiction either includes no felonies or is limited to less than all felonies and which may or may not hear appeals.

Credit card fraud   The use or attempted use of a credit card in order to obtain goods or services with the intent to avoid payment.

Crime (criminal offense)   An act committed or omitted in violation of a law forbidding or commanding it for which an adult can be punished, upon conviction, by incarceration and other penalties, or for which a corporation can be penalized, or for which a juvenile can be brought under the jurisdiction of a juvenile court and adjudicated a delinquent or transferred to adult court.

Crime Index offenses, (index crimes)   A UCR classification that includes all Part I offenses with the exception of involuntary (negligent) manslaughter.

Crimes against business (business crimes, commercial crimes)   A summary term used by the National Crime Panel reports, including burglary and robbery (against businesses).

Crimes against households (household crimes)   A summary term used by the National Crime Panel reports, including burglary (against households), household larceny, and motor vehicle theft.

Crimes against persons   A summary term used by UCR and the National Crime Panel reports, but with different meanings:

       UCR
       Murder
       Nonnegligent (voluntary) manslaughter
       National Crime Panel
       Forcible rape
       Robbery (against persons)
       Aggravated assault
       UCR
       Negligent (involuntary) manslaughter
       Forcible rape
       Aggravated assault
       National Crime Panel
       Simple assault
       Personal larceny

Crimes against property (property crime)   A summary term used by UCR, both as a subclass of the Part I offenses and as a subclass of Crime Index offenses, but with different meanings:

       As a subset of UCR Part I offenses
       Robbery
       Burglary
       Larceny-theft
       Motor vehicle theft
       As a subset of UCR Crime Index offenses
       Burglary
       Larceny-theft
       Motor vehicle theft

Crimes of violence (violent crime)   A summary term used by UCR and the National Crime Panel, but with different meanings:

       As a subset of UCR Index Crimes
       Murder
       Nonnegligent (voluntary) manslaughter
       Forcible rape
       Robbery
       Aggravated assault
       As a subset of National Crime Panel crimes
       against persons
       Forcible rape

Robbery (against persons)

Aggravated assault

Simple assault

Criminal history record information Information collected by criminal justice agencies on individuals, consisting of identifiable descriptions and notations of arrests, detentions, indictments, informations, or other formal criminal charges, and any disposition(s) arising therefrom, including sentencing, correctional supervision, and release.

Criminal justice agency Any court with criminal jurisdiction and any other government agency or subunit that defends indigents, or of which the principal functions or activities consist of the prevention, detection, and investigation of crime; the apprehension, detention, and prosecution of alleged offenders; the confinement or official correctional supervision of accused or convicted persons; or the administrative or technical support of the above functions.

Criminal proceedings Proceedings in a court of law undertaken to determine the guilt or innocence of an adult accused of a crime.

Culpability The state of mind of one who has committed an act that makes him or her liable to prosecution for that act.

Defendant A person against whom a criminal proceeding is pending.

Defense attorney An attorney who represents the defendant in a legal proceeding.

Delinquency Juvenile actions or conduct in violation of criminal law and, in some contexts, status offenses.

Delinquent A juvenile who has been adjudicated by a judicial officer of a juvenile court as having committed a delinquent act, which is an act for which an adult could be prosecuted in a criminal court.

Delinquent act An act committed by a juvenile for which an adult could be prosecuted in a criminal court but for which a juvenile can be adjudicated in a juvenile court or prosecuted in a criminal court if the juvenile court transfers jurisdiction.

De novo Anew, afresh, as if there had been no earlier decision.

Dependency The legal status of a juvenile over whom a juvenile court has assumed jurisdiction because the court has found his or her care by parent, guardian, or custodian to fall short of a legal standard of proper care.

Dependent A juvenile over whom a juvenile court has assumed jurisdiction because the court has found his or her care by parent, guardian, or custodian to fall short of a legal standard of proper care.

Detention The legally authorized holding in confinement of a person subject to criminal or juvenile court proceedings until the point of commitment to a correctional facility or release.

Detention center   A government facility that provides temporary care in a physically restricting environment for juveniles in custody pending court disposition.

Detention facility   A generic name proposed in this terminology as a cover term for those facilities that hold adults or juveniles in confinement pending adjudication, adults sentenced for a year or less of confinement, and in some instances post-adjudicated juveniles, including facilities called "jails," "county farms," "honor farms," "work camps," "road camps," "detention centers," "shelters," "juvenile halls," and the like.

Detention facility, adult   A confinement facility of which the custodial authority is forty-eight hours or more and in which adults can be confined before adjudication or for sentences of a year or less.

Detention facility, juvenile   A confinement facility having custodial authority over juveniles confined pending and after adjudication.

Detention hearing   In juvenile proceedings, a hearing by a judicial officer of a juvenile court to determine whether a juvenile is to be detained, to continue to be detained, or to be released, while juvenile proceedings are pending in his or her case.

Diagnosis or classification center   A functional unit within a correctional institution, or a separate facility, that holds persons held in custody in order to determine to which correctional facility or program they should be committed.

Dismissal   A decision by a judicial officer to terminate a case without a determination of guilt or innocence.

Disposition   The action by a criminal or juvenile justice agency that signifies that a portion of the justice process is complete and jurisdiction is relinquished or transferred to another agency or that signifies that a decision has been reached on one aspect of a case and a different aspect comes under consideration, requiring a different kind of decision.

Disposition, court   The final judicial decision, which terminates a criminal proceeding by a judgment of acquittal or dismissal or which states the specific sentence in the case of a conviction.

Disposition hearing   A hearing in juvenile court, conducted after an adjudicatory hearing and subsequent receipt of the report of any predisposition investigation, to determine the most appropriate disposition of a juvenile who has been adjudicated a delinquent, a status offender, or a dependent.

Disposition, juvenile court   The decision of a juvenile court, concluding a disposition hearing, that a juvenile be committed to a correctional facility, placed in a care or treatment program, required to meet certain standards of conduct, or released.

Diversion   The official halting or suspension, at any legally prescribed processing point after a recorded justice system entry, of formal criminal or juvenile justice proceedings against an alleged offender, and referral of that person to a treatment or care program administered by a nonjustice agency or a private agency, or no referral.

Driving under the influence—alcohol (drunk driving) The operation of any vehicle after having consumed a quantity of alcohol sufficient to potentially interfere with the ability to maintain safe operation.

Driving under the influence—drugs The operation of any vehicle while attention or ability is impaired through the intake of a narcotic or an incapacitating quantity of another drug.

Drug law violation The unlawful sale, transport, manufacture, cultivation, possession, or use of a controlled or prohibited drug.

Early release Release from confinement before the sentence has been completed. Early release to supervision means less jail time and, with more rapid turnover, lower jail populations and capacity requirements. Early release may come about through parole, time off for good behavior or work performed, or modification of the sentence by the court. The last procedure is usually associated with sentences to jail with a period of probation to follow. Although there are some objections to its use, "probation with jail" is a common disposition in some jurisdictions. More often than not, these sentences are in lieu of a state prison term.

Embezzlement The misappropriation, misapplication, or illegal disposal of legally entrusted property with intent to defraud the legal owner or intended beneficiary.

Escape The unlawful departure of a lawfully confined person from a confinement facility or from custody while being transported.

Expunge The sealing or purging of arrest, criminal, or juvenile record information.

Extortion Unlawful obtaining or attempting to obtain the property of another by the threat of eventual injury or harm to that person, the person's property, or another person.

Felony A criminal offense punishable by death or by incarceration in a state or federal confinement facility for a period of which the lower limit is prescribed by statute in a given jurisdiction, typically one year or more.

Field citation Citation and release in the field by police as an alternative to booking and pretrial detention. This practice reduces law enforcement costs as well as jail costs.

Filing The commencement of criminal proceedings by entering a charging document into a court's official record.

Finding The official determination of a judicial officer or administrative body regarding a disputed matter of fact or law.

Fine The penalty imposed on a convicted person by a court requiring that he or she pay a specified sum of money. The fine is a cash payment of a dollar amount assessed by the judge in an individual case or determined by a published schedule of penalties. Fines may be paid in installments in many jurisdictions.

Forgery   The creation or alteration of a written or printed document that, if validly executed, would constitute a record of a legally binding transaction, with the intent to defraud by affirming it to be the act of an unknowing second person. Defining features: Making or altering a written or printed document or record. Act being falsely attributed to an unknowing second person. Intent being to deprive illegally a person of property or legal rights.

Fraud   An element of certain offenses consisting of deceit or intentional misrepresentation with the aim of illegally depriving a person of property or legal rights.

Fugitive   A person who has concealed himself or herself or fled a given jurisdiction in order to avoid prosecution or confinement.

Group home   A nonconfining residential facility for adjudicated adults or juveniles or those subject to criminal or juvenile proceedings, intended to reproduce as closely as possible the circumstances of family life and at the minimum, providing access to community activities and resources.

Recommended conditions of use. Classify government facilities fitting this definition as community facilities.

Annotation. Group home is variously defined in different jurisdictions. Most of the facilities known by this name are privately operated, though they may be financed mainly from government funds. Classification problems unique to private facilities have not been dealt with in this terminology, although most recommended standard descriptors for publicly operated facilities are also applicable to the private sector. See *correctional facility* for recommended standard descriptors. The data collection questionnaire for the LEAA (Law Enforcement Assistance Administration) series "Children in Custody" defines *group home* as one which allows juveniles extensive contact with the community, such as through jobs and schools, so long as none or fewer than half are placed there on probation or "aftercare/parole." It is distinguished from *halfway house* in this series by the percentage of residents on probation or parole.

Halfway house   A nonconfining residential facility for adjudicated adults or juveniles or those subject to criminal or juvenile proceedings, intended as an alternative to confinement for persons not suited for probation or needing a period of readjustment to the community after confinement.

Recommended conditions of use. Classify government facilities fitting this definition as *community facilities*.

Annotation. Halfway house is variously defined in different jurisdictions. Most of the facilities known by this name are privately operated, though they may be financed mainly from government funds. Classification problems unique to private facilities have not been dealt with in this terminology, although most recommended standard descriptors for publicly operated facilities are also applicable to the private sector. See *correctional facility* for recommended standard descriptors. The data collection questionnaire for the LEAA series "Children in Custody" defines *halfway house* as one which has 50 percent or more juveniles on probation or aftercare/parole, allowing them extensive contact with the community, such as through "jobs and schools." It is distinguished from group home in this series by the percentage of residents on probation or parole.

Hearing   A proceeding in which arguments, evidence, or witnesses are heard by a judicial officer or administrative body.

Hearing, probable cause   A proceeding before a judicial officer in which arguments, evidence, or witnesses are presented and in which it is determined whether there is sufficient cause to hold the accused for trial or whether the case should be dismissed.

Homicide   Any killing of one person by another.

Homicide, criminal   The causing of the death of another person without justification or excuse. Equivalent terms (defined for the Uniform Crime Reports): criminal homicide, murder (often used as a cover term for murder and nonnegligent manslaughter), nonnegligent manslaughter, voluntary manslaughter, negligent manslaughter, and vehicular manslaughter.

Homicide, excusable   The intentional but justifiable causing of the death of another or the unintentional causing of the death of another by accident or misadventure, without gross negligence. Not a crime.

Homicide, justifiable   The intentional causing of the death of another in the legal performance of an official duty or in the circumstances defined by law as constituting legal justification. Not a crime.

Homicide, willful   The intentional causing of the death of another person, with or without legal justification.

Indictment   A formal written accusation made by a grand jury and filed in a court, alleging that a specified person(s) has committed a specific offense(s).

Information   A written formal accusation, filed in a court by a prosecutor, that alleges a specific person has committed a specific offense.

Infraction   An offense punishable by fine or other penalty, but not by incarceration.

Inmate   A person in custody in a confinement facility.

Institutional capacity   The officially stated number of inmates or residents that a correctional facility is designed to house, exclusive of extraordinary arrangements to accommodate overcrowded conditions.

Intake   The process during which a juvenile referral is received and a decision is made by an intake unit to file a petition in juvenile court, to release the juvenile, to place the juvenile under supervision, or to refer the juvenile elsewhere.

Intake unit   A government agency or agency subunit that receives juvenile referrals from police, other government agencies, private agencies, or persons, and screens them, resulting in closing of the case, referral to care or supervision, or filing of a petition in juvenile court.

Jail   A confinement facility, usually administered by a local law enforcement agency, intended for adults but sometimes also containing juveniles, that holds persons detained pending adjudication and/or persons committed after adjudication for sentences of a year or less.

Jail (sentence)   The penalty of commitment to the jurisdiction of a confinement facility system for adults, of which the custodial authority is limited to persons sentenced to a year or less of confinement.

Judge   A judicial officer who has been elected or appointed to preside over a court of law, whose position has been created by statute or by constitution and whose decisions in criminal and juvenile cases may only be reviewed by a judge or a higher court and may not be reviewed de novo.

Judgment   The statement of the decision of a court that the defendant is convicted or acquitted of the offense(s) charged.

Judicial officer   Any person exercising judicial powers in a court of law.

Jurisdiction   The territory, subject matter, or person over which lawful authority may be exercised.

Jurisdiction, original   The lawful authority of a court or an administrative agency to hear or act upon a case from its beginning and to pass judgment on it.

Jury, grand   A body of persons who have been selected and sworn to investigate criminal activity and the conduct of public officials and to hear the evidence against an accused person(s) to determine whether there is sufficient evidence to bring that person(s) to trial.

Jury, trial (jury, petit, jury)   A statutorily defined number of persons selected according to law and sworn to determine certain matters of fact in a criminal action and to render a verdict of guilty or not guilty.

Juvenile   A person subject to juvenile court proceedings because a statutorily defined event was alleged to have occurred while his or her age was below the statutorily specified limit of original jurisdiction of a juvenile court.
  Annotation. Jurisdiction is determined by age at the time of the event, not at the time of judicial proceedings, and continues until the case is terminated. Thus a person may be described in a given data system as a juvenile because he or she is still subject to juvenile court proceedings, even though his or her actual age may be several years over the limit. Conversely, criminal process data systems may include juveniles if the juvenile court has waived jurisdiction. Although the age limit varies in different states, it is most often the eighteenth birthday. The variation is small enough to permit nationally aggregated data to be meaningful, although individual states should note their age limit in communications with other states. UCR defines a juvenile as anyone under eighteen years of age. *See* youthful offender.

Juvenile court   A cover term for courts that have original jurisdiction over persons statutorily defined as juveniles and alleged to be delinquents, status offenders, or dependents.

Juvenile justice agency A government agency, or subunit thereof, of which the functions are the investigation, supervision, adjudication, care or confinement of juveniles whose conduct or condition has brought or could bring them within the jurisdiction of a juvenile court.

Juvenile record An official record containing, at a minimum, summary information pertaining to an identified juvenile concerning juvenile court proceedings, and, if applicable, detention and correctional processes.

Kidnapping Unlawful transportation of a person without his or her consent or without the consent of his or her guardian, if a minor.

Larceny (larceny-theft) Unlawful taking or attempted taking of property, other than a motor vehicle, from the possession of another.

Law enforcement agency A federal, state, or local criminal justice agency of which the principal functions are the prevention, detection, and investigation of crime and the apprehension of alleged offenders.

Law enforcement agency, federal A law enforcement agency that is an organizational unit, or subunit, of the federal government.

Law enforcement agency, local A law enforcement agency that is an organizational unit, or subunit, of local government.

Law enforcement agency, state A law enforcement agency that is an organizational unit, or subunit, of state government.

Law enforcement officer (peace officer, police officer) An employee of a law enforcement agency who is an officer sworn to carry out law enforcement duties or is a sworn employee of a federal prosecutorial agency who primarily performs investigative duties.

Law enforcement officer, federal An employee of a federal law enforcement agency who is an officer sworn to carry out law enforcement duties or is a sworn employee of a federal prosecutorial agency who primarily performs investigative duties.

Law enforcement officer, local An employee of a local law enforcement agency who is an officer sworn to carry out law enforcement duties or is a sworn employee of a local prosecutorial agency who primarily performs investigative duties.

Law enforcement officer, state An employee of a state law enforcement agency who is an officer sworn to carry out law enforcement duties or is a sworn employee of a state prosecutorial agency who primarily performs investigative duties.

Level of government The federal, state, regional, or local county or city location of administrative and major funding responsibility of a given agency.

Manslaughter, involuntary (negligent manslaughter) Causing the death of another by recklessness or gross negligence.

Manslaughter, vehicular   Causing the death of another by the grossly negligent operation of a motor vehicle.

Manslaughter, voluntary (nonnegligent manslaughter)   Intentionally causing the death of another with reasonable provocation.

Misdemeanor   An offense usually punishable by incarceration in a local confinement facility for a period of which the upper limit is prescribed by statute in a given jurisdiction, typically limited to a year or less.

Model Penal Code   A generalized modern codification of that which is considered basic to criminal law, published by the American Law Institute in 1962.

Monitored release   Recognizance release with the addition of minimal supervision of service; that is, the defendant may be required to keep a pretrial services agency informed of his or her whereabouts, and the agency reminds the defendant of court dates and verifies the defendant's appearance.

Motion   An oral or written request made by a party to an action, before, during, or after a trial, that a court issue a rule or order.

Motor vehicle theft   Unlawful taking, or attempted taking, of a motor vehicle owned by another with the intent to deprive the owner of it permanently or temporarily.

Murder   Intentionally causing the death of another without reasonable provocation or legal justification, or causing the death of another while committing or attempting to commit another crime.

Nolo contendere   A defendant's formal answer in court to the charges in a complaint, information, or indictment in which the defendant states that he or she does not contest the charges and which, though not an admission of guilt, subjects the defendant to the same legal consequences as does a plea of guilty.

Offender (criminal)   An adult who has been convicted of a criminal offense.

Offender, alleged   A person who has been charged with a specific criminal offense(s) by a law enforcement agency or court but has not been convicted.

Offense   An act committed or omitted in violation of a law forbidding or commanding it.

Offenses, Part I   A class of offenses selected for use in UCR, consisting of those crimes that are most likely to be reported, that occur with sufficient frequency to provide an adequate basis for comparison, and that are serious crimes by nature and/or volume.

    Annotation.

    The Part I offenses are

        1. Criminal homicide.

           a. Murder and nonnegligent (voluntary) manslaughter

           b. Manslaughter by negligence (involuntary manslaughter)

2. Forcible rape
   a. Rape by force
   b. Attempted forcible rape
3. Robbery
   a. Firearm
   b. Knife or cutting instrument
   c. Other dangerous weapon
   d. Strongarm
4. Aggravated assault
   a. Firearm
   b. Knife or cutting instrument
   c. Other dangerous weapon
   d. Hands, fist, feet, etc.—aggravated injury
5. Burglary
   a. Forcible entry
   b. Unlawful entry—no force
   c. Attempted forcible entry
6. Larceny-theft (larceny)
7. Motor vehicle theft
   a. Autos
   b. Trucks and buses
   c. Other vehicles
8. Arson

Offenses, Part II   A class of offenses selected for use in UCR, consisting of specific offenses and types of offenses that do not meet the criteria of frequency and/or seriousness necessary for Part I offenses.

Annotation.

The Part II offenses are

Other assaults (simple,* nonaggravated)
Arson*
Forgery* and counterfeiting*
Fraud*
Embezzlement*
Stolen property: buying, receiving, possessing
Vandalism
Weapons; carrying, possessing, etc.
Prostitution and commercialized vice
Sex offenses (except forcible rape, prostitution, and commercialized vice)

Terms marked with an asterisk (*) are defined in this glossary, though not necessarily in accord with UCR usage. UCR does not collect reports of Part II offenses. Arrest data concerning such offenses, however, are collected and published.

Narcotic drug law violations
Gambling
Offenses against the family and children
Driving under the influence*
Liquor law violations
Drunkenness
Disorderly conduct
Vagrancy
All other offenses (except traffic law violations)
Suspicion*
Curfew and loitering law violations (juvenile violations)
Runaway* (juveniles)

Pardon   An act of executive clemency that absolves the party in part or in full from the legal consequences of the crime and conviction.

Annotation.   Pardons can be full or conditional. The former generally applies to both the punishment and the guilt of the offender and blots out the existence of guilt in the eyes of the law. It also removes his or her disabilities and restores civil rights. The conditional pardon generally falls short of the remedies of the full pardon, is an expression of guilt, and does not obliterate the conviction. (U.S. Supreme Court decisions on pardons and their effects are directly contradictory, and thus state laws usually govern pardons.)

Parole   The status of an offender conditionally released from a confinement facility, prior to the expiration of his or her sentence, and placed under the supervision of a parole agency.

Parole agency   A correctional agency, which may or may not include a parole authority and of which the principal function is the supervision of adults or juveniles placed on parole.

Parole authority   A person or a correctional agency that has the authority to release on parole those adults or juveniles committed to confinement facilities, to revoke parole, and to discharge from parole.

Parolee   A person who has been conditionally released from a correctional institution before the expiration of his or her sentence and who has been placed under the supervision of a parole agency.

Parole violation   A parolee's act or a failure to act that does not conform to the conditions of his or her parole.

Partial confinement   An alternative to the traditional jail sentence, consisting of "weekend" sentences, that permit offenders to spend the work week in the community, with their families, and at their jobs; furloughs, which enable offenders to leave the jail for a period of a few hours to a few days for specified purposes—to seek employment, take care of personal matters or family obligations, or engage in community service; or work/study release, under which offenders work or attend school during the day and return to the detention facility at night and on weekends.

Penalty   The punishment annexed by law or judicial decision to the commission of a particular offense, which may be death, imprisonment, fine, or loss of civil privileges.

Percentage bail   A publicly managed bail service arrangement that requires the defendant to deposit a percentage (typically 10 percent) of the amount of bail with the court clerk. The deposit is returned to the defendant after scheduled court appearances are made, although a charge (usually 1 percent) may be deducted to help defray program costs.

Person   A human being, or a group of human beings considered a legal unit, which has the lawful capacity to defend rights, incur obligations, prosecute claims, or be prosecuted or adjudicated.

Personally secured bail   Security that is put up by the defendant or the defendant's family. This arrangement is generally out of reach of the less affluent defendant.

Petition (juvenile)   A document filed in juvenile court alleging that a juvenile is a delinquent, a status offender, or a dependent and asking that the court assume jurisdiction over the juvenile or that the juvenile be transferred to a criminal court for prosecution as an adult.

Petition not sustained   The finding by a juvenile court in an adjudicatory hearing that there is not sufficient evidence to sustain an allegation that a juvenile is a delinquent, status offender, or dependent.

Plea   A defendant's formal answer in court to the charges brought against him or her in a complaint, information, or indictment.

Plea bargaining   The exchange of prosecutorial and/or judicial concessions, commonly a lesser charge, the dismissal of other pending charges, a recommendation by the prosecutor for a reduced sentence or a combination thereof, in return for a plea of guilty.

Plea, final   The last plea to a given charge, entered in a court record by or for a defendant.

Plea, guilty   A defendant's formal answer in court to the charges in a complaint, information, or indictment, in which the defendant states that the charges are true and that he or she has committed the offense as charged.

Plea, initial   The first plea to a given charge, entered in a court record by or for a defendant.

Plea, not guilty   A defendant's formal answer in court to the charges in a complaint, information, or indictment, in which the defendant states that he or she is not guilty.

Police department   A local law enforcement agency directed by a chief of police or a commissioner.

Police officer   A local law enforcement officer employed by a police department.

Population movement   Entries and exits of adjudicated persons, or persons subject to judicial proceedings, into or from correctional facilities or programs.

Predisposition report   The document resulting from an investigation by a probation agency or other designated authority, which has been requested by a juvenile court, into the past behavioral, family background, and personality of a juvenile who has been adjudicated a delinquent, a status offender, or a dependent, in order to assist the court in determining the most appropriate disposition.

Presentence report   The document resulting from an investigation undertaken by a probation agency or other designated authority, at the request of a criminal court, into the past behavior, family circumstances, and personality of an adult who has been convicted of a crime, in order to assist the court in determining the most appropriate sentence.

Prior record   Criminal history record information concerning any law enforcement, court, or correctional proceedings that have occurred before the current investigation of, or proceedings against, a person; or statistical descriptions of the criminal histories of a set of persons.

Prison   A confinement facility having custodial authority over adults sentenced to confinement for more than a year.

Prisoner   A person in custody in a confinement facility or in the personal custody of a criminal justice official while being transported to or between confinement facilities.

Prison (sentence)   The penalty of commitment to the jurisdiction of a confinement facility system for adults, whose custodial authority extends to persons sentenced to more than a year of confinement.

Privately secured bail   An arrangement similar to the bail bondsman system except that bail is provided without cost to the defendant. A private organization provides bail for indigent arrestees who meet its eligibility requirements.

Probable cause   A set of facts and circumstances that would induce a reasonably intelligent and prudent person to believe that an accused person had committed a specific crime.

Probation   The conditional freedom granted by a judicial officer to an alleged offender, or adjudicated adult or juvenile, as long as the person meets certain conditions of behavior. One requirement is to report to a designated person or agency over some specified period of time. Probation may contain special conditions, as discussed in the definition of suspended sentence. Probation often includes a suspended sentence but may be used in association with the suspension of a final judgment or a deferral of sentencing.

Probation agency (probation department)   A correctional agency of which the principal functions are juvenile intake, the supervision of adults and juveniles placed on probation status, and the investigation of adults or juveniles for the purpose of preparing presentence or predisposition reports to assist the court in determining the proper sentence or juvenile court disposition.

Probationer   A person required by a court or probation agency to meet certain conditions of behavior who may or may not be placed under the supervision of a probation agency.

Probation officer   An employee of a probation agency whose primary duties include one or more of the probation agency functions.

Probation (sentence)   A court requirement that a person fulfill certain conditions of behavior and accept the supervision of a probation agency, usually in lieu of a sentence to confinement but sometimes including a jail sentence.

Probation violation   An act or a failure to act by a probationer that does not conform to the conditions of his or her probation.

Prosecutor   An attorney employed by a government agency or subunit whose official duty is to initiate and maintain criminal proceedings on behalf of the government against persons accused of committing criminal offenses.

Prosecutorial agency   A federal, state, or local criminal justice agency whose principal function is the prosecution of alleged offenders.

Pro se (in propria persona)   Acting as one's own defense attorney in criminal proceedings; representing oneself.

Public defender   An attorney employed by a government agency or subdivision, whose official duty is to represent defendants unable to hire private counsel.

Public defender's officer   A federal, state, or local criminal justice agency or subunit of which the principal function is to represent defendants unable to hire private counsel.

Purge (record)   The complete removal of arrest, criminal, or juvenile record information from a given records system.

Rape   Unlawful sexual intercourse with a female [or person], by force or without legal or factual consent.

Rape, forcible   Sexual intercourse or attempted sexual intercourse with a female [or person] against her or his will, by force or threat of force.

Rape, statutory   Sexual intercourse with a female [or person] who has consented in fact but is deemed, because of age, to be legally incapable of consent.

Rape without force or consent   Sexual intercourse with a female [or person] legally of the age of consent but who is unconscious or whose ability to judge or control her conduct is inherently impaired by mental defect or intoxicating substances.

Recidivism   The repetition of criminal behavior; habitual criminality.

   Annotation.   In statistical practice, a recidivism rate may be any of a number of possible counts of instances of arrest, conviction, correctional commitment, and correctional status changes, related to the numbers of repetitions of these events within a given period of time. Efforts to arrive at a single standard statistical description of recidivism have been hampered by the fact that the term's correct referent is the actual repeated criminal or delinquent behavior of a given person or group; yet the only available statistical indicators of that behavior are records of such system events as rearrests, reconvictions, and probation or parole violations or revocations. It is recognized that these data reflect agency decisions about events and may or may not closely correspond with actual criminal behavior. Different conclusions about degrees of correspondence between system decisions and actual behavior consequently produce different definitions of recidivism, that is, different judgments of which system event repetition rates best measure actual recidivism rates. This is an empirical question, and not one of definition to be resolved solely by analysis of language usage and system logic. Resolution has also been delayed by the limited capacities of most criminal justice statistical systems, which do not routinely make available the standardized offender-based transaction data (OBTD) that may be needed for the best measurement of recidivism. Pending the adoption of a standard statistical description of recidivism and the ability to implement it, it is recommended that recidivism analyses include the widest possible range of system events that can correspond with actual recidivism and that sufficient detail of offenses charged be included to enable discrimination among degrees of gravity of offenses. The units of count should be clearly identified and the length of community exposure time of the subject population stated.

Recidivism is measured by: (1) criminal acts that resulted in a conviction by a court, when committed by individuals who are under correctional supervision or who have been released from correctional supervision within the previous three years, and by (2) technical violations of probation or parole in which a sentencing or paroling authority took action that resulted in an adverse change in the offender's "legal status."

Neither of these formulations is endorsed as adequate for all purposes. Both limit the measure and concept of recidivism to populations that are or have been under correctional supervision. Yet the ultimate significance of data concerning the repetition of criminal behavior often depends on the comparison of the behavior of unconfined or unsupervised offenders with the behavior of those with correctional experience.

Referral to intake   In juvenile proceedings, a request by the police, parents, or other agency or person that a juvenile intake unit take appropriate action concerning a juvenile alleged to have committed a delinquent act or status offense or to be dependent.

Release from detention   The authorized exit from detention of a person subject to criminal or juvenile justice proceedings.

Release from prison   A cover term for all lawful exits from federal or state confinement facilities primarily intended for adults serving sentences of more than a year, including all conditional and unconditional releases, deaths, and transfers to other jurisdictions, excluding escapes.

>   Transfer of jurisdiction
>   Release on parole
>   Conditional release

Release while still under jurisdiction of correctional agency, before
expiration of sentence

Discretionary

Release date determined by parole authority

Mandatory

Release date determined by statute

Discharge from prison

Release ending all agency jurisdiction

Unconditional release

Discretionary

Pardon, commutation of sentence

Mandatory

Expiration of sentence

Temporary release

Authorized, unaccompanied temporary departure for educational,
employment, or other authorized purposes

Transfer of jurisdiction

Transfer to jurisdiction of another correctional agency or a court

Death

Death from homicide, suicide, or natural causes

Execution

Execution of sentence of death

In some systems, release on "parole" represents only discretionary conditional
release. It is recommended that mandatory conditional releases be included, as both
types describe conditional releases with subsequent parole status.

Release on bail The release by a judicial officer of an accused person who has been
taken into custody, upon the accused's promise to pay a certain sum of money or
property if he or she fails to appear in court as required, a promise that may or
may not be secured by the deposit of an actual sum of money or property.

Release on own recognizance The release, by a judicial officer, of an accused person who has been taken into custody, upon the accused's promise to appear in
court as required for criminal proceedings.

Release, pretrial A procedure whereby an accused person who has been taken into
custody is allowed to be free before and during his or her trial.

Release to third party The release, by a judicial officer, of an accused person who
has been taken into custody, to a third party who promises to return the accused
to court for criminal proceedings.

Residential treatment center A government facility that serves juveniles whose
behavior does not necessitate the strict confinement of a training school, often
allowing them greater contact with the community.

Restitution   Usually a cash payment by the offender to the victim of an amount considered to offset the loss incurred by the victim or the community. The amount of the payment may be scaled down to the offender's earning capacity, and/or payments may be made in installments. Sometimes services directly or indirectly benefiting the victim may be substituted for cash payment.

Retained counsel   An attorney, not employed or compensated by a government agency or subunit or assigned by the court, who is privately hired to represent a person(s) in a criminal proceeding.

Revocation   An administrative act performed by a parole authority removing a person from parole, or a judicial order by a court removing a person from parole or probation, in response to a violation by the parolee or probationer.

Revocation hearing   An administrative and/or judicial hearing on the question of whether or not a person's probation or parole status should be revoked.

Rights of defendant   Those powers and privileges that are constitutionally guaranteed to every defendant.

Robbery   The unlawful taking or attempted taking of property that is in the immediate possession of another, by force or the threat of force.

Robbery, armed   The unlawful taking or attempted taking of property that is in the immediate possession of another, by the use or threatened use of a deadly or dangerous weapon.

Robbery, strongarm   The unlawful taking or attempted taking of property that is in the immediate possession of another by the use or threatened use of force, without the use of a weapon.

Runaway   A juvenile who has been adjudicated by a judicial officer of a juvenile court as having committed the status offense of leaving the custody and home of his or her parents, guardians, or custodians without permission and failing to return within a reasonable length of time.

Seal (record)   The removal, for the benefit of the subject, of arrest, criminal, or juvenile record information from routinely available status to a status requiring special procedures for access.

Security   The degree of restriction of inmate movement within a correctional facility, usually divided into maximum, medium, and minimum levels.

Security and privacy standards   A set of principles and procedures developed to ensure the security and confidentiality of criminal or juvenile record information in order to protect the privacy of the persons identified in such records.

Sentence   The penalty imposed by a court on a convicted person, or the court decision to suspend imposition or execution of the penalty.

Sentence, indeterminate   A statutory provision for a type of sentence to imprisonment in which, after the court has determined that the convicted person shall be imprisoned, the exact length of imprisonment and parole supervision is afterward fixed within statutory limits by a parole authority.

Sentence, mandatory A statutory requirement that a certain penalty shall be imposed and executed upon certain convicted offenders.

Sentence, suspended The court decision postponing the pronouncement of sentence upon a convicted person or postponing the execution of a sentence that has been pronounced by the court.

Sentence, suspended execution The court decision setting a penalty but postponing its execution.

Sentence, suspended imposition The court decision postponing the setting of a penalty.

Shelter A confinement or community facility for the care of juveniles, usually those held pending adjudication.

Sheriff The elected or appointed chief officer of a county law enforcement agency, usually responsible for law enforcement in unincorporated areas and for operation of the county jail.

Sheriff, deputy A law enforcement officer employed by a county sheriff's department.

Sheriff's department A law enforcement agency organized at the county level, directed by a sheriff, that exercises its law enforcement functions at the county level, usually within unincorporated areas, and operates the county jail in most jurisdictions.

Speedy trial The right of the defendant to have a prompt trial.

State highway patrol A state law enforcement agency whose principal functions are the prevention, detection, and investigation of motor vehicle offenses and the apprehension of traffic offenders.

State highway patrol officer An employee of a state highway patrol who is an officer sworn to carry out law enforcement duties, primarily traffic code enforcement.

State police A state law enforcement agency whose principal functions may include maintaining statewide police communications, aiding local police in criminal investigations, training police, guarding state property, and patroling highways.

State police officer An employee of a state police agency who is an officer sworn to carry out law enforcement duties, sometimes including traffic enforcement duties.

Stationhouse citation An alternative to pretrial detention, whereby the arrestee is escorted to the precinct police station or headquarters rather than the pretrial detention facility. Release, which may occur before or after booking, is contingent upon the defendant's written promise to appear in court as specified on the release form.

Status offender A juvenile who has been adjudicated by a judicial officer of a juvenile court as having committed a status offense, which is an act or conduct that is an offense only when committed or engaged in by a juvenile.

Status offense   An act or conduct that is declared by statute to be an offense, but only when committed or engaged in by a juvenile, and that can be adjudicated only by a juvenile court.

Subjudicial officer   A judicial officer who is invested with certain judicial powers and functions but whose decisions in criminal and juvenile cases are subject to *de novo* review by a judge.

Subpoena   A written order issued by a judicial officer requiring a specified person to appear in a designated court at a specified time in order to serve as a witness in a case under the jurisdiction of that court or to bring material to that court.

Summons   A written order issued by a judicial officer requiring a person accused of a criminal offense to appear in a designated court at a specified time to answer the charge(s). The summons is a request or instruction to appear in court to face an accusation. As an alternative to the arrest warrant, it is used in cases on which complaints are registered with the magistrate or prosecutor's office.

Supervised release   A type of release requiring more frequent contact than monitored release does. Typically, various conditions are imposed and supervision is aimed at enforcing these conditions and providing services as needed. Some form of monetary bail also may be attached as a condition of supervised release, especially in higher-risk cases.

Suspect   A person, adult or juvenile, considered by a criminal justice agency to be one who may have committed a specific criminal offense but who has not been arrested or charged.

Suspended sentence   Essentially a threat to take more drastic action if the offender again commits a crime during some specified time period. When no special conditions are attached, it is assumed that the ends of justice have been satisfied by conviction and no further action is required, as long as the offender refrains from involvement in new offenses. Suspended sentences may be conditioned on various limitations as to mobility, associates, or activities or on requirements to make reparations or participate in some rehabilitation program.

Suspicion   Belief that a person has committed a criminal offense, based on facts and circumstances that are not sufficient to constitute probable cause.

Theft   Larceny, or in some legal classifications, the group of offenses including larceny, and robbery, burglary, extortion, fraudulent offenses, hijacking, and other offenses sharing the element of larceny.

Third-party release   A release extending to another person the responsibility for ensuring the defendant's appearance in court. This may be a person known to the defendant or a designated volunteer. Third-party release may be a condition of unsecured bail, with the third party as a cosigner.

Time served   The total time spent in confinement by a convicted adult before and after sentencing, or only the time spent in confinement after a sentence of commitment to a confinement facility.

Training school   A correctional institution for juveniles adjudicated to be delinquents or status offenders and committed to confinement by a judicial officer.

Transfer hearing   A preadjudicatory hearing in juvenile court in order to determine whether juvenile court jurisdiction should be retained or waived for a juvenile alleged to have committed a delinquent act(s) and whether he or she should be transferred to criminal court for prosecution as an adult.

Transfer to adult court   The decision by a juvenile court, resulting from a transfer hearing, that jurisdiction over an alleged delinquent will be waived and that he or she should be prosecuted as an adult in a criminal court.

Trial   The examination of issues of fact and law in a case or controversy, beginning when the jury has been selected in a jury trial, the first witness is sworn, or the first evidence is introduced in a court trial and concluding when a verdict is reached or the case is dismissed.

Trial, court (trial, judge)   A trial in which there is no jury and a judicial officer determines the issues of fact and law in a case.

Trial, jury   A trial in which a jury determines the issues of fact in a case.

UCR   An abbreviation for the Federal Bureau of Investigation's uniform crime reporting program.

Unconditional discharge   As a posttrial disposition, essentially the same as unconditional diversion. No savings are obtained in criminal justice processing costs, but jail populations may be reduced; conditions of release are imposed for an offense in which the defendant's involvement has been established.

Unconditional diversion   The cessation of criminal processing at any point short of adjudication with no continuing threat of prosecution. This type of diversion may be a voluntary referral to a social service agency or program dealing with a problem underlying the offense.

Unsecured bail   A form of release differing from release on recognizance only in that the defendant is subject to paying the amount of bail if he or she defaults. Unsecured bail permits release without a deposit or purchase of a bondsman's services.

Venue   The geographical area from which the jury is drawn and in which trial is held in a criminal action.

Verdict   In criminal proceedings, the decision made by a judicial officer in a court trial, that a defendant is either guilty or not guilty of the offense(s) for which he or she has been tried.

Verdict, guilty   In criminal proceedings, the decision made by a jury in a jury trial, or by a judicial officer in a court trial, that the defendant is guilty of the offense(s) for which he or she has been tried.

Verdict, not guilty   In criminal proceedings, the decision made by a jury in a jury trial, or by a judicial officer in a court trial, that the defendant is not guilty of the offense(s) for which he or she has been tried.

Victim   A person who has suffered death, physical or mental suffering, or loss of property as the result of an actual or attempted criminal offense committed by another person.

Warrant, arrest   A document issued by a judicial officer that directs a law enforcement officer to arrest a person who has been accused of an offense.

Warrant, bench   A document issued by a judicial officer directing that a person who has failed to obey an order or notice to appear be brought before the court.

Warrant, search   A document issued by a judicial officer that directs a law enforcement officer to conduct a search for specified property or persons at a specific location, to seize the property or persons, if found, and to account for the results of the search to the issuing judicial officer.

Witness   A person who directly perceives an event or thing or who has expert knowledge relevant to a case.

Youthful offender   A person, adjudicated in criminal court, who may be above the statutory age limit for juveniles but is below a specified upper age limit, for whom special correctional commitments and special record sealing procedures are made available by statute.

Security Resources

PROFESSIONAL RESOURCES

Jerry L. Wright, CPP, CFE
Certified Protection Professional
Certified Fraud Examiner

Security Trade & Interest Organizations

Security Periodicals

Training Programs & Resources

Audio-Visual Distributors

Computer Resources on the Internet

Today's Safety Manager now in many cases also serves as the Corporate Security Manager. In order to manage the several tasks that are assigned each day, it is important to know as many resources as possible so that the Safety Manager can respond to a crisis professionally. It is impossible for any one professional to be an expert on every aspect of their assigned position. Fortunately, there are many resources that are available to assist during times of crisis. Keep this chapter available as a handy resource to help put out fires that occur during each day that you are responsible for security.

Security Trade and Interest Organizations

ACADEMY OF CRIMINAL JUSTICE SCIENCES (ACJS)
Northern Kentucky Univ.,
402 Nunn Hall,
Highland Heights, KY 41076
(606) 572-5634 Fax: (606) 572-6665
Officer: Patricia DeLancey, Exec. Sec.

ACADEMY OF SECURITY EDUCATORS AND TRAINERS (ASET)
Route 2, Box 3644
Berryville, VA 22611
(540) 955-1129 Fax: (540) 955-0255
Officer: Richard D. Kobetz, Dir.

AIR TRANSPORT ASSOCIATION OF AMERICA
1709 New York Ave., N.W.
Washington, D.C. 20006-5206
(202) 626-4000 Fax: (202) 626-4166
Officer: Mrs. Carol Hallett, Pres.

AMERICAN ACADEMY OF FORENSIC SCIENCES
P.O. Box 669
Colorado Springs, CO 80901-0669
(719) 636-1100 Fax: (719) 636-1993
Officer: Ann H. Warren, Exec. Dir.

AMERICAN BANKERS ASSOCIATION (ABA)
1120 Connecticut Ave., N.W.
Washington, D.C. 20036
(202) 663-5000 Fax: (202) 296-9258
Officer: Donald G. Ogilvie, Exec. V.P.

AMERICAN CORRECTIONAL ASSN. (ACA)
4380 Forbes Blvd.
Lanham, MD 20706
(301) 918-1800 Fax: (301) 918-1900
Officer: James A. Gondles, Jr., Exec. Dir.

AMERICAN CRIMINAL JUSTICE ASSN. (ACJA)
P.O. Box 601047
Sacramento, CA 95860
(916) 484-6553 Fax: (916) 488-2227
Officer: Karen K. Campbell, Exec. Sec.

AMERICAN DEFENSE PREPAREDNESS ASSN.
2101 Wilson Blvd., Suite 400
Arlington, VA 22201-3061
(703) 522-1820 Fax: (703) 522-1885
Officer: Lt. Gen. Lawrence F. Skibbie

AMERICAN ELECTRONICS ASSOCIATION
5201 Great America Pkwy., Suite 520
Santa Clara, CA 95054
(408) 987-4200 Fax: (408) 970-8565
Officer: William Archey, Pres.

AMERICAN FEDERATION OF POLICE
3801 Biscayne Blvd.
Miami, FL 33137
(305) 573-0202 Fax: (305) 573-9819
Officer: Gerald S. Arenberg, Exec. Dir.

AMERICAN FIRE SPRINKLER ASSN.
12959 Jupiter Road, Suite 142
Dallas, TX 75238
(214) 349-5965 Fax: (214) 343-8898
Officer: Steve Muncy, Pres.

AMERICAN HARDWARE MFRS. ASSN.
801 N. Plaza Drive
Schaumburg, IL 60173-4977
(847) 605-1025 Fax: (847) 605-1093
Officer: William P. Farrell, Pres/CEO

AMERICAN INSTITUTE OF CERTIFIED PUBLIC ACCOUNTANTS (AICPA)
1211 Ave. of the Americas
New York, NY 10036-8775
(212) 596-6200 Fax: (212) 596-6213
Officer: Barry Melancon, Pres.

AMERICAN LIGHTING ASSN.
P.O. Box 420288
Dallas, TX 75342-0288
(214) 698-9898 Fax: (214) 698-9899
Officer: Richard D. Upton

AMERICAN MANAGEMENT ASSN. (AMA)
135 West 50th Street
New York, NY 10020
(212) 586-8100 Fax: (212) 903-8168
Officer: David Fagiano, Pres./CEO

AMERICAN POLYGRAPH ASSN. (APA)
P.O. Box 8037
Chattanooga, TN 37414-0037
(800) 272-8037 Fax: (423) 894-5435
Officer: Robbie Bennett, Mgr.

THE AMERICAN SAFE DEPOSIT ASSN. (TASDA)
330 West Main Street
Greenwood, IN 46142
(317) 888-1118 Fax: (317) 888-1787
Officer: Joyce A. McLin, Exec. Dir.

AMERICAN SECURITY EDUCATORS
P.O. Box 1337
Downey, CA 90240
(310) 928-1847 Fax: (310) 869-6906
Officer: James W. Gonos, Pres.

AMERICAN SOCIETY FOR AMUSEMENT PARK SECURITY & SAFETY (ASAPSS)
Universal Studios Florida
1000 Universal Studios Plaza
Orlando, FL 32819
(407) 363-8381 Fax: (407) 354-6747
Officer: Robert Brauner

AMERICAN SOCIETY FOR INDUSTRIAL SECURITY (ASIS)
1655 N. Ft. Myer Drive., Suite 1200
Arlington, VA 22209
(703) 522-5800 Fax: (703) 243-4954
Officer: Michael J. Stack, Exec. Dir.

AMERICAN SOCIETY FOR TESTING AND MATERIALS (ASTM)
100 Barr Harbor Drive
West Conshohocken, PA 19428
(610) 832-9500 Fax: (610) 832-9555
Officer: James A. Thomas, Pres.

AMERICAN SOCIETY FOR TRAINING AND DEVELOPMENT (ASTD)
1640 King Street, Box 1443
Alexandria, VA 22313
(703) 683-8100 Fax: (703) 683-8103
Officer: Curtis E. Plott, Pres.

AMERICAN SOCIETY OF LAW ENFORCEMENT TRAINERS (ASLET)
P.O. Box 361
Lewes, DE 19958
(302) 645-4080 Fax: (302) 645-4084
Officer: Steve Bunting, Exec. Dir.

AMERICAN TRUCKING ASSOCIATION (ATA)
2200 Mill Road
Alexandria, VA 22314
(703) 838-1700 Fax: (703) 684-5751
Officer: Thomas J. Donohue, Pres/CEO

ARMED FORCES COMMUNICA-TIONS & ELECTRONICS ASSOCIATION (AFCEA)
4400 Fair Lakes Court
Fairfax, VA 22033-3899
(703) 631-6100 Fax: (703) 631-4693
Officer: Lt. Gen. Norman Wood, USAF Ret.

ASSOCIATED CREDIT BUREAUS
1090 Vermont Ave., N.W., Suite 200
Washington, D.C. 20005-4905
(202) 371-0910 Fax: (202) 371-0134
Officer: D. Barry Connelly, Pres.

ASSOCIATED LOCKSMITHS OF AMERICA
3003 Live Oak Street
Dallas, TX 75204
(214) 827-1701 Fax: (214) 827-1810
Officer: Ellie Wooderson, Controller

ASSOCIATION OF CERTIFIED FRAUD EXAMINERS
716 West Avenue
Austin, TX 78701
(512) 478-9070 Fax: (512) 478-9297
Officer: James D. Ratley, Program Dir.

ASSN. OF FORMER AGENTS OF THE U.S. SECRET SERVICE
P.O. Box 848
Annandale, VA 22003
(703) 256-0188
Officer: P. Hamilton Brown, Exec. Sec.

ASSN. OF FORMER INTELLIGENCE OFFICERS
6723 Whittier Avenue, Suite 303A
McLean, VA 22101
(703) 790-0320
Officer: David D. Whipple, Exec. Dir.

ASSOCIATION FOR INFORMATION TECHNOLOGY (AIT)
P.O. Box 626
Kings Park, NY 11754-0626
(516) 269-3881 Fax: (516) 269-3881
Officer: Mike Lackey, Pres.

ASSOCIATION OF OLD CROWS
The AOC Bldg., 1000 N. Payne Street
Alexandria, VA 22314-1696
(703) 549-1600 Fax: (703) 549-2489
Officer: Vern Luke, Exec. Dir.

ASSOCIATION OF RECORDS MANAGERS & ADMINISTRATORS (ARMA)
P.O. Box 8540, 4200 Somerset Drive,
Suite 215
Prairie Village, KS 66208-0540
(913) 341-3808 Fax: (913) 341-3742
Officer: James P. Souders, Exec. Dir.

ASSOCIATION OF STATE CORRECTIONAL ADMINISTRATORS
Spring Hill West, South Salem, NY 10590
(914) 533-2562
Officer: Camille G. Camp, Exec. Dir.

AUTOMATIC IDENTIFICATION MFRS, INC. (AIM USA)
634 Alpha Drive
Pittsburgh, PA 15238
(412) 963-8588 Fax: (412) 963-8753
Officer: Larry Roberts, Pres.

BANK ADMINISTRATION INSTITUTE (BAI)
1 N. Franklin Street, 10th Floor
Chicago, IL 60606
(312) 553-4600 Fax: (312) 683-2426
Officer: Ronald G. Burke, Pres.

BUSINESS ESPIONAGE CONTROLS AND COUNTER-MEASURES ASSN. (BECCA)
P.O. Box 55582
Seattle, WA 98155-0582
(206) 364-4672 Fax: (206) 367-3316
Officer: Will Johnson, Exec. Dir.

BUSINESS SOFTWARE ALLIANCE (BSA)
1150 18th Street, N.W., Suite 700
Washington, D.C. 20036
(202) 872-5500 Fax: (202) 872-5501
Officer: Robert W. Holleyman II, Pres.

CENTRAL STATION ALARM ASSN. (CSAA)
7101 Wisconsin Ave., Suite 901
Bethesda, MD 20814-4805
(301) 907-0045 Fax: (301) 907-2930
Officer: Ron LaFontaine, Pres.
Stephen Paul Doyle, E.V.P.

COMMUNICATIONS FRAUD CONTROL ASSOCIATION (CFCA)
1990 M Street, N.W., Suite 508
Washington, DC 20036
(202) 296-3225 Fax: (202) 296-3268
Officer: Ms. Frances Feld, CAE, Exec. Dir.

COMPUTER & COMMUNICATIONS INDUSTRY ASSOCIATION
666 11th Street, N.W., Suite 600
Washington, DC 20001-4542
(202) 783-0070 Fax: (202) 783-0534
Officer: Edward Block, Pres.

COMPUTER SECURITY INSTITUTE
600 Harrison Street
San Francisco, CA 94107
(415) 905-2310 Fax: (415) 905-2218
Officer: Patrice Rapalus, Exec. Dir.

COUNCIL OF INTERNATIONAL INVESTIGATORS (CII)
P.O. Box 61
Ambler, PA 19002
(800) 759-8884 Fax: (215) 540-0486
Officer: Norman A. Willox, Jr., Exec. Secy/Treas.

DATA PROCESSING MANAGEMENT ASSOCIATION (DPMA)
505 Busse Highway
Park Ridge, IL 60068
(847) 825-8124 Fax: (847) 825-1693
Officer: Mike Wukitsch, Exec. Dir.

DOOR AND HARDWARE INSTITUTE
14170 Newbrook Drive
Chantilly, VA 22021-2010
(703) 222-2010 Fax: (703) 222-2410
Officer: Jerry Heppes, Exec. Dir.

ELECTRONIC FUNDS TRANSFER ASSOCIATION (EFTA)
950 Herndon Parkway, Suite 390
Herndon, VA 22070
(703) 435-9800 Fax: (703) 435-7157
Officer: Kurt Helwig, Exec. Dir.

ELECTRONIC INDUSTRIES ASSN. (EIA)
2500 Wilson Blvd.
Arlington, VA 22201
(703) 907-7500 Fax: (703) 907-7501
Officer: Peter F. McCloskey, Pres.

ETHICS RESOURCE CENTER, INC.
1120 G Street, N.W., Suite #200
Washington, DC 20005
(202) 737-2258 Fax: (202) 737-2227
Officer: Michael G. Daigneault,
   Esq., Pres.

FEDERAL EMERGENCY MANAGEMENT AGENCY (FEMA)
16825 S. Seton Avenue
Emmitsburg, MD 21727
(202) 646-3923
Officer: James L. Witt, Exec. Dir.

FEDERAL LAW ENFORCEMENT OFFICERS ASSOCIATION
P.O. Box 508
E. Northport, New York 11731-0472
(516) 368-6117 Fax: (516) 368-6429

FIRE EQUIPMENT MANUFACTURERS ASSN.
1300 Sumner Avenue
Cleveland, OH 44115-2851
(216) 241-7333 Fax: (216) 241-0105
Officer: John H. Addington, Exec. Dir.

FIRE SUPPRESSION SYSTEMS ASSN.
5024-R Campbell Blvd.
Baltimore, MD 21236
(410) 931-8100 Fax: (410) 931-8111
Officer: Calvin K. Clemons, CAE,
   Exec. Dir.

FIREARM & SECURITY TRAINER MANAGEMENT ASSN.
P.O. Box 326
Willow Grove, PA 19090-0326
(800) 673-7825 Fax: (215) 657-1579
Officer: Joseph L. Chernicoff, Dir.

HOME AUTOMATION ASSOCIATION
808 17th Street, N.W., Suite 200
Washington, D.C. 20006
(202) 223-9669 Fax: (202) 223-9569
Officer: Charlie McGrath

INDEPENDENT ARMORED CAR OPERATORS ASSOCIATION (IACOA)
102 East Avenue J
Lancaster, CA 93535
(805) 726-9864 Fax: (805) 949-7877
Officer: John Margaritis, Secy.

INFORMATION SYSTEMS AUDIT & CONTROL ASSOCIATION
3701 Algonquin Road, Suite 1010
Rolling Meadows, IL 60008
(847) 253-1545 Fax: (847) 253-1443
Officer: Susan Caldwell, Exec. Dir.

INFORMATION TECHNOLOGY INDUSTRY COUNCIL (ITI)
1250 I Street, Suite 200
Washington, DC 20005
(202) 737-8888 Fax: (202) 638-4922
Officer: John L. Pickitt, Pres.

INSTITUTE OF ELECTRICAL & ELECTRONICS ENGINEERS (IEEE)
345 East 47th Street
New York, NY 10017-2394
(212) 705-7900 Fax: (212) 752-4929
Officer: Theodore Hissey, Exec. Dir.

INSTITUTE OF INTERNAL AUDITORS
249 Maitland Avenue
Altamonte Springs, FL 32701-4201
(407) 830-7600 Fax: (407) 831-5171
Officer: Willliam Bishop, Pres.

INSTITUTE OF NUCLEAR MATERIALS MANAGEMENT
60 Revere Drive, Suite 500
Northbrook, IL 60062
(847) 480-9573 Fax: (847) 480-9282
Officer: Barbara A. Scott, Exec. Dir.

INTERNATIONAL ASSOCIATION FOR COMPUTER SYSTEMS SECURITY (IACSS)
Six Swarthmore Lane
Dix Hills, NY 11746
(516) 499-1616 Fax: (516) 462-9178
Officer: Robert J. Wilk, Pres.

INTERNATIONAL ASSOCIATION FOR HEALTHCARE SECURITY AND SAFETY (IAHSS)
P.O. Box 637
Lombard, IL 60148
(630) 953-0990 Fax: (630) 950-1786
Officer: Bonnie Michelman, Pres.

INTERNATIONAL ASSOCIATION OF CAMPUS LAW ENFORCEMENT ADMINISTRATORS (IACLEA)
638 Prospect Avenue
Hartford, CT 06105-4298
(860) 586-7517 Fax: (860) 586-7550
Officer: Peter Berry, Exec. Dir.

INTERNATIONAL ASSOCIATION OF CHIEFS OF POLICE (IACP)
515 N. Washington Street
Alexandria, VA 22314
(703) 836-6767 Fax: (703) 836-4543
Officer: Daniel N. Rosenblatt, Exec. Dir.

INTERNATIONAL ASSOCIATION OF CREDIT CARD INVESTIGATORS (IACCI)
1620 Grant Avenue
Novato, CA 94947
(415) 897-8800 Fax: (415) 898-0798
Officer: Susan Race-Sylstra, Exec. Dir.

INTERNATIONAL ASSOCIATION OF PROFESSIONAL SECURITY CONSULTANTS (IAPSC)
808 17th Street, N.W., Suite 200
Washington, DC 20006
(202) 223-9669 Fax: (202) 223-9569
Officer: Claire Shanley, Exec. Dir.

INTERNATIONAL ASSOCIATION OF SECURITY SERVICES
P.O. Box 8202
Northfield, IL 60093
(312) 973-7712
Officer: Howard W. Ross, Exec. Dir.

INTERNATIONAL FENCE INDUSTRY ASSOCIATION (IFIA)
5300 Memorial Drive, Suite 116
Stone Mountain, GA 30083
(404) 299-5413 Fax: (404) 299-8927
Officer: Frederic G. Dempsey, Jr., CAE, Exec. VP

INTERNATIONAL GRAPHOANALYSIS SOCIETY
111 N. Canal Street
Chicago, IL 60606
(312) 930-9446 Fax: (312) 930-5903
Officer: Brett Hallongren

INTERNATIONAL NARCOTIC ENFORCEMENT OFFICERS ASSN.
112 State Street
Albany, NY 12207
(518) 463-6232 Fax: (518) 432-3378
Officer: John J. Bellizzi, Exec. Dir.

INTERNATIONAL MASS RETAILING ASSOCIATION (IMRA)
1700 N. Moore Street, Suite 2250
Arlington, VA 22209
(703) 841-2300 Fax: (703) 841-1184
Officer: Robert Verdisco, Pres.

INTERNATIONAL PERSONNEL MANAGEMENT ASSN.

1617 Duke Street
Alexandria, VA 22314
(703) 549-7100 Fax: (703) 684-0948
Officer: Donald T. Tichenor, CAE,
Exec. Dir.

INTERNATIONAL SECURITY MANAGEMENT ASSN. (ISMA)

P.O. Box 623
Buffalo, IA 52728
(319) 381-4008 Fax: (800) 568-1894
Officer: Gary Balonier, Pres.

INTERNATIONAL SOCIETY OF FIRE SERVICE INSTRUCTORS

50 Main Street
Ashland, MA 01721
(508) 881-5800 Fax: (508) 881-6829
Officer: Kristine Meyer, CEO

JEWELERS SECURITY ALLIANCE OF U.S.

6 E. 45th Street
New York, NY 10017
(212) 687-0328 Fax: (212) 808-9168
Officer: John J. Kennedy

JUSTICE RESEARCH & STATISTICS ASSOCIATION

444 North Capitol Str., N.W., Suite 445
Washington, DC 20001
(202) 624-8560 Fax: (202) 624-5269

NATIONAL ALARM ASSOCIATION OF AMERICA

811 East Third
Dayton, OH 45402
(800) 283-6285
Officer: Gene Riddlebaugh

NATIONAL ARMORED CAR ASSN., INC. (NACA)

1023 15th Street, N.W., Suite 700
Washington, DC 20005
(202) 289-1780 Fax: (202) 842-3275
Officer: Larry Sabbath

NATIONAL ASSOCIATION OF CHIEFS OF POLICE (NACP)

3801 Biscayne Blvd.
Miami, FL 33137
(305) 573-0202 Fax: (305) 573-9819
Officer: Donna Shepherd, Exec. Dir.

NATIONAL ASSOCIATION OF LEGAL INVESTIGATORS (NALI)

4 South 29th Street
Belleville, IL 62223-6714
(800) 266-6254
Officer: Anthony M. Golec

NATIONAL ASSOCIATION OF PRIVATE SECURITY INDUSTRIES (NAPSI)

P.O. Box 59349
Dallas, TX 75229
(214) 404-9191 Fax: (214) 404-8997
Officer: Walter Neuls, Exec. Dir.

NATIONAL ASSOCIATION OF SECURITY COMPANIES (NASCO)

2670 Union Avenue, Extd., Suite 710
Memphis, TN 38112
(901) 323-0173
Officer: Gayle M. Simonton, Exec. Dir.

NATIONAL ASSOCIATION OF SURETY BOND PRODUCERS

5301 Wisconsin Ave., N.W., Suite 450
Washington, D.C. 20015
(202) 686-3700 Fax: (202) 686-3656
Officer: J. Martin Huber, Exec. V.P.

NATIONAL BURGLAR AND FIRE ALARM ASSOCIATION (NBFAA)

7101 Wisconsin Avenue, Suite 901
Bethesda, MD 20814-4805
(301) 907-3202 Fax: (301) 907-7897
Officer: James A. Synk, Exec. Dir.

NATIONAL CABLE TELEVISION ASSN.

1724 Massachusetts Ave., N.W.
Washington, D.C. 20036-1969
(202) 775-3550 Fax: (202) 775-3604
Officer: Decker Anstrom, Pres.

NATIONAL COMPUTER SECURITY ASSOCIATION (NCSA)

10 S. Courthouse Avenue
Carlisle, PA 17013
(717) 258-1816 Fax: (717) 243-8642
Officer: Robert C. Bales, Exec. Dir.

NATIONAL CONSUMERS LEAGUE

1701 K Street, Suite 1200
Washington, DC 20006
(202) 835-3323 Fax: (202) 835-0747
Officer: Linda F. Golodner, Pres.

NATIONAL COORDINATING COUNCIL ON EMERGENCY MANAGEMENT

111 Park Place
Falls Church, VA 22046-4513
(703) 538-1795 Fax: (703) 241-5603
Officer: Elizabeth Armstrong, Exec. Dir.

NATIONAL COUNCIL OF INVESTIGATION & SECURITY SERVICES (NCISS)

P.O. Box 755
Des Moines, Iowa 50303
(800) 445-8408 Fax: (515) 224-1014
Officer: Gary Kuty, Pres.

NATIONAL CRIME PREVENTION INSTITUTE (NCPI)

University of Louisville
Louisville, Kentucky 40292
(502) 852-6987 Fax: (502) 852-6990
Officer: Wilbur Rykert, PhD., Dir.

NATIONAL FIRE PROTECTION ASSN. (NFPA)

P.O. Box 9101 Batterymarch Park
Quincy, MA 02269
(617) 770-3000 Fax: (617) 770-0700
Officer: Anthony R. O'Neill, V.P.

NATIONAL FIRE SPRINKLER ASSN.

Route 22 & Robin Hill Park, Box 1000
Patterson, NY 12563
(914) 878-4200 Fax: (914) 878-4215
Officer: John A. Viniello, Pres.

NATIONAL INSTITUTE OF STANDARDS & TECHNOLOGY

Building 820, Room 426
Gaithersburg, MD 20899
(301) 975-3411 Fax: (301) 948-0279
Officer: Stuart Katzke, Div. Chief, Comp. Sec.

NATIONAL FORENSIC CENTER

17 Temple Terrace
Lawrenceville, NJ 08648
(609) 883-0550 Fax: (609) 883-7622
Officer: Betty S. Lipscher, Dir.

NATIONAL INDEPENDENT BANK EQUIPMENT & SYSTEMS ASSN.

1411 Peterson
Park Ridge, IL 60068
(847) 825-8419 Fax: (847) 825-8445
Officer: Ann Walk, Exec. Dir.

NATIONAL INSURANCE CRIME BUREAU

10330 S. Roberts Road, Suite 3A
Palos Hills, IL 60465
(708) 430-2430 Fax: (708) 430-2446
Officer: John Diliberto, Pres.

NATIONAL SAFETY COUNCIL

1121 Spring Lake Drive
Itasca, IL 60143-3201
(708) 285-1121 Fax: (708) 285-1315
Officer: Jerry Scannell, Pres.

NATIONAL SECURITY INDUSTRIAL ASSN.

1025 Connecticut Ave., N.W., Suite 300
Washington, DC 20036
(202) 775-1440 Fax: (202) 775-1309
Officer: Thomas C. Richards, Pres.

PETROLEUM INDUSTRY SECURITY COUNCIL

P.O. Box 73567
Houston, TX 77273-3567
(713) 397-7464 Fax: (713) 397-7531
Officer: Betty Burdett, Exec. Dir.

RISK & INSURANCE MANAGEMENT SOCIETY (RIMS)

655 Third Avenue, 2nd Floor
New York, NY 10017
(212) 286-9292 Fax: (212) 986-9716
Officer: Gene Ricci, Exec. Dir.

SECURITY COMPANIES ORGANIZED FOR LEGISLATIVE ACTION (SCOLA)

1023 15th Street, N.W., 7th Floor
Washington, DC 20005
(202) 289-1780 Fax: (202) 842-3275
Officer: Lawrence Sabbath, V.P.

SECURITY INDUSTRY ASSOCIATION (SIA)

635 Slaters Lane, Suite 110
Alexandria, VA 22314
(703) 683-2075 Fax: (703) 683-2469
Officer: Bob Ensinger, Dir. of Comm.

SOCIETY FOR HUMAN RESOURCE MANAGEMENT

606 N. Washington Street
Alexandria, VA 22314-1914
(703) 548-3440 Fax: (703) 836-0367
Officer: Michael R. Losey, Pres.

SOCIETY OF COMPETITIVE INTELLIGENCE PROFESSIONALS (SCIP)

1700 Diagonal Road, Suite 520
Alexandria, VA 22314
(703) 739-0696 Fax: (703) 739-2524
Officer: Guy Kolb, Exec. Dir.

SOCIETY OF FIRE PROTECTION ENGINEERS

One Liberty Square
Boston, MA 02109
(617) 482-0686 Fax: (617) 482-8184
Officer: D. Peter Lund, Exec. Dir.

WORLD ASSN. OF DETECTIVES (WAD)

P.O. Box 22022
San Francisco, CA 94122
(800) 962-0516 Fax: (415) 342-1002
Officer: Sam Webster, Exec. Dir.

WORLD ASSOCIATION OF DOCUMENT EXAMINERS (WADE)

111 N. Canal Street
Chicago, IL 60606
(312) 930-9446 Fax: (312) 930-5903
Officer: Corinne Lamb, Admin.

CANADA

THE INTERNATIONAL FOUNDATION FOR PROTECTION OFFICERS

105-150 Crowfoot Crescent, N.W.,
    Suite 1015
Calgary, Canada T3G 3T2
(403) 932-7785 Fax: (403) 932-9521
U.S. Address:
Bellingham Business Park
4200 Meridian, Suite 200
Bellingham, WA 98226
(360) 733-1571 Fax: (360) 671-4329
Officer: Sandy Davies, Exec. Dir.

Security Periodicals

ANNUALS/BIENNIALS

BEST SAFETY DIRECTORY

A. M. Best Company
Ambest Road
Oldwick, NJ 08858
(908) 439-2200 Fax: (908) 439-3296
Two-volume set: $50

FORENSIC SERVICES DIRECTORY

National Forensic Center
17 Temple Terrace
Lawrenceville, NJ 08648
(609) 883-0550 Fax: (609) 883-7622
Editor: Betty S. Lipscher

INSURANCE FACTS

Insurance Information Institute
110 William Street
New York, NY 10038
(212) 669-9200 Fax: (212) 732-1916

LEGAL NEWSLETTERS IN PRINT
Infosources Publishing
140 Norma Road
Teaneck, NJ 07666
(201) 836-7072
Editor: Arlene L. Eis
Subscription: $90/yr.

SECURITY LETTER SOURCE BOOK
Security Letter
166 East 96th Street
New York, NY 10128
(212) 348-1553 Fax: (212) 534-2957
Editor: Robert D. McCrie, CPP
Biennial: $75

JOURNALS

BUSINESS INSURANCE WEEKLY
Crain Communications
740 N. Rush Street
Chicago, IL 60611
(312) 649-5398 Fax: (312) 280-3174
Editor: Paul Winston
Weekly

CAMPUS LAW ENFORCEMENT JOURNAL
International Association of Campus Law
   Enforcement Administrators
638 Prospect Avenue
Hartford, CT 06105
(860) 586-7517 Fax: (860) 586-7550
Editor-in-Chief: Peter Berry, CAE
Bi-monthly

CONSTRUCTION RISK MANAGEMENT
International Risk Management
   Institute, Inc.
12222 Merit Drive, Suite 1660
Dallas, TX 75251-2217
(214) 960-7693 Fax: (214) 960-6037
Editor: W. Jeffrey Woodward, CPCU
Updated quarterly; Subscription:
$226/yr.

CRYPTOLOGIA
U. S. Military Academy
Dept. of Mathematical Sciences
West Point, NY 10996
(914) 938-3200
Editor: Brian J. Winkel
Subscription: Quarterly; $44/yr.

DISASTER RECOVERY JOURNAL
P.O. Box 510110, 11337 St. Johns
   Church Road
St. Louis, MO 63151-0110
(314) 894-0276
Editor: Richard L. Arnold
Subscription: Quarterly; Free

FBI LAW ENFORCEMENT BULLETIN
FBI Academy, Madison Bldg., Room 209
Quantico, VA 22135
(703) 640-8666 Fax: (703) 640-1474
Subscription: Monthly; $19.00/yr.
 Professional journal for civilian and law
enforcement community.

INFORMATION SYSTEMS SECURITY
Auerbach Publications
31 St. James Avenue
Boston, MA 02116
(617) 423-2020
Subscription: Quarterly; $125/yr.

THE LEGAL INVESTIGATOR
National Association of Legal
   Investigators
P.O. Box 3254
Alton, IL 62002
(800) 266-6254 Fax: (618) 465-1506
Subscription: Quarterly; $45/yr.

LIBRARY & ARCHIVAL SECURITY
The Haworth Press, Inc.
10 Alice Street
Binghamton, NY 13904
(607) 722-5857
Editor: Bruce A. Shuman
Subscription: Quarterly; $95/yr.

MILITARY POLICE JOURNAL
U.S. Army M.P. School
Ft. McClellan, AL 36205-5030
(205) 848-4326
Editor: Kay Mundy
Biannual

SECURITY TECHNOLOGY & DESIGN
850 Busse Highway
Park Ridge, IL 60068
(847) 692-5940 Fax: (847) 692-4604
Editor: Steve Lasky
Subscription: Monthly; Free

NEWSLETTERS/NEWS SERVICES

ACJS TODAY
Academy of Criminal Justice Sciences
Northern Kentucky University
402 Nunn Hall
Highland Heights, KY 41076
(606) 572-5634 Fax: (606) 572-6665
Subscription included in ACJS
    membership.

AMERICAN POLYGRAPH ASSOCIATION NEWSLETTER, AND POLYGRAPH JOURNAL QUARATERLY
American Polygraph Association
P.O. Box 1061
Severna Park, MD 21146
(800) 272-8037
Editor: Norman Ansley
Subscription: Bi-monthly newsletter

BANK FRAUD
Bank Administration Institute
    Foundation
One North Franklin
Chicago, IL 60606
(312) 553-4600 Fax: (312) 683-2379
Managing Editor: Richard G. Kemmer
Subscription: Monthly; $174/yr.

BANK SECURITY REPORT
R.I.A. Group
395 Hudson Street
New York, NY 10014
(212) 971-5000
Editor: Susan Gordon
Subscription: Monthly

CAMPUS SECURITY REPORT
Rusting Publications
402 Main Street, P.O. Box 190
Fort Washington, NY 11050
(516) 883-1440
Editor: Robert R. Rusting
Subscription: Monthly; $199/yr.

CARD TECHNOLOGY TODAY
Publ. by SJB Services
576 Fifth Avenue, Suite 1103
New York, NY 10036
(212) 221-5000 Fax: (212) 221-5958
Subscription: Monthly; $674/yr.

CKC REPORT
The Hotel Technology Newsletter
Chervenak, Keane & Co.
307 E. 44th Street
New York, NY 10017
(212) 966-8230 Fax: (212) 983-5275
Editor: Larry Chervenak
Subscription: 10 issues; $180/yr.

CODES AND STANDARDS
Kelly P. Reynolds & Assoc., Inc.
833 W. Chicago Avenue, Suite 2000
Chicago, IL 60622
(312) 829-6000, (800) 950-CODE,
Fax: (312) 829-8855
Editor: Kelly Reynolds
Subscription: Monthly; $75/yr.

COMPUTER SECURITY
Computer Security Institute
600 Harrison Avenue
San Francisco, CA 94107
(415) 905-2310
Subscription: Bimonthly; part of membership services.

COMPUTER SECURITY DIGEST
Computer Protection Systems, Inc.
12275 Appletree
Plymouth, MI 48170
(313) 459-8787 Fax: (313) 459-2720
Editor: Jack Bologna
Subscription: Monthly; $125/yr.

DRUG ABUSE & ALCOHOLISM NEWSLETTER
Vista Hill Foundation
2355 Northside Drive, 3rd Floor
San Diego, CA 92108
(619) 563-1770
Editor: Marc A. Schuckit, MD
10 months; Free

EDPACS
The EDP Audit Control and Security
  Newsletter
P.O. Box 129
Hillsboro, TN 37342
(615) 728-2421
Editor: Belden Menkus
Subscription: Monthly, $152/yr.

THE EXPERT AND THE LAW
National Forensic Center
17 Temple Terrace
Lawrenceville, NJ 08648
(609) 883-0550, (800) 526-5177
Editor: Betty Lipscher
Subscription: Bimonthly; $100/yr.

THE EXPERT WITNESS JOURNAL
Seak, Inc.
P.O. Box 729
Falmouth, MA 02541
(508) 548-7023
Editor: Steven Babitsky, JD
Subscription: Monthly; $95/yr.

FORENSIC ACCOUNTING REVIEW
Computer Protection Systems, Inc.
12275 Appletree
Plymouth, MI 48170
(313) 459-8787 Fax: (313) 459-2720
Editor: Jack Bologna
Subscription: Monthly; $125/yr.

HOSPITAL SECURITY & MANAGEMENT
Rusting Publications
402 Main Street, P.O. Box 190
Fort Washington, NY 11050
(516) 883-1440
Editor: Robert R. Rusting
Subscription: Monthly; $189/yr.

IFAREPORTS
(Formerly The Stolen Art Alert)
International Foundation for Art
  Research
500 Fifth Avenue, Suite 1234
New York, NY 10110
(212) 391-6234
Editor: Dr. Constance Lowrenthal
Subscription: 10 issues; $65/yr.

THE JOURNAL OF POLYGRAPH SCIENCE
National Training Center of Polygraph
  Science
200 W. 57th Street, Suite 1400
New York, NY 10019
(212) 755-5241
Editor: Richard O. Arther
Subscription: Bimonthly; $76/yr.

LIPMAN REPORT
Guardsmark, Inc.
22 S. 2nd Street
Memphis, TN 38103
(901) 522-6000 Fax: (901) 522-6013
Editor: Ira A. Lipman
Subscription: Monthly; $60

NATIONAL CRIMINAL JUSTICE REFERENCE SERVICE
User Services, Dept. 2
Rockville, MD 28050
(301) 251-5500, (800) 732-3277

PERSONAL IDENTIFICATION NEWS
Warfel & Miller
12300 Twinbrook Parkway, Suite #300
Rockville, MD 20852
(301) 881-6668 Fax: (301) 881-2554
Editor: Ben Miller
Subscription: Monthly; $345/yr.

THE PETER BERLIN REPORT ON SHRINKAGE CONTROL
Peter Berlin Consulting Group
380 N. Broadway
Jericho, NY 11753
(516) 932-0450 Fax: (516) 932-9393
Editor: Peter Berlin
Subscription: 10 issues; $135

PRIVATE SECURITY CASE LAW REPORTER
Strafford Publications, Inc.
590 Dutch Valley Road, N.E.
Atlanta, GA 30324-0729
(404) 881-1141 Fax: (404) 881-0074
Editor: Jennifer Vaughan
Subscription: 10 issues; $292/yr.

PROTECTION OF ASSETS BULLETIN
The Merritt Company
P.O. Box 955
Santa Monica, CA 90406
(800) 638-7597, (310) 450-7234
Fax: (310) 396-4563
Editor: Timothy J. Walsh, CPP
Subscription: Monthly; $397/yr.

THE RISK REPORT
International Risk Management
    Institute, Inc.
12222 Merit Drive, Suite 1660
Dallas, TX 75251-2217
(214) 960-7693 Fax: (214) 960-6037
Editor: Jack P. Gibson, CPCU, CLU
Subscription: Monthly; $159/yr.

SIA
Security Industry Association
635 Slaters Lane, Suite 110
Alexandria, VA 22314
(703) 683-2075 Fax: (703) 683-2469
Monthly for the members of SIA.

SECURITY DIRECTORS DIGEST
Washington Crime News Services
3918 Prosperity Avenue, Suite 318
Fairfax, VA 22031-3334
(703) 573-1600

Editor: Betty B. Bosarge
Subscription: Weekly; $345/yr.
Publishes also: *Narcotics Control Digest;
Enforcement & Prevention Digest; C.J.
Training & Management Digest.*

SECURITY LAW NEWSLETTER
Crime Control Research Corp.
1063 Thomas Jefferson Street, N.W.
Washington, DC 20007
(202) 337-2700
Editor: Eva F. Sherman
Subscription: Monthly; $297/yr.

SECURITY LETTER
166 E. 96th Street
New York, NY 10128
(212) 348-1553 Fax: (212) 534-2957
Editor: Robert D. McCrie, CPP
Subscription: Semimonthly; $188/yr.

SECURITY MANAGEMENT BULLETIN
Protecting Property, People & Assets
Bureau of Business Practice
24 Rope Ferry Road
Waterford, CT 06386
(203) 442-4365
Subscription: Bi-monthly; $120/yr.

SECURITY & SPECIAL POLICE LEGAL UPDATE
Americans for Effective Law Enforcement
5519 N. Cumberland Avenue, Suite 1008
Chicago, IL 60656-1471
(312) 763-2800
Editor: Bernard J. Farber
Subscription: Monthly; $188/yr.

SPARKS OF INTEREST
ANSUL Fire Protection
1 Stanton Street
Marinette, WI 54143-2542
(715) 735-7411 Fax: (715) 732-3477
Editor: Paul Gregory
Quarterly
For distributors, customers, and friends
of ANSUL.

TRADE PUBLICATIONS

ASSETS PROTECTION
Assets Protection Publishing
P.O. Box 5323
Madison, WI 53705
(608) 877-1409
Editor: Paul Shaw
Subscription: 6 issues; $72/yr.

COMPUTING & COMMUNICATIONS LAW & PROTECTION
Assets Protection Publishing
P.O. Box 5323
Madison, WI 53705
(608) 877-1409
Editor: Paul Shaw
Subscription: Monthly; $84/yr.

ID SYSTEMS
Helmers Publishing, Inc.
174 Concord Street, P.O. Box 874
Peterborough, NH 03458-0874
(603) 924-9631 Fax: (603) 924-7408
Editor: Mary Langen
Subscription: Monthly; $55/yr.

INFOSECURITY NEWS
498 Concord Street
Framingham, MA 01701-2357
(508) 879-9792 Fax: (508) 872-1153
Editor: David Bernstein
Subscription: Monthly; Free for anyone in security.

LAW AND ORDER
Hendon, Inc.
1000 Skokie Blvd.
Wilmette, IL 60091
(847) 256-8555 Fax: (847) 256-8574
Editor: Bruce W. Cameron
Subscription: Monthly; $22/yr.

LAW ENFORCEMENT NEWS
John Jay College of Criminal Justice
899 Tenth Avenue
New York, NY 10019
(212) 237-8442
Editor: Peter Dodenhoff
Subscription: $22/yr.

LOCKSMITH LEDGER INTERNATIONAL
Locksmith Publishing Corp.
850 Busse Highway
Park Ridge, IL 60068-2382
(847) 692-5940 Fax: (847) 692-4604
Editor: Gale Johnson
Subscription: 15 issues; $38/yr.

THE NATIONAL LOCKSMITH
National Publishing Company
1533 Burgundy Parkway
Streamwood, IL 60107
(630) 837-2044 Fax: (630) 837-1210
Editor: Marc Goldberg
Subscription: $38/yr.

POLICE THE LAW OFFICER MAGAZINE
Hare Publications
6300 Yarrow Drive
Carlsbad, CA 92009
(619) 438-2511 Fax: (619) 931-5809
Editor: Randall Resch
Subscription: Monthly; $21.95/yr.

POLICE & SECURITY NEWS
Days Communications, Inc.
1690 Quarry Road
Kulpsville, PA 19443
(215) 538-1240
Editor: James Devery
Subscription: Bi-monthly; $14.00/yr.

RECORD
Factory Mutual Engineering Corp.
1151 Boston-Providence Turnpike
P.O. Box 9102
Norwood, MA 02062
(617) 762-4300
Editor: Amy Mastrodomenico
Subscription: Quarterly; $25/yr.

SECURITY
Cahners Publishing Co.
P.O. Box 5080, 1350 E. Touhy Avenue
Des Plaines, IL 60018
(847) 635-8800
Editor: Bill Zalud
Subscription: Monthly; $79.90/yr. Free to qualified subscribers.

SECURITY DEALER

PTN Publishing Corp.
445 Board Hollow Road, Suite 21
Melville, NY 11747
(516) 845-2700 Fax: (516) 845-2736
Editor: Susan A. Brady
Subscription: Monthly; $50/yr.

SECURITY DISTRIBUTING & MARKETING

Cahners Publishing
P.O. Box 5080, 1350 E. Touhy Avenue
Des Plaines, IL 60018
(847) 635-8800
Editor: Bill Zalud
Subscription: Monthly; $79.90/yr. Free to
qualified subscribers.

SECURITY MANAGEMENT

American Society of Industrial Security
   (ASIS)
1655 N. Ft. Myer Drive, Suite 1200
Arlington, VA 22209
(703) 522-5800 Fax: (703) 243-4954
Editor: Mary Alice Crawford
Subscription: Monthly

SECURITY NEWS

Terra Publishing
P.O. Box 460 Center Street Ext.
Salamanca, NY 14779
(800) 992-3488
Editor: Sandra Jackson
Subscription: Monthly; Free

SECURITY SALES

Bobit Publishing Co.
2512 Artesia Blvd.
Redondo Beach, CA 90278
(310) 376-8788 Fax: (310) 376-9043
Editor: Jason Knott
Subscription: Monthly; $35/yr.

SOUND & VIDEO CONTRACTOR

Intertec Publishing Corp.
P.O. Box 12901
Overland Park, KS 66282-2901
(913) 341-1300 Fax: (913) 967-1905
Editor: Ted Uzzle
Subscription: Monthly; $65/yr.

SECURITY LITERATURE

HIGHWAY LOSS REDUCTION STATUS REPORT

Insurance Institute for Highway Safety
1005 N. Glebe Road
Arlington, VA 22201
(703) 247-1500
Editor: Anne Fleming
Subscription: Monthly; Free

TRAINING PROGRAMS & RESOURCES

ALLIANCE OF AMERICAN INSURERS

1501 Woodfield Road, Suite 400 West
Schaumburg, IL 60173-4980
(847) 330-8500 Fax: (847) 330-8602
Contact: Roger S. Lawson, Pres.

AMERICAN MANAGEMENT ASSOCIATION

135 W. 50th Street
New York, New York 10020-1201
(212) 586-8100 Fax: (212) 903-8168
Contact: David Fagiano, Pres.

AMERICAN SECURITY EDUCATORS

P.O. Box 1337
Downey, CA 90240
(310) 928-1847 Fax: (310) 869-6906
Contact: James W. Gonos, Pres.

AMERICAN SOCIETY FOR INDUSTRIAL SECURITY (ASIS)

1655 N. Ft. Myer Drive, Suite 1200
Arlington, VA 22209
(703) 522-5800 Fax: (703) 243-4954
Contact: Michael J. Stack, Exec. Dir.

AMERICAN SOCIETY OF LAW ENFORCEMENT TRAINERS (ASLET)

P.O. Box 361
Lewes, DE 19958
(302) 645-4080 Fax: (302) 645-4084
Contact: Steve Bunting, Exec. Dir.

ANSUL FIRE SCHOOL

One Stanton Street
Marinette, WI 54143
(715) 735-7411
Contact: James Anderla
Services: Hands-on fire training for over
35 years. An extensive program of seminars and training resources available
throughout the year. First aid fire training
schools conducted May through October.

BANK ADMINISTRATION INSTITUTE

1 North Franklin Street, 10th Floor
Chicago, IL 60606
(312) 553-4600 Fax: (312) 683-2426
Contact: Ronald G. Burke, Pres/CEO

COMPUTER SECURITY INSTITUTE

600 Harrison Street
San Francisco, CA 94107
(415) 905-2310 Fax: (415) 905-2218
Contact: Patrice Rapalus

CRIMINAL JUSTICE CENTER

John Jay College of Criminal Justice
899 10th Avenue
New York, NY 10019
(212) 237-8000
See also: Security Management Institute

CRIMINAL JUSTICE INSTITUTE

Broward Community College
3501 S. W. Davie Road
Ft. Lauderdale, FL 33314
(954) 475-6793 Fax: (954) 475-6796
Contact: Wayne Madole

EASTERN KENTUCKY UNIVERSITY

Training Resource Center
300 Stratton Bldg.
Richmond, KY 40475
(606) 622-1498 Fax: (606) 622-6399
Contact: Bruce Wolford

EXECUTIVE PROTECTION INSTITUTE

(Formerly N. Mountain Pines Training
    Center)

Arcadia Manor, Route 2, Box 3645
Berryville, VA 22611
(540) 955-1128
Contact: Richard W. Kobetz, Exec. Dir.
Services: Managing security systems,
workplace violence, executive VIP protection, business intelligence, yacht and mar-
itime security, 7-day program on providing
exec. protection in May & October.

FEDERAL EMERGENCY MANAGEMENT AGENCY (FEMA)

500 C Street, S. W.
Washington, D.C. 20472
(202) 646-4600
Contact: Office of Public Affairs
Operates a training school in
Emmitsburg, MD. Maintains regional
offices for local assistance.

HORIZON INSTITUTE, INC.

P.O. Box 5757
Deltona, FL 32728-5757
(904) 789-3225 Fax: (904) 532-5969
Contact: Kathy Keller

INTERNATIONAL ASSOCIATION FOR HEALTHCARE SECURITY & SAFETY (IAHSS)

P.O. Box 637
Lombard, IL 60148
(630) 953-0990 Fax: (630) 950-1786
Contact: Bonnie Michelman, Pres.

INTERNATIONAL ASSOCIATION OF CHIEFS OF POLICE

515 N. Washington Street
Alexandria, VA 22314
(703) 836-6767 Fax: (703) 836-4543
Contact: Daniel N. Rosenblatt, Exec. Dir.

INVESTIGATION TRAINING INSTITUTE

P.O. Box 669
Shelburne, VT 05482
(802) 985-9123 Fax: (802) 985-9121
Contact: Edward R. Burke

JARVIS INTERNATIONAL INTELLIGENCE, INC.
11720 East 21st Street
Tulsa, OK 74129
(918) 437-1100 Fax: (918) 437-1191
Contact: Ray Jarvis, Pres; Cindy Jarvis, Exec. Asst.

JUSTICE RESEARCH AND STATISTICS ASSOCIATION
444 N. Capitol Street, N.W., Suite 445
Washington, DC 20001
(800) 732-3277 Fax: (202) 624-5269

MIS TRAINING INSTITUTE, INC.
498 Concord Street
Framingham, MA 01701-2357
(508) 879-7999 Fax: (508) 872-1153
Contact: Michael Sobol, Dir.

MSI
Formerly Mosler Anti-Crime Bureau
160 Benmont Avenue
Bennington, VT 05201
(802) 447-1503 Fax: (802) 442-3823
Contact: Bill Hogan

NATIONAL BURGLAR & FIRE ALARM ASSN.
7101 Wisconsin Avenue, Suite 901
Bethesda, MD 20814-4805
(301) 907-3202 Fax: (301) 907-7897
Contact: James A. Synk, Exec. Dir.

NATIONAL CRIME PREVENTION COUNCIL
1701 K Street, N.W., 2nd Floor
Washington, D.C. 20006
(202) 466-6272 (202) 296-1356
Contact: John A. Calhoun, Exec. Dir.

NATIONAL CRIME PREVENTION INSTITUTE
University of Louisville
Shelby Campus, Burhans Hall
Louisville, KY 40292
(502) 852-6987 Fax: (502) 852-6990
Contact: Wilbur Rykert, Ph.D., Dir.

NATIONAL CRISIS PREVENTION INSTITUTE
3315-K North 124th Street
Brookfield, WI 53005
(414) 783-5787 Fax: (414) 783-5906
Contact: Gail Zimdars

NATIONAL FIRE PROTECTION ASSN.
1 Batterymarch Park
Quincy, MA 02269
(617) 770-3000 Fax: (617) 770-0700
Contact: Anthony R. O'Neill, V.P.

NATIONAL RIFLE ASSOCIATION OF AMERICA (NRA)
11250 Waples Mill Road
Fairfax, VA 22030
(703) 267-1000 Fax: (703) 267-3957
Contact: Marion Hammer, Pres.

NATIONAL SAFETY COUNCIL
1121 Spring Lake Drive
Itasca, IL 60143
(708) 285-1121 Fax: (708) 285-1315
Contact: Jerry Scannell, Pres.

NOR-CAL TRAINING ACADEMY
NOR-CAL Bldg., 2016 Oakdale Avenue
San Francisco, CA 94124-2098
(415) 550-8282 Fax: (415) 821-1164
Contact: Robert A. Borisoff, CPP, Pres.
Moura Borisova, V.P.
Services: State licensing: firearms, baton, tear gas, hunter safety, security guards, firearm instructor, self-defense, rape prevention, loss prevention, security training, process serving. Also expert witness and court interpreter in Russian and Japanese.

PADGETT-THOMPSON
P.O. Box 8297
Overland Park, KS 66208
(800) 255-4141 or (913) 451-2900
Fax: (913) 491-2664

**PINKERTON CONSULTING &
INVESTIGATION SERVICES**
3100 West End Avenue, Suite 550
Nashville, TN 37203
(615) 385-3777 Fax: (615) 297-3901
Contact: Tom Newkirk

**PROFESSIONAL SECURITY TELEVISION
NETWORK (PSTN)**
Wescott Communications
1303 Marsh Lane
Carrollton, TX 75006-9977
(214) 417-4100

ROSS ENGINEERING, INC.
1400 Shepard Drive, #100
Sterling, VA 20164
(703) 450-2200 Fax: (703) 450-2204
Contact: James A. Ross, Pres.

SECURITY MANAGEMENT INSTITUTE
John Jay College of Criminal Justice
899 Tenth Avenue, Room 636
New York, NY 10019
(212) 237-8638 Fax: (212) 237-8637

SMITH & WESSON ACADEMY
2100 Roosevelt Avenue
Springfield, MA 01101
(413) 781-8300 Fax: (413) 736-0776
Contact: Barbara Grissom
Services: Offers training year around on
law enforcement firearms and defensive
tactics. Also offers civilian firearms
training.

WACKENHUT EDUCATION SERVICES
4200 Wackenhut Drive, #100
Palm Beach Gardens, FL 33410-4243
(561) 622-5656 Fax: (561) 691-6700
Contact: Dr. Michael Goodboe
Services: Conducts training and educational programs, instruction in firearms,
driving techniques, crisis and hostage
negotiations. Trains their own security
officers, supervisors, and managers. Also
does training for private locations.

Audio-Visual Distributors

ABBOTT, LANGER & ASSOCIATES
548 First Street
Crete, IL 60417
Tel: (708) 672-4200
Fax: (708) 672-4674

AIMS MEDIA
9710 DeSoto Avenue
Chatsworth, CA 91311
Tel: (800) 367-2467
Fax: (818) 341-6700

**ALA VIDEO/LIBRARY VIDEO
NETWORK**
320 York Road
Towson, MD 21204
Tel: (800) 441-TAPE
Fax: (410) 887-2091

**ALTERNATIVE COMPUTER
TECHNOLOGY**
7908 Cin-Day Road, Suite W
West Chester, OH 45069
Tel: (513) 755-1957
Fax: (513) 755-1958

AMERICAN HOSPITAL ASSOCIATION
1 North Franklin Street
Chicago, IL 60606
Tel: (312) 422-3000
Fax: (312) 422-4796

AMERICAN MEDIA, INC.
4900 University Avenue
W. Des Moines, IA 50266-6769
Tel: (515) 224-0919 and
(800) 262-2557
Fax: (515) 224-0256

AMERICAN POLYGRAPH ASSOCIATION
P.O. Box 8037
Chattanooga, TN 37414-0037
Tel: (800) 272-8037
Fax: (423) 894-5435

AMERICAN SOCIETY FOR INDUSTRIAL SECURITY
1655 N. Ft. Myer Drive, Suite 1200
Arlington, VA 22209
Tel: (703) 522-5800
Fax: (703) 243-4954

AMERICAN TRUCKING ASSOCIATION
2200 Mill Road
Alexandria, VA 22314
Tel: (703) 838-1700 and (800) ATA-LINE
Fax: (703) 548-1841

ARMA INTERNATIONAL
4200 Somerset Drive, Suite 215
Prairie Village, KS 66208
Tel: (800) 422-2762

ASSOCIATED GENERAL CONTRACTORS OF AMERICA
1957 E Street, N.W.
Washington, DC 20006
Tel: (202) 393-2040
Fax: (202) 347-4004

ASSOCIATION OF CERTIFIED FRAUD EXAMINERS
716 West Avenue
Austin, TX 78701
Tel: (512) 478-9070 and (800) 245-3321
Fax: (512) 478-9297

BANK ADMINISTRATION INSTITUTE
1 North Franklin Street, 10th Floor
Chicago, IL 60606
Tel: (312) 553-4600
Fax: (312) 683-2426

BANKERS TRAINING AND CONSULTING COMPANY
744 Office Parkway, Suite 150
St. Louis, MO 63141
Tel: (314) 567-6760 and (800) 264-7600
Fax: (800) 844-3637

BNA COMMUNICATIONS, INC.
9439 Key West Avenue
Rockville, MD 20850

Tel: (301) 948-0540 and
(800) 233-6067
Fax: (301) 294-6795

BUREAU OF BUSINESS PRACTICE
Prentice Hall
24 Rope Ferry Road
Waterford, CT 06386
Tel: (800) 876-9105
Fax: (860) 437-3555

BUSINESS & LEGAL REPORTS
39 Academy Street
Madison, CT 06443
Tel: (203) 245-7448 and (800) 727-5257
Fax: (203) 245-2559

BUTCHER COMPANIES
311 E. Thayer Avenue
Bismarck, ND 58501
Tel: (701) 224-1541
Fax: (701) 224-1097

BUTTERWORTH-HEINEMANN
225 Wildwood Avenue, Unit B
Woburn, MA 01601
Tel: (617) 928-2500 and (800) 366-2665
Fax: (617) 933-6333

CK COMMUNICATIONS
31 N. Erie
Toledo, OH 43624
Tel: (419) 243-7821
Fax: (419) 243-7826

COMMONWEALTH FILMS, INC.
223 Commonwealth Avenue
Boston, MA 02116
Tel: (617) 262-5634 and (800) 237-2244
Fax: (617) 262-6948

CORONET/MTI FILM & VIDEO
Processing Center
P.O. Box 2649
Columbus, OH 43216
Tel: (800) 777-8100
Fax: (614) 771-7364

CORVISION MEDIA
1359 Barclay Blvd.
Buffalo Grove, IL 60089
Tel: (847) 537-3100 and (800) 537-3130
Fax: (847) 537-3353

CRM FILM & VIDEO
2215 Faraday Avenue
Carlsbad, CA 92008
Tel: (800) 421-0833
Fax: (619) 931-5792

**EDUCATIONAL INSTITUTE OF THE
AMERICAN HOTEL & MOTEL ASSN.**
P.O. Box 1240
1407 S. Harrison Road
East Lansing, MI 48826
Tel: (517) 353-5500 and (800) 752-4567
Fax: (517) 353-5527

EDUCATIONAL RESOURCES, INC.
557 Whiteford Way
Lexington, SC 29072
Tel: (800) 333-8822
Fax: (803) 356-1946

ERNST & YOUNG
787 7th Avenue
New York, NY 10019
Tel: (212) 773-3000

EXCELLENCE IN TRAINING CORP.
11358 Aurora Avenue
Des Moines, IA 50322
Tel: (515) 276-6569 and (800) 747-6569
Fax: (515) 276-9476

**FILM LIBRARY—GREATER LOS
ANGELES CHAPTER, NATIONAL
SAFETY COUNCIL**
3450 Wilshire Blvd., Suite 700
Los Angeles, CA 90010
Tel: (213) 385-6461 and (800) 421-9585
Fax: (213) 385-8405

FOOD MARKETING INSTITUTE
800 Connecticut Avenue, N.W.
Washington, DC 20006
Tel: (202) 452-8444
Fax: (202) 429-4550

GOAL PRODUCTIONS, INC.
2623 E. Foothill Blvd., #101
Pasadena, CA 91107
Tel: (818) 584-9515
Fax: (818) 792-2709

GRIGGS PRODUCTIONS, INC.
5616 Geary
San Francisco, CA 94121
Tel: (415) 668-4200
Fax: (415) 668-6004

HOME CENTER INSTITUTE
5822 W. 74th Street
Indianapolis, IN 46278
Tel: (317) 299-0339
Fax: (317) 328-4354

HORIZON INSTITUTE, INC.
P.O. Box 5757
Deltona, FL 32728-5757
Tel: (904) 789-3225
Fax: (904) 532-5969

INDUSTRY TRAINING SYSTEMS CORP.
1303 Marsh Lane
Carrollton, TX 75006
Tel: (800) 727-2487
Fax: (214) 716-5352

INSTRUCTIONAL MEDIA CENTER
California State University—Hayward
Hayward, CA 94542
Tel: (510) 885-3778

JAMES C. SHAEFFER & ASSOC., INC.
655 Fairfield Court
Ann Arbor, MI 48108
Tel: (800) 968-9527
Fax: (313) 741-9528

JOHN E. REID & ASSOCIATES
250 S. Wacker Drive, Suite 1100
Chicago, IL 60606
Tel: (312) 876-1600 and (800) 255-5747
Fax: (312) 876-1743

LOSS PREVENTION SPECIALISTS
5415 Lake Howell Road, Suite 236
Winter Park, FL 32792-1088
Tel: (407) 671-8226 and (800) 366-5774
Fax: (407) 671-8249

MEDIAMIX PRODUCTIONS, INC.
180 Blackburn Road
Summit, NJ 07901
Tel: (908) 277-0058
Fax: (908) 277-0119

MIS TRAINING INSTITUTE
498 Concord Street
Framingham, MA 01702
Tel: (508) 879-7999
Fax: (508) 872-1153

MOSLER ANTI-CRIME BUREAU
160 Benmont Avenue
Bennington, VT 05201
Tel: (802) 442-6725
Fax: (802) 442-3823

NATIONAL ASSOCIATION OF CONVENIENCE STORES
1605 King Street
Alexandria, VA 22314-2792
Tel: (703) 684-3600
Fax: (703) 836-4564

NATIONAL BURGLAR & FIRE ALARM ASSN.
7101 Wisconsin Avenue, Suite 901
Bethesda, MD 20814
Tel: (301) 907-3202
Fax: (301) 907-7897

NATIONAL COMPUTER SECURITY ASSN.
10 S. Courthouse Avenue
Carlisle, PA 17013
Tel: (717) 258-1816 and (800) 488-4595
Fax: (717) 243-8642

NATIONAL COMPUTER SECURITY CENTER
Awareness Division
Attn: Y13/IAOC
Fort G.G. Meade, MD 20755-6000
Tel: (410) 766-8729

NATIONAL CRIME PREVENTION COUNCIL
1700 K Street, N.W., 2nd Floor
Washington, DC 20006-3817
Tel: (202) 466-6272
Fax: (202) 296-1356

NATIONAL CRIMINAL JUSTICE REFERENCE SERVICE
P.O. Box 6000
Rockville, MD 20849-6000
Tel: (301) 251-5500 and (800) 851-3420
Fax: (301) 953-3848

NATIONAL CRISIS PREVENTION INSTITUTE
3315-K N. 124th Street
Brookfield, WI 53005
Tel: (414) 783-5906
(800) 558-8976

NATIONAL FIRE PROTECTION ASSN.
P.O. Box 9101
1 Batterymarch Park
Quincy, MA 02269-9101
Tel: (617) 770-3000 and (800) 344-3555
Fax: (617) 770-0700

NATIONAL RETAIL FEDERATION
701 Pennsylvania Ave., N.W., Suite 710
Washington, DC 20004
Tel: (202) 783-7971
Fax: (202) 737-2849

NATIONAL SAFETY COUNCIL
1121 Spring Lake Drive
Itasca, IL 60143-3201
Tel: (708) 285-1121
Fax: (708) 285-1315

**NATIONAL TECHNICAL INFORMATION
SERVICES**
5285 Port Royal Road
Springfield, VA 22161
Tel: (703) 487-4650

NATIONAL TRAUMA SERVICES
3554 Front Street
San Diego, CA 92103
Tel: (619) 296-2811 and
(800) 398-2811

**PERFORMANCE DIMENSIONS
PUBLISHING**
P.O. Box 502
Powers Lake, WI 53159-0502
Tel: (800) 877-7413
Fax: (414) 279-3850

**PROFESSIONAL SECURITY TELEVISION
NETWORK**
1303 Marsh Lane
Carrollton, TX 75006
Tel: (800) 942-7786
Fax: (214) 716-5352

**PROFESSIONAL TRAINING
RESOURCES**
P.O. Box 439
Shaftsbury, VT 05262
Tel: (802) 447-7832
Fax: (800) 998-9400

PSYCHEMEDICS CORPORATION
5832 Uplander Way
Culver City, CA 90230
Tel: (310) 216-7776 and
(800) 522-7424
Fax: (310) 216-6662

PUBLIC RISK MANAGEMENT ASSN.
1815 N. Ft. Myer Drive, Suite 1020
Arlington, VA 22209-1805
Tel: (703) 528-7701
Fax: (703) 528-7966

RESOURCE NETWORK
122 S. Main Street, Suite 208
Harrisonburg, VA 22801
Tel: (540) 433-5750
Fax: (540) 433-5640

ROSS ENGINEERING, INC.
1400 Sheperd Drive
Sterling, VA 20164
Tel: (703) 450-2200
Fax: (703) 450-2204

**SCOTTI SCHOOL OF DEFENSIVE
DRIVING**
10 High Street, Suite 15
Medford, MA 02155
Tel: (617) 395-9156 and (800) 343-0046
Fax: (617) 391-8252

SECURESEARCH, INC.
3500 Pharmacy Avenue, Unit 4
Scarborough, Ontario, Canada
M1W 2T6
Tel: (416) 492-5349
Fax: (416) 492-3656

SECURITY TRAINING CORP.
P.O. Box 150310
Longview, TX 75615
Tel: (903) 759-6619
Fax: (903) 759-9208

**SOUTHWEST COOPERATIVE
FOUNDATION**
6020 W. 151st Street
Oak Forest, IL 60452
Tel: (708) 687-0900

VARIED DIRECTIONS, INC.
69 Elm Street
Camden, ME 04843
Tel: (207) 236-8506 and (800) 888-5236
Fax: (207) 236-4512

VIDEO PUBLISHING HOUSE, INC.
930 N. National Parkway, Suite 505
Schaumburg, IL 60173
Tel: (847) 517-8744 and (800) 824-8889
Fax: (847) 517-8750

VIDEO TRAINING, INC.
911 Western Avenue, Suite 210
Seattle, WA 98104
Tel: (800) 600-1555
Fax: (206) 682-1865

WICKERSTY & ASSOCIATES
P.O. Box 646
Bladensburg, MD 20710-0646
Tel: (301) 386-5425 and (800) 966-3866
Fax: (301) 386-5427

COMPUTER RESOURCES ON THE INTERNET

SECURITY MAGAZINE
http://www.secmag.com
Security products and services.

SECURITY MANAGEMENT
http://www.securitymanagement.com
The magazine for the American Society for Industrial Security. Has product,security services and membership information.

FRAUD INFORMATION FROM THE ASSOCIATION OF CERTIFIED FRAUD EXAMINERS
http://www.acfe.org

FRAUD INFORMATION FROM THE ALABAMA CHAPTER OF CFE'S ON FRAUD & INVESTIGATIONS
http://www.bham.net/users/jwrhymes/Fraud/Fraud.htm1

The Association of Certified Fraud Examiners and their Alabama chapter can provide information on fraud issues and investigative resources.

FEDERAL BUREAU INVESTIGATIONS
http://www.fbi.gov
The Federal Bureau Investigation (FBI) will identify how their resources can be used by the general public.

PRIVATE INVESTIGATOR MALL
http://www.pimall.com
The PI Mall can identify private investigation resources and other services.

SWITCHBOARD
http://www.switchboard.com
This switchboard can assist you in finding names associated with a telephone number. There are many other safety, security and investigative resources which can be searched on the Internet by searching the topic name or area of interest.

SIMON INFORMATION CENTER
http://www.simon-net.com
If you want to keep track of industry trends and happenings, this information service will help you do that. One of its most popular sections is the Employment Section. This center has more than 500 articles on security related issues on-line. The e-mail center for this service is simon@simon-net.com. To access this system you need either Netscape 2.0 browser or higher or AOL version 3.0.

BULLETIN BOARD SYSTEMS & DATA SERVICES

ASISNET
Information, Inc.
7700 Old Georgetown Road, 7th Floor
Bethesda, MD 20814
(301) 215-4688

Subject Index

A

Access cards, 252
Access control, 205, 256–22
  access control panel (ACP), 256–59
  access points:
    alarm masking, 263–64
    area loading, 264
    elevator, 263
    guard tour, 263
    time and attendance, 265–67
  alarms/codes by categories, 259–62
  antipassback (APB), 262–63
  authorized presence required, 265
  automated, 332
  building barrier elements, 329
  card reader access systems, 256, 258, 298–99
    card-encoding technologies, 298–99
    with keypad, 259
    magnetic stripe, 298–99
    proximity cards, 298–99
    Wiegand access card, 298–99
  cost of, 328
  defined, 328
  distributed processing systems, 258
  enable second authenticator, 265
  example of, 267–69
  fingerprinting, 331
  future of, 308–9
  hand geometry, 305, 330
  handwriting verification systems, 330
  and parking facilities, 337
  personal identification number (PIN), 330
  products/vendors, 298–99
  retinal scan, 331
  secondary verifications, examples of, 329
  smart cards, 331–32
  speech measurements, 331
  system coding, 259
  technologies, 328–34
  two-person control point, 264
  video comparator systems, 330
  See also Physical security
Acts between consenting adults, 275
Addressable vs. analog fire alarm systems, 169
Administrative countermeasures, 253–55
Aggravated assault, 273
Airports/aviation security, 116
  airborne terrorism, 111–12
  airport personnel, 114–16
    baggage/passenger matching, 115
    originating passenger/bag match, 115
    profile selectee or random
      passenger/baggage match, 115–16
    skycaps, 114
    ticket agents, 114
  baggage universe, 111
  explosives, detection of, 112–14
  profiling, 112
  skyjacking, 111–12
  unaware passengers, 112
Alarm masking access point, 263–64
Alarms, 62, 208, 251
  addressable vs. analog fire alarm systems, 169
  false, 64, 68–71
  separated by categories, 259–62
  silent, 251
Alaska, security licensing requirements, 39
American criminal justice system, 21–22
American Division Telegraph (ADT), 16

American Society for Industrial Security
  (ASIS), 22, 28–30, 67, 109, 310, 316
    and biometrics, 124
    Code of Ethics, 32
    Hallcrest II as reviewed by, 60–64
    Law Enforcement Council (1991), 97
    and professional standards, 42–43
Anglo-Saxon tithing system, 11
Antipassback (APB), 262–63
Applicants, screening requirements for, 38
Aquinas, Thomas, 9
Archive security, 141
Area loading access point, 264
Armed gate guards, 247
Armstrong v. *Sundance Entertainment Inc.*, 229
Arson, 56, 277, 283–85
ASIS, *See* American Society for Industrial
  Security (ASIS)
Assault, 277, 283
    aggravated, 273
Assessment/surveillance technologies, 326–28
Assets, definition of, 201
Assets protection, 187
Attorney, as investigative team member, 167
Audio-visual distributors, 408–13
Authorized presence required, 265
Automated access control, 332
Automated gates, 247
Automatic handguns, 281
Automatic handwriting verification systems, 330
Automatic teller machines (ATMs), 333–34
    fraud, 116, 117–19
Auto thefts, 274
Aviation security, *See* Airports/aviation security

B

Babylonian code, 4–5
Back-alley justice, 83
Background investigations, 288
    computerized, 255
Bad checks, 119–20, 286–88
Badges, 252
Baggage/passenger matching, 115
Baggage universe, 111
Banking/financial services security, 116–23
    and computers/computer security principles,
      123
    fraud, 116–20, 350, 353
      automatic teller machine (ATM) fraud,
        116, 117–19
      check fraud, 119–20

credit card fraud, 119
    inside abuse (defalcation), 119
    loan fraud, 119
  role of, 120–23
  smart cards, 117
Bank Protection Act (1968), 116
Bar code systems, 298–99, 310
Behavior, continuum of, 2–3
Bible, 4
Biometrics, 22, 124, 304–5
    fingerprinting, 124, 304, 331
    hand geometry, 305, 330
    keyboard rhythms, 305
    palm prints, 305
    retinal scans, 305, 331
    signature dynamics, 305
    voiceprint, 304
Blood feud, 3
Bobbies, 13
Bond servants, punishments applied to, 5
Bow Street Runners, 13
Branding, 8
Brank, 8
Brink's Armored Car service, 16
Brinks, Washington Perry, 16
Building barrier elements, 329
Building envelope, 249–51
Bureaucratic control, 184
Burglary, 56, 274–75, 277–78
Burlary Protection Council (1921), 17
Burns International, 16
Businesses/institutions:
    arson, 283–85
    assault, 283
    burglary, 277–78
    computer crime, 160–64, 291–93
    drugs in the workplace, 293
    falsified overtime, 290
    impact of crime on, 275–94
    larceny/theft, 277
    personal use of company supplies/equip-
      ment, 290–91
    robbery, 279–81, 283
    trespassing, 281–82
    vandalism, 282–83
    white-collar crime, 285–93
Butler v. *Acme Market*, 228

C

Cadix International Inc., 124
California, security licensing requirements, 40

Card Application Technology Center (Florida State University), 138
Card reader access systems, 256, 258, 298–99
 card-encoding technologies, 298–99
 with keypad, 259
 magnetic stripe, 298–99
 proximity cards, 298–99
 Wiegand access card, 298–99
Cargo seals, 159–60
Cash cards, 117
Cat-o'-nine tails, 8
Cause in fact, 224
CCTV, See Closed circuit television (CCTV)
Cellular phones, fraud in use of, 141
Central control technologies, 335–36
Certified Fraud Examiner (CFE), 316
Certified Fraud Investigator (CFI), 30
Certified Hospital Protection Administrator (CHPA), 30
Certified Protection Officer (CPO), 316
Certified Protection Professional (CPP), 30, 43
Changes in behavioral definitions, 31–33
Check fraud, 119–20, 277, 286–88
Check-kiting, 290
Child molesters, 275
Church law, 5
 free will concept, 6–7
 Inquisition, 6–7
 ordeal, 6
Citizen patrols, 62
Citizen's arrest, 11
Civil death, 5
Civil Service Act (1883), 15
Clearance by arrest, 80, 87
Clear zones, 246–47
Closed circuit television (CCTV), 247, 251, 253, 326–28, 335, 341
 color monitors at central stations, 302
 and employee privacy, 302
 miniaturization of cameras, 300–302
 products/vendors, 300–302
 solid-state cameras:
  advantages of, 300, 327–28
  cost of, 327
 video, operational requirements, 302
Code of conduct, police, 101–2
Code of Draco, 6
Code of ethics, 34–35
 ASIS, 32
Code of Justinian, 6
Colonial experience, and mutual protection concept, 14–15

Color of law, 100–101
Commercial burglary, 278
Commercial office building security, 137–41
 patrol, 139–41
 targets of theft, 139
 tenants, involvement in security program, 140–41
 See also Businesses/institutions
Commonwealth v. Leone, 102–3
Communications, 208
Communications security, 306
Communications technologies, 334–35
Community policing, 86–90
 community-based deployment strategies, 89–90
 community involvement, 89
 increased police accountability, 90
 problem-solving orientation, 89–90
Compensatory damages, 233–36
Compliance responsibility, hospitals, 129
Computer crime, 64, 65, 160–64, 277, 291–93
 accountability for, 165, 167
 computer manipulation crimes, 162–63
 data diddling, 291–92
 detecting, 165, 167
 hackers, 291
 hardware/software thefts, 163
 internal, 161–62
 logic bombs, 292
 preventing, 165, 167
 protecting/correcting, 165, 167
 salami slicing, 292
 scavenging, 292
 support of criminal enterprises, 163
 telecommunications crime, 162
 Trojan horse, 292
Computerized background investigations, 255
Computer manipulation crimes, 162–63
Computer security, 160–68
 and banks/financial services, 123
 computer crime, 160–64, 291–93
 e-commerce, 164
 environment, 22, 165–68
 environment for, 165–68
 investigative team, 166–67
  attorney, 167
  coordinator, 166–67
  information systems specialist, 167
  investigator, 167
  keys to success of, 173
Consensus decisions, 182
Constable, 11

Continuum of behavior, 2–3
Contract security, 46–47
    organizational placement, 190
Control Screening (manufacturer), 257
Coordinator, as investigative team member,
    166–67
Coppers, use of term, 13
Copyright and trademark infringement, 65
Corporal punishment, 8
Corrections Corporation of America, 105
Cost:
    of access control, 328
    of crime, 55–57, 197
    of downtime, 204
    of litigation, 225–26
    replacement cost, 203
    temporary replacement cost, 204
Countermeasures, 202–3
Crash bars, 249
Credit card fraud, 119, 277, 288
Crime:
    common-law origins of, 271–75
    cost of, 55–57, 197
    economic, 55–56
    external threats, 58
    and fear, 1, 59
    headline, 58, 272
    internal threats, 60
    ordinary, 56
    and sin, 5
    white-collar, 56, 285–93, 350
Crime-concealment arsonists, 284
Crime prevention, 271–95
    businesses/institutions, impact of crime on,
        275–94
    common-law origins of crime, 271–75
        crimes against morality and decency,
            275
        crimes against the person, 272–73
        crimes against property, 273–75
        other reported crime, 275
    as police work, 276
Criminal homicide, 273
Criminal victimization, 53–55
Crisis management, 145–53
    anticipating crises, 149
    assessing the situation, 149
    audience, identifying, 149
    checklist, 156
    communication methods, deciding on, 150
    communication protocols, establishing, 148
    crisis management team, identifying, 148

disasters, 150–54
    planning for, 153
    and vulnerability, 151–52
highlights, 145–53
key messages, identifying, 149
man-made disasters, 147
onion model of, 151
planning, 148–50
pyramid, 146
riding out the storm, 150
spokespersons:
    identifying, 148
    training, 148
vulnerability catalog, 152
Cultural differences in definitions, 33

D

Damages, compensatory/punitive, 233–36
Dante, 9
D.A.R.E. program, 188
Data diddling, 291–92
DataLink, 70, 124
Death penalty, 7–8
Defalcation, 119
Delayed egress, 127–28
Department-level security, 189
Designated employee entrances/exits, 248
Deterrence, 8, 211
Discounted cash, 204
Discretionary power, 82–83
Distributed processing systems, 258
Division-level security, 189
Doors, securing, 249
Downtime, cost of, 204
Drug abuse, 81
    in the workplace, 62, 293
Drug trafficking, 65–66
Duarte v. *State of California*, 228, 231
Ducking stools, 8
Due process, 11
Duraproxy (Garon Product), 91

E

Earldoms, 11
E-commerce, 164
Economic crime, 55–56
Educational institution security, 135–37
Eighteenth Amendment, 31
Electronic card readers, 247
Electronic fund transfers, 116
Elevator access point, 263

E-mail, 176
Embezzlement, 65, 277, 288–91
   check-kiting, 290
   kick-backs, 290
   lapping, 289
Emergency plans/operations, 209
Employee Polygraph Protection Act (1988), 255
Employee theft, 56, 64, 134
Enable second authenticator, 265
English common law, 272
Enhanced x-ray detection, and explosives, 114
Entrance control, *See* Access control
Entrapment portals, 265
Entry point lighting, 247
Ethics:
   and changes in behavioral definitions, 31–33
   code of, 34–35
   cultural differences in definitions, 33
   organizational, 33
   professional, 33
   and security profession, 31–45
   situational, 33
   standards, 35–36
   standards legislation, 37–39
      Washington State, 39–42
   and training, 367
ETRUST Internet Privacy Study, 164
Examination of losses/incidents, 205
Excitement arsonists, 284–85
Explosives, detection of, 112–14, 257–58
Explosives Detection System (EDS), 115
External threats, 58
"Eye for an eye, tooth for a tooth" doctrine, 4
EyeDentify, 124

F

False alarms, 64, 68–71
Falsification of documents, 155
Falsified overtime, 290
FAR 107.14, 110
Fargo, William G., 16, 17
Fast neutron analysis, and explosives, 114
Fear:
   of arbitrary power in police practice, 82–83
   and crime, 1, 59
Federal law 42 US Code section 1983, 100
Felonies, 11, 271–72
   definition of, 272
   distinction between misdemeanors and, 272
Fences, 247–49, 340
Fiber optics, 141, 305–6, 335

Fielding, Henry, 13
Financial fraud, 350, 353
Financial services security, *See* Banking/financial services security
Fines, 4
Fingerprinting, 124, 304, 331
Firearms, and training, 72–73
Fire safety, 168–73
   addressable vs. analog fire alarm systems, 169
   fire annunciation, 171
   fire drills, 168, 170–72
   firefighting equipment, 170
   inspections/maintenance, 172
   postfire investigation, 172
   prevention, 169–70
   program responsibility, 172–73
Flogging, 8
Floor, securing, 249–51
Florida, security licensing requirements, 40
Folkways, 2
   changes in, 31
Forcible rape, 273
Foreseeability, 59–60
Foreseeable cause, 224–25
Forgery, bad checks compared to, 286–88
Fortress hospital, 126
Four-stage systems model, of police productivity, 87–88
Fourth Amendment, 100
Frances T. v. Village Green Owners' Association, 231
Frankpledge, 11
Fraud, 64, 65
   banking/financial services security, 116–20, 350, 353
      automatic teller machine (ATM) fraud, 116, 117–19
      check fraud, 119–20
      credit card fraud, 119
      inside abuse (defalcation), 119
      loan fraud, 119
   cellular phones, 141
Free will, 6–7
Friedensgeld, 5, 7
Functional work area, 251–52

G

Gangs, and vandalism, 282–83
Gate controls, 247–48
George II, king of England, 12
Get tough sentencing attitudes, 78

Government, impact of crime on, 276
Graffiti, 91
Grand jury, 11
Grand larceny, 277
Greek law, early, 6
Gross negligence, 226
Guard houses, lighting of, 247
Guard tour access point, 263
Gun sheet, 281

H

Hallcrest II, 37, 46–47, 51–52, 55–60, 63, 66, 104–5, 134, 179, 343
  as reviewed by ASIS, 60–64
Hallcrest Report, 51–60, 275, 343
Hammurabic Code, 4–5
Hand geometry, 305, 330
Handguns, 281
Handwriting verification systems, 330
Hardware, 310
Hardware/software thefts, 163
Headline crimes, 58
Healthcare, security in, *See* Hospital security
Henry VIII, kind of England, 10
Hidden business tax, 57
Holmes, Edwin, 16
Homicide, 273
Hospital security, 123–32
  delayed egress, 127–28
  development of, 130–31
  fortress hospital, 126
  litigation in, 128
  need for, 128–30
    compliance responsibility, 129
    and economic foundation for organization, 129
    legal responsibility, 129
    moral responsibility, 128
    and public-employee relations, 130
  and violence, 132
Hudson v. *Americus/Sumpter County Hospital Authority*, 125
Hurricane Andrew, 145

I

IACP, *See* International Association of Chiefs of Police (IACP)
IAHSS, *See* International Association for Healthcare Security and Safety (IAHSS)
Idaho, security licensing requirements, 39

Identification (ID), 304–5
  biometrics, 124, 304–5
    fingerprinting, 124, 304
    hand geometry, 305
    keyboard rhythms, 305
    palm prints, 305
    retinal scans, 305
    signature dynamics, 305
    voiceprint, 304
  picture ID, 304
Illinois, security licensing requirements, 41
Inadequate security, 125
Incrementalism, 192
Indentix Inc., 124
Independent security zones, 252
Indermann v. *Domes*, 229
Industrial espionage, 65
Industrial Security Manual (ISM), 212
Infant monitoring, 127
Informal organization, 180
Information systems specialist, as investigative team member, 167
Infrastructure, American transportation, 160
In loco parentis, 137
Inquisition, 6–7
Inside abuse (defalcation), 119
Institutions, impact of crime on, 275–94
Insurance-claim arsonists, 284
Insurance rate changes, and loss, 204
Integrated partnership, 187
Integrated security packaging, 157
Integrated systems, 303
Intermodal cargo containers, 155
Internal computer crimes, 161–62
Internal threats, 60
International Association of Chiefs of Police (IACP), 22, 67, 83
  Law Enforcement Code of Ethics, 84
International Association for Healthcare Security and Safety (IAHSS), 130, 316
  code of ethics, 131
  and professional standards, 44–45
  training, 45
International Consultants on Targeted Security (ICTS), 112
International Foundation for Protection Officers (IFPO), and professional standards, 43
Internet resources, security, 413–14
Intrusion detection, 247, 305–6 technologies, 326
Investigation, 80

Investigative team, 166–67
  attorney, 167
  coordinator, 166–67
  information systems specialist, 167
  investigator, 167
  keys to success of, 173
Investigator, as investigative team member, 167
Ion Trap Mobility Spectrometry, 257
IriScan, 124, 333

J

Jails, overcrowding, 78, 105

K

Keyboard rhythms, 305
Kick-backs, 290
King, Rodney, 21, 83, 145
Kline v. *1500 Massachusetts Ave. Apartment Corp.*, 230
Knor v. *Parking Co. of Am.*, 227
Known to the police, use of term, 87

L

Lapping, 289
Larceny, 277
Law:
  church, 5
  Code of Draco, 6
  Code of Justinian, 6
  defined, 3
  development of, 2–10
  early Greece, 6
  English common law, 272
  fines, 4
  Hammurabic Code, 4–5
  Middle Ages, 6–7
  punishment, 4, 7–8
  retaliation, 3–4
  Roman Empire, 5–6
  secular, emergence of, 9–10
  state, 5
Law Enforcement Assistance Administration (LEAA), 26
Law Enforcement Code of Ethics:
  IACP, 84
    evolution of, 85
Law Enforcement Education Program (LEEP), 26
Layered approach to security, 253
Laz v. *Dworman*, 230–31

Legal responsibility, for hospital security, 129
Lex eterna, 9
Lex humana, 9
Lex naturalis, 9
Lex salica, 4
Lex talionis, 4
Library security, 141
Lighting:
  on rooftops, 251
  security, 62, 246–47
Line-of-protection concept, 245, 252, 253
Litigation, 222–42
  breach of duty, 223–24
  cause in fact, 224
  cost of, 225–26
  damages, 233–36
  definition of, 223–25
  duty to protect, 226–28
  duty to provide reasonable security, 223
  foreseeable cause, 224–25
  injury to plaintiff, 225
  negligent security litigation, 231–33
  policies/procedures, 236–38
  statistics/trends in, 237
  status of the plaintiff, 228–29
  tort rules, 229–31
  vicarious, 238–39
Loading areas, lighting, 251
Loan fraud, 119
Locking turnstiles, 247
Lodging industry:
  assaults, 283
  burglaries, 278
  security, 141
Logic bombs, 292
Loss prevention, 22–23, 187
  dimensions of, 77–108
Loss Prevention Specialists (LPS), 136
Lynching, 8

M

Magna Carta, 11–13
Maintenance, as security effort, 197
Man-made disasters, 147
Mantraps, 247, 253, 265
Metal detectors, 235
Metropolitan Police Act (1829), 13
Michigan Molecular Institute (MMI), 91
Middle Ages, 6–7
Military model, and security officers, 184–86

Misdemeanors, 11, 271–72
    definition of, 272
    distinction between felonies and, 272
Model muddle, 183
Monitoring, 208
Moonlighting, 64, 71
Moral responsibility, for hospital security, 128
Mores, 3
    changes in, 31
More, Sir Thomas, 9
Motion Picture Association of America
    (MPAA), Anti-Piracy Operation, 219–20
Museum security, 141
Mutilation, 8

N

National Burglar and Fire Alarm Association,
    71
National Fire Protection Association (NFPA),
    169
National Institute of Justice (NIJ), 51, 67 and
    private security, 64–73
Negligent security litigation, 231–33
    employment practices, 232
    environmental conditions, 232–33
    management-related issues, 233
    physical security measures, 232
    prior crime activity, 232
    security operations, 232
Negligent training, 128
Nested security zones, 252
Networking, 205
New York, security licensing requirements, 41
Norman period, 11
North West Police Agency, 15
Nuclear magnetic resonance, and explosives,
    114

O

Oklahoma City bombing, 145
On-line information services, and private
    security/public law enforcement, 70
Operational security (OPSEC), 253
Ordeal, 6
Ordinary crime, 56
Organizational ethics, 33
Originating passenger/bag match, 115
Outer perimeter, 245
Outlaws, 4

P

PageLink, 70
Palm prints, 305
Pan American flight 103, 110, 326
Parallel development, and private security,
    15–16
Parking lot lighting, 247
Partnership with people, 89
Patrol services, 47
Peel, Robert, 13–14, 15
Penal servitude, 5
Personal identification number (PIN), 265, 330
Personal property, 2
Personnel, as security effort, 197
Personnel screening, 208
Personnel subsystems, 255
Petty larceny, 277
Physical security, 243–70
    access control, 256–67
    administrative countermeasures, 253–55
    alarms, 251
    assessment of, 208
    building envelope, 249–51
    concentric rings of security, 256–69
    fences, 247–49
    five Ds, 208, 244
    functional work area, 251–52
    layered approach to security, 253
    line-of-protection concept, 245, 252, 253
    outer perimeter, 245
    personnel subsystems, 255
    security lighting, 246–47
    specific room/asset, 253
    specific system countermeasures, 256
    See also Access control
Picture ID, 304
Pillory, 8–9
PIN, 265, 330
Pinkerton, Allen, 15
Pinkerton Protection Patrol, 15
Piracy, film studios, 219–20
Plant equipment/facilities inventory, 173–76
    corrective action, 175
    inspection checklists, 174–75
    inspection schedule, 174
    inventory records, 174
    program evaluation, 175–76
    work requests, 175
Police code of conduct, 101–2
Police moonlighting, 64, 71
Police-private security issues, 68–72

commercial office building security, 137–41
computer security, 160–68
educational institution security, 135–37
library security, 141
lodging industry security, 141
museum security, 141
retail security, 133–35
service-oriented security, 132–33
telecommunications security, 141
Security hardware, 209
Security Internet resources, 413–14
Security licensing requirements, comparison of, 39–41
Security lighting, 246–47
Security management, 180–83
characteristics of, 191–95
development of science of management, 194–95
evolution of, 187–91
gradualist approach to program development/change, 191–92
and integration of services, 193–94
management theory, 182–83
models of, 183–87
bureaucratic control, 184
military model, 184–86
security officers, 184
upgrading security personnel, 186–87
organizational environment, influence of, 190–91
recent developments in, 180–81
Security Management magazine, 60
Security Network, 70
Security officers, 184
Security periodicals, 399–405
annuals/biennials, 399–400
journals, 400–401
newsletters/news services, 401–3
security literature, 405
trade publications, 404–5
Security personnel, upgrading, 186–87
Security-police cooperation, 67–68
Security products/vendors, 296–315
access control, 298–99
closed circuit television (CCTV), 300–302
communications security, 306
hardware, 310
identification (ID), 304–5
integrated systems, 303
intrusion detection, 305–6
technology, 310–14
Security-related lawsuits, 125

Security review, stages of, 212–13
Security tasks, 144–78
computer security, 160–68
computer crime, 160–64
environment, 22, 165–68
crisis management, 145–53
highlights, 147
man-made disasters, 147
planning, 148–50
pyramid, 146
fire safety, 168–73
addressable vs. analog fire alarm systems, 169
fire annunciation, 171
fire drills, 168, 170–72
firefighting equipment, 170
inspections/maintenance, 172
postfire investigation, 172
prevention, 169–70
program responsibility, 172–73
plant equipment/facilities inventory, 173–76
corrective action, 175
inspection checklists, 174–75
inspection schedule, 174
inventory records, 174
program evaluation, 175–76
work requests, 175
substance abuse, identifying, 176
transportation facilities/equipment, 154–60
break bulk, 155
cargo seals, 159–60
falsification of documents, 155
intermodal cargo containers, 155
loading onto local transportation for delivery, 158
loading onto mode of transportation, 155
movement from storage to docking area, 155
movement to destination, 155
movement to storage area prior to shipment, 154
transport and delivery to ultimate receiver, 158–60
unloading and storage at destination site, 157
Security trade and interest organizations, 391–99
Security training programs/resources, 405–8
Security zones, 252
Self-actualization, 181
Semiautomatic handguns, 281
Seniority system, 185
Sensar, 333–34

Sensormatic Electronics Corp., 337
Service-oriented security, 132–33
Sexual harassment, 347–51
Shared services, 47
Sheriff, origin of term, 11
Shipping, as security effort, 197
Shire-reeve, 11
Shires, 11
Shoplifters, 56, 134–35
Shotguns, 281
Signature dynamics, 305
Signature verification, 124
Silent alarms, 251
Situational ethics, 33
Skycaps, and airports/aviation security, 114
Skyjacking, 111–12
    See also Airports/aviation security
Slaves, punishments applied to, 5
Smart Buyer's Checklist, 307
Smart cards, 117, 298–99, 331–32
Social control, 2
Software thefts, 163
Solid-state charged coupled device (CCD)
    cameras, 300, 327–28
    cost of, 327
Sovereign Immunity, 11
Special police officers, 97–105
    administrative responsibility for, 104
    authority, increase in, 98
    as control mechanism, 103
    deterrence to crime, 99
    enhanced powers:
        advantages to, 98–99
        disadvantages of, 99–100
    and increased liability, 104
    and inequitable performance, 104–5
    negative image of, 99
    public officials:
        issues of concern to, 104–5
        issues favoring, 103–4
    and reduced crime, 104
    and reduced overtime, 103
    relationship with law enforcement, 99
    as revenue source, 103
    risk of liability, reduction in, 98
    security employee morale, 98
    staff, quality of, 99
    as supplemental police personnel, 103
    undesirable candidates for, 100
    and unnecessary arrests, 100
Specific system countermeasures, 256
Speech measurements, 331

Standard operating procedures (SOPs), 191
Standards, 35–36
    and training, 72
Standards legislation, 37–39
State law, 5
Status of the plaintiff, 228–29
Statute of Westminster (1285), 12
Statutory rape, 273
Stocks, 8
Subpoenas, 92
Substance abuse, identifying, 176
Summerian codes, 4–5
Surveillance, 208
    technologies, 326–28
Suspect description form, 280
Synergism, 182
System coding, 259
Systems integration, 303, 317, 320–42
    access control technologies, 328–34
    advent of, 322–23
    assessment/surveillance technologies,
        326–28
    central control technologies, 335–36
    communications technologies, 334–35
    fences, 340
    initial building security considerations, 324
    integrated systems model, 321
    intrusion detection technologies, 326
    technology design considerations, 324–25

T

Task analyses, for security positions, 186
Technology, 310–14
    access control, 328–34
    Smart Buyer's Checklist, 307
Telecommunications crime, 162
Telecommunications security, 141
TeleLink, 70
Tenant-in-chief, 11
Territoriality, 2
Terrorism, 250
    airborne, 111–12
Texas, security licensing requirements, 41
Theft, 277
    auto, 274
Thermal neutron activation, and explosives,
    114
Thompson v. *McCoy*, 100–101
Threat, definition of, 203
3M Corporation, 91
Three-stage systems model, 80–83

Three strikes and you're out sentencing practices, 78
Ticket agents, and airports/aviation security, 114
Time and attendance access point, 265–67
Tire rippers, 247
Tithing, 11
Tithingman, 11
TouchLock II, 124
Training, 95, 184–85, 367
    Certified Protection Officer (CPO) program, 95
    and firearms, 72–73
    IAHSS, 45
    negligent, 128
    and standards, 72
Transportation facilities/equipment, 154–60
    break bulk, 155
    falsification of documents, 155
    intermodal cargo containers, 155
    loading onto local transportation for delivery, 158
    loading onto mode of transportation, 155
    movement from storage to docking area, 155
    movement to destination, 155
    movement to storage area prior to shipment, 154
    transport and delivery to ultimate receiver, 158–60
    unloading and storage at destination site, 157
Trespass citations, 282
Trespassing, 277, 281–82
Trojan horse, 292
Tucker v. *Sandlin*, 228
TWA Flight 800, 110
Two-person control point, 264

U

Unarmed gate guards, 247
Unaware passengers, 112
Uniform Crime Reports, 52, 71, 80, 272, 275
Unisys Corporation, 138
United Airlines, security training, 114–15
unmanned gates, 247
Unnecessary arrests, and special police officers, 100
US Investigations Services, Inc., 288

V

Vandalism, 56, 277, 282–83
Vandalism arsonists, 284
Vapor detection system, and explosives, 114
Vendetta, 3
Vicarious litigation, 238–39
Victimization, criminal, 53–55
Video assessment, 327
Video comparator systems, 330
Violence:
    in hospitals, 132
    in the workplace, 20, 61–62
Voiceprint, 304
Volstead Act, 31
Vulnerability, definition of, 201

W

Wackenhut, Inc., 16, 105
War on drugs, 81
Warrants/subpoenas, 92
Washington, security licensing requirements, 39
Watch and ward, 12, 14
Wells Fargo, 16, 17
Wells, Henry, 16, 17
Wergeld, 4, 5, 7
Whipping, 8
Whistle-blowers, 35, 119
White-collar crime, 56, 277, 285–93, 350
    check fraud, 286–88
    credit card fraud, 119, 288
    definition of, 285
    embezzlement, 288–91
    white-collar offenders, 286
Wiegand access card, 298
Wild West, 15–16
William, duke of Normandy, 11
Windows, securing, 249
Work doubles, 186
Workplace:
    drugs in, 293
    sexual harassment, 347–51
    violence, 20, 61–62
WSE License Plate Reader (Westinghouse Security Electronics), 337

X

X-ray absorption, and explosives, 112

Author Index